lonely planet

Paris

Steve Fallon
Tony Wheeler
Daniel Robinson

D0188585

Paris

2nd edition

Published by
  Lonely Planet Publications
  Head Office: PO Box 617, Hawthorn, Vic 3122, Australia
  Branches: 150 Linden Street, Oakland, CA 94607, USA
                   10a Spring Place, London NW5 3BH, UK
                   71 bis rue du Cardinal Lemoine, 75005 Paris, France

Printed by
  Colorcraft Ltd, Hong Kong

Photographs by

Rachel Black	Simon Bracken	Bethune Carmichael
Mark Honan	James Lyon	Richard Nebesky
Brenda Turnnidge	Tony Wheeler	

Front cover: Acrobat in front of the Eiffel Tower (Jacques Cochin, The Image Bank)

First Published
  November 1996

This Edition
  November 1998

Although the authors and publisher have tried to make the information as accurate as possible, they accept no responsibility for any loss, injury or inconvenience sustained by any person using this book.

National Library of Australia Cataloguing in Publication Data

  Fallon, Steve
  Paris

  2nd ed.
  Includes index
  ISBN 0 86442 622 4

  1. Paris (France) – Guidebooks. I. Title.
  (Series: Lonely Planet city guide).

914.436104839

text & maps © Lonely Planet 1998
photos © photographers as indicated 1998

Steve Fallon

Born in Boston, Massachusetts, Steve can't remember a time when he was not obsessed with travel, other cultures and languages. As a teenager he worked an assortment of jobs to finance trips to Europe and South America, and he graduated from Georgetown University with a Bachelor of Science in modern languages. The following year he taught English at the University of Silesia near Katowice, Poland. After he had worked for several years for a Gannett newspaper and obtained a master's degree in journalism, his fascination with the 'new' Asia took him to Hong Kong, where he lived and worked for 13 years. In 1987, he put journalism on hold when he opened Wanderlust Books, Asia's only travel bookshop. Steve lived in Budapest for 2½ years before moving to London in 1994. He has written or contributed to a number of Lonely Planet titles.

Daniel Robinson

Daniel was raised in the USA (the San Francisco Bay area and Glen Ellyn, IL) and Israel. Before, during and after his BA studies in Near Eastern Studies (Arab and Islamic history) at Princeton University, he spent several years backpacking around Asia, parts of the Middle East and Europe.

His previous work for Lonely Planet includes the Vietnam and Cambodia sections of the award-winning *Vietnam, Laos & Cambodia* guide and all three editions of *France*. Daniel lives in Tel Aviv with his wife Yael and, between Lonely Planet assignments, is working on a PhD in Israeli history at Tel Aviv University.

Tony Wheeler

Tony was born in England but grew up in Pakistan, the Bahamas and the USA. He returned to England to do a degree in engineering at Warwick University, worked as an automotive design engineer, returned to London Business School to complete an MBA, then set out on an Asian overland trip with his wife, Maureen. That trip led to Tony and Maureen founding Lonely Planet Publications in Australia in 1973, and they've been travelling, writing and publishing guidebooks ever since. In 1996 they spent a year in Paris, with their children Tashi and Kieran.

From Steve Fallon

Once again, my share of this guidebook is dedicated to Michael Roths-child, a star that is always in reach, a star that never falls. He has my undying admiration, gratitude and affection. A number of people helped in the updating of *Paris* and I would like to thank all the staff at the Lonely Planet Paris office for help beyond the call of duty, especially *ma copine de table*, Zahia Hafs, and the very active Laurence Billiet. Thanks too to Brenda Turnnidge, Frank Viviano, Chew Terrière and particularly Danielle 'Pixie' Garno (née Garnaut) for assistance, encouragement and companionship. Much appreciated. And to all those wonderful, infuriating Parisians I met along the way – elegant and stylish, cultured and entertaining, bitchy and full of attitude – *merci*. They're just what the world needs more of.

This Book

The 1st edition of Paris was written and researched by Tony Wheeler and Daniel

Robinson. Steve Fallon updated, expanded and revised this 2nd edition.

From the Publisher
This book was edited at Lonely Planet's Melbourne office by Sarah Mathers, with help from Carolyn Bain, and proofed by Craig MacKenzie. Quentin Frayne checked the language section. Anthony Phelan drew the maps and, along with Jane Hart, handled the book's design and layout. Thanks to Tim Uden for advice on Quark and Katie Cody for her help with checking layout. The cover was designed by David Kemp. A special thanks to Christian Vuaillet from the RATP for supplying the Paris metro map.

Warning & Request
Things change – prices go up, schedules change, good places go bad and bad places go bankrupt – nothing stays the same. So, if you find things better or worse, recently opened or long since closed, please tell us and help make the next edition even more accurate and useful.

We value all of the feedback we receive from travellers. Julie Young coordinates a small team who read and acknowledge every letter, postcard and email, and ensure that every morsel of information finds its way to the appropriate authors, editors and publishers.

Everyone who writes to us will find their name in the next edition of the appropriate guide and will also receive a free subscription to our quarterly newsletter, *Planet Talk*. The very best contributions will be rewarded with a free Lonely Planet guide.

Excerpts from your correspondence may appear in new editions of this guide; in our newsletter, *Planet Talk*; or in updates on our Web site – so please let us know if you don't want your letter published or your name acknowledged.

Thanks Many thanks to the travellers who used the last edition and wrote to us with helpful hints, useful advice and interesting anecdotes. Your names follow:

Keleigh Ahmann, J Bain, Victoria Bayman, Robert Bougras, Tulani Bridgewater, Jan Buruma, Mickey Coburn, SD Cook, Jim Delaney, Ronald Denomme, David Fisher, Sue Foley, Rodney Gray, Anthony Hadj, Allen Heloise, Nick, Tom & Anna Hodgson, Martha Holloway, M Johnstone, Emma Laney, Simon Li, Christina Mariani, Virginie Menage, Dermott Monaham, Kevin Phua, Vanessa Pollett, Jenny Scholin, Carole Testwuide, Bill Turner, Bart Vabin, Paul Walleck, Michael Wise, Carla Zecher.

Contents

Introduction

Paris has just about exhausted the superlatives that can reasonably be applied to any city. Notre Dame and the Eiffel Tower – at sunrise, at sunset, at night – have been described countless times, as have the Seine and the subtle (and not-so-subtle) differences between the Left and Right banks. But what writers have been unable to capture is the grandness and even magic of strolling along the city's broad avenues, which lead from impressive public buildings and exceptional museums to parks, gardens and esplanades.

Paris probably has more landmarks familiar to people who have never visited the place than any other city in the world. As a result, first-time visitors often arrive in the French capital with all sorts of expectations: of grand vistas, of intellectuals discussing weighty matters in cafés, of romance along the Seine, of naughty nightclub revues, of rude people who won't speak English. If you look hard enough, you can probably find all of those things. But another approach is to set aside the preconceptions of Paris that are so much a part of English-speaking culture, and to explore the city's avenues and backstreets as if the tip of the Eiffel Tower or the spire of Notre Dame wasn't about to pop into view at any moment.

Paris is enchanting almost everywhere, at any time, in every season. And, like a good meal, it excites, it satisfies, the memory lingers ... In *A Moveable Feast*, his book of recollections of Paris in the 1920s, the American author Ernest Hemingway wrote: 'If you are lucky to have lived in Paris as a young man, then wherever you go for the rest of your life, it stays with you, for Paris is a moveable feast.' Those of us who took Hemingway's advice in our salad days could not agree more. We're still dining out on the memories.

Facts about Paris

HISTORY
The Romans & the Gauls

The Celtic Gauls moved into what is now France between 1500 and 500 BC. Some time during the 3rd century BC, members of a Celtic tribe called the Parisii set up a few huts made of wattle and daub on what is now the Île de la Cité and engaged in fishing and trading.

Centuries of conflict between the Gauls and Rome ended between 55 and 52 BC, when Julius Caesar's legions took control of the territory, and the settlement on the Seine prospered as the Roman town of Lutetia (from the Latin meaning 'Midwater Dwelling'), counting some 10,000 inhabitants by the 3rd century AD. A temple to Jupiter was established where Notre Dame cathedral (Map 6) now stands, and the Roman town spread to the south bank, with Rue Saint Jacques as the main thoroughfare and a forum at the corner of today's Rue Soufflot (Map 6), near the Panthéon and the Jardin du Luxembourg. Traces of this Roman Paris can be seen in the Crypte Archéologique (Map 6) under the square in front of Notre Dame, in the Arènes de Lutèce (Map 5) and at the Roman baths in the Musée National du Moyen Age, formerly known as the Musée de Cluny (Map 6).

The Great Migrations, beginning in the mid-3rd century with raids by the Franks and then the Alemanii from the east, left the settlement on the south bank scorched and pillaged, and its inhabitants fled to the island, which was subsequently fortified by stone walls. Christianity had been introduced early in the 2nd century AD, and the first church, probably made of wood, was built on the Île de la Cité two centuries later.

The Merovingians & Carolingians

Roman occupation of what had by then become known as Paris (after its first settlers) ended in the late 5th century when a second wave of Franks and other Germanic groups under Merovius, overran the territory. In 508, Merovius' grandson, Clovis I, made Paris his seat. Childeric II, Clovis' son and successor, founded the Abbey of Saint Germain des Prés and the dynasty's most productive ruler, Dagobert, established an abbey at Saint Denis, which would soon become the richest and most important monastery in France and the final resting place of its kings for a time.

The militaristic rulers of the Carolingian dynasty, beginning with Charles Martel (688-741), were almost permanently away fighting wars in the east, and Paris became something of a backwater, controlled for the most part by the Counts of Paris. When Charles Martel's grandson, Charlemagne (768-814), moved his capital to Aix-la-Chapelle (today's Aachen in Germany), Paris' fate was sealed. Basically a group of separate villages with its centre on the island, Paris was badly defended throughout the second half of the 9th century and suffered a succession of raids by the Scandinavian Vikings.

The Middle Ages

The Counts of Paris, whose powers had increased as the Carolingians feuded among themselves, elected one of their own, Hugh Capet, as king at Senlis (see the Excursions chapter) in 987. He then made Paris the royal seat; under Capetian rule, which would last for the next 800 years, Paris prospered as a centre of politics, commerce, trade, religion and culture.

By the time Hugh Capet had assumed the throne, the Vikings (also known as the Norsemen, ie Normans) were in control of the north and west of French territory. In 1066 they mounted a successful invasion – the so-called Norman Conquest – of England from their base in today's Normandy. This would lead to almost 300 years of conflict between the Normans and the Capetians.

Paris' strategic riverside position ensured importance throughout the Middle Ages, although settlement remained centred on the Île de la Cité and the *rive gauche* (left bank). The Marais area north of the Seine on the *rive droite* (right bank) was exactly what its French name suggests, a waterlogged 'marsh'. The first guilds were established in the 11th century and rapidly grew in importance; in the middle of the 12th century the ship merchants' guild bought the principal river port, by today's Hôtel de Ville (Map 8), from the crown.

This was a time of frenetic building activity in Paris. Abbot Suger, both confessor and minister to several Capetian kings, was one of the powerhouses of this period, and in 1135 he commissioned the basilica at Saint Denis (see the Excursions chapter). It was the first major structure to be built in the Gothic style and would serve as a model for many other 12th-century French cathedrals. Less than three decades later, work started on the cathedral of Notre Dame, the greatest creation of medieval Paris. Construction continued for nearly two centuries.

The marshes of the Marais were drained and settlement finally moved to the north bank of the Seine, the area known today as the Right Bank, which would become the mercantile centre, especially around Place de Grève (today's Place de l'Hôtel de Ville). The food markets at Les Halles (Map 7) first came into existence around 1110, the beautiful Sainte Chapelle (Map 6) on the Île de la Cité was consecrated in 1248 and the Louvre (Map 7) began its existence as a riverside fortress in the 1200s.

In a bid to do something about the city's horrible traffic congestion and stinking mud and excrement, Philippe-August (1180-1223) paved some of Paris' streets for the first time since the Romans.

Meanwhile, the area south of the Seine – today's Left Bank – was developing as a centre of learning and erudition, particularly in the area known as the Latin Quarter, where students and their independent teachers spoke only in that language. The ill-fated lovers Abélard and Héloïse (see the boxed text) wrote their treatises on philosophy and finest poetry at this time; Thomas Aquinas taught at the new University of Paris (founded under papal protection in about

---

Abélard & Héloïse

He was a brilliant 39-year-old philosopher and logician who had gained something of a reputation for controversial ideas. She was the beautiful niece of a clergyman at Notre Dame. And like Bogart and Bergman in Casablanca and Romeo and Juliet in Verona, they had to fall in love in – of all damn places – medieval Paris.

In 1118, the wandering scholar Pierre Abélard (1079-1142) returned to Paris, having clashed with yet another theologian in the provinces. There he was employed by Canon Fulbert of Notre Dame to tutor his niece Héloïse (1098-1164). One thing led to another and a son called Astrolabe was born. Abélard did the gentlemanly thing and married his sweetheart secretly, but when Fulbert learned of it he was outraged. The canon sent Héloïse packing to a nunnery and had Abélard castrated.

Abélard took monastic vows at the abbey in Saint Denis and continued his studies and controversial writings, falling foul of several clergymen of the day and even being branded as a heretic by the pope at one point. Héloïse, meanwhile, was made abbess of a congregation of nuns.

All the while, however, the star-crossed lovers continued to correspond: he sending tender advice on how to run the convent and she writing passionate, poetic letters to her lost lover. The two were reunited only in death; in 1817 their remains were disinterred and brought to Cimitière Père Lachaise, 20e (Map 1), where they lie today beneath a neo-Gothic tombstone.

1215); and numerous other colleges were established, including the Sorbonne (Map 6) by Robert de Sorbon, confessor to King Louis IX, in 1253.

In 1337, some three centuries of hostility between the Capetians and the Normans degenerated into the Hundred Years' War, which would be fought on and off until 1453. The Black Death (1348-49) killed about a third of Paris' population (which numbered about 80,000 at the time) but only briefly interrupted the fighting. These two events, along with the development of free, independent cities in Italy and the Low Countries, brought political tension and open insurrection to Paris. In 1356, the provost of the merchants, a wealthy draper named Étienne Marcel, allied himself with peasants revolting against the dauphin (the future King Charles V) and seized Paris in a bid to limit the power of the throne and secure a city charter. But the dauphin's supporters recaptured the city within two years, and Marcel and his followers were executed.

After the French forces were defeated by the English at Agincourt in 1415, Paris was once again embroiled in revolt. The Dukes of Burgundy, allied with the English, occupied the capital in 1420. Two years later John Plantagenet, Duke of Bedford, was installed as regent of France for England's King Henry VI, then an infant. Henry was crowned as king of France at Notre Dame less than 10 years later, but Paris remained under siege by the French almost continuously for much of that time.

In 1429 a 17-year-old peasant girl known to history as Jeanne d'Arc (Joan of Arc) persuaded the French legitimist Charles VII that she had received a divine mission from God to expel the English from France and bring about Charles' coronation. She rallied the French troops and defeated the English at Patay, north of Orléans, and Charles was crowned at Reims. However, Joan of Arc failed in her attempt to capture Paris. In 1430 she was captured by the Burgundians and sold to the English. She was convicted of witchcraft and heresy by a tribunal of French ecclesiastics and burned at the stake

two years later at Rouen. Charles VII returned to Paris in 1437, but the English were not entirely driven from French territory (with the exception of Calais) until 1453.

The occupation had left Paris a disaster zone. While the restored monarchy moved to consolidate its power, conditions improved under Louis XI (1461-81), during whose reign the city's first printing press was installed at the Sorbonne. Churches were rehabilitated or built in the Flamboyant Gothic style at this time and a number of *hôtels particuliers* (private mansions) such as the Hôtel de Cluny and the Hôtel de Sens (Map 8; now the Bibliothèque Forney at 1 Rue du Figuier, 4e) were erected.

The Renaissance

The culture of the Italian Renaissance (French for 'rebirth') arrived in full swing in France in the early 16th century, during the reign of François I (1515-47) partly because of a series of indecisive French military operations in Italy. For the first time, the French aristocracy was exposed to Renaissance ideas of scientific and geographic scholarship and discovery, and the value of secular over religious life.

Writers such as Rabelais, Marot and Ronsard were influential as were the architectural disciples of Michelangelo and Raphael. Around Paris evidence of this architectural influence can be seen in François I's château at Fontainebleau and the Petit Château at Chantilly. In the city proper, Renaissance-era structures include the Tour Saint Jacques (Maps 6 and 8) with elements of Flamboyant Gothic; the Église Saint Eustache (Map 7) on the Right Bank; and Église Saint Étienne du Mont (Map 6) on the Left. The oldest bridge in Paris, the Pont Neuf (new bridge; Map 6), is another prime example of the architecture of the period. The Marais remains the best area for spotting reminders of Renaissance Paris, with fine hôtels particuliers such as the Hôtel (now Musée) Carnavalet (Map 8).

This new architecture was meant to reflect the splendour of the monarchy, which was fast moving toward absolutism, and

Paris as the capital of a powerful centralised state. But all this grandeur and show of strength was not enough to stem the tide of Protestantism that was flowing into France.

The Reformation
By the 1530s the position of the Protestant Reformation sweeping Europe had been strengthened in France by the ideas of John Calvin, a Frenchman exiled to Geneva. The Edict of January (1562), which afforded the Protestants certain rights, was met by violent opposition from ultra Catholic nobles whose fidelity to their religion was mixed with a desire to strengthen their power base in the provinces. Paris remained very much a Catholic stronghold, and trials and executions by burning at the stake in the Place de Grève continued apace up to the religious civil war.

The Wars of Religion (1562-98) involved three groups: the Huguenots (French Protestants who received help from the English), the Catholic League and the Catholic king. The fighting severely weakened the position of the monarchy and brought the French state close to disintegration. The most deplorable massacre took place in Paris in 1572, when some 3000 Huguenots who had come to Paris to celebrate the wedding of the Protestant Henri of Navarre (the future Henri IV) were slaughtered in what is now called the Saint Bartholomew's Day Massacre (23-24 August). In 1588 on the so-called Day of the Barricades the Catholic League rose up against Henri III and forced him to flee the royal court at the Louvre; he was assassinated the following year.

Henri III was succeeded by Henri IV, starting the Bourbon dynasty. In 1598 he promulgated the Edict of Nantes, which guaranteed the Huguenots freedom of conscience and many civil and political rights, but this was not universally accepted. Ultra Catholic Paris refused to allow its new Protestant king entry to the city, and a siege of the capital continued for almost five years. Only when Henri IV embraced Catholicism at Saint Denis – *'Paris vaut bien une messe'* (Paris is well worth a Mass), he is reputed to have said upon taking communion there – did the capital submit to him.

Henri IV's rule was characterised by the consolidation of the monarchy's power and the rebuilding of Paris (population about 400,000) after more than three decades of fighting. The magnificent Place Royale (Map 8; today's Place des Vosges), built in the Marais in the early 1600s, and Place Dauphine (Map 6) at the western end of Île de la Cité are prime examples of the new era of town planning.

The reign of Henri IV ended as abruptly and tragically as that of his predecessor. In 1610 he was assassinated by a Catholic fanatic named François Ravaillac as his coach drove along Rue de la Ferronnerie (Map 7) in the Marais.

Henri IV's son, the future Louis XIII (1601-43), was too young to assume the throne at the time of his father's death so his mother, Marie de Médecis, was named regent. She set about building the magnificent Palais de Luxembourg (Map 6) and its enormous gardens, just outside the city wall, for herself.

Louis XIII assumed royal power in 1617 but throughout most of his undistinguished reign remained under the control of his ruthless chief minister, Cardinal Richelieu. Richelieu is best known for his untiring efforts to establish an all-powerful monarchy in France – opening the door to the absolutism of Louis XIV, and French supremacy in Europe, which would see France fighting Holland, Austria and England almost continuously. Under Louis XIII's reign two uninhabited islets in the Seine were joined to form the Île de Saint Louis, and Richelieu commissioned a number of palaces and churches, including the Palais Royal (Map 7) and the Val-de-Grâce (Map 6).

Louis XIV & the Ancien Régime
Le Roi Soleil (the Sun King, 1638-1715) ascended the throne in 1643 at the age of five. His mother, Anne of Austria, was appointed

regent and Cardinal Mazarin, a protégé of Richelieu, was named chief minister. One of the decisive events of Louis XIV's early reign was the War of the Fronde (1648-53), a rebellion of the bourgeoisie and some of the nobility opposed to taxation and the increasing power of the monarchy. The revolt forced the royal court to flee Paris for a time.

When Mazarin died in 1661, Louis XIV assumed absolute rule until his own death in 1715. Throughout his long reign, he sought to project the power of the French monarchy – bolstered by claims of divine right – both at home and abroad. He involved France in a long series of costly wars which gained it territory but terrified its neighbours and nearly bankrupted the treasury. State taxation to fill the coffers caused widespread poverty and vagrancy in Paris.

But Louis XIV – whose widely quoted saying *'L'État c'est moi'* (I am the State) is often taken out of historical context – was able to quash the ambitious, feuding aristocracy and create the first truly centralised French state, elements of which can still be seen in France today. He did pour huge sums of money into building his extravagant palace at Versailles, 23km south-west of Paris, but by doing so was able to sidestep the endless intrigues of the capital, by then a city of 600,000 people. And by turning his nobles into courtiers, Louis XIV forced them to compete with each other for royal favour, reducing them to ineffectual sycophancy. Though he hated Paris (due largely to his experiences during the War of the Fronde), Louis XIV commissioned the fine Place Vendôme (Map 2), Place des Victoires (Map 7), Invalides (Map 4) and the Cour Carrée at the Louvre (Map 7).

Louis XIV mercilessly persecuted the Protestant minority, which he considered a threat to the unity of the state (and thus his power). In 1685 he revoked the Edict of Nantes, which had guaranteed the Huguenots freedom of conscience.

Louis XIV's successor, his grandson Louis XV (1710-74), turned out to be an oafish buffoon though his regent, the Duke of Orléans, did move the court from Versailles back to Paris; in the Age of the Enlightenment, the French capital had become, in effect, the centre of Europe. It was Louis XIV who said *'Après moi, le déluge'* (After me, the flood); in hindsight his words were more than prophetic. He was followed by the incompetent – and later universally despised and powerless – Louis XV.

As the 18th century progressed, new economic and social circumstances rendered the *ancien régime* (old order) dangerously out of step with the needs of the country. The regime was further weakened by the anti-establishment and anticlerical ideas of the Enlightenment, whose leading lights included Voltaire, Rousseau and Montesquieu. But entrenched vested interests, a cumbersome power structure and royal lassitude prevented change from starting until the 1770s, by which time the monarchy's moment had passed.

The Seven Years' War (1756-63) was only one of a series of ruinous military engagements pursued by Louis XV, and it had led to the loss of France's flourishing colonies in Canada, the West Indies and India. It was in part to avenge these losses that Louis XVI sided with the colonists in the American War of Independence. But the Seven Years' War cost a fortune and, even more disastrous for the monarchy, it helped to disseminate in France the radical democratic ideas which were thrust upon the world stage by the American Revolution.

The French Revolution & the First Republic

By the late 1780s, the indecisive Louis XVI (1754-1793) and his dominating queen, Marie-Antoinette, had managed to alienate virtually every segment of society – from enlightened groups to conservatives – and he became increasingly isolated as unrest neared boiling point. When the king tried to neutralise the power of the more reform-minded delegates at a meeting of the *États Généraux* (Estates General) at the Jeu de Paume at Versailles in May/June 1789, the urban masses took to the streets and, on 14

July, a Parisian mob raided the Hôtel des Invalides for weapons and then stormed the prison at Bastille – the ultimate symbol of the despotism of the ancien régime.

At first, the Revolution was in the hands of relative moderates. France was declared a constitutional monarchy and various reforms were made, including the adoption of the Declaration of the Rights of Man. But as the masses armed themselves against the external threat to the new government posed by Austria, Prussia and the many exiled French nobles, patriotism and nationalism mixed with revolutionary fervour, then popularising and radicalising the Revolution. It was not long before the moderate republican Girondins lost power to the radical Jacobins, led by Robespierre, Danton and Marat, who abolished the monarchy and declared the First Republic in September 1792 after Louis XVI proved unreliable as a constitutional monarch. The National Assembly was replaced by a Revolutionary Convention.

In January 1793, Louis XVI, who had tried to flee the country with his family but only got as far as Varennes, was convicted of 'conspiring against the liberty of the nation' and guillotined at Place de la Révolution (Map 2; today's Place de la Concorde), followed by his queen in October. In March the Jacobins set up the notorious Committee of Public Safety to deal with national defence and to apprehend and try 'traitors'. This body virtually had dictatorial control over the city and the country during the so-called Reign of Terror (September 1793 to July 1794), which saw religious freedoms revoked, churches desecrated and closed and cathedrals turned into 'Temples of Reason'.

By autumn, following Marat's assassination by the Girondin Charlotte Corday in July, the Reign of Terror was in full swing, and by the middle of 1794 some 2500 people had been beheaded in Paris and more than 14,500 elsewhere in France. In the end, the Revolution turned on itself, 'devouring it's own children' in the words of the Jacobin Saint-Just. Robespierre sent Danton

to the guillotine, and Saint-Just and even Robespierre himself ended their lives with their heads separated from their bodies.

After the Reign of Terror, a five-man delegation of moderate Republicans led by Paul Barras, who had seen to the arrests of Robespierre and Saint-Just among others, set themselves up as a Directoire (Directory) to rule the Republic. On 13 Vendémiaire in the year 6 (ie 5 October 1795; see the boxed text 'Republican Calendar'), a group of Royalist rebels bent on overthrowing the Directory was intercepted on the Rue Saint Honoré by loyalist forces led by a dashing young Corsican general named Napoleon Bonaparte. For his efforts, Napoleon was put in command of the army in Italy, where he was particularly successful in the campaign against Austria. His victories soon turned him into an independent political force.

Napoleon & the First Empire

The post-revolutionary government was far from stable, and when Napoleon returned to Paris in 1799, he found a chaotic republic in which few had any faith. In November, when it appeared that the Jacobins were again on the ascendancy in the legislature, Napoleon tricked the delegates into leaving Paris for Saint Cloud to the south-west 'for their own protection', overthrew the discredited Directory and assumed power himself.

At first, Napoleon took the title of First Consul. In 1802, a referendum declared him 'Consul for Life' and his birthday became a national holiday. By 1804, when he had himself crowned 'Emperor of the French' by Pope Pius VII at Notre Dame, the scope and nature of Napoleon's ambitions were obvious to all. But to consolidate and legitimise his authority, Napoleon needed more victories on the battlefield. So began a seemingly endless series of wars and victories by which France came to control most of Europe.

In 1812, in an attempt to do away with his last major rival on the continent – the tsar – Napoleon invaded Russia. Although his Grande Armée captured Moscow, it was

Republican Calendar

During the Revolution, the Convention adopted a new, more 'rational' calendar from which all 'superstitious' associations (eg saints' days) were removed. Year I began on 22 September 1792, the day the Republic had been proclaimed. The 12 months – renamed Vendémaire, Brumaire, Frimaire, Nivôse, Pluviôse, Ventôse, Germinal, Floréal, Prairial, Messidor, Thermidor and Fructidor – were divided into three 10-day weeks called *décades*. Based on the cult of nature, the poetically inspired names of the months were chosen according to the seasons: the autumn months, for instance, were Vendémaire, derived from *vendange* (grape harvest or vintage), Brumaire from *brume* (mist or fog), and Frimaire from *frimas* (frost). The last day of each décade was a rest day, and the five or six remaining days of the year were used to celebrate Virtue, Genius, Labour, Opinion and Rewards. These festivals were initially called *sans-culottides* in honour of the *sans-culottes*, the extreme Revolutionaries who wore pantaloons rather than the short breeches favoured by the upper classes. While the Republican calendar worked well in theory, it caused no end of confusion for France in its communication and trade abroad as the months and days kept on changing in relation to those of the Gregorian calendar. Napoleon re-introduced the Gregorian calendar on 1 January 1806.

wiped out shortly after by the brutal Russian winter. Prussia and Napoleon's other enemies quickly recovered from their earlier defeats, and less than two years after the fiasco in Russia, the allied armies entered Paris. Napoleon abdicated and left France for the tiny Mediterranean island-kingdom of Elba.

At the Congress of Vienna (1814-15), the Allies restored the House of Bourbon to the French throne, installing Louis XVI's brother as Louis XVIII (the second son of Louis XVI had been declared Louis XVII by monarchist exiles and died in 1795). But in March 1815, Napoleon escaped from Elba, landed in southern France and gathered a large army as he marched northward towards Paris. His 'Hundred Days' back in power ended, however, when his forces were defeated by the English under the Duke of Wellington at Waterloo in Belgium. Napoleon was exiled to the remote South Atlantic island of Saint Helena, where he died in 1821.

Although reactionary in some ways – he re-established slavery in the colonies, for example – Napoleon instituted a number of important reforms, including a reorganisation of the judicial system, the promulgation of a new legal code, the Code Napoléon (or civil code), which forms the basis of the French legal system (and many others in Europe) to this day, and a new education system. More importantly, he preserved the essence of the changes brought about by the Revolution. Napoleon is therefore remembered by the French as a great hero.

Few of Napoleon's grand plans for Paris were completed, but the Arc de Triomphe (Map 2), the Arc de Triomphe du Carrousel (Map 7), La Madeleine (Map 2), the Pont des Arts (Map 7), the Rue de Rivoli (Map 8) and the Canal Saint Martin (Map 3) date from this period.

The Second Republic

The reign of Louis XVIII (ruled 1814-24) was dominated by the struggle among extreme monarchists who wanted to return to the *ancien régime*, liberals who saw the changes wrought by the Revolution as irreversible and the radicals of the working-class neighbourhoods of Paris. Charles X (ruled 1824-30) handled the struggle among them with great ineptitude and was overthrown in the so-called July Revolution of 1830 when a motley group of revolutionaries seized the Hôtel de Ville. The Colonne de Juillet in the centre of the

Place de la Bastille (Map 5) honours those killed in the street battles that accompanied the revolution; they are buried in vaults under the column.

Louis-Philippe (1773-1850), an ostensibly constitutional monarch of bourgeois sympathies and tastes, was then chosen by Parliament to head what became known as the July Monarchy. He was in turn overthrown in the February Revolution of 1848, and the Second Republic was established.

The Second Empire

In presidential elections held in 1848, Napoleon's useless nephew Louis Napoleon Bonaparte was overwhelmingly elected. Legislative deadlock caused Louis Napoleon to lead a coup d'état in 1851, after which he was proclaimed Emperor Napoleon III and moved into the Palais des Tuileries, which would be destroyed during the Paris Commune two decades later.

The Second Empire lasted from 1852 until 1870. During this period, France enjoyed significant economic growth and Paris was transformed under Baron Haussmann (see The Architecture of Paris section following Facts for the Visitor). In 17 years he oversaw the construction of a new city – displacing hundreds of thousands of poor people in the process – of wide boulevards, fine public buildings and beautiful parks, serviced, not insignificantly, by a modern sewerage system. The 12 avenues leading out from the Arc de Triomphe, for example, were his work. The city's first department stores were also built at this time (eg Au Bon Marché in 1852).

Unfortunately, Napoleon III – like his uncle before him – embroiled France in a number of conflicts, including the disastrous Crimean War (1853-56). In 1870, Prussian Prime Minister Otto von Bismarck goaded Napoleon III into declaring war on Prussia. Within months the thoroughly unprepared French army was defeated and the emperor taken prisoner. When news of the debacle reached Paris, the masses took to the streets and demanded that a republic be declared.

The achievements of Napoleon Bonaparte (1769-1821) were of lasting significance to France.

The Third Republic & the Belle Époque

The Third Republic began as a provisional government of national defence in September 1870. The Prussians were, at the time, advancing on Paris and would subsequently lay siege to the capital, forcing starving Parisians to bake bread laced with sawdust and consume most of the animals in the menagerie at the Jardin des Plantes (Map 5). In January 1871 the government negotiated an armistice with the Prussians, who demanded that Assemblée Nationale (National Assembly) elections be held immediately. The republicans, who had called on the nation to continue to resist and were overwhelmingly supported by Parisians, lost to the monarchists, who had campaigned on a peace platform.

As expected, the monarchist-controlled assembly ratified the Treaty of Frankfurt (1871). However, when ordinary Parisians heard of its harsh terms – a 5FF billion war indemnity and surrender of the provinces of Alsace and Lorraine – they revolted against the government.

The Communards, as the supporters of the Paris Commune were known, took over the city in March and the French government moved to Versailles. In May, the government launched a week-long offensive, now known as La Semaine Sanglante (Bloody Week), on the Commune in which several thousand rebels were killed. After a mop up of the Parc des Buttes-Chaumont (Maps 1 and 3), the last of the Communard insurgents, cornered by government forces in the Cimetière Père Lachaise (see map on page 134, and Map 1), fought a hopeless, all-night battle among the tombstones. In the morning, the 147 survivors were lined up against the Mur des Fédérés (Wall of the Federalists), shot and buried where they fell in a mass grave. A further 20,000 or so Communards, mostly from the working class, were rounded up throughout the city and summarily executed. Karl Marx interpreted the Communard insurrection as the first great proletarian uprising against the bourgeoisie, and socialists came to see its victims as martyrs of the class struggle. Among the buildings destroyed in the fighting were the Hôtel de Ville, the Palais des Tuileries and the Cours des Comptes (Map 4; site of the present-day Musée d'Orsay).

Despite this disastrous start, the Third Republic ushered in the glittering *belle époque* (beautiful age), with Art Nouveau architecture, a whole field of artistic 'isms' from impressionism onwards (best seen at the Musée d'Orsay) and advances in science and engineering, including the construction of the first metro line. Expositions Universelles (World Exhibitions) were held in Paris in 1889 (showcasing the Eiffel Tower, which was much maligned at the time) and again in 1901 in the purpose-built Petit Palais (Map 2). The Paris of nightclubs and artistic cafés made its first appearance around this time.

France was obsessed with a desire for revenge after its defeat by Germany, and jingoistic nationalism, scandals and accusations were the order of the day. But the greatest moral and political crisis of the Third Republic was the infamous Dreyfus Affair, which began in 1894 when a Jewish army officer, Captain Alfred Dreyfus, was accused of betraying military secrets to Germany, court-martialled and sentenced to life imprisonment on Devil's Island, the French penal colony off the northern coast of South America. Despite bitter opposition from the army command, right-wing politicians and many Catholic groups, leftists and liberals in Paris, including the novelist Émile Zola, succeeded in having the case reopened and Dreyfus vindicated in 1900. When he died in 1935 he was laid to rest in the Cimetière de Montparnasse (see map on page 117, and Map 1). The Dreyfus affair greatly discredited both the army and the Catholic Church. The result was more rigorous civilian control of the military and, in 1905, the legal separation of church and state.

WWI & the Inter-War Period

Central to France's entry into WWI was the desire to regain Alsace and Lorraine, lost to Germany in 1871. Indeed, Raymond Poincaré, president of the Third Republic from 1913 to 1920 and later prime minister, was a native of Lorraine and a firm supporter of war with Germany. But when the heir to the Austrian throne, Archduke Franz Ferdinand, was assassinated by Serbian nationalists at Sarajevo on 28 June 1914, precipitating what would erupt into a global war,

Germany jumped the gun. Within a month, it had declared war on Russia and France.

In early September German troops had reached the Marne River, a mere 15km east of Paris, and the government was moved to Bordeaux. But Maréchal Joffre's troops, transported to the front by Parisian taxis, brought about the 'Miracle of the Marne', and Paris was safe within a month. In November 1918 the armistice was finally signed in a railway carriage in a clearing of the Forêt de Compiègne, 82km north-east of Paris.

The defeat of Austria-Hungary and Germany in WWI, which regained Alsace and Lorraine for France, was achieved at an unimaginable human cost. Of the eight million French men who were called to arms, 1.3 million were killed and almost one million crippled. In other words, two of every 10 Frenchmen aged between 20 and 45 years of age were killed in WWI. At the Battle of Verdun (1916) alone, the French (led by Général Philippe Pétain) and the Germans each lost about 400,000 men.

The 1920s and 1930s saw Paris as a centre of the avant-garde, with artists pushing into the new fields of cubism and surrealism, Le Corbusier rewriting the architectural text book, foreign writers like Ernest Hemingway and F Scott Fitzgerald attracted by the city's liberal atmosphere, and nightlife establishing a cutting-edge reputation for everything from jazz clubs to striptease.

France's efforts to promote a separatist movement in the Rhineland and its occupation of the Ruhr in 1923 to enforce reparations payments proved disastrous. But it did lead to almost a decade of accommodation and compromise with border guarantees and Germany's admission to the League of Nations. The naming of Adolf Hitler as chancellor in 1933, however, changed all that.

WWII

During most of the 1930s, the French, like the British, had done their best to appease Hitler, but two days after Berlin's invasion of Poland in 1939, the two countries declared war on Germany. By June 1940 France had capitulated and Paris was occupied; almost half the population of five million fled the city by car, on bicycle or on foot. The British expeditionary force sent to help the French barely managed to avoid capture by retreating to Dunkerque and crossing the English Channel in small boats. The expensive Maginot Line, a supposedly impregnable wall of fortifications along the Franco-German border, had proved useless. The German armoured divisions simply outflanked it by going through Belgium.

The Germans divided France into a zone under direct German occupation (along the west coast and in the north, including Paris) and a puppet state based in the spa town of Vichy, which was led by Pétain, the ageing WWI hero of the Battle of Verdun. Both Pétain's collaborationist government, whose leaders and supporters assumed that the Nazis were Europe's new masters and had to be accommodated, and French police forces in German-occupied areas including Paris helped the Nazis round up French Jews and others for deportation to Auschwitz and death camps elsewhere.

After the fall of Paris, Général Charles de Gaulle, France's under-secretary of war, fled to London and, in a famous radio broadcast on 18 June 1940, appealed to French patriots to continue resisting the Germans. He also set up a French government-in-exile and established the Forces Françaises Libres (Free French Forces), a military force dedicated to continuing the fight against the Germans.

The underground movement known as the Résistance, which never included more than perhaps 5% of the population – the other 95% were either collaborators (eg the film stars Maurice Chevalier and Arletty and the designer Coco Chanel), or did nothing at all – engaged in such activities as railway sabotage, collecting intelligence for the Allies, helping Allied airmen who had been shot down and publishing anti-German leaflets. Paris was the centre for the activities of the Resistance movement.

Général Charles de Gaulle served as president of the Fifth Republic (1959-69)

The liberation of France began with the US, British and Canadian landings in Normandy on D-day (6 June 1944). On 15 August, Allied forces also landed in southern France. After a brief insurrection by the Resistance, Paris was liberated on 25 August by an Allied force spearheaded by Free French units led by General Leclerc, who were sent in ahead of the Americans so the French would have the honour of liberating the capital. Hitler, who visited Paris in June 1940 and loved it, ordered that the city be torched toward the end of the war. It was an order that, gratefully, had not been obeyed.

The Fourth Republic
De Gaulle returned to Paris and set up a provisional government, but in January 1946 he resigned as president, miscalculating that such a move would provoke a popular outcry for his return. A few months later, a new constitution was approved by referendum.

The Fourth Republic was a period of unstable coalition cabinets which followed one another with bewildering speed (on average, once every six months) and eco-

nomic recovery, helped immeasurably by massive American aid. The war to reassert French colonial control of Indochina ended with the French defeat at Dien Bien Phu in 1954. France also tried to suppress an uprising by Arab nationalists in Algeria, whose population included over one million French settlers.

The Fifth Republic
The Fourth Republic came to an end in 1958, when extreme right-wingers, furious at what they saw as defeatism rather than tough action in dealing with the uprising in Algeria, began conspiring to overthrow the government. De Gaulle was brought back to power to prevent a military coup and possible civil war. He soon drafted a new constitution that gave considerable powers to the president at the expense of the National Assembly.

The Fifth Republic (which continues to this day) was rocked in 1961 by an attempted coup staged in Algiers by a group of right-wing military officers. When it failed, the Organisation de l'Armée Secrète (OAS; a group of French settlers and sympathisers opposed to Algerian independence) turned to terrorism, trying several times to assassinate de Gaulle. The book and film *The Day of the Jackal* portrayed a fictional OAS attempt on de Gaulle's life.

In 1962, de Gaulle negotiated an end to the war in Algeria. Some 750,000 *pieds noirs* (meaning 'black feet' – as Algerian-born French people are known in France) flooded into France and the capital. In the meantime, almost all of the other French colonies and protectorates in Africa had demanded and achieved independence. Shrewdly, the French government began a program of economic and military aid to its former colonies in order to bolster France's waning importance internationally and create a bloc of French-speaking nations in the Third World.

Paris maintained its position as an artistic and creative centre, and the 1960s saw large parts of the Marais beautifully restored. But the loss of the colonies, the surge in immigration and economic difficulties, including an increase in unemployment, weakened de Gaulle's government.

A large anti-Vietnam war demonstration in Paris in March 1968, led by student Daniel Cohn-Bendit ('Danny the Red'), now a European Parliament Member representing the German Green Party, gave impetus to the student movement and protests were staged throughout the spring. A seemingly insignificant incident in May, in which police broke up yet another in a long series of demonstrations by students of the University of Paris, sparked a violent reaction on the streets of the capital; students occupied the Sorbonne and barricades were erected in the Latin Quarter. Workers joined in the protests and some six million people nation-wide participated in a general strike that virtually paralysed both the country and the city.

It was a period of much creativity and new ideas with slogans appearing everywhere like 'L'Imagination au Pouvoir' (Put Imagination in Power) and 'Sous les Pavés, la Plage' (Under the Cobblestones, the Beach), a reference to Parisians' favoured material for building barricades and what they could expect to find beneath them.

The alliance between workers and students couldn't last long. While the former wanted a greater share of the consumer market, the latter wanted to destroy it. De Gaulle took advantage of this division and appealed to people's fear of anarchy. Just as Paris and the rest of France seemed on the brink of revolution and an overthrow of the Fifth Republic imminent, stability was restored. The government made a number of immediate changes, including the decentralisation of the higher education system, and reforms (eg lowering the voting age to 18, an abortion law, workers' self-management) continued through the 1970s.

1969 to the Present

In 1969 de Gaulle was succeeded as president by the Gaullist leader Georges Pompidou, who was in turn succeeded by Valéry Giscard d'Estaing in 1974. François Mitterrand, long-time head of the Parti Socialiste (PS), was elected president in 1981 and, as the business community had feared (the Paris stock market index fell by 30% on news of his victory), immediately set out to nationalise 36 privately owned banks, large industrial groups and various other parts of the economy, increasing the state-owned share of industrial production from 15% to over 30%. During the mid-1980s, however, Mitterrand followed a generally moderate economic policy and in 1988, at the age of 69, was re-elected for a second seven-year term. In the 1986 parliamentary elections, the right-wing opposition led by Jacques Chirac, mayor of Paris from 1977, received a majority in the National Assembly, and for the next two years Mitterrand was forced to work with a prime minister and cabinet from the opposition, an unprecedented arrangement known as cohabitation.

During this period the leaders' passion for nominal immortalisation through grands projets (great works) took hold, starting with the Centre Pompidou (Map 8). Mitterrand took the enthusiasm to great heights, with the Opéra Bastille (Map 5), the Grande Arche de La Défense (see the La Défense map on page 138), the Cité des Sciences (Map 1), the Musée d'Orsay, the Bibliothèque Nationale de France (Map 1) and the controversial glass pyramid in the forecourt of the Louvre all on his building list.

In the May 1995 presidential elections Chirac – the ailing Mitterrand, who would die in January 1996, decided not to run again – walked away with a comfortable electoral victory. In his first few months in office, Chirac received high marks for his direct words and actions in matters relating to European Union (EU) and the war raging in Bosnia. His Cabinet choices, including the selection of 'whiz kid' Foreign Minister Alain Juppé as prime minister, were well received. But Chirac's decision to resume nuclear testing on the Polynesian island of Mururoa and a nearby atoll was met with outrage both in France and abroad.

On the home front, Chirac's moves to restrict welfare payments (a move designed to bring France closer to meeting the criteria of European Monetary Union) led to the largest protests since 1968. For three weeks in late 1995 Paris was crippled by public sector strikes, leaving the economy battered.

In 1997 Chirac took a big gamble and called an early parliamentary election for June. The move backfired. Chirac remained president but his party, the Rassemblement pour la République (RPR; Rally for the Republic) lost support and a coalition of Socialists, Communists and Greens, led by Lionel Jospin, a former minister of education in the Mitterrand government (who, most notably, promised the French people a shorter working week for the same pay), became prime minister. France had once again entered into a period of cohabitation – with Chirac on the other side this time around.

A year into office, Jospin and his government continued to enjoy the electorate's broad trust and approval, not the least due to his political skill and perceived lack of public arrogance (a most unusual trait among French politicians). As president, Chirac retains the power to dissolve Parliament after two years of a government's mandate (ie mid-1999) has elapsed. But with the fractious right unable to agree on whether or not to opt for economic liberalism and the absence of a uniting leader, this appears unlikely.

GEOGRAPHY
The city of Paris, which is both the national capital and that of the historic Île de France region, measures approximately 9.5km (north to south) by 11km (west to east), not including the Bois de Boulogne and the Bois de Vincennes; its total area is 105 sq km. Within central Paris – which the French call *intra-muros* (within the walls) – the Rive Droite (Right Bank) is north of the Seine, while the Rive Gauche (Left Bank) is south of the river.

Paris is a relatively easy city to come to terms with. The ring road known as the Périphérique makes a neat oval containing the whole central area. The Seine cuts an arc across the oval, and the terrain is so flat that Montmartre hill, in the central north of the city, really stands out.

CLIMATE
The Paris basin lies midway between Brittany and Alsace, and is affected by the climates of both. The Île de France region records the nation's lowest annual precipitation (about 575mm) but rainfall patterns are erratic; you're just as likely to be caught in a heavy spring or autumn downpour as in a sudden summer cloudburst. Paris' average yearly temperature is 12°C (3° in January, 19° in July), but the mercury sometimes drops below zero in winter and can climb to the mid-30s or higher in the middle of summer.

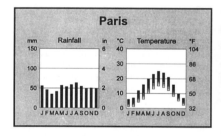

ECOLOGY & ENVIRONMENT
The French are regularly criticised for not being very environmentally sensitive – they've embraced nuclear power without a thought for the dangers, strung unsightly power lines across beautiful country and blithely tested their nuclear weapons in other peoples' backyards.

In Paris, environmental apathy is most clearly revealed in poor air quality. Fly over Paris on the wrong day and you'll see an LA-style brown cloud hanging ominously over the city. Too many cars is the primary cause of this problem, and though certain restrictions are placed on driving in the city during the worst periods, in general there's a curious reluctance to confront car pollution. Public health authorities in Paris say some 350 people die prematurely each year from heart problems triggered by air pollution. Parking restrictions appear to be very feebly enforced; enormous numbers of parking attendants, usually working in packs of two or three, scatter parking tickets like confetti, but Parisian drivers seem to simply ignore them. Perhaps the fees are so low that the odd parking ticket is not worth worrying about.

On the brighter side, some positive steps are being taken. There are now pedestrian-only and bicycle routes – Mayor Jean Tiberi is very *pro-vélo* (pro-bicycle) – along the Seine and the Canal Saint Martin, open on Sunday between 10 am and 5 pm, a network of almost 100km of inner-city bicycle lanes and lanes in the Bois de Boulogne and Bois de Vincennes. Steady efforts have been made to clean up the Seine; these days it's muddy rather than dirty.

FLORA & FAUNA
Flora
At first glance Paris does not appear to have much parkland. There are no great inner-city green spaces like London's Hyde Park or Central Park in Manhattan, although there is the Bois de Boulogne on the western edge of the city and the Bois de Vincennes to the south-east. Other parks tend to be small or, like the famous Jardin du Luxembourg and Jardin des Tuileries, formal affairs, often with more statuary, fountains and paths than grass. Nevertheless, there are splashes of green, many of them the work of Baron Haussmann's urban planning, which produced interesting parks like the Parc des Buttes-Chaumont and the Parc de Monceau. In virtually every park in Paris, regardless of the size, you'll see a signboard illustrating and explaining the trees, plants and flowers of the city.

Fauna
The parks of Paris are particularly rich in birdlife, including magpies, jays, blue and great tits and even woodpeckers. In winter, seagulls are sometimes seen on the Seine and a few hardy ducks also brave the river's often swift-flowing waters. Year round, kestrels nest in the towers of Notre Dame (see the boxed text 'Notre Dame's Kestrels' in the Things to See & Do chapter), but in built-up areas the only birds you're likely to encounter are those ubiquitous rats-on-wings, pigeons. Believe it or not, there are actually crayfish in the city's canals.

GOVERNMENT & POLITICS
The city is run by the *maire* (mayor) who is elected by the 163 members of the Conseil de Paris (Council of Paris), who are elected for six-year terms. The mayor has 18 *adjoints* (deputy mayors), whose offices are in the Hôtel de Ville (city hall).

The first mayor of Paris to be elected with real powers was Chirac in 1977. From 1871 until 1977, the mayor was nominated by the government since Paris was considered a dangerous and revolutionary city. Since the 1995 election of Chirac as president, the Council of Paris has elected Jean Tiberi – a man who is very close to the president and is from the same party, RPR. Tiberi was the former mayor of the 5e *arrondissement* (district) and former deputy mayor for housing.

The mayor has many powers, but they do not include control of the police; that office is handled by the Préfet de Police, part of the Ministry of the Interior. Ever since Chirac won the mayoralty election in 1977, the Council of Paris has been run by right-wing parties, either the Union for French Democracy (UDF) or, more frequently, the RPR.

Paris is a *département* (department or county) as well as a city and the mayor is also the head of that division. The city is divided into 20 arrondissements and each has its own *maire d'arrondissement* (mayor of the arrondissement) and *conseil d'arrondissement* (council of the arrondissement), which are also elected for six-year terms. They have very limited powers, principally administering local cultural, sporting and social activities.

ECONOMY

France's economy may not be the power-house of Europe – Germany can lay claim to that distinction – but French financial leaders have enough clout to determine the shape of European Monetary Union in 1999. EMU, as it is known, has been the driving force behind much of Europe's financial direction as the millennium nears.

For the traveller the most important consequence will be the disappearance of many of Europe's banknotes and bills beginning in 2002, when the euro becomes the standard European currency.

At the heart of financial policy making will be a central bank. Although Paris had hoped that its half-hearted attempts at becoming a regional financial centre would result in the city being selected as the bank's headquarters, the French capital lost out to Frankfurt. But in May 1998 the French won a victory which surprised many European observers: the central bank's chief would have a much shorter reign than originally envisaged, and its second head would be a French official.

Germans were upset, not so much in losing out to their age-old rivals, but because French financial planners have a reputation for being led by their politicians. The Germans fear that a French central bank chief would be ruled more by the ballot box than by firm economic fundamentals.

Most outsiders are surprised by the degree to which the French state still owns much of France. While French bankers are advising many countries around the world on how to sell off state-owned companies, the French themselves have been slow to privatise their own industry. When the So-cialist-dominated government announced in 1998 that France Telecom would be sold to the public in a stock market issue financial markets were relieved. But the sale was contingent on the findings of a special com-mittee that included the trade unions, which were afraid of the negative impact a partial sale would have on jobs.

Pragmatism had something to do with the Socialists going back on their word and opting for privatisation. France continually wrestles with a budget deficit, and in the late 1990s there were fears that the government would overspend to such a degree that France would not be eligible to join the first wave of EMU. Selling off state assets was one way for France to ensure that it met the criteria.

The French economy is growing at about the EU average. This sluggish rise in annual gross domestic product – estimated at just under 3% in 1999 – will keep France's rela-tively high unemployment at around 12%, a figure that has not budged in years.

About 20% of all economic activity in France takes place in the Paris region. Because of the centralised bureaucracy, the capital counts for 40% of the nation's white-collar jobs. Estimates number the homeless on the streets of Paris at upwards of 50,000.

A planned 35-hour work week by the year 2000 might not mean more holiday time for the average employee. Some companies are expected to rely more on part-time workers while other employers will be forced to pay overtime rates to staff.

POPULATION & PEOPLE

The population of Paris is about 2.2 million, although the Île de France, the greater metro-politan area of Paris, has about 10 million inhabitants, or about 17% of France's total population of 58 million people. Paris today is a very cosmopolitan city with many resi-dents from other nations of the EU and a large English-speaking constituency.

France has had waves of immigration, particularly from former French colonies in North Africa and French-speaking sub-Saharan Africa. During the late 1950s and early 1960s, over one million French settlers returned to metropolitan France from Algeria, other parts of Africa and Indochina.

In recent years there has been a racist backlash against the country's non-white immigrant communities, especially Mus-lims from North Africa. In 1993, the French government changed its immigration laws to make it harder for immigrants to get French citizenship or bring their families into the country.

ARTS
Dance
The first *ballet comique de la reine* (dramatic ballet) in France was performed at an aristocratic wedding at the French court in 1581. In 1661 Louis XIV founded the Académie Royale de Danse (Royal Dance Academy), from which ballet around the world developed.

By the end of the 1700s choreographers like Jean-Georges Noverre became more important than the musicians, poets and dancers themselves. In the early 19th century, romantic ballets such as *Giselle* and *Les Sylphides* were more popular than opera in Paris.

Between 1945 and 1955, Roland Petit created such innovative ballets as *Turangalila*. Maurice Béjart shocked the public with his *Symphonie pour un Homme Seul* (danced in black, 1955), *Le Sacre du Printemps* and *Le Marteau sans Maître*, with music by Pierre Boulez.

Music
In the 17th and 18th centuries, French baroque music influenced and informed much of the European musical output. Composers François Couperin and Jean Philippe Rameau were two major players in this field.

France produced and cultivated a number of musical luminaries in the 19th century. Among these were Hector Berlioz, Charles Gounod, César Franck, Camille Saint-Saëns and Georges Bizet. Berlioz was the founder of modern orchestration, while Franck's organ compositions sparked a musical renaissance in France that would produce such greats as Gabriel Fauré and the impressionists Claude Debussy and Maurice Ravel. Two contemporary composers include Olivier Messiaen, who combines modern, almost mystical music with natural sounds such as birdsong, and his student, the radical Pierre Boulez, who includes computer-generated sound in his compositions.

Jazz hit Paris in the 1920s with a bang and has remained popular ever since. France's contribution to the world of jazz has been great: the violinist Stéphane Grappelli and the legendary three-fingered Gypsy guitarist Django Reinhardt.

The most appreciated form of indigenous music is the *chanson française*, with a tradition going back to the troubadours of the Middle Ages. French songs have always favoured lyrics over music and rhythm, which partially explains the enormous popularity of rap in France today.

The chanson tradition was revived from the 1930s by such singers as Edith Piaf (see the boxed text in the Entertainment chapter) and Charles Trenet. In the 1950s singers such as Georges Brassens, Léo Ferré, Claude Nougaro, Jacques Brel and Barbara became national stars.

Today's popular music has come a long way since the *yéyé* (imitative rock) of the 1960s sung by Johnny Halliday – though you might not think so listening to middle-of-the-roaders Vanessa Paradis and Patrick Bruel. Watch out for rappers MC Solaar, Doc Gynéco and I Am from Marseille. Evergreen balladeers/folk singers include Francis Cabrel, Julien Clerc, Jean-Jacques Goldman and Jacques Higelin, while the late Serge Gainsbourg remains enormously popular. Some people like the New Age space music of Jean-Michel Jarre; others say his name fits his sound.

France's claim to fame over the past decade has been *sono mondial* (world music) – from Algerian *raï* and other North African music (Cheb Khaled, Natache Atlas, Jamel, Cheb Mami, Racid Taha) to Senegalese *mbalax* (Youssou N'Dour), West Indian *zouk* (Kassav, Zouk Machine) and Cuban salsa. Mano Negra and Les Négresses Vertes were two bands in the late 1980s that combined many of these elements – often with brilliant results. Watch for their successors Noir Désir.

Literature
The great landmarks of French Renaissance literature are the works of Rabelais, La Pléiade and Montaigne. François Rabelais' exuberant narrative blends coarse humour with encyclopaedic erudition in a vast

oeuvre which seems to include every kind of person, occupation and jargon to be found in mid-16th century France. Rabelais had friends in high places in Paris, including Archbishop Jean du Bellay, whom he accompanied to Rome on two occasions. But some of Rabelais' friends and associates fell foul of the clergy, including his publisher, Étienne Dolet, who, after being convicted of heresy and blasphemy in 1546, was hanged and then burned at Place Maubert (5e).

During the 17th century, known as *le grand siècle*, François de Malherbe brought a new rigour to the treatment of rhythm in literature. Transported by the perfection of Malherbe's verses, Jean de La Fontaine recognised his vocation and went on to write his charming *Fables* in the manner of Aesop. The mood of classical tragedy permeates *La Princesse de Clèves* by Marie de La Fayette, which is widely regarded as the first major French novel.

The literature of the 18th century is dominated by philosophers, among them Voltaire and Jean-Jacques Rousseau. Voltaire's political writings, in which is argued that society is fundamentally opposed to nature, were to have a profound and lasting influence. Rousseau's sensitivity to landscape and its moods anticipates romanticism, and the insistence on his own singularity in *Les Confessions* makes it the first modern autobiography.

The 19th century brought Victor Hugo, widely acclaimed for his poetry as well as for his novels. *Les Misérables* (1862) describes life among the poor and marginalised of Paris during the first half of the 19th century. The flight of the central character, Jean Valjean, through the sewers of the capital is memorable as are Hugo's descriptions (all 20 pages of them). *The Hunchback of Notre Dame* (see the boxed text in the Things to See & Do chapter), published three decades earlier, had made Hugo the key figure of French romanticism.

Other 19th-century novelists include Stendhal, Honoré de Balzac, Aurore Dupain, better known as George Sand, and

of course Alexandre Dumas the elder, who wrote the swashbuckling adventures *The Count of Monte Cristo* and *The Three Musketeers*. The much loved latter tells the story of d'Artagnan (based on the historical personage Charles de Baatz d'Artagnan, 1623-73), who arrives in Paris determined to become one of Louis XIII's guardsmen.

In 1857 two landmarks of French literature appeared: *Madame Bovary* by Gustave Flaubert and *Les Fleurs du Mal* by Charles Baudelaire. Both writers were tried for the supposed immorality of their works. Flaubert won his case, and his novel was distributed without cuts. Baudelaire, who moonlighted as a translator in Paris (he introduced the works of the American writer Edgar Allan Poe to Europe in translations which have since become French classics), was obliged to cut several poems from *Les Fleurs du Mal*, and he died an early and painful death, practically unknown. Flaubert's second most popular novel, *L'Éducation Sentimentale*, presents a vivid picture of life among Parisian dilettantes, intellectuals and revolutionaries at the decline and fall of Louis-Philippe's monarchy and the February Revolution of 1848.

The aim of Émile Zola, who came to Paris in 1858 with his close friend Paul Cézanne, was to convert novel writing from an art to a science by the application of experimentation. His theory may seem naive, but his work influenced all the significant French writers of the late 19th century and is reflected in much 20th-century fiction as well. *Nana* tells the decadent tale of a young woman who resorts to prostitution to survive in the Paris of the Second Empire.

Paul Verlaine and Stéphane Mallarmé created the symbolist movement, which strove to express states of mind rather than simply detail daily reality. Arthur Rimbaud, apart from crowding an extraordinary amount of rugged, exotic travel into his 37 years and having a tempestuous homosexual relationship with Verlaine, produced two enduring pieces of work: *Illuminations* and *Une Saison en Enfer* (A Season in Hell).

Marcel Proust dominated the early 20th century with his giant seven-volume novel, *À la Recherche du Temps Perdu* (Remembrance of Things Past); it is largely autobiographical and explores in evocative detail the true meaning of past experience recovered from the unconscious by 'involuntary memory'. In 1907, Proust moved from the family home near the Ave des Champs-Élysées to the apartment on Blvd Haussmann famous for the cork-lined bedroom from which he almost never stirred. The original room is now on display in the Musée Carnavalet in the Marais (3e). André Gide found his voice in the celebration of homosexual sensuality and, later, left-wing politics. *Les Faux-Monnayeurs* (The Counterfeiters) exposes the hypocrisy and self-deception with which people try to avoid sincerity – a common theme with Gide.

André Breton ruled the surrealist group and wrote its three manifestoes, although the first use of the word 'surrealist' is attributed to the writer Guillaume Apollinaire, a fellow traveller. As a poet, Breton was overshadowed by Paul Éluard and Louis Aragon, whose most famous surrealist novel was *Le Paysan de Paris*.

Colette enjoyed tweaking the nose of conventionally moral readers with titillating novels which detailed the amorous exploits of such heroines as the schoolgirl Claudine. One of her most interesting works concerned the German occupation of Paris, *Paris de Ma Fenêtre* (Paris from My Window). Her view, by the way, was from 9 Rue de Beaujolais (1er).

After WWII, existentialism, a significant literary movement, developed around Jean-Paul Sartre, Simone de Beauvoir and Albert Camus, who worked and conversed in the cafés of Saint Germain des Prés. All three stressed the importance of the writer's political engagement. De Beauvoir, author of the ground-breaking study *The Second Sex*, had a profound influence on feminist thinking.

In the late 1950s, some younger novelists

Strangers in Paris

Foreigners *(ètrangers,* or strangers, to the French) have found inspiration in Paris since Charles Dickens used it alongside London as the backdrop to his novel on the French Revolution, *A Tale of Two Cities* (1859). The glory days of Paris as a literary setting, however, were without a doubt the interwar years.

Hemingway's *A Moveable Feast* portrays bohemian life in Paris between the wars and many of the vignettes – climbing to the rooftop of his apartment on Rue du Cardinal Lemoine with a prostitute to avoid his wife at the front door, overhearing Gertrude Stein and her lover, Alice B Toklas, battle it out from the sitting room of her salon near the Jardin du Luxembourg – are classic and very Parisian.

Language guru Stein, who could be so tiresome with her word plays and endless repetitions ('A rose is a rose is a rose is a rose') in books like *The Making of Americans*, was able to let her hair down by assuming her lover's identity in *The Autobiography of Alice B Toklas*. It's a fascinating account of the author's many years in Paris, her salon on the Rue de Fleurus and her friendships with Matisse, Picasso, Braque, Hemingway and others. It's also where you'll find that classic recipe for hashish brownies. Stein's *Wars I Have Seen* is a personal account of life in German-occupied Paris.

Down and Out in Paris and London, George Orwell's account of the time he spent living with tramps in Paris and London in the late 1920s, introduces the reader to another side of Paris altogether. Both *Tropic of Cancer* and *Tropic of Capricorn* by Henry Miller are steamy novels set in the French capital. They were published in France in the 1930s but banned under obscenity laws in the UK and USA until the 1960s.

began to look for new ways of organising the narrative. The so-called *nouveau roman* (new novel) refers to the works of Nathalie Sarraute, Alain Robbe-Grillet, Boris Vian, Julien Gracq and Michel Butor, among others. However, these writers never formed a close-knit group, and their experiments have taken them in divergent directions. Today the nouveau roman is very much out of favour in France.

Mention must also be made of *Histoire d'O*, the highly erotic sadomasochistic novel (written under a pseudonym in 1954) by Dominique Aury (1907-98). It sold more copies than any other contemporary French novel outside France.

In 1980 Marguerite Yourcenar, best known for her memorable historical novels such as *Mémoires d'Hadrien*, became the first woman to be elected to the French Academy.

Marguerite Duras came to the notice of a larger public when she won the prestigious Prix Goncourt for her novel *L'Amant* (The Lover) in 1984. She was also noted for the screenplays of *India Song* and *Hiroshima Mon Amour*, described by one critic as part nouveau roman, part Mills & Boon.

Philippe Sollers was one of the editors of *Tel Quel*, a highbrow, then left-wing Paris-based review which was very influential in the 1960s and early 1970s. His 1960s novels were highly experimental, but with *Femmes* (Women) he returned to a conventional narrative style.

Another editor of *Tel Quel* was Julia Kristeva, best known for her theoretical writings on literature and psychoanalysis. In recent years she has turned her hand to fiction, and *Les Samuraï*, a fictionalised account of the heady days of *Tel Quel*, is an interesting document on the life of the Paris intelligentsia. Roland Barthes and Michel Foucault are other authors and philosophers associated with this period.

More accessible authors who enjoy a wide following include Françoise Sagan, Patrick Modiano, Yann Queffélec, Pascal Quignard and Denis Tillinac. The *roman policier* (detective novel) has always been a great favourite with the French and among its greatest exponents has been the Belgian-born Georges Simenon and his novels featuring Inspector Maigret *(Maigret at the Crossroads* portrays Montmartre at its sleaziest and seediest best).

Architecture
See the Architecture of Paris section beginning on page 63.

Painting
Voltaire wrote that French painting began with Nicolas Poussin (1594-1665), a baroque painter who frequently set scenes from classical mythology and the Bible in ordered landscapes bathed in golden light.

In the 18th century, Jean-Baptiste Chardin brought the humbler domesticity of the Dutch masters to French art. In 1785 the public reacted with enthusiasm to two large paintings with clear republican messages: *The Oath of the Horatii* and *Brutus Condemning His Son* by Jacques Louis David. David became one of the leaders of the Revolution, and a virtual dictator in matters of art, where he advocated a precise, severe classicism. He was made official state painter by Napoleon. He is perhaps best remembered for the famous painting of Marat lying dead in his bath.

Jean Auguste Dominique Ingres, David's most gifted pupil, continued in the neoclassical tradition. The historical pictures to which he devoted most of his life are now generally regarded as inferior to his portraits.

The gripping *Raft of the Medusa* by Théodore Géricault is on the threshold of romanticism; if Géricault had not died young, he would probably have become a leader of the movement, along with his friend Eugène Delacroix. Delacroix's most famous picture, perhaps, is *La Liberté Conduisant le Peuple* (Freedom Leading the People), which commemorates the July Revolution of 1830.

The members of the Barbizon School brought about a parallel transformation of landscape painting. The school derived its name from the village of Barbizon near the Forêt de Fontainebleau, where Camille

Corot and Jean-François Millet, among others, gathered to paint in the open air. Corot is best known for his landscapes, while Millet took many of his subjects from peasant life and had a strong influence on van Gogh.

Millet anticipated the realist programme of Gustave Courbet, a prominent member of the Paris Commune, whose paintings show the misery of manual labour and the cramped lives of the working class.

Édouard Manet used realism to depict the life of the Parisian middle classes, yet he included in his pictures numerous references to the old masters. His *Déjeuner sur l'Herbe* and *Olympia* were considered scandalous, largely because they broke with the traditional treatment of their subject matter.

Impressionism, initially a term of derision, was taken from the title of an 1874 experimental painting by Claude Monet, *Impression: Soleil Levant* (Impression: Sunrise). Monet was the leading figure of the school, which counted among its members Alfred Sisley, Camille Pisarro, Berthe Morisot and Pierre-Auguste Renoir. The impressionists' main aim was to capture fleeting light effects, and light came to dominate the content of their painting.

Edgar Degas was a fellow traveller, but he preferred his studio to open-air painting. He found his favourite subjects at the racecourse and the ballet. Henri de Toulouse-Lautrec was a great admirer of Degas and chose similar subjects: people in the bars, brothels and music halls of Montmartre. He is best known for his posters and lithographs in which the distortion of the figures is both caricatural and decorative.

Paul Cézanne is celebrated for his still lifes and landscapes depicting the south of France, while the name of Paul Gauguin immediately conjures up his studies of Tahitian women. Both he and Cézanne are usually referred to as postimpressionists, something of a catch-all term for the diverse styles which flowed from impressionism.

In the late 19th century, Gauguin worked for a time in Arles in Provence with the Dutch artist Vincent van Gogh, who spent most of his painting life in France. A brilliant, innovative artist, van Gogh produced haunting self-portraits and landscapes in which colour assumes an expressive and emotive quality. His later technique paralleled pointillism, developed by Georges Seurat. Seurat applied paint in small dots or uniform brush strokes of unmixed colour, producing fine mosaics of warm and cool tones.

Henri Rousseau was a contemporary of the postimpressionists but his 'naive' art was totally unaffected by them. His dreamlike pictures of the Paris suburbs, jungle and desert scenes have had a lasting influence on 20th-century art.

Gustave Moreau was a member of the symbolist school. His eerie treatment of mythological subjects can be seen in his old studio (now the Musée Gustave Moreau) in Paris.

Fauvism took its name from the slur of a critic who compared the exhibitors at the 1906 autumn salon with *fauves* (wildcats) because of their radical use of intensely bright colours. Among these 'wild' painters were Henri Matisse, André Derain and Maurice de Vlaminck.

Cubism was effectively launched in 1907 by the Spanish prodigy Pablo Picasso with his *Les Demoiselles d'Avignon*. Cubism, as developed by Picasso, Georges Braque and Juan Gris, deconstructed the subject into a system of intersecting planes and presented various aspects simultaneously.

After WWI, the School of Paris was formed by a group of expressionists, mostly foreign-born, like Amedeo Modigliani from Italy and the Russian Marc Chagall. Chagall's pictures combine fantasy and folklore.

Dada, a literary and artistic movement of revolt, started in Germany and Switzerland during WWI. In France, one of the principal Dadaists was Marcel Duchamp, whose *Mona Lisa* adorned with moustache and goatee epitomises the spirit of the movement.

Surrealism, an offshoot of Dada, flourished between the wars. Drawing on the theories of Freud, it attempted to reunite the conscious and unconscious realms, to permeate everyday life with fantasies and dreams.

WWII ended Paris' role as the world's artistic capital. Many artists left France, and though some returned after the war, the city never regained its old magnetism.

Sculpture

By the 14th century, sculpture was increasingly commissioned for the tombs of the nobility. In Renaissance France, Pierre Bontemps decorated the beautiful tomb of François I at Saint Denis, and Jean Goujon created the Fontaine des Innocents in central Paris. The baroque style is exemplified by Guillaume Coustou's *Horses of Marly* at the entrance to the Ave des Champs-Élysées.

In the 19th century, memorial statues in public places came to replace sculpted tombs. One of the best artists in the new mode was François Rude, who sculpted the statue of Marshall Ney outside the Closerie des Lilas and the relief on the Arc de Triomphe. Another sculptor was Jean-Baptiste Carpeaux who began as a romantic, but whose work such as *The Dance* on the Opéra Garnier and his fountain in the Jardin du Luxembourg look back to the warmth and gaiety of the baroque era.

At the end of the 19th century, Auguste Rodin's work overcame the conflict of neoclassicism and romanticism. His sumptuous bronze and marble figures of men and women did much to revitalise sculpture as an expressive medium. One of Rodin's most gifted pupils was Camille Claudel, whose work can be seen along with that of Rodin in the Musée Rodin.

Braque and Picasso experimented with sculpture, and in the spirit of Dada, Marcel Duchamp exhibited 'found objects', such as a urinal, which he titled *Fountain* and signed.

One of the most influential sculptors to emerge after WWII was César Baldaccini, using iron and scrap metal to create his imaginary insects and animals, later graduating to pliable plastics.

Cinema

France's place in the film history books was firmly ensured when the Lumière brothers invented 'moving pictures' and organised the world's first paying (1FF) public movie screening – a series of two-minute reels – in Paris' Grand Café on the Blvd des Capucines on 28 December 1895.

In the 1920s and 1930s avant-garde directors such as René Clair, Marcel Carné and the intensely productive Jean Renoir, son of the famous artist, searched for new forms and subjects.

In the late 1950s a large group of new generation directors burst onto the scene with a new genre, the *nouvelle vague* (new wave). This group included Jean-Luc Godard, François Truffaut, Claude Chabrol, Eric Rohmer, Jacques Rivette, Louis Malle and Alain Resnais. This disparate group of directors believed in the primacy of the film-maker, giving rise to the term *film d'auteur*.

Many films followed, among them Alain Resnais' *Hiroshima Mon Amour* and *L'Année Dernière à Marienbad* (Last Year in Marienbad). François Truffaut's *Les Quatre Cents Coups* (The 400 Blows) was partly based on his own rebellious adolescence. Jean-Luc Godard made such films as *À Bout de Souffle* (Breathless), *Alphaville* and *Pierrot le Fou* (1965), which showed even less concern for sequence and narrative. The new wave continued until the 1970s, by which stage it had lost its experimental edge.

Of the non-new wave directors of the 1950s and 1960s, one of the most notable was Jacques Tati, who made many comic films based around the charming, bumbling figure of Monsieur Hulot and his struggles to adapt to the modern age.

The most successful directors of the 1980s and 1990s include Jean-Jacques Beineix, who made *Diva* and *Betty Blue*, and Jean-Luc Besson who made *Subway*, *The Big Blue* and *The Fifth Element*.

In 1986 Claude Berri came up with *Jean de Florette* followed by *Manon des Sources*, modern versions of writer/film-maker Marcel Pagnol's original works, which proved enormously popular both in France and abroad. Léos Carax, in his *Boy Meets Girl*, creates a kind of Parisian purgatory of souls lost in the eternal night.

Jacques Tati and Nathalie Pascaud in *Les Vacances de Monsieur Hulot*

Light social comedies like *Trois Hommes et un Couffin* (Three Men and a Cradle), *Romuald et Juliette* by Coline Serreau and *La Vie est un Long Fleuve Tranquille* (Life is a Long Quiet River) by Étienne Chatiliez have been among the biggest hits in France in recent years.

Other well regarded directors today include Bertrand Blier (*Trop Belle pour Toi*), Eric Klapisch (*Un Air de Famille*), Claude Sautet and André Téchiné. Matthieu Kassovitz's award-winning *La Haine* examines the prejudice and violence of the world of the 'Beurs' – young, French-born Algerians. Alain Renais' *On Connaît la Chanson*, based on the life of the late British television playwright Dennis Potter, received international acclaim and six Césars in 1997.

Theatre

Molière, an actor, became the most popular comic playwright of *le grand siècle*. Plays such as *Tartuffe* are staples of the classical repertoire. The playwrights Pierre Corneille and Jean Racine, by contrast, drew their sub-jects from history and classical mythology. For instance, Racine's *Phèdre*, taken from Euripides, is a story of incest and suicide among the descendants of the Greek gods.

SOCIETY & CONDUCT
Dos & Donts

Some visitors to Paris conclude that it would be a lovely place if it weren't for the Parisians. As in other cities around the world, however, the more tourists a particular area or district attracts, the less patience the locals tend to have for them.

A few dos:

- The easiest way to improve the quality of your relations with Parisians is always to say 'Bonjour, monsieur/madame/mademoiselle' when you walk into a shop, and 'Merci, monsieur ... au revoir' when you leave. 'Monsieur' means 'sir' and can be used with any male person who isn't a child. 'Madame' is used where 'Mrs' would apply in English, whereas 'mademoiselle' is used when talking to un-married women. When in doubt, use 'madame'.

- It is customary for people who know each other to exchange *bises* (kisses) as a greeting, though rarely men with men unless they are related. The usual ritual is one glancing peck on each cheek, but some people go for three or even four kisses. People who don't kiss each other will almost always shake hands.

- If invited to someone's home or a party, always bring some sort of gift, such as good wine (not some 10FF *vin de table*). Flowers are another good standby, but chrysanthemums are only taken to cemeteries.

- Many French people seem to feel that 'going Dutch' (ie splitting the bill) at restaurants is an uncivilised custom. In general, the person who did the inviting pays for dinner, though close friends and colleagues will sometimes share the cost.

A few don'ts:

- When buying fruit and vegetables anywhere except at supermarkets, do not touch the produce unless invited to do so. Show the shopkeeper what you want and he or she will choose the vegetables or fruit for you.

- In a restaurant, do not summon the waiter by shouting 'garçon', which means 'boy'. Saying 's'il vous plaît' (please) is the way it's done nowadays.

- When you're being served cheese (eg as the final course for dinner), remember two cardinal rules: never cut off the tip of the pie-shaped soft cheeses (eg Brie, Camembert) and cut cheeses whose middle is the best part (eg blue cheese) in such a way as to take your fair share of the crust.
- Money, particularly income, is a subject that is simply not discussed in France.
- In general, lawns in France are meant to be looked at and praised for their greenness, not sat upon; watch out for *pelouse interdite* (Keep off the Grass!) signs. But this has been changing in recent years, with such signs being removed and replaced with *pelouse autorisée*, meaning tourists and locals alike are permitted to sit, eat, play and walk on the grass of certain parks (with some exceptions such as the Jardin des Tuileries and Jardin du Luxembourg).

RELIGION
Roman Catholics
Some 80% of French people identify themselves as Roman Catholic but, although most have been baptised, very few go to church much less attend Mass. *Conversion*, such as that experienced by the poet Paul Claudel (1868-1955) and the novelist Henry de Montherlant (1896-1972), thus actually means 're-conversion' in English. The Catholic Church in France is generally very progressive and ecumenically minded. Cardinal Jean-Marie Lustiger, archbishop of Paris since 1981, was born to Jewish parents from Poland in Paris in 1926. He converted to Catholicism at age 14. His mother died in the Nazi extermination camp at Auschwitz in 1942.

Protestants
France's Protestants (Huguenots), who were severely persecuted during much of the 16th and 17th centuries, now number about one million. They are concentrated in Alsace, the Jura, the south-eastern part of the Massif Central and along the Atlantic coast.

Muslims
Islam has between four and five million nominal adherents in France, and they now make up the country's second-largest religious group. The vast majority are immigrants or their offspring who came from North Africa during the 1950s and 1960s.

In recent years, France's Muslim community has been the object of racist agitation by right-wing parties and extremist groups. Many North Africans complain of discrimination by the police and employers.

Jews
There has been a Jewish community in France for most of the time since the Roman period. During the Middle Ages, the community suffered persecution and there were a number of mass expulsions. French Jews, the first in Europe to achieve emancipation, were granted full citizenship in 1790-91. Since 1808, the French Jewish community has had an umbrella organisation known as the Consistoire based in Paris.

The country's Jewish community, which now numbers some 650,000 (the largest in Europe), grew substantially during the 1960s as a result of immigration from Algeria, Tunisia and Morocco.

LANGUAGE
Around 122 million people worldwide speak French as their first language; it is one of the official languages in Belgium, Switzerland, Luxembourg, the Canadian province of Québec and over two dozen other countries, most of them former French colonies in Africa. It is also spoken in the Val d'Aosta region of north-western Italy. Various forms of Creole are used in Haiti, French Guiana and parts of Louisiana. France has a special government ministry (Ministère de la Francophonie) to deal with the country's relations with the French-speaking world.

French was *the* international language of culture and diplomacy until WWI, and the French are somewhat sensitive to this fact. Your best bet is always to approach people politely in French, even if the only words you know are *Pardon, parlez-vous anglais?*, 'Excuse me, do you speak English?'.

For more useful words and phrases than we have space for here, see Lonely Planet's *French phrasebook*.

Grammar

An important distinction is made in French between *tu* ('you' singular) and *vous* ('you' plural). *Tu* is only used when addressing children or people you know well. When addressing someone who is not a personal friend, *vous* should be used unless the person invites you to use *tu*. In this case they will say *'Tu peux me tutoyer'*. In general, younger people are less insistent on this formality, and they'll usually use *tu* from the beginning of an acquaintance. In this book, however, we have used the more polite *vous* form. (When using *vous*, remember that verbs must also be conjugated in the second person plural, eg *vous aimez*, and not *vous aimes*, 'you like').

All nouns in French are either masculine or feminine and adjectives must reflect the gender of the noun they modify. The feminine form of many nouns and adjectives is indicated by an *e* added to the masculine form – a male student is *un étudiant*, a female student is *une étudiante*. The gender of a noun is often indicated by a preceding article: 'the' is *le* (m) and *la* (f); 'a' is *un* (m) and *une* (f); 'some' is *du* (m) and *de la* (f). In this book, where both masculine and feminine forms of a word are given, the masculine appears first, separated from the feminine by a slash.

Pronunciation

French has a number of sounds that may be unfamiliar to Anglophones:

- The distinction between the 'u' sound (as in *tu*) and the 'oo' sound (as in *tout*). For both sounds, the lips are rounded and pushed forward, but to achieve the 'u' sound, try to say 'ee' while keeping the lips rounded and forward.

- The nasal vowels. In producing nasal vowels, the breath escapes partly through the nose and partly through the mouth. There are no nasal vowels in English. In French there are three:

bon vin blanc, 'good white wine'. These sounds mostly occur where a syllable ends in a single 'n' or 'm'; the 'n' or 'm' is silent but indicates the nasalisation of the preceding vowel.

- The standard 'r' of Parisian French is produced by moving the bulk of the tongue backwards to constrict the airflow in the pharynx while the tip of the tongue rests behind the lower front teeth. It's similar to the noise made by some people before spitting, but with much less friction.

- The French 'j', as in the word *jour*, 'day', is pronounced as the 's' in 'leisure'.

Greetings & Civilities

Hello/ Good morning.	*Bonjour.*
Good evening.	*Bonsoir.*
Goodbye.	*Au revoir.*
Yes.	*Oui.*
No.	*Non.*
Maybe.	*Peut-être.*
Please.	*S'il vous plaît.*
Thank you.	*Merci.*
You're welcome.	*Je vous en prie.*
Excuse me.	*Excusez-moi.*
I'm sorry/ Forgive me.	*Pardon.*
Just a moment.	*Attendez un moment.*

Language Difficulties

Do you speak English?	*Parlez-vous anglais?*
I understand.	*Je comprends.*
I don't understand.	*Je ne comprends pas.*
Could you write it down please?	*Est-ce-que vous pouvez l'écrire?*
How do you say ... in French?	*Comment dit-on ... en français?*

Small Talk

How are you?	*Comment allez-vous?* (formal) *(Comment) ça va?* (informal)
Fine, thanks.	*Bien, merci.*
What's your name?	*Comment vous appelez-vous?*
My name is ...	*Je m'appelle ...*

Pleased to meet you.	*Enchanté/ée.*
What country are you from?	*De quel pays venez-vous?*
I'm from ...	*Je viens d'/du/des ...*
How old are you?	*Quel âge avez-vous?*
I'm ... years old.	*J'ai ... ans.*
Do you like ...?	*Aimez-vous ...?*
I like ... very much.	*J'aime beaucoup ...*
I don't like ...	*Je n'aime pas ...*

Getting Around

I want to go to ...	*Je voudrais aller à ...*
I'd like to book a seat to ...	*Je voudrais réserver une place pour ...*
Where is the (bus/tram) stop?	*Où est l'arrêt (de bus/de tramway)?*
What time does the next train (leave/arrive)?	*À quelle heure (part/arrive) le prochain train?*

aeroplane	*l'avion*
boat	*le bateau*
bus (city)	*le bus*
bus (intercity)	*le car*
ferry	*le ferry*
tram	*le tramway*

I'd like a ... ticket.	*Je voudrais un billet ...*
one-way	*aller simple*
return	*aller-retour*
How long does the trip take?	*Combien de temps dure le trajet?*
Do I need to change trains/platform?	*Est-ce que je dois changer de train/de quai?*

1st class	*première classe*
2nd class	*deuxième classe*
left-luggage office	*consigne manuelle*
platform	*le quai*
ticket	*le billet*
ticket window	*le guichet*
timetable	*l'horaire*

I'd like to hire a bicycle/car.	*Je voudrais louer un vélo/une voiture.*

Directions

How do I get to ...?	*Comment-dois je faire pour arriver à ...?*

Is it near/far?	*Est-ce que c'est près/loin?*
I want to go to ...	*Je veux aller à ...*
I'm looking for ...	*Je cherche ...*
Can you show me (on the map)?	*Est-ce que vous pouvez me le montrer (sur la carte)?*
Go straight ahead.	*Continuez tout droit.*
Turn left.	*Tournez à gauche.*
Turn right.	*Tournez à droite.*
at the traffic lights	*aux feux*
at the next corner	*au prochain coin*
behind	*derrière*
in front of	*devant*
opposite	*en face de*
north/south	*nord/sud*
east/west	*est/ouest*

Around Town

I'm looking for ...	*Je cherche ...*
a bank	*une banque*
the city centre	*le centre-ville*
an exchange office	*un bureau de change*
the ... embassy	*l'ambassade de ...*
my hotel	*mon hôtel*
the market	*le marché*
the police	*la police*
the post office	*la poste/le bureau de poste*
a public telephone	*une cabine téléphonique*
the public toilet	*les toilettes*
the railway station	*la gare*
the tourist office	*l'office de tourisme*
the metro station	*le métro*
the bridge	*le pont*
the castle/vineyard	*le château*
the cathedral	*la cathédrale*
the church	*l'église*
the island	*l'île*
the lake	*le lac*
the main square	*la place centrale*
the museum	*la musée*
the old city	*la vieille ville*
the palace	*le palais*
the quay/bank	*le quai/la rive*
the square	*la place*
the tower	*la tour*

Top: Champ de Mars with the Eiffel Tower in the background
Bottom: Maintenance work on a facade in the Marais

MARK HONAN

SIMON BRACKEN

MARK HONAN

BRENDA TURNNIDGE

Top: Selling roasted chestnuts
Middle & Bottom: Faces of Paris
Right: Carnival along Boulevard Beaumarchais, near Bastille

SIMON BRACKEN

RACHEL BLACK

SIMON BRACKEN

Top: Model sailboats in the Jardin du Luxembourg
Bottom Left: Bois de Boulogne
Bottom Right: Church in Châteaux de Vincennes

Top: Parc des Buttes-Chaumont
Bottom Left: Musée d'Orsay
Bottom Right: Église St Eustache

| I'd like to make a telephone call. | *Je voudrais utiliser le téléphone.* |
| I'd like to change some money/ travellers cheques. | *Je voudrais changer de l'argent/ des chèques de voyage.* |

Accommodation

I'm looking for ...	*Je cherche ...*
a campground	*un camping*
a hostel	*une auberge de jeunesse*
a hotel	*un hôtel*

| Do you have any rooms available? | *Est-ce que vous avez des chambres libres?* |

I'd like ...	*Je voudrais ...*
a bed	*un lit*
a single room	*une chambre simple*
a double room	*une chambre double*
a room with shower and toilet	*une chambre avec douche et WC* (pron: 'vay-say')
to stay in a dormitory	*coucher dans un dortoir*

How much is it ...?	*Quel est le prix ...?*
per night	*par nuit*
per person	*par personne*
Is breakfast included?	*Est-ce que le petit déjeuner est compris?*
Can I see the room?	*Je peux voir la chambre?*
Where is the bathroom?	*Où est la salle de bain?*
shower?	*la douche?*
I'll be staying ...	*Je resterai ...*
for one day	*un jour*
for one week	*une semaine*

Paperwork

Surname	*Nom de famille*
Given name	*Prénom*
Date of birth	*Date de naissance*
Place of birth	*Lieu de naissance*
Nationality	*Nationalité*
Sex	*Sexe*
Passport	*Passeport*
Driver's Licence	*Permis de conduire*

Food

breakfast	*le petit déjeuner*
lunch	*le déjeuner*
dinner	*le dîner*

I'd like the set lunch.	*Je prends le menu.*
I'm a vegetarian.	*Je suis végétarien/ végétarienne.*
Some water, please.	*Une carafe d'eau, s'il vous plaît.*
the bill, please	*l'addition, s'il vous plaît*

Shopping

How much is it?	*C'est combien?*
It's too expensive for me.	*C'est trop cher pour moi.*
Can I look at it?	*Est-ce que je peux le/la voir?*
Can I pay by credit card?	*Est-ce que je peux payer avec ma carte de crédit?*
Do you take travellers cheques?	*Est-ce que vous prenez des chèques de voyage?*
Do you have another colour/ size?	*Est-ce que vous avez d'autres couleurs/ tailles?*

Health

I'm ...	*Je suis ...*
diabetic	*diabétique*
epileptic	*épileptique*
asthmatic	*asthmatique*
anaemic	*anémique*

I'm allergic ...	*Je suis allergique ...*
to antibiotics	*aux antibiotiques*
to penicillin	*à la pénicilline*
to bees	*aux abeilles*

antiseptic	*l'antiseptique*
aspirin	*l'aspirine*
condoms	*préservatifs*
contraceptive	*le contraceptif*
medicine	*le médicament*
sunblock cream	*la crème solaire haute protection*
tampons	*tampons hygiéniques*

Time & Dates

What time is it?	*Quelle heure est-il?*
today	*aujourd'hui*
tonight	*ce soir*
tomorrow	*demain*
day after tomorrow	*après-demain*
yesterday	*hier*
every day	*tous les jours*
in the morning	*le matin*
in the afternoon	*l'après-midi*
in the evening	*le soir*

Monday	*lundi*
Tuesday	*mardi*
Wednesday	*mercredi*
Thursday	*jeudi*
Friday	*vendredi*
Saturday	*samedi*
Sunday	*dimanche*

Numbers

0	*zéro*
1	*un*
2	*deux*
3	*trois*
4	*quatre*
5	*cinq*
6	*six*
7	*sept*
8	*huit*
9	*neuf*
10	*dix*
11	*onze*
12	*douze*
13	*treize*
14	*quatorze*
15	*quinze*
16	*seize*
17	*dix-sept*
18	*dix-huit*
19	*dix-neuf*
20	*vingt*
21	*vingt-et-un*
22	*vingt-deux*
30	*trente*
40	*quarante*
50	*cinquante*
60	*soixante*
70	*soixante-dix*
80	*quatre-vingt*
90	*quatre-vingt-dix*
100	*cent*
1000	*mille*
one million	*un million*

Emergencies

Help!	*Au secours!*
Call a doctor!	*Appelez un médecin!*
Call the police!	*Appelez la police!*
Go away!	*Laissez-moi tranquille!*
Leave me alone!	*Fichez-moi la paix!*

Facts for the Visitor

WHEN TO GO

As all the old songs tell us, Paris is at its best in spring – though winter-like relapses are not unknown in the otherwise beautiful month of April. Autumn is also pleasant, but of course the days are fairly short. In winter Paris has all sorts of cultural events going on, while in July and August the weather is warm and even hot. Most Parisians leave the city in August for their annual vacation; as a result many places will be closed, although visitors will be as thick on the ground as ever. If you understand French you can find out the weather forecast for Paris and its vicinity by calling ☎ 08 36 68 02 75. The national forecast in French and English can be heard on ☎ 08 36 70 12 34.

ORIENTATION

The location of every museum, hotel, restaurant etc mentioned in this book is referenced to one of the colour maps (numbered 1 to 9).

Arrondissements

For more than a century Paris has been divided into 20 arrondissements (districts) which spiral out from the city centre clockwise like a conch shell. Paris addresses *always* include the arrondissement numbers and they're very important as streets with the same names exist in different districts.

In this book, arrondissement numbers follow the usual French notation: 1er for *premier* (1st), 4e for *quatrième* (4th), 16e for *seizième* (16th) and so on.

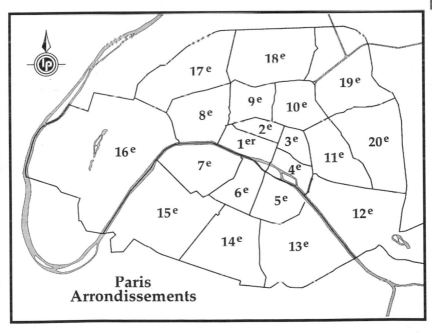

Paris
Arrondissements

MAPS

The most useful map of Paris is the 1:10,000-scale *Paris Plan* published by Michelin. It comes in booklet form, large format and sheet form; the last two are particularly useful if you're driving.

Many Parisians swear by the hand-drawn, pocket-sized map book called *Paris par Arrondissement* (60FF), which has a double-page street plan of each arrondissement; others find it confusing and difficult to use though it does list the appropriate metro stop next to streets in the index. Perhaps a more realistic choice is *Paris Practique* (36FF), in a larger format though slimmer.

TOURIST OFFICES
Local Tourist Offices

Paris' main tourist office (Map 2; main ☎ 01 49 52 53 54 or ☎ 01 44 29 12 12 for information in English; fax 01 49 52 53 00; www.paris-promotion.fr; metro George V) is at 127 Ave des Champs-Élysées (8e). It's open every day of the year, except on 1 May and Christmas Day, from 9 am to 8 pm (11 am to 6 pm on Sunday in winter).

There are tourist office annexes in the Gare du Nord (☎ 01 45 26 94 82) and the Gare de Lyon (☎ 01 43 43 33 24) open daily, except Sunday and holidays, from 8 am to 8 pm. The annexe (☎ 01 45 51 22 15) at the base of the Eiffel Tower is open from 2 May to September daily (including holidays) from 11 am to 6 pm.

The Île de France tourist office (☎ 01 42 44 10 50) is in the lower level of the Carrousel du Louvre shopping mall next to I M Pei's inverted glass pyramid. It is open daily, except Tuesday and three public holidays, from 10 am to 7 pm.

Tourist Offices Abroad

French government tourist offices (usually called Maisons de la France) can provide every imaginable sort of tourist information on Paris as well as the rest of the country, most of it in the form of brochures. Offices include the following:

Australia
  (☎ 02-9231 5244; fax 02-9221 8682; frencht@ozermail.com.au), 25 Bligh St, Sydney, NSW 2000. Weekdays 9 am to 5 pm.
Belgium
  (☎ 0902 88 025; fax 02-502 0410; maisonde-lafrance@pophost.eunet.be), 21 Ave de la Toison d'Or 1050 Brussels. Weekdays 10 am to 5 pm.
Canada
  (☎ 514-288 4264; fax 514-845 4868; mfrance@passeport.com), 1981 McGill College Ave, Suite 490, Montreal, Que H3A 2W9. Weekdays 9 am to 4 pm.
  (☎ 416-593 4723; fax 416-979 7587; french.tourist@sympatico.ca), 30 Saint Patrick St, Suite 700, Toronto, Ont Map M5T 3A3. Weekdays 9 am to 4 pm.
Germany
  (☎ 069-758 021; fax 069-745 556; maison_de_la_France@t-online.de), Westendstrasse 47, D-60325 Frankfurt. Weekdays 9 am to 4.30 pm.
  (☎ 030-218 2064; fax 030-214 1238), Keithstrasse 2-4, D-10787 Berlin. Weekdays 9 am to 1 pm and 2 to 5.30 pm (4.30 pm on Friday).
Hong Kong
  (☎ 2501 9548; fax 2536 2868), c/o Air France, Alexandra House, 21st floor, Chater Road, Central. Weekdays 9 am to 1 pm and 2 to 6 pm.
Ireland
  (☎ 01-703 4046; fax 01-874 7324), 35 Lower Abbey St, Dublin 1. Weekdays 9.30 am to 1.30 pm and 2 to 5 pm.
Italy
  (☎ 02-584 861; fax 02-5848 6222; entf@enter.it), Via Larga 7, 20122 Milan. Weekdays 9.30 am to 5.30 pm.
Japan
  (☎ 03-3582 6965; fax 03-3505 2873), Akasaka Building, 10-9 Akasaka 2-chome, Minato-ku, Tokyo 107. Weekdays 9 am to 5 pm.
Netherlands
  (☎ 0900 112 2332; fax 020-620 3339; fra_vvv@euronet.nl), Prinsengracht 670, 1017 KX Amsterdam. Weekdays 10 am to 5 pm.
Singapore
  (☎ 326 0784; fax 221 5012; mdlfsin@pacfic.net.sg), 89 Neil Rd, Singapore 088849. Weekdays 9 am to 1 pm.
South Africa
  (☎ 011-880 8062; fax 011-880 7722; mdfsa@frenchdoor.co.za), Oxford Manor, 1st floor, 196 Oxford Road, Illovo 2196. Weekdays 9 am to 1 pm and 2 to 4.30 pm.

Spain
(☎ 91-541 8808; fax 91-541 2412; maisonde-lafrance@mad.sericom.es), Alcalá 63, 28013 Madrid. Weekdays 9 am to 1.30 pm and 4 to 7 pm (8 am to 3 pm in summer).

Switzerland
(☎ 01-211 3085; fax 01-212 1644), Löwen-strasse 59, 8023 Zürich. Weekdays 10 am to 1 pm and 2 to 5.30 pm.
(☎ 022-732 8610; fax 022-731 5873), 2 Rue Thalberg, Geneva 1201. Weekdays 9 am to noon and 1 to 5.45 pm (5 pm on Friday).

UK
☎ 0891-244 123; fax 0171-493 6594; piccadil-ly@mdlf.demon.co.uk), 178 Piccadilly, London W1V 0AL. Weekdays 9 am to 5.30 pm.

USA
(☎ 212-838 7800; fax 212-838 7855; info@francetourism.com), 444 Madison Ave, 16th floor, New York, NY 10022-6903. Week-days 9 am to 5 pm.

DOCUMENTS

By law, everyone in France, including tourists, must carry some sort of ID at all times. For foreign visitors, this means a passport or, for citizens of the European Union (EU), a national ID card.

Visas

There are no entry requirements or restrictions on nationals of the EU. Citizens of the USA, Canada, New Zealand, Israel and, since August 1998, Australia do not need visas to visit France as tourists for up to three months. Except for people from a handful of other European countries, everyone else must have a visa.

Among those who need visas are South Africans. Visa fees depend on the current exchange rate but a transit visa should cost about £7/65FF, a visa valid for stays of up to 30 days with one or two entries around £18/165FF, and a single/multiple entry visa of up to three months £21.50/25.50, 195/230FF. You will need your passport (valid for a period of three months beyond the date of your departure from France), a ticket in and out of France, proof of money and possibly of accommodation, two passport-size photos and the visa fee in cash.

If all the forms are in order, your visa will be issued on the spot. You can also apply for a French visa after arriving in Europe – the fee is the same, but you may not have to produce a return ticket. If you enter France overland, your visa may not be checked at the border, but major problems can arise if you don't have one later on (eg at the airport as you leave the country).

Long Stay If you'd like to work or study in Paris or stay for over three months, apply to the French consulate nearest where you live for the appropriate sort of *long séjour* (long-stay) visa. Unless you live in the EU, it is extremely difficult – if not impossible – to get a visa that will allow you to work in France. For any sort of long-stay visa, begin the paperwork in your home country several months before you plan to leave (applications cannot usually be made in a third country).

If you are issued a long-stay visa valid for six or more months, you'll probably have to apply for a *carte de séjour* (residence permit) within eight days of arrival in France. EU passport holders seeking a carte de séjour should apply to the visa office in the Salle Europe on the ground floor next to *escalier* (stairway) C in the Préfecture de Police at 1 Place Louis Lépine, 4e (Map 6; metro Cité), which keeps the same hours. Foreigners staying in arrondissements 8e, 9e, 11e and 17e to 20e must go to the Hôtel de Police at 19-21 Rue Truffaut, 17e (metro Place Clichy or La Fourche) weekdays between 9 am and 4.30 pm. For those foreigners in the other districts, the correct address is the Hôtel de Police at 114-116 Avenue du Maine, 14e (Map 1; metro Gaîté). Details are available from the Préfecture de Police on ☎ 01 53 71 51 68.

Student If you'd like to study in France, you must apply for a student visa in your country of residence; tourist visas cannot be turned into student visas after you arrive in France. Students of all nationalities must apply for a carte de séjour to the office at 13 Rue Miollis, 15e (Map 4; metro Cambronne or Ségur), open weekdays from 8.45 am to 4.30 pm (4 pm on Friday). People with student visas can apply for permission to work part-time (enquire at your place of study).

Au Pair For details on au pair visas, which must be arranged *before* you leave home (unless you're an EU resident), see Au Pair under Work later in this chapter.

Visa Extensions

Tourist visas *cannot* be extended except in emergencies (eg medical problems). You might try going to the appropriate Hôtel de Police depending on which arrondissement you're staying in (see the previous Long-Stay section) or calling the Préfecture de Police (☎ 01 53 71 51 68) for guidance.

If you don't need a visa to visit France, you'll almost certainly qualify for another automatic three-month stay if you take the train to Geneva or Brussels and then re-enter France. The fewer recent French entry stamps you have in your passport the easier this is likely to be. If you needed a visa the first time around, one way to extend your stay is to go to a French consulate in a neighbouring country and apply for another one there.

Travel Insurance

If you require a visa to enter France you may need to provide evidence that you have travel insurance to the consulate at which you apply. Even if you don't, you should seriously consider taking out a policy to cover theft, loss and medical problems. The policies handled by STA Travel and other international student travel organisations are usually good value.

Some policies offer lower and higher medical-expense options; the higher ones are chiefly for countries such as the USA which have extremely high medical costs. There is a wide variety of policies available so check the small print. Some policies specifically exclude 'dangerous activities', which can include scuba diving, motorcycling, skiing – even trekking. A locally acquired motorcycle licence is not valid under some policies.

You may prefer a policy which pays doctors or hospitals directly rather than you having to pay on the spot and claim later. If you have to claim later make sure you keep all documentation. Some policies ask you to call back (reverse charges) to a centre in your home country where an immediate assessment of your problem is made.

Check that the policy covers ambulances or an emergency flight home.

Paying for your airline ticket with a credit card often provides limited travel accident insurance, and you may be able to reclaim the payment if the operator doesn't deliver.

Driving Licence

If you don't hold a European driving licence and plan to drive – God forbid! – in Paris, obtain an International Driving Permit (IDP) from your local automobile association before you leave – you'll need a passport photo and a valid licence. They are usually inexpensive and valid for one year only. An IDP is not valid unless accompanied by your original driver's licence.

Hostelling International Card

A Hostelling International card is necessary only at official *auberges de jeunesse* (hostels), of which there are few in Paris, but it may get you small discounts at other hostels. If you don't pick one up before leaving home, you can buy one at almost any official French hostel for 70/100FF if you're under/over 26 years of age. One night membership (where available) is about 10FF and a family card is 100FF.

Student & Youth Cards

An International Student Identity Card (ISIC) can pay for itself through half-price admissions, discounted air and ferry tickets, and cheap meals in student cafeterias. Many places stipulate a maximum age, usually 24 or 25. Accueil des Jeunes en France (AJF) and other student travel agencies (see that section) issue ISIC cards for 60FF.

If you're under 26 but not a student, you can apply for a GO25 card issued by the Federation of International Youth Travel Organisations (FIYTO; 60FF), which entitles you to much the same discounts as an ISIC and is also issued by student unions or student travel agencies.

A Carte Jeunes (120FF for one year) is available to anyone under 26 who has been in France for at least six months. It gets you discounts on things like air tickets, car rental, sports events, concerts and movies. You can pick one up at AJF and student travel agencies.

Teachers, professional artists, museum conservators and certain categories of students are admitted to some museums free. Bring along proof of affiliation, eg an International Teacher Identity Card (ITIC; 60FF).

Seniors' Cards

Reduced entry prices are charged for people over 60 at most cultural centres, including museums, galleries and public theatres. SNCF (Sociéte Nationale des Chemins de Fer; state owned railway company) issues the Carte Senior to those over 60, which gives reductions of 20 to 50% on train tickets. It costs 140FF for a card valid for purchasing four tickets or 285FF for a card valid for one year.

Photocopies

The hassles brought on by losing your passport can be considerably reduced if you have a record of its number and issue date, or even better, photocopies of the relevant data pages. A photocopy of your birth certificate can also be useful.

Also add the serial numbers of your travellers cheques (cross them off as you cash them) and photocopies of your credit cards, airline ticket and other travel documents. Keep all this emergency material separate from your passport, cheques and cash, and leave extra copies with someone you can rely on back home. Add some emergency money, say US$50 in cash, to this separate stash as well. If you do lose your passport, notify the police immediately to get a statement, and contact your nearest consulate.

EMBASSIES
French Embassies & Consulates

Addresses include the following:

Australia
    Embassy: (☎ 02-6270 5111; fax 02-6273 3193), 6 Perth Ave, Yarralumla, Canberra, ACT 2600.
    Consulates: (☎ 03-9820 0944 or 03-9820 0921;
fax 03-9820 9363), 492 St Kilda Rd, Level 4, Melbourne, Vic 3004.
    (☎ 02-9262 5779; fax 02-9283 1210), St Martin's Tower, 20th floor, 31 Market St, Sydney, NSW 2000.
Belgium
    Embassy: (☎ 02-548 8711; fax 02-513 6871), 65 Rue Ducale, 1000 Brussels.
    Consulate: (☎ 02-229 8500; fax 02-229 8510), 12A Place de Louvain, 1000 Brussels.
Canada
    Embassy: (☎ 613-789 1795; fax 613-789 0279), 42 Sussex Drive, Ottawa, Ont K1M 2C9.
    Consulates: (☎ 514-878 4385; fax 514-878 3981), 1 Place Ville Marie, 26th floor, Montreal, Que H3B 4S3.
    (☎ 416-925 8041; fax 416-925 3076) 130 Bloor St West, Suite 400, Toronto, Ont Map M5S 1N5.
Germany
    Embassy: (☎ 0228-955 6000; fax 0228-955 6055), An der Marienkapelle 3, 53179 Bonn.
    Consulates: (☎ 030-885 90243; fax 030-885 5295), Kurfürstendamm 211, 10719 Berlin.
    (☎ 089-419 4110; fax 089-419 41141), Möhlstrasse 5, 81675 Munich.
Ireland
    Embassy: (☎ 01-260 1666; fax 01-283 0178), 36 Ailesbury Rd, Ballsbridge, Dublin 4.
Israel
    Embassy: (☎ 03-524 5371; fax 03 522 6094), 112 Herbert Samuel Drive, Tel Aviv 63572.
    Consulate: (☎ 03 510 1415; fax 03-510 4370), Migdalor Building, 11th floor, 1-3 Ben Yehuda St, 63801 Tel Aviv.
Italy
    Embassy: (☎ 06-686 011; fax 0-686 01360), Piazza Farnese 67, 00186 Rome.
    Consulate: (☎ 06-6880 6437; fax 06-6860 1260), Via Giulia 251, 00186 Rome.
Japan
    (☎ 03-5420 8800; fax 03-5420 8847), 11-44 4-chome, Minami Azabu, Minato-ku, Tokyo 106.
Netherlands
    Embassy: (☎ 070-312 5800; fax 070-312 5854), Smidsplein 1, 2514 BT The Hague.
    Consulate: (☎ 020-624 8346; fax 020-626 0841), Vijzelgracht 2, 1000 HA Amsterdam.
New Zealand
    Embassy: (☎ 04-472 0200; fax 04-472 5887), 1-3 Willeston St, Wellington.
Singapore
    Embassy: (☎ 65-466 4866; fax 65-469 0907), 5 Gallop Rd, Singapore 258960.
South Africa
    Embassy: January-June (☎ 021-212 050; fax 021-261 996), 1009 Main Tower, Cape Town Center, Heerengracht, 8001 Cape Town.

FACTS FOR THE VISITOR

July-December (☎ 012-435 564; fax 012-433 481), 807 George Ave, Arcadia, 0132 Pretoria.

Spain
Embassy: (☎ 91-435 5560; fax 91-435 6655), Calle de Salustiano Olozaga 9, 28001 Madrid. Consulates: (☎ 91-319 7188; fax 91-308 6273), Calle Marques de la Ensen10, 28004 Madrid.
(☎ 93-317 8150; fax 93-412 4282), Ronda Universitat 22, 08007 Barcelona.

Switzerland
Embassy: (☎ 031-359 2111; fax 031-352 2191), Schosshaldenstrasse 46, 3006 Berne. Consulates: (☎ 022-311 3441; fax 022-310 8339), 11 Rue Imbert Galloix, 1205 Geneva. (☎ 01-268 8585; fax 01-268 8500), Mühlebachstrasse 7, 8008 Zürich.

UK
Embassy: (☎ 0171-201 1000; fax 0171-201 1004), 58 Knightsbridge, London SW1X 7JT. Consulate: (☎ 0171-838 2000; fax 0171-838 2001), 21 Cromwell Rd, London SW7 2DQ. The visa section is at 6A Cromwell Place, London SW7 2EW (☎ 0171-838 2051; fax 01711-838 2001). Dial ☎ 0891-887733 for general information on visa requirements.

USA
Embassy: (☎ 202-944 6000; fax 202-944 6166), 4101 Reservoir Rd NW, Washington, DC 20007. Consulates: (☎ 212-606 3688; fax 202-606 3620), 934 Fifth Ave, New York, NY 10021. (☎ 415-397 4330; fax 415-433 8357), 540 Bush St, San Francisco, CA 94108.
Other consulates: Atlanta, Boston, Chicago, Houston, Los Angeles, Miami and New Orleans.

Embassies & Consulates in Paris

Addresses include the following:

Australia
(Map 4; ☎ 01 40 59 33 00; also functions as an emergency number after hours; metro Bir Hakeim), 4 Rue Jean Rey, 15e. The consular section, which handles matters concerning Australian nationals, is open Monday to Friday from 9.15 am to noon and 2 to 4.30 pm.

Belgium
(☎ 01 44 09 39 39; metro Charles de Gaulle-Étoile), 9 Rue de Tilsitt, 17e.

Canada
(Map 2; ☎ 01 44 43 29 00, also good for emergencies; metro Alma Marceau or Franklin D Roosevelt), 35 Ave Montaigne, 8e. Canadian citizens in need of consular services should call the embassy Monday to Friday from 9.30 to 11 am or 2 to 4.30 pm to set up a weekday appointment.

Czech Republic
(☎ 01 40 65 13 00; metro Bir Hakeim), 15 Ave Charles Floquet, 7e.

Germany
Consulate: (Map 2; ☎ 01 53 83 46 40; Minitel 3615 ALLEMAGNE; metro Iéna), 34 Ave d'Iéna, 16e.

Ireland
(Map 2; ☎ 01 44 17 67 00; Minitel 3615 IRLANDE; metro Argentine), 4 Rue Rude (16e), between Ave de la Grande Armée and Ave Foch; open Monday to Friday from 9.30 am to noon (or by appointment). The phone is staffed on weekdays from 9.30 am to 1 pm and 2.30 to 5.30 pm; the after-hours emergency number is ☎ 01 44 17 67 67.

Israel
(☎ 01 40 76 55 00; metro Franklin D Roosevelt), 3 Rue Rabelais, 8e.

Italy
Consulate: (☎ 01 44 30 47 00; metro Muette), 5 Blvd Émile Augier, 16e.

Japan
(☎ 01 48 88 62 00; metro Courcelles), 7 Ave Hoche, 8e.

New Zealand
(Map 2; ☎ 01 45 00 24 11 for 24-hour voice mail and emergencies; metro Victor Hugo), 7ter Rue Léonard de Vinci (16e), one block south of Ave Foch across Place du Venezuela from 7 Rue Léonard de Vinci; open Monday to Friday from 9 am to 1 pm for routine matters and 2 to 5.30 pm for emergencies. In July and August, Friday hours are 8.30 am to 2 pm.

South Africa
(☎ 01 53 59 23 23; metro Invalides), 59 Quai d'Orsay (7e), near the American Church.

Spain
(☎ 01 44 43 18 00; metro Alma Marceau), 22 Ave Marceau, 8e.

Switzerland
(☎ 01 49 55 67 00; metro Varenne), 142 Rue de Grenelle, 7e.

UK
Consulate: (Map 2; ☎ 01 44 51 31 00 or, 24 hours a day in an emergency, ☎ 01 42 66 29 79; Minitel 3615 GBRETAGNE; metro Concorde), 16 Rue d'Anjou (8e), open weekdays except on bank holidays from 9.30 am to 12.30 pm and 2.30 to 5 pm.

USA
Consulate: (Map 2; ☎ 01 43 12 23 47 for a recording, ☎ 01 43 12 49 48 in an emergency, 24 hours; Minitel 3614 ETATS-UNIS; metro Concorde), 2 Rue Saint Florentin, 1er. Except on French and US holidays, the American Services section is open Monday to Friday from 9 am to 3 pm.

CUSTOMS

If you are not a resident of the EU, you can get a TVA (*taxe sur la valeur agoutée*; VAT in English) refund provided that: you're over 15; you'll be spending less than six months in France; you purchase goods (not more than 10 of the same item) worth at least 1200FF (tax included) at a single shop; and the shop offers *vente en détaxe* (duty-free sales).

Present a passport at the time of purchase and ask for a *bordereau de détaxe* (export sales invoice). Some shops may refund 14% of the purchase price rather than the full 17.1% you are entitled to in order to cover the time and expense involved in the refund procedure.

As you leave France or another EU country, have all three pages (two pink and one green) of the bordereau validated by the country's customs officials at the airport or border. Customs officials will take the two pink sheets and the stamped self-addressed envelope provided by the store; the green sheet is your receipt. One of the pink sheets will then be sent to the shop where you made your purchase, which will then send you a *virement* (transfer of funds) in the form you have requested, such as by French-franc cheque, or directly into your account. Be prepared for a long wait.

Instant Refunds

If you're flying out of Orly or Charles de Gaulle airports certain stores can arrange for you to receive your refund as you're leaving the country. You must make such arrangements at the time of purchase.

When you arrive at the airport you have to do three things:

- Up to three hours before your flight leaves, bring your bordereau, passport, air ticket and the things you purchased (don't put them in your checked luggage) to the *douane* (customs) office so they can stamp all three copies of the bordereau (one of which they keep).
- Go to an Aéroports de Paris (ADP) information counter, where they will check the figures and put another stamp on the documents.
- Go to the *douane de détaxe* (customs refund) window or the exchange bureau indicated on your bordereau to pick up your refund.

MONEY
Cash

Bringing along the equivalent of about US$100 in low-denomination notes will make it easier to change a small sum of money when an inferior rate is on offer or you need just a few francs. Keep the equivalent of about US$50 separate from the rest of your money as an emergency stash.

Travellers Cheques

Except at exchange bureaus and the Banque de France, you have to pay to cash travellers cheques: at banks, expect a charge of 22 to 30FF per transaction; the post office charges a minimum of 16FF. A percentage fee may apply for large sums. American Express offices do not charge a commission on their own travellers cheques but holders of other brands must pay 3% on top (minimum charge 40FF).

The travellers cheques offering the greatest degree of flexibility are those issued by American Express (in US dollars or French francs) and Visa (in French francs) because they can be changed at many post offices.

Keep a record of cheque numbers, where they were purchased and which ones were cashed. Obviously, you should keep all such information separate from the cheques themselves.

Lost or Stolen Travellers Cheques If your American Express travellers cheques are lost or stolen in Paris, call ☎ 0800 90 86 00, a 24-hour toll-free number. The main American Express office (Map 2; ☎ 01 47 77 77 07; metro Auber or Opéra) is at 11 Rue Scribe (9e). Reimbursements are available Monday to Saturday from 9 am to 6.30 or 7 pm (5.30 pm on Saturday).

Other American Express outlets are at 38 Ave de Wagram, 8e (Map 2; ☎ 01 42 27 58 80); 5 Rue St Eleuthère, 18e (☎ 01 42 23 93 52); and 26 Ave de l'Opéra, 1er (☎ 01 53 29 40 39).

If you lose your Thomas Cook cheques, contact any Thomas Cook bureau – eg in a major train station or at 4 Blvd Saint Michel, 6e (☎ 01 46 34 23 81) – for replacements.

Adieu Franc, Bonjour Euro

Don't be surprised if you come across two sets of prices for goods and services in Paris. From 1 January 1999 both the franc and Europe's new currency – the euro (€) – are legal tender here. It's all part of the harmonisation of the EU. Along with national borders, venerable currencies like the franc are also being phased out. Not all EU members have agreed to adopt the euro, but the franc, Deutschmark and lira are among the first of 11 currencies to go the way of the dodo.

No actual coins or banknotes will be issued until 1 January 2002; until that time, the euro is in effect 'paperless'. Prices can now be quoted in euros, but there aren't actually any euros in circulation. Companies use the new European currency for their accounting, banks now offer euro accounts and credit card companies can bill in euros. Essentially, the euro can be used any time it is not necessary to hand over hard cash.

This can lead to confusion, and travellers should be aware that the scheme is open to abuse. For instance, a restaurant may list prices in both francs and euros. Check the bill carefully – your total might have the amount in francs, but a credit card might have the euro equivalent.

Things will probably get worse during the first half of 2002. There will be a six-month period when countries can use both their old currencies and the newly issued euro notes and coins.

Coins and notes have already been designed. The banknotes come in denominations ranging from €5 to €500. All bills feature a generic 'European' bridge on one side and a vaguely familiar but unidentifiable 'European' arch on the reverse. Each country is permitted to design coins with one side standard for all euro coins and the other bearing a national emblem.

The euro will have the same value in all member countries of the EU; the euro 5 note in France is the same euro 5 note you will use in Italy. The official exchange rates, set in January 1999, pitch euro 1 as roughly equal in value to US$1.

Their customer service bureau can be contacted toll-free by dialling ☎ 0800 90 83 30.

Eurocheques Eurocheques, available if you have a European bank account, are guaranteed up to a certain limit. When cashing them (eg at post offices), you will be asked to show your Eurocheque card bearing your signature and registration number, and perhaps a passport or ID card. Your Eurocheque card should be kept separately from the cheques. Many hotels and merchants refuse to accept Eurocheques because of the relatively large commissions.

ATMs

Automatic teller machines (ATMs) are known in French as DABs (*distributeurs automatiques de billets*) or *points d'argent*. ATM cards can give you direct access to your cash reserves back home at a superior exchange rate. Most ATMs will also give you cash advances through your Visa or MasterCard although they may reject some foreign PIN codes.

Some ATMs won't accept PIN codes with more than four digits – ask your bank how to handle this, and while you're at it find out about withdrawal fees and daily limits. There are plenty of ATMs in Paris linked to the international Cirrus and Maestro networks. If you normally remember your PIN code as a string of letters, translate it back into numbers, as keyboards may not have letters indicated.

Credit Cards

The cheapest way to take your money with you to France is by using a credit or debit card to get cash advances. Visa (Carte Bleue) is the most widely accepted, followed by MasterCard (Access or Eurocard). American Express cards are not very useful except at upmarket establishments, but they do allow you to get cash at certain ATMs and over a dozen American Express offices in France.

In general, all three cards can be used to pay for travel by train and in many restaurants.

Exchange rates may vary – to your advantage or disadvantage – between the day you use the card and the date of billing.

It may be impossible to get a lost Visa or MasterCard reissued until you get home (American Express and Diners Club offer on-the-spot replacement cards); hence, two different credit cards are safer than one. Always keep some spare travellers cheques or cash on hand in the event of such an emergency.

Lost or Stolen Cards If your Visa card is lost or stolen in Paris, call Carte Bleue on ☎ 01 42 77 11 90, 24 hours a day. To get a replacement card you'll have to deal with the issuer.

Report a lost MasterCard, Access or Eurocard to Eurocard France (☎ 01 45 67 53 53) and, if you can, to your credit card issuer back home (for cards from the USA, call ☎ 314-275 6690). Eurocard France is at 16 Rue Lecourbe, 15e (metro Sèvres Lecourbe) and is open Monday to Friday from 9.30 am to 5.30 pm.

If your American Express card is lost or stolen, call ☎ 01 47 77 70 00 or ☎ 01 47 77 72 00, both staffed 24 hours a day. In an emergency, American Express card holders from the USA can call collect on ☎ 202-783 7474 or ☎ 202-677 2442. Replacements can be arranged at any American Express office (see Lost or Stolen Travellers Cheques earlier).

A lost Diners Club card should be reported on ☎ 01 47 62 75 75.

International Transfers

Telegraphic transfers are not very expensive but, despite their name, can be quite slow. Be sure to specify the name of the bank and the name and address of the branch where you'd like to pick it up.

It's quicker and easier to have money wired via an American Express (US$50 for US$1000). Western Union's Money Transfer system (☎ 01 43 54 46 12) and Thomas Cook's MoneyGram service (☎ 0800 90 83 30) are also popular.

Currency

The national currency is the French franc, abbreviated in this book by the letters 'FF'. One franc is divided into 100 centimes.

French coins come in denominations of 5, 10, 20 and 50 centimes (0.5FF) and 1, 2, 5, 10 and 20FF. Banknotes are issued in denominations of 20, 50, 100, 200 and 500FF. It is sometimes difficult to get change for a 500FF bill.

Exchange Rates

Australia	A$1	=	3.77FF
Canada	C$1	=	4.12FF
EU	€1	=	6.63FF
Germany	DM1	=	3.34FF
Ireland	IR£1	=	8.42FF
Japan	¥100	=	4.38FF
New Zealand	NZ$1	=	3.17FF
Spain	100 pta	=	3.95FF
UK	UK£1	=	9.96FF
USA	US$1	=	6.08FF

Changing Money

Banks and exchange bureaus often give a better rate for travellers cheques than for cash. Major train stations and fancy hotels have exchange facilities which operate evenings, weekends and holidays.

Banque de France Banque de France, France's central bank, offers the best exchange rates in the country. It does not accept Eurocheques or provide credit card cash advances. Most do not accept US$100 notes due to the preponderance of counterfeit ones.

Post Offices Many post offices perform exchange transactions for a middling rate. The commission for travellers cheques is 1.2% (minimum 16FF).

Post offices accept banknotes in a variety of currencies as well as travellers cheques issued by American Express (denominated in either US dollars or French francs) or Visa (in French francs only). If you have any other kind of travellers cheques, you're out of luck – except at Disneyland Paris.

Commercial Banks Commercial banks usually charge between 22 and 50FF per foreign currency transaction. The rates offered vary, so it pays to compare.

Commercial banks are generally open either from Monday to Friday or Tuesday to Saturday. Hours are variable but are usually from 8 or 9 am to sometime between 11.30 and 1 pm and 1.30 or 2 to 4.30 or 5 pm. Exchange services may end half an hour before closing time.

Exchange Bureaus In Paris, *bureaux de change* are faster, easier, open longer and usually give better rates than the banks.

Exchange bureaus at both airports are open daily from 6 or 6.30 am until 11 or 11.30 pm. All of Paris' six major train stations have exchange bureaus – some run by Thomas Cook – but their rates are less than stellar. Changing money at the bureau de change chains like Chequepoint and Exact Change is only slightly less foolish than making your travellers cheques into paper aeroplanes and launching them into the Seine; they offer about 10% less than a fair rate. When using bureaux de change, shop around and beware of the small print – for example, bureaus on the Rue de Rivoli specialise in offering good rates which only apply if you're changing US$3000 or more. The CCF exchange office at the main tourist office takes no commission, offers a decent rate and is open daily from 9 am to 7.30 pm.

Costs

If you stay in hostels or showerless, toilet-less rooms in bottom-end hotels and have picnics rather than dining out, it is possible to stay in Paris for US$40 a day per person. A couple staying in two-star hotels and eating one cheap restaurant meal each day should count on spending at least US$65 a day per person.

Tipping & Bargaining

French law requires that restaurant, café and hotel bills include the service charge (usually 10 to 15%), so a *pourboire* (tip)

is neither necessary nor expected in most cases. However, most people leave a few francs in restaurants, unless the service was bad. They rarely tip in cafés and bars when they've just had a coffee or a drink.

In taxis, the usual tip is 2FF no matter what the fare, with the maximum about 5FF. People in France rarely bargain except at flea markets.

Discounts

Museums, cinemas, SNCF, ferry companies and other institutions offer all sorts of price breaks to:

- people under the age of either 25 or 26
- students with ISIC cards (age limits may apply) or holders of the GO25 or Euro<26 card
- *le troisième âge* (senior travellers), ie people over 60 (or, in certain cases, 65)

Look for the words *demi-tarif* or *tarif réduit* (half-price tariff or reduced rate) on rate charts and then ask if you qualify. Some senior discounts have been done away with recently.

Those under 18 get an even wider range of discounts, including free entry to *musées nationaux* (museums run by the French government).

For more information see Student & Youth Cards and Seniors' Cards earlier in this chapter and for information on the Carte Musées et Monuments, which allows entry to around 70 venues in Paris, see the Things to See & Do chapter.

Taxes & Refunds

France's TVA (VAT) is 20.6% on most goods except food, medicine and books, for which it's 5.5%; it goes as high as 33% on such items as watches, cameras and video cassettes. Prices which include TVA are often marked TTC (*toutes taxes comprises*, ie 'all taxes included'). For details on TVA refunds up to 17.1% available to tourists, see the Customs section earlier in this chapter.

POST & COMMUNICATIONS
Post
Most post offices in Paris are open Monday to Friday from 8 am to 7 pm and on Saturday from 8 am to noon.

The main post office (Map 7; ☎ 01 40 28 20 00; metro Sentier or Les Halles) at 52 Rue du Louvre (1er), five blocks north of the east end of the Louvre, is open 24 hours a day, seven days a week – but only for sending mail, telegrams and domestic faxes, picking up poste restante mail (3FF for up to 20g, 4FF for up to 100g) and making calls with *télécartes* (phonecards). Other services, including currency exchange, are available only during regular post office hours. Be prepared for long queues after 7 pm. Poste restante not specifically addressed to a particular branch post office is delivered here.

The post office (Map 2; ☎ 01 42 56 13 71; metro George V), at 71 Ave des Champs-Élysées (8e) has slightly extended hours (weekdays from 8 am to 7.30 pm and Saturday from 10 am to 7 pm) when you can send letters, telegrams and faxes, make télécarte calls and change money.

Postal Rates Domestic letters up to 20g cost 3FF. Postcards and letters up to 20g cost 3FF within the EU; 3.80FF to most of the rest of Europe and Africa; 4.40FF to the USA, Canada and the Middle East; and 5.20FF to Australasia. Aerograms cost 5FF to all destinations.

In Paris packages weighing over 2kg are handled by the *poste principale* of each arrondissement.

Telephone
Almost all public telephones in France require a phonecard, which can be purchased at post offices, *tabacs* (tobacconists), supermarket check-out counters, SNCF ticket windows, Paris metro stations and anywhere you see a blue sticker reading *'télécarte en vente ici'*. Cards worth 50 calling units cost 40.60FF; those worth 120 units are 97.50FF.

Many cafés and restaurants have privately owned and coin-operated Point Phones.

To find a Point Phone, look for blue-on-white window stickers bearing the Point Phone emblem.

All public phones except Point Phones can receive both domestic and international calls. If you want someone to call you back, just give them France's country code, the area code (where relevant) and the number, usually written after the words *Ici le ...* or *No d'appel* on the tariff sheet or on a little sign inside the phone box. When there's an incoming call, the words *décrochez – appel arrivé* will appear in the LCD window.

For France Telecom's *service des renseignements* (directory enquiries or assistance), dial ☎ 12. Don't be surprised if the operator does not speak English. The call is free from public phones but costs 3.71FF from private lines.

Calling Paris To call the Paris area from outside France, dial your country's international access code, then 33 (France's country code), 1 and finally the eight-digit number.

Calls Abroad To call someone outside France, dial the international access code (00), the country code, the area code (without the initial zero if there is one) and the local number. International direct dial (IDD) calls to almost anywhere in the world can be placed from public telephones.

To make a reverse-charges (collect) or person-to-person call, dial 00 then 33 plus the country code of the place you're calling (for the USA and Canada, dial 11 instead of 1).

For directory enquiries concerning subscriber numbers outside France, dial 00 then 3312 and finally the relevant country code (again, 11 instead of 1 for the USA and Canada).

International Rates Daytime calls to other parts of Europe cost from 2.47 to 4.45FF a minute. Reduced tariffs (1.98 to 3.46FF) generally apply on weekdays from 9.30 pm to 8 am and on weekends and public holidays from 2 pm on Saturday to 8 am on Monday.

Nondiscount calls to continental USA and Canada are 2.97FF a minute on weekdays from 2 to 8 pm. The price then drops to 2.35FF. The rate to Alaska, Hawaii and the Caribbean is a whopping 9.77FF a minute (7.79FF discount rate).

Full-price calls to Australia, New Zealand, Japan, Hong Kong or Singapore are 6.55FF a minute. A discount rate of 5.20FF a minute applies daily from 9.30 pm (Saturday from 2 pm) to 8 am and all day on Sunday and public holidays.

Calls to Asia, non-Francophone Africa and South America are generally 6.55 to 9.77FF a minute, though to some countries a rate of 5.20 to 7.79FF will apply at certain times.

Country Direct Services Country Direct lets you phone home by billing the long-distance carrier you use at home. The numbers can be dialled from public phones without inserting a phonecard; with some models, you're meant to dial even if there's no dial tone. The numbers listed below will connect you, free of charge, with an operator in your home country, who will verify your method of payment ie credit card, reverse charges etc.

Australia	
Telstra	☎ 0800 99 00 61
Optus	☎ 0800 99 20 61
Canada	☎ 0800 99 00 16
	☎ 0800 99 02 16
Hong Kong	☎ 0800 99 08 52
	☎ 0800 99 28 52
	☎ 0800 99 18 52
Ireland	☎ 0800 99 03 53
New Zealand	☎ 0800 99 00 64
Singapore	☎ 0800 99 00 65
UK	
BT	☎ 0800 99 00 44
	☎ 0800 99 02 44
Mercury	☎ 0800 99 09 44
USA	
AT&T	☎ 0800 99 00 11
MCI	☎ 0800 99 00 19
Sprint	☎ 0800 99 00 87
Worldcom	☎ 0800 99 00 13

Domestic Calls Local calls are quite cheap, from 0.74FF (from a subscriber phone, 0.81FF from a phone box), depending on the time the call was made, the length of time taken, and the distance covered. To call the provinces from Paris, dial the area code (02 to 05, depending on the area) and the local eight-digit number. To call the Paris area from the provinces, dial the 10-digit number, which always starts with 01.

Minitel Minitel is an extremely useful telephone-connected, computerised information service though it can be expensive to use and is being given a run for its money by the Internet. The most basic Minitels, equipped with a B&W monitor and a clumsy keyboard, are available for no charge to telephone subscribers. Newer models have colour screens, and many people now access the system with a home computer and a modem.

Minitel numbers consist of four digits (eg 3611, 3614, 3615 etc) and a string of letters. Home users pay a per-minute access charge, but consulting the *annuaire* (directory) is free. Most of the Minitels in post offices are also free for directory enquiries (though some require a 1 or 2FF coin), and many of them let you access pay-as-you-go on-line services.

Fax, Telegraph & Email
Virtually all Parisian post offices can send and receive domestic and international faxes, telexes and telegrams. It costs about 80FF (20FF within France) to send a one-page fax.

ONLINE SERVICES
Useful Web sites on both Paris and France in general in English include:

www.paris-promotion.fr
    Paris tourist office Web site.
www.francetourism.com
    All manner of information on and about travel in France from the French Government Tourism Office.
www.maison-de-la-france.fr
    Maison de la France homepage.

www.guideweb.com
   Information about selected regions in France.
www.realfrance.com
   'Inside' information on Art de Vivre (arts and crafts, nature, leisure); Art de la Table (food, restaurants, wine); Art et Culture (museums, sights, events); and Art de Voyager (hotels, guesthouses, châteaux).
www.skifrance.fr
   Information about ski resorts, services, conditions etc.
www.france.qrd.org
   Queer resources directory for gay and lesbian travellers.

Both La Poste and France Telecom have set their sights on the Internet. At the time of going to print, La Poste was setting up Internet access centres at 1000 post offices around France; a chip card costing 90FF would get you three hours' access. France Telecom, meanwhile, has been sponsoring 'Internet stations' around France, including one in Paris called Cyber Espace (☎ 01 40 51 96 16) at 35 Rue du Cherche Midi (6e). These are not cybercafés as such but high-tech centres where people can surf the Internet, send emails and take free beginners' courses on how to use the Net. Access rates are cheaper than commercial cybercafés – 20/30FF for a half-hour/hour.

Internet devotees can also have their hunger satiated at a number of cybercafés in and around Paris. Venues include the following:

Café Orbital
   (Map 6; ☎ 01 43 25 76 77; metro Odéon), 13 Rue de Médicis (6e). Open daily 10 am to 10 pm; 55FF per hour, 200/300FF for five/10 hours. Student discount available.
Hi Tech Café
   (Map 4; ☎ 01 45 38 67 61; metro Montparnasse), 10 Rue de Départ (15e). Open Monday to Saturday from noon to 2 am; 40FF per hour or 320FF for 10 hours.
Web Bar
   (Map 8; ☎ 01 42 72 66 55; webbar@webbar.fr; metro Filles du Calvaire), 32 Rue de Picardie (3e). Open daily from 11.30 am to 2 am; 40FF per hour or 250FF for 10 hours.

TRAVEL AGENCIES
General Travel Agencies
The following agencies are among the largest in Paris and offer the best services and deals.

Anyway
   (☎ 08 03 00 80 08; Minitel 3615 ANYWAY), which no longer has any consumer branches but does all it's ticketing by telephone or Minitel, offers some highly competitive fares. You can call Monday to Saturday between 9 am and 7 pm.
Forum Voyages
   (☎ 01 53 32 71 72 or ☎ 08 36 68 12 02 for information and reservations; Minitel 3615 FV) has 11 branches in Paris proper including one (☎ 01 42 61 20 20; metro Pyramides) at 11 Ave de l'Opéra (1er) and another (☎ 01 43 25 54 54; metro Cardinal Lemoine) at 28 Rue Monge (5e). They are open weekdays from 9.30 am to 7 pm and on Saturday from 10 am to 6 pm.
Havas Voyages
   This large group has almost two dozen branches around the city. There's a branch (☎ 01 53 29 40 00; metro Pyramides) at 26 Ave de l'Opéra (1er); and another (☎ 01 44 41 68 68; metro Place Monge) 4 Rue Monge (5e).
Maison de la Chine
   (Map 6; ☎ 01 40 51 95 00; Minitel 3615 MAISON DE LA CHINE; metro Saint Sulpice), 76 Rue Bonaparte on the western side of Place Saint Sulpice, has package tours as well as competitive air fares to China, Indochina and South America. It is open Monday to Saturday from 10 am to 7 pm.
Nouvelles Frontières
   (☎ 08 03 33 33 33; Minitel 3615 NF; www.nouvelles-frontieres.com), has some 13 outlets around the city including one at 5 Ave de l'Opéra, 1er (metro Pyramides) open weekdays from 9 am to 8 pm (7 pm on Saturday) and another at 66 Blvd Saint Michel, 6e (metro Luxembourg) open Monday to Saturday from 9 am to 7 pm.
Voyageurs du Monde
   (Map 7; ☎ 01 42 86 16 00; metro Pyramides), at 55 Rue Sainte Anne (2e) is an enormous place with seven different departments dealing with different destinations (eg North America, China, Latin America, Asia etc). There's also a good travel bookshop (☎ 01 42 86 17 38) here and the Voyageurs du Monde has its own restaurant (☎ 01 49 26 06 73), serving exotic daily specialities (open at lunch only), next door.

Student Travel Agencies

Paris travel agencies catering to students and young people can supply discount tickets to travellers of all ages. Most issue ISIC student ID cards (60FF), the Carte Jeunes (120FF) and sell Eurolines tickets.

Accueil des Jeunes en France
(AJF; Map 8; ☎ 01 42 77 87 80; metro Rambuteau), 119 Rue Saint Martin (4e) across the square from the Centre Pompidou. This place does more than find travellers places to stay (see Accommodation Services in the Places to Stay chapter), it also functions as a travel agency for people of all ages. AJF is open Monday to Friday from 10 am to 6.45 pm and on Saturday to 5.45 pm.

Council Travel
(Map 7; ☎ 01 44 55 55 44; metro Pyramides), 22 Rue des Pyramide, 1er. Holders of plane tickets issued by Council Travel (the US student travel company) and Travel CUTS (its Canadian counterpart) can come here to get lost tickets replaced, make reservations for tickets with open returns and change flight dates (but not routes). Refunds are available from the issuing office only. It is open Monday to Friday from 9.30 am to 6.30 pm and on Saturday from 10 am to 5.30 pm. Council Travel's second bureau (Map 6; ☎ 01 44 41 89 80; metro Odéon) at 1 Place de l'Odéon (6e) is open weekdays from 9.30 am to 6.30 pm and Saturday from 11 am to 3 pm.

OTU Voyages
(Map 6; ☎ 01 44 41 38 50; metro Port Royal), 39 Ave Georges Bernanos, 5e. This branch of the French student travel agency is open weekdays from 10 am (11 am on Monday) to 6.45 pm.

USIT
(Map 6; ☎ 01 42 34 56 90; metro Luxembourg), 6 Rue de Vaugirard, 6e. Ireland's student travel outfit is open weekdays from 9.30 am to 6.30 pm and on Saturday from 10 am to 6 pm. For telephone sales, ring ☎ 01 42 44 14 00. For information and reservations by Minitel, dial 3615 USIT.

USIT has three other branches including those at (Map 7; ☎ 01 42 44 14 00; metro Bourse) 12 Rue Vivienne (2e), open Monday to Friday from 9.30 am to 6 pm (8 pm on Thursday in summer); (☎ 01 43 29 69 50; metro Luxembourg) 85 Blvd Saint Michel (5e), open Monday to Saturday from 10 am to 6 pm; and (☎ 01 44 08 71 20; metro Jussieu) 31 bis Rue Linné (5e), open Monday to Saturday from noon to 7 pm.

BOOKS

Most books are published in different editions by different publishers in different countries. As a result, a book might be a hardcover rarity in one country, yet be readily available in paperback in another. Fortunately, bookshops and libraries search by title or author, so your local bookshop or library is best placed to advise you on the availability of the following recommendations. See the Shopping chapter for details on bookshops in Paris.

Lonely Planet

Lonely Planet's *France*, *Western Europe* and *Mediterranean Europe* guides all deal with Paris and the country as a whole.

Guidebooks

Walking guides on Paris include *Paris Step by Step* by Christopher Turner, *Walking Paris* by Gilles Desmons, *Paris Walks* by Alison and Sonia Landes and *Frommer's Walking Tours Paris* by Lisa Legarde. *The Paris Literary Companion* by Ian Littlewood escorts you past the buildings where literary personalities once lived. *Paris Pas Cher*, updated annually, lists inexpensive shopping options. Another source of information on penny-wise living in Paris is *Paris aux Meilleurs Prix*.

History

The Sun King by Nancy Mitford is a classic work on Louis XIV and the country he ruled from Versailles. Alistair Horne's *The Fall of Paris* deals with the Commune of 1870-71; *Citizens* by Simon Schama is a highly acclaimed and truly monumental work which examines the first few years after the storming of the Bastille in 1789. Christopher Hibbert's *A Social History of the French Revolution* is a highly readable social account of the same period.

Larry Collins and Dominique Lapierre's *Is Paris Burning?* is a dramatic account of the liberation of Paris in 1944. Horne's *To Lose a Battle* deals with the defeat and capitulation of Paris in 1940. *Paris after the Liberation* by Anthony Beevor and Artemis

Cooper brings postwar Paris to life. One of the most interesting recent books on Paris and France in general is Julian Barnes' *Cross Channel*, a witty collection of key moments in shared Anglo-French history – from Joan of Arc to travelling from London to Paris on Eurostar.

General

The French by Theodore Zeldin is a highly acclaimed survey of French passions, peculiarities and perspectives. *France Today* by John Ardagh is a good introduction to modern-day France, its politics, its people and their idiosyncrasies. Fernand Braudel's two-volume *The Identity of France* is a comprehensive look at the country and its people.

Past Imperfect: French Intellectuals, 1944-1956 by Tony Judt is an examination of the lively intellectual life of postwar France. *The Food of France* by Waverley Root is a superb introduction to French cuisine.

NEWSPAPERS & MAGAZINES

France's main daily newspapers are *Le Figaro* (right wing; aimed at professionals, business people and the bourgeoisie), *Le Monde* (centre-left; very popular with business people, professionals and intellectuals), *Le Parisien* (centre; middle-class, easy to read if your French is basic), *France Soir* (right; working and middle-class), *Libération* (left; popular with students and intellectuals) and *L'Humanité* (communist; working-class). *L'Équipe* is a daily devoted exclusively to sport.

Among English-language newspapers widely available in Paris are the *International Herald Tribune* (10FF), which is edited in Paris and has very good coverage of French news; the *Guardian*; the *Financial Times*; *The Times*; and the colourful *USA Today*. The *European* weekly newspaper is also readily available, as are *Newsweek*, *Time* and the *Economist*. One of the best places to buy foreign newspapers is La Maison de l'Expatriée in the 7e (Map 4). See Bookshops in the Shopping chapter for details.

Paris-based *France USA Contacts* (or *FUSAC*), issued every fortnight, consists of hundreds of ads placed by both companies and individuals. It is distributed free at Paris' English-language bookshops, Anglophone embassies and the American Church (Map 4; ☎ 01 47 05 07 99; metro Pont de l'Alma) at 65 Quai d'Orsay (7e) and can be very helpful if you're looking for au pair work, short-term accommodation etc. To place an ad, contact FUSAC Centre d'Annonces (☎ 01 45 38 56 57; fax 01 45 38 98 94; metro Gaîté or Edgar Quinet) at 3 Rue Larochelle (14e) weekdays from 10 am to 7 pm.

RADIO

AM & FM Radio

You can pick up a mixture of the BBC World Service and BBC for Europe on 648kHz AM. The Voice of America (VOA) is on 1197kHz AM but reception is often poor.

In Paris, you can pick up an hour of Radio France Internationale (RFI) news in English every day at 4 pm on 738kHz AM. Radio Netherlands often has programming in English on 1512kHz AM.

France Info broadcasts the news headlines in French every few minutes. It can be picked up on 105.5MHz FM in Paris.

Short & Long-Wave Radio

Pocket-size digital short-wave radios, such as those made by Sony and Phillips, make it easy to keep abreast of the world news in English wherever you are.

The BBC World Service can be heard on 6195, 9410, 11955, 12095 (a good daytime frequency) and 15575kHz, depending on the time of day. BBC Radio 4 broadcasts on 198kHz long-wave. It carries BBC World Service programming in the wee hours of the morning.

The VOA broadcasts in English at various times of the day on 7170, 9535, 9680, 9760, 9770, 11805, 15135, 15205, 15255, 15410 and 15580kHz.

Radio Canada International's half-hour English-language broadcasts, including relays of domestic CBC programs such as the World at Six, often come in loud and clear on one or more of the following frequencies: 5995, 7235, 11690, 11890, 11935, 13650, 13670, 15150, 15325, 17820 and 17870kHz.

Although Radio Australia directs most of its broadcasts to the Asia-Pacific region, it can sometimes be picked up in western Europe. Frequencies to try include 9500, 11660 and 11880kHz.

RFI can be picked up in English on 6175 kHz at 2 pm and at 6 pm (Central European Time).

Internet

Local and international radio stations from every corner of the globe now 'broadcast' their programs via the Internet, to be picked up by Net surfers using software like RealAudio that can be easily downloaded. Station Web sites often include write-ups of the latest news and are an excellent source of short-wave schedules. TRS Consultants' Hot Links (www.trsc.com) has dozens of hypertext links relevant to Internet radio.

Stations with Internet relays include the BBC World Service (www.bbc.co.uk/worldservice), Radio Australia (www.abc.net.au/ra), Radio Canada International (www.rcinet.ca), CBC Radio (www.radio.cbc.can), Radio France Internationale (www.rfi.fr) and the Voice of America (www.voa.gov).

TV

Upmarket hotels often offer cable and satellite TV access to CNN, BBC Prime, Sky and other networks. Canal+ (pronounced 'ka-NAHL ploose'), a French subscription TV station available in many mid-range hotels, sometimes screens nondubbed English movies.

A variety of weekend-to-weekend TV listings are sold at newsstands. Foreign movies which haven't been dubbed and are shown with subtitles are marked 'VO' or 'v.o.' *version originale*.

VIDEO SYSTEMS

Unlike the rest of western Europe and Australia, which use PAL (phase alternation line),

French TV broadcasts are in SECAM (*système électronique couleur avec mémoire*). North America and Japan use a third incompatible system, NTSC (National Television Systems Committee). Non-SECAM TVs will not work in France, and French videotapes cannot be played on videocassette recorders and TVs that lack a SECAM capability.

PHOTOGRAPHY & VIDEO

Be prepared to have your camera and film run through x-ray machines at airports and the entrances to sensitive public buildings. The gadgets are ostensibly film-safe up to 1000 ASA, and laptops and computer disks appear to pass through without losing data, but there is always some degree of risk.

Colour-print film produced by Kodak and Fuji is widely available in supermarkets, photo shops and FNAC stores. At FNAC, a 36-exposure roll of Kodacolor costs 37/46FF for 100/400 ASA. One-hour developing is widely available.

For *diapositives* (slides), count on paying at least 48/60/70FF for a 36-exposure roll of Ektachrome rated at 100/200/400 ASA; developing costs 28/32FF for 24/36 exposures.

Kodachrome costs 92FF for a 36-exposure roll of 64 ASA, including processing, but it may be a bit difficult to find now that it's no longer developed in France. Processing can take several weeks.

Properly used, a video camera can give a fascinating record of your holiday. Unlike still photography, video 'flows' so, for example, you can shoot scenes of Paris city life rolling past the bus window to give an overall impression that isn't possible with ordinary photos.

Video cameras these days have very sensitive microphones, and you might be surprised how much sound will be picked up. This can also be a problem if there is a lot of ambient noise – filming by the side of a busy road might seem OK when you do it, but viewing it back home might simply give you a cacophony of traffic noise. One good rule to follow for beginners is to try to film in long takes, and don't move the camera around too much. If your camera has a stabiliser, you can use it to obtain good footage while travelling on various means of transport, even on bumpy roads.

Make sure you keep the batteries charged and have the necessary charger, plugs and transformer for France. You can obtain video cartridges easily in Paris, but make sure you buy the correct format. It is usually worth buying at least a few cartridges duty-free to start off your trip.

Photography is rarely forbidden, except in museums and art galleries. When photographing people, it is a basic courtesy to ask permission. If you don't know any French, smile while pointing at your camera and they'll get the picture.

TIME
France uses the 24-hour clock, with the hours separated from the minutes by a lower-case letter 'h'. Thus, 15h30 is 3.30 pm, 21h50 is 9.50 pm, 00h30 is 12.30 am etc.

France is one hour ahead of (ie later than) GMT/UTC. During daylight-saving (or summer) time, which runs from the last Sunday in March to the last Sunday in OCTOBER (not September as previous), France is two hours ahead of GMT/UTC. The UK and France are almost always one hour apart – when it's 6 pm in London, it's 7 pm in Paris.

New York is generally six hours behind Paris. This may fluctuate a bit depending on exactly when daylight-saving time begins and ends on both sides of the Atlantic.

The Australian east coast is between eight and 10 hours ahead of (later than) France.

ELECTRICITY
France runs on 220V at 50Hz AC. Old-type wall sockets, often rated at 600 watts, take two round prongs. The new kinds of sockets take fatter prongs and a protruding earth (ground) prong. Adapters to make new plugs fit into the old sockets are said to be illegal but are available at most electricians' shops and the BHV department store (Map 8; ☎ 01 42 74 90 00; metro Hôtel de Ville) at 52-64 Rue de Rivoli, 4e. Tape recorders not equipped with built-in adapters may function poorly.

There are two types of adapters; mixing them up will destroy either the transformer or your appliance. The 'heavy' kind, usually designed to handle 35 watts or less (see the tag) and often metal-clad, is designed for use with small electric devices such as radios, tape recorders and razors. The other kind, which weighs much less but is rated for up to 1500 watts, is for use only with appliances that contain heating elements, such as hair dryers and irons.

WEIGHTS & MEASURES
Metric System
France uses the metric system, which was invented after the Revolution by the French Academy of Sciences at the request of the National Assembly and adopted by the French government in 1795. Inspired by the same rationalist spirit in whose name churches were ransacked and turned into 'Temples of Reason', the metric system replaced a confusing welter of traditional units of measure that lacked all logical basis and made conversion complicated and commerce chaotic.

Numbers
For numbers with four or more digits, the French use full stops (periods) or spaces where writers in English would use commas – one million therefore usually appears as 1.000.000 or 1 000 000. For decimals, on the other hand, the French use commas, so 1.75 comes out as 1,75.

LAUNDRY
There are countless *laverie libre-service* (unstaffed, self-service laundrettes) in Paris; your hotel or hostel can suggest one in the neighbourhood. French laundrettes are not cheap – count on 20FF for a 6 or 7kg machine and 2/5FF for five/12 minutes of drying. Some laundrettes have self-service *nettoyage à sec* (dry-cleaning) machines.

Change machines are often out of order, so come prepared. Coins of 2FF are especially handy for the *séchoirs* (dryers) and the *lessive* (laundry powder) dispenser. In general, you deposit coins into a *monnayeur central* (central control box) – not the machine itself – and push a button that corresponds to the number of the machine you wish to operate. These gadgets are sometimes programmed to deactivate the washing machines an hour or so before closing time.

PUBLIC BATHS

Before WWII, a very high percentage of Paris' working-class flats lacked bathroom facilities. Even today, a fair number of Parisians live in showerless flats, which is why the municipality runs 20 or so *bains-douches municipaux* (municipal bathhouses), where a shower costs 7.50FF. Facilities for both men and women are available.

Near the Centre Pompidou, the Bains-Douches Municipaux (Map 8; ☎ 01 42 77 71 90; metro Rambuteau) at 18 Rue du Renard (4e) is open on Wednesday from noon to 7 pm; Thursday and Saturday from 7 am to 7 pm; Friday from 9 am to 7 pm; and on Sunday from 8 am to noon.

On Île Saint Louis, the Bains-Douches Municipaux (Map 8; ☎ 01 43 54 47 40; metro Pont Marie) at 8 Rue des Deux Ponts (4e) is open on Thursday from noon to 7 pm, on Friday from 8 am to 7 pm, on Saturday from 7 am to 7 pm and on Sunday from 8 am to noon.

The Bains-Douches Municipaux (Map 5; ☎ 01 45 35 46 63; metro Monge) at 50 Rue Lacépède (5e), just east of Place de la Contrescarpe, and the Bains-Douches Oberkampf (Map 3; metro Parmentier) at 42 Rue Oberkampf (11e) are open the same hours as the one on Île Saint Louis.

TOILETS

French bathrooms – both public and private – hold a few surprises for the uninitiated.

Bidets

In many private homes and hotel rooms – even those without toilets or showers – you will find a bidet, a porcelain fixture that looks like a shallow toilet with a pop-up stopper. Originally conceived to improve the personal hygiene of aristocratic women, its primary purpose is for washing the genitals and anal area, though its uses have expanded to include everything from hand-washing laundry to soaking your feet.

Public Toilets

Public toilets are signposted as *toilettes* or *WC*. Gone are the days of the *vespassiennes* (urinals) in the street, but Paris still has a number of fine-looking public toilets from the *belle époque* (at Place de la Madeleine, for example). You're more likely to come upon one of the tan-coloured, self-disinfecting toilet pods scattered around the city. Get your change ready – many public toilets cost 2 to 2.50FF. Some café toilets have the washbasins and urinals in a common area through which you pass to get to the closed toilet stalls.

In older cafés and hotels, the amenities may consist of a *toilette à la turque* (Turkish-style toilet), a squat toilet.

Café owners do not appreciate you using their facilities if you are not a paying customer. Options when you're desperate include ducking into a fast-food joint, a major department store, Forum des Halles or the underground toilets in front of Notre Dame.

HEALTH

Your main health risk in Paris is likely to be an upset stomach from eating and drinking too much. You might experience mild stomach problems if you're not used to copious amounts of rich cream and olive oil-based sauces, but you'll get used to it after a while.

Organise a visit to your dentist before departure and arrange travel insurance with good medical cover. If you wear glasses, take along a spare pair and your prescription. If you require a particular medication, take an adequate supply (though in our experience French pharmacies will sometimes dispense medication available by prescription only in the UK and USA). No jabs are required to travel to France.

Travel with Children by Maureen Wheeler (Lonely Planet) includes basic advice on travel health for young children.

EU residents are covered for emergency medical treatment throughout the European Union. The coverage provided by most private US health insurance policies continues if you travel abroad, at least for a limited period. Canadians covered by the Régie de l'Assurance-Maladie du Québec, and who have a valid Assurance-Maladie du Québec card, can benefit from certain reimbursement agreements with France's national health-care system. Australian Medicare provides absolutely no coverage in France.

France has an extensive public health-care system. Anyone (including foreigners) who is sick, even mildly so, can receive treatment in the *service des urgences* (casualty ward or emergency room) of any public hospital.

Medical Services

There are some 50 *assistance publique* (public health service) hospitals in Paris. If you need an ambulance, call ☎ 15 or ☎ 01 45 67 50 50. For emergency treatment, call Urgences Médicales on ☎ 01 48 28 40 04 or SOS Médecins on ☎ 01 47 07 77 77. Both offer 24-hour house calls. Some possibilities are:

Hospitals

American Hospital (Map 1; ☎ 01 46 41 27 37; fax 01 46 41 27 00), at 63 Blvd Victor Hugo offers emergency medical and dental care 24 hours a day.

Hôpital Franco-Britannique (Map 1; ☎ 01 46 39 22 22; metro Anatole France), at 3 Rue Barbès is a less expensive English-speaking option. People from outside the EU are asked to pay up front.

Hôtel Dieu (Map 6; ☎ 01 42 34 82 34; metro Cité), on the north side of Place du Parvis Notre Dame (4e). After 10 pm use the emergency entrance on Rue de la Cité. The 24-hour emergency room can refer you to the hospital's emergency gynaecological services in case of sexual assault.

Dental services

La Pitié-Salpêtrière hospital (Maps 1 and 5; metro Chevaleret) on Rue Bruand (13e) is the only dental hospital with extended hours. The after-hours entrance, open from 5.30 pm to 8.30 am, is at 47 Blvd de l'Hôpital (Map 5; metro Gare d'Austerlitz).

SOS Dentaire (Map 1; ☎ 01 43 37 51 00; metro Port Royal) at 87 Blvd de Port Royal (13e) is a private dentists' office that offers its services when most dentists are off duty: Monday to Friday from 8 to 11.40 pm and on weekends and holidays from 9 am to 12.10 pm, 2.20 to 7.10 pm and 8 to 11.40 pm. If you have an urgent problem, call to set up an appointment. A consultation and treatment generally costs 300 to 600FF. Payment must be made in cash or by personal cheque in francs.

Pharmacies

Pharmacie des Champs (Map 2; ☎ 01 45 62 02 41; metro George V), inside the shopping arcade at 84 Ave des Champs-Élysées (8e), is open 24 hours a day year round.

Pharmacie Européenne de la Place de Clichy (Map 2; ☎ 01 48 74 65 18; metro Place de Clichy), 6 Place de Clichy (17e), is open round the clock every day of the year.

Pharmacie des Halles (Map 8; ☎ 01 42 72 03 23; metro Châtelet), at 10 Blvd de Sébastopol (4e), is open daily from 9 am (noon on Sunday and holidays) to midnight.

HIV/AIDS Organisations

For information on free and anonymous HIV-testing centres *(centres de dépistage)* in and around Paris, ring the SIDA Info Service toll-free, 24 hours a day, on ☎ 0800 84 08 00. Information is also available in the Marais quarter at Le Kiosque (☎ 01 44 78 00 00; metro Saint Paul) at 36 Rue Geoffroy l'Asnier (4e) and at another Le Kiosque in the Latin Quarter at 6 Rue Dante, 5e (☎ same; metro Maubert Mutualité). Both are open weekdays from 10 am to 12.30 pm and 1 to 7 pm and on Saturday from 2 to 7 pm.

The offices of AIDES (☎ 01 44 52 00 00; metro Télégraphe) at 247 Rue de Belleville (19e), an organisation which works for the prevention of AIDS and assists AIDS sufferers, are staffed on weekdays from 2 to 6 pm.

FACTS-Line (☎ 01 44 93 16 69), in operation Monday, Wednesday and Friday from 6 to 10 am, is an English-language help line for those with HIV or AIDS.

WOMEN TRAVELLERS

Women attract more unwanted attention than men, but female travellers need not walk around Paris in fear as people are rarely assaulted on the street. However, the French seem to have given relatively little thought to *harcèlement sexuel* (sexual harassment), and many men still think that to stare suavely at a passing woman is to pay her a flattering compliment.

Assault

Using the metros until late at night is generally OK, as stations are rarely deserted.

France's national rape-crisis hotline (☎ 0800 05 95 95) can be reached toll-free from any telephone without using a phonecard. Staffed by volunteers Monday to Friday from 10 am to 6 pm, it's run by a women's organisation called Viols Femmes Informations, whose Paris office is at 9 Villa d'Este, 13e (metro Porte d'Ivry).

In an emergency, you can always call the police (☎ 17), who will take you to the hospital. Medical, psychological and legal services are available to people referred by the police at the 24-hour Service Médico-Judiciaire of the Hôtel Dieu (☎ 01 42 34 82 34).

Women's Movement

Women were given the right to vote in 1945 by De Gaulle's short-lived postwar government, but until 1964 a woman needed her husband's permission to open a bank account or even get a passport. It was in such an environment that Simone de Beauvoir wrote *Le Deuxième Sexe* (The Second Sex) in 1949.

For reasons that have more to do with French society than anything else, few women's groups function as the kind of supportive social institutions that have been formed in the most English-speaking countries.

Maison des Femmes

The women-only Maison des Femmes (Maps 1 and 5; ☎ 01 43 43 41 13; metro Reuilly Diderot) at 163 Rue Charenton (12e) is the main meeting place for women of all ages and nationalities. It is staffed on Wednesday from 4 to 7 pm and on Saturday from 3 to 6 pm.

GAY & LESBIAN TRAVELLERS

France is one of Europe's most liberal countries when it comes to homosexuality, in part because of the long French tradition of public tolerance towards groups of people who choose not to live by conventional social codes. France's lesbian scene is much less public than its gay counterpart and is centred mainly around women's cafés and bars.

Organisations

Most of France's major gay organisations are based in Paris and include the following:

ActUp Paris
  (☎ 01 48 06 13 89 for a recording; Minitel 3615 ACTUPP; actupp@compuserve.com; www.actupp.org; metro Voltaire), 45 Rue Sedaine (11e). Meetings are held every Tuesday night at 7.30 pm at the École des Beaux-Arts at 14 Rue Bonaparte, 6e (Map 6; metro Saint Germain des Prés).

Association des Médecins Gais
  (☎ 01 48 05 81 71), BP 433, 75527 Paris CEDEX 11. The Association of Gay Doctors, based in the CGL, deals with health issues of special importance to gays. It's staffed on Wednesday from 6 to 8 pm and on Saturday from 2 to 4 pm.

Centre Gai et Lesbien
  (CGL; Map 5; ☎ 01 43 57 21 47; metro Ledru Rollin), 3 Rue Keller (11e). The bar, library etc are open Monday to Saturday from 2 to 8 pm; Café Positif, open on Sunday from 2 to 7 pm, is mainly for people who are HIV positive.

Écoute Gaie
  (☎ 01 44 93 01 02), a hotline for gays and lesbians. Staffed on weekdays from 6 to 10 pm and on Saturday from 6 to 8 pm.

Gay Publications

Among the more serious gay publications are the CGL's monthly called *3 Keller* (15FF) and Act Up's monthly called *Action* (free). *Gay* is a monthly national magazine available at newsstands everywhere (35FF).

Published weekly, *e.m@le* has interviews, gossip and articles (in French), among the best listings of gay clubs, bars and associations and personal classifieds. It is available free at gay venues or for 8FF at newsagents. *VIP*, published monthly, has fewer listings and more articles (20FF; free at gay venues). *Hyzberg*, the 'free gay and lesbian monthly magazine' contains listings and articles on Paris and selected areas in the rest of France – mostly about and for men. The semi-monthly *Homosphere* (free) is essentially just a listing of personal ads. *Le Nouveau HH* (22FF; free at gay venues) has personals and some articles.

Guidebooks listing pubs, restaurants, discotheques, beaches, saunas, sex shops and cruising areas include those appearing below. Most of these titles are available from Les Mots à la Bouche (Map 8; see Bookshops in the Shopping chapter).

Guide Exes
   An annual guide (60FF) for both gays and lesbians published by Exes.
Guide Gai Pied
   A predominantly male, French and English-language annual guide (79FF) to France (about 80 pages on Paris) that is published by Les Éditions du Triangle Rose (☎ 01 43 14 73 00).
Spartacus International Gay Guide
   A male-only guide (180FF; US$32.95) to the world with more than 100 pages devoted to France and 28 pages on Paris.

Lesbian Publications

The monthly national magazine, *Lesbia* (25FF; ☎ 01 43 48 89 54), gives a rundown of what's happening around the country. *Les Nanas*, a freebie appearing every other month, is for women only. *Dyke Guide* is a new bilingual guide (59FF) for lesbians published by AT Productions.

DISABLED TRAVELLERS

France is not particularly well equipped for the *handicapés* (disabled people): kerb ramps are few and far between, older public facilities and bottom-end hotels often lack lifts, and the Paris metro, most of it built decades ago, is hopeless. But physically challenged people who would like to visit Paris can overcome these problems. Most hotels with two or more stars are equipped with lifts, and Michelin's *Guide Rouge* indicates hotels with lifts and facilities for disabled people. Both the Foyer International d'Accueil de Paris Jean Monnet and the Centre International de Séjour de Paris Kellermann have facilities for disabled travellers (see Hostels & Foyers in the Places to Stay chapter).

In recent years the SNCF has made efforts to make its trains more accessible to people with physical disabilities. A traveller in a wheelchair (*fauteuil roulant*) can travel in the wheelchair in both TGV and non-TGV trains provided they make a reservation by phone or at a train station at least a few hours before departure. Details are available in SNCF's booklet *Guide du Voyageur à Mobilité Réduite*. You can also contact SNCF Accessibilité on ☎ 0800 15 47 53 (toll-free).

In some places vehicles outfitted for people in wheelchairs provide transport within the city. Details are available from the Groupement pour l'Insertion des Personnes Handicapées Physiques (☎ 01 41 83 15 15) at 98 Rue de la Porte Jaune, 92210 Saint Cloud).

General publications you might look for include:

Holidays and Travel Abroad: A Guide for Disabled People
   An annual publication (UK£5) providing a good overview of facilities available to disabled travellers in Europe). Published in even-numbered years by the Royal Association for Disability & Rehabilitation (RADAR; ☎ 0171-250 3222), based at 12 City Forum, 250 City Rd, London EC1V 8AF.
Paris & Île de France pour Tous
   Available from the Paris tourist office for 60FF.

PARIS FOR CHILDREN

Paris abounds in places that will delight children. Family visits to many areas of the city can be designed around a rest stop (or picnic) at the following attractions (see the

BETHUNE CARMICHAEL

Children's playground in the Parc de la Villette

Things to See & Do chapter for further details):

- Bastille Area, 4e, 11e and 12e (Map 5): playground at the Port de Plaisance de Paris-Arsenal
- Bois de Boulogne (Map 1): Jardin d'Acclimatation
- Bois de Vincennes (Map 1): zoo
- Champs-Élysées Area, 8e (Map 2): Palais de la Découverte
- 19e arrondissement (Map 1): Parc de la Villette, Cité des Enfants in the Cité des Sciences et de l'Industrie
- Eiffel Tower Area, 7e (Map 4): Champ de Mars
- Jardin des Plantes Area, 5e (Map 5): Grande Galerie de l'Évolution, zoo, playground
- Montmartre, 18e (Map 9): playground
- 6e arrondissement (Map 6): Jardin du Luxembourg

The weekly entertainment magazine *L'Officiel des Spectacles* (2FF), which comes out on Wednesday, lists *gardes d'enfants* (babysitting services) available in Paris, including:

Après la Classe (☎ 01 44 78 05 05), from 39.50FF an hour.

Étudiants de l'Institut Catholique (☎ 01 45 48 31 70), from 34FF an hour plus 10FF for each session.

Laureats (☎ 01 40 29 44 44), available seven days a week round the clock; from 35FF an hour.

Au P'tit Môme (☎ 01 47 00 61 54), open from 8 am to 8 pm, seven days a week; from 34FF an hour plus 40FF administration cost.

For more information on travelling *en famille* consult *Travel with Children* by Maureen Wheeler (Lonely Planet).

LIBRARIES

The free Bibliothèque Publique d'Information (BPI; ☎ 01 44 78 12 33; www.bpi.fr), a huge, noncirculating library usually spread over three floors of the Centre Pompidou, has been relocated to 11 Rue Brantôme, 3e (Map 8; metro Rambuteau) until the renovation of the centre is completed in late 1999. The 2300 periodicals include quite a few English-language newspapers and magazines from around the world. It is open daily, except Tuesday, from noon (10 am on weekends and public holidays) to 10 pm. The BPI is so popular that, from 2 to 4 pm, you sometimes have to wait in line to get in.

The Bibliothèque Nationale de France François Mitterrand (Map 1; ☎ 01 53 79 53 79; metro Quai de la Gare) at 11 Quai FrancMauriac (13e) contains some 10 million tomes over more than 400km of shelves and can accommodate 3000 readers. The library is open to the general public (20FF for a day pass, 200FF for an annual one) Tuesday to Saturday from 10 am to 7 pm and on Sunday from noon to 6 pm. The specialist research library will open in late 1998.

The British Council (Map 4; ☎ 01 49 55 73 00; metro Invalides), on the east side of Esplanade des Invalides at 9-11 Rue de Constantine (7e), has a lending library (☎ 01 49 55 73 23; 250FF a year for membership, 200FF with a student card) and a reference library (30FF per day) open weekdays from 11 am to 6 pm (to 7 pm on Wednesday). See Cultural Centres for more information on the council.

The American Library in Paris (Map 4; ☎ 01 53 59 12 60; metro Pont de l'Alma or École Militaire) at 10 Rue du Général Camou (7e) is among the largest English-language lending libraries in Europe with some 90,000 volumes of classic and contemporary fiction, non-fiction and some 450 magazines. Annual membership costs 570FF (460FF for students), 240FF for three months in summer and 70FF a day (library reading privileges only). It is open Tuesday to Saturday from 10 am to 7 pm with limited hours on Sunday and Monday and in August.

CULTURAL CENTRES

The British Council (Map 4; ☎ 01 49 55 73 00; metro Invalides) at 11 Rue de Constantine (7e), whose mission is 'to promote British culture and civilisation', has reference and lending libraries (see above), and also runs language courses through the British Institute. The café in the basement is open weekdays from 9.30 am to 6.45 pm.

The American Church (Map 4; ☎ 01 47 05 07 99; metro Pont de l'Alma) at 65 Quai d'Orsay (7e) functions as a community centre for English speakers and is an excellent source of information on flats, jobs etc. Reception is staffed daily from 9 am to 1 pm and 2 to 10.30 pm (7.30 pm on Sunday). The church has three bulletin boards: an informal board downstairs on which people post all sorts of announcements (for no charge), and two identical official bulletin boards – one near reception, the other outside – listing flats, things for sale and jobs, especially work for au pairs, babysitters and English-language teachers. The American Church sponsors a variety of classes, workshops, concerts (on Sunday at 6 pm from September to May) and other cultural activities.

The English-speaking Saint Joseph's Church (Map 2; ☎ 01 42 27 28 56; metro Charles de Gaulle Étoile) is two blocks north-east of the Arc de Triomphe at 50 Ave Hoche (8e). It also has a bulletin board with information on work, apartments, cultural events etc.

The offices of the Service Culturel (French Cultural Service), many of them attached to embassies or consulates, provide information to people who would like to study in France.

Australia
(☎ 06-6216 0100; fax 06-6273 5450), 6 Perth Ave, Yarralumla, Canberra, ACT 2600.
Canada
(☎ 416-925 0025; fax 416-925 2560), 175 Bloor St East, Suite 606, Toronto, Ont Map M4W 3R8.

Ireland
(☎ 01-676 2197; fax 01-676 9403), 1 Kildare St, Dublin 2.
New Zealand
(☎ 04-494 1320; fax 04-499 0546), 1-3 Willeston St, PO Box 53, Wellington.
Singapore
(☎ 468 4663; fax 466 32965), Gallop Rd, Singapore 258960.
South Africa
(☎ 012-435 658), 795 George Ave, Arcadia, 0132 Pretoria.
UK
(☎ 0171-838 2055; fax 0171-838 2088), 23 Cromwell Rd, London SW7 2EL.
USA
(☎ 212-439 1400), 972 Fifth Ave, New York, NY 10021.

DANGERS & ANNOYANCES

In general, Paris is a safe city and occurrences of random street assaults are rare. La Ville Lumière (the City of Light), as Paris is called, is generally well lit, and there's no reason not to use the metro until it stops running at around 12.45 am. As you'll notice, women *do* travel alone on the metro late at night in most areas, though not all who do so report feeling 100% comfortable. The Bois de Boulogne and Bois de Vincennes are best avoided after dark.

Nonviolent crime (such as pickpocketing and thefts from handbags or packs) is a problem wherever there are crowds, especially crowds of tourists. Places to be especially careful include Montmartre, Pigalle, the areas around Forum des Halles and the Centre Pompidou, on the metro at rush hour and even the Latin Quarter. Be especially wary of children; kids who jostle up against you in the crowds may be diving into your bag with professional aplomb at the same instant.

Metro stations which are probably best avoided late at night include Châtelet-Les Halles and its seemingly endless corridors, Château Rouge in Montmartre; Gare du Nord, Strasbourg Saint Denis, Réaumur Sébastopol, and Montparnasse Bienvenüe. *Bornes d'alarme* (alarm boxes) are located in the centre of each metro/RER platform and in some station corridors.

LOST & FOUND

All lost objects found anywhere in Paris – except those discovered on trains or in railway stations – are eventually brought to the city's infamous Bureau des Objets Trouvés (Lost Property Office; Map 1; ☎ 01 55 76 20 20; metro Convention) at 36 Rue des Morillons (15e), run by the Préfecture de Police. Since telephone enquiries are impossible, the only way to find out if your lost item has been located is to go all the way down there and fill in the forms. The office is open on weekdays from 8.30 am to 5 pm (on Monday, Wednesday and Friday), to 8 pm (on Tuesday and Thursday). In July and August, daily closing time is 5 pm.

Items lost in the metro (☎ 01 40 06 75 27 for information) are held by station agents for one day before being sent to the Bureau des Objets Trouvés. Anything found on trains or in railway stations is taken to the *objets trouvés* bureau – usually attached to the left-luggage office – of the relevant train station. Telephone enquiries (in French) are possible:

Gare d'Austerlitz	☎ 01 53 60 71 98
Gare de l'Est	☎ 01 40 18 88 73
Gare de Lyon	☎ 01 40 19 67 22
Gare Montparnasse	☎ 01 40 48 14 24
Gare du Nord	☎ 01 53 90 20 20
Gare Saint Lazare	☎ 01 53 42 01 44

LEGAL MATTERS
Police
Thanks to the Napoleonic Code (on which the French legal system is based), the police can pretty much search anyone they want to at any time – whether or not there is probable cause. They have been known to stop and search chartered coaches solely because they are en route from Amsterdam.

France has two separate police forces. The Police Nationale, under the command of departmental prefects (and, in Paris, the Préfet de Police), includes the Police de l'Air et des Frontières (PAF), the border police. The Gendarmerie Nationale, a paramilitary force under the control of the Ministry of Defence, handles airports, borders etc. During times of crisis (eg a wave of terrorist attacks), the army may be called in to patrol public places.

The dreaded Compagnies Républicaines de Sécurité (CRS), riot police heavies, are part of the Police Nationale. You often see hundreds of them, equipped with the latest riot gear, at strikes or demonstrations.

Police with shoulder patches reading 'Police Municipale' are under the control of the local mayor.

If asked a question, cops are likely to be correct and helpful but no more than that (though you may get a salute). If the police stop you for any reason, be polite and remain calm. They have wide powers of search and seizure and, if they take a dislike to you, they may choose to use them. The police can, without any particular reason, decide to examine your passport, visa, carte de séjour etc.

French police are very strict about security, especially at airports. Do not leave baggage unattended; they're serious when they warn that suspicious objects will be summarily blown up.

Drinking & Driving
As elsewhere in the EU, the laws are very tough when it comes to drinking and driving, and for many years the slogan has been: *'Boire ou conduire, il faut choisir'* (To drink or to drive, you have to choose). The acceptable blood-alcohol limit is 0.05%, and drivers exceeding this amount face fines of up to 30,000FF (two years in jail maximum). Licences can also be immediately suspended.

Drugs
Importing or exporting drugs can lead to a 10 to 30-year jail sentence. The fine for possession of drugs for personal use can be as high as 500,000FF.

Littering
The fine for littering is about 1000FF.

Smoking
By nature many French people do not take seriously laws they consider stupid or intrusive; whether others feel the same is

another matter. Laws banning smoking in public places do exist, for example, but no one pays much attention to them. Diners will often smoke in the nonsmoking sections of restaurants – and the waiter will happily bring them an ashtray.

BUSINESS HOURS
Most museums are closed on either Monday or Tuesday, though in summer some open daily. A few places (eg the Louvre) stay open until almost 10 pm on one or two nights a week.

Small businesses are open daily, except Sunday and often Monday. Hours are usually 9 or 10 am to 6.30 or 7 pm, with a midday break from noon or 1 pm to 2 or 3 pm.

Supermarkets and hypermarkets are open Monday to Saturday; a few open on Sunday morning in July and August. Small food shops are mostly closed on Sunday morning or afternoon and Monday, so Saturday afternoon may be your last chance to stock up on provisions until Tuesday, unless you come across a supermarket, seven-day grocery or a boulangerie on duty by rotational agreement. Many restaurants in Paris are closed on Sunday.

Local laws require that most business establishments close for one day a week. Exceptions include family-run businesses, such as grocery stores and small restaurants, and places large enough to rotate staff so everyone has a day off. Since you can never tell which day of the week a certain merchant or restaurateur has chosen to take off, this book includes, where possible, details on weekly closures.

In August, lots of establishments shut down so owners and employees alike can head for the hills or the beaches.

PUBLIC HOLIDAYS & SPECIAL EVENTS
The following holidays are observed in Paris:

1 January
    Jour de l'An – New Year's Day
Late March/April
    Pâques – Easter Sunday
    lundi de Pâques – Easter Monday

1 May
    Fête du Travail – May Day
8 May
    Victoire 1945 – Victory in Europe Day
May (40th day after Easter)
    L'Ascension – Ascension Thursday
Mid-May to mid-June (7th Sunday after Easter)
    Pentecôte – Pentecost/Whit Sunday
    lundi de Pentecôte – Whit Monday
14 July
    Fête Nationale – Bastille Day/National Day
15 August
    L'Assomption – Assumption Day
1 November
    La Toussaint – All Saints' Day
11 November
    Le onze Novembre – Armistice Day 1918/ Remembrance Day
25 December
    Noël – Christmas

The following are *not* public holidays: Shrove Tuesday (*Mardi Gras*; the first day of Lent); Maundy (or Holy) Thursday (*jeudi saint*) and Good *Friday (vendredi saint)* just before Easter; Boxing Day (26 December).

The school holidays *(vacances scolaires)* in France, during which time millions of families take domestic vacations, generally fall as follows:

Christmas and New Year
    Schools all over the country are closed from 20 December to 4 January.
February/March
    The February holidays last from about 11 February to 11 March; pupils in each of three zones are off for overlapping 15-day periods.
Easter
    The month-long spring break, which begins a week before Easter, also means pupils have overlapping 15-day holidays.
Summer
    The nationwide summer recess lasts from the tail end of June until very early September.

Innumerable cultural and sporting events take place in Paris throughout the year; details appear in *Pariscope* and *L'Officiel des Spectacles* (see Listings in the Entertainment chapter) or are available from the tourist office. The following abbreviated list gives you a taste of what to expect.

31 December/1 January
New Year's Eve the places to be are Ave des Champs-Élysées (8e), Blvd Saint Michel (5e) and Place de la Bastille, 11e.
La Grande Parade de Montmartre New Year's Day parade in Montmartre that wends its way from Place Pigalle northward to Place Jules Joffrin, 18e.

Late January/early February
Chinese New Year Dragon parades and other festivities are held in Chinatown, the area of the 13e between Ave d'Ivry and Ave de Choisy (metro Tolbiac) as well as along Rue Au Maire, 3e (metro Arts et Métiers), which is south-east of the Conservatoire des Arts et Métiers.

Late February/early March
Salon International de l'Agriculture A huge 10-day international agricultural fair with lots to eat, including dishes from all over France. Held at the Parc des Expositions at Porte de Versailles, 15e (metro Porte de Versailles).

Early March
Jumping International de Paris Show jumping tournament at the Palais Omnisports de Paris-Bercy, 12e (metro Bercy).

Late March/mid-April
Banlieues Bleues Jazz festival held in Saint Denis and other Paris suburbs attracts big-name talent.

Mid-April
Marathon International de Paris Paris International Marathon which starts on the Place de la Concorde (1er) and finishes on the Ave Foch, 16e.

Late April/early May
Foire de Paris Huge food and wine fair at the Parc des Expositions at Porte de Versailles, 15e (metro Porte de Versailles).

Late May/early June
Internationaux de France de Tennis (French Open Tennis Tournament) A glitzy tennis tournament held in Stade Roland Garros (metro Porte d'Auteuil) at the southern edge of the Bois de Boulogne, 16e.

Mid-June in odd-numbered years
Paris Air Show The world's premier exposition of civilian and military air and space technology. Held at Le Bourget airport, in Paris' northern suburbs

Around 20 June
Gay Pride A colourful, Saturday afternoon parade through the Marais to celebrate Gay Pride Day. Various bars and clubs sponsor floats.

21 June
Fété de la Musique A music festival that caters to a great diversity of tastes and features impromptu live performances all over the city.

Late June/early July
La Course des Garçons de Café A Sunday afternoon foot race through central Paris whose participants – hundreds of waiters and waitresses – carry a glass and a bottle balanced on a tray. Spilling or breaking anything results in disqualification.

Early July
La Goutte d'Or en Fête World music festival (raï, reggae, rap etc) at Place de Léon, 18e (metro Barbès Rouchechouart).

14 July
Bastille Day Paris is *the* place to be on France's National Day. Late on the night of the 13th, about a dozen *bals des sapeurs-pompiers* (dances sponsored by Paris' fire brigades – considered sex symbols in France) are held at fire stations around the city. At 10 am on the 14th, there's a military and fire brigade parade along Ave des Champs-Élysées, accompanied by a flyover of fighter aircraft and helicopters. Reviewing stands line the Ave des Champs-Élysées, so the only way to get a halfway decent view is to arrive early. Much of the city centre, temporarily pedestrianised, fills with strollers out to celebrate *liberté*, *égalité* and *fraternité* amid the omnipresent riot police. On the night of the 14th, a huge display of *feux d'artifice* (fireworks) is held at around 11 pm either near the Eiffel Tower or at the Invalides.

3rd or 4th Sunday in July
Tour de France The last stage of the world's most prestigious cycling event always ends with a dash up the Ave des Champs-Élysées.

Mid-September to December
Festival d'Automne Autumn Festival of music and theatre held in venues throughout the city.

Early October
Foire Internationale d'Art Contemporain (FIAC) Huge contemporary art fair with some 150 galleries represented at the Espace Eiffel Branly, 29-55 Quai Branly, 7e (metro Pont de l'Alma).

24-25 December
Christmas Eve Mass at Notre Dame Midnight Mass is celebrated on Christmas Eve at many Paris churches, including Notre Dame (get there by 11 pm to find a place in a pew).

DOING BUSINESS

France is not the easiest country in which to do business, as the legal and tax systems are quite complicated. The best advice is to find a lawyer who specialises in international matters.

To rent a fully equipped office, you can

expect to pay around 500FF a day. Faxes cost 15FF per page; the rate for a bilingual secretary is around 160FF an hour; an English translator charges around 400FF per page, 600FF for Japanese; and the services of an interpreter are around 5000FF a day. The major luxury hotels offer fully serviced business centres but they can be quite expensive. For example, the Disneyland Paris Centre de Convention (☎ 01 60 45 75 00; fax 01 60 45 76 91) has a seminar package which costs between 1200 and 1400FF per person per day.

The Chambre de Commerce et d'Industrie de Paris (CCI; ☎ 01 42 89 70 00; fax 01 42 89 78 68), 27 Ave de Friedland, 75008 Paris, has lists of organisations providing translation, secretarial, fax, answering and message services. It also has a legal department (☎ 01 42 89 75 75).

The American Chamber of Commerce (☎ 01 40 73 89 90; fax 01 47 20 18 62), 21 Ave George V, 75008 Paris, offers a commercial information service for 350FF and use of its research library, open Tuesday and Thursday from 10 am to 12.30 pm, for 100FF (50FF for students with ID). It also publishes Commerce in France eight times a year and a directory called Guide to Doing Business in France (350FF); its membership directory costs 650FF. Once you are in Paris, you will discover that Minitel is a great tool for tracking down information.

Before you leave home, it's a good idea to contact one of the main commercial offices or your embassy's trade office in Paris. They include:

Franco-British Chamber of Commerce & Industry
 (☎ 01 53 30 81 30; fax 01 53 30 81 35), 31 Rue Boisy d'Anglas, 75008.
Service de Documentation Commerciale
 (☎ 01 43 12 25 32; fax 01 43 12 21 72).
Trade Office of the Australian Embassy
 (☎ 01 40 59 33 00; fax 01 40 59 33 10), 4 Rue Jean Rey, 75017 Paris.
Trade Office of the Japanese Embassy
 (☎ 01 48 88 62 00; fax 01 42 27 50 81) 7 Ave Hoche, 75008 Paris.
Trade Office of the UK Embassy
 (☎ 01 44 51 31 00; fax 01 44 51 34 01), 35 Rue du Faubourg Saint Honoré, 75008 Paris.

Trade Office of the US Embassy
 (☎ 01 43 12 21 72; fax 01 42 66 97 83), 2 Ave Gabriel, 75008 Paris.

WORK

Despite France's unemployment rate of over 12% and laws that forbid people who aren't EU nationals from taking employment in France, working 'in the black' (ie without documents) is still possible. Au pair work is popular and can be done legally even by non-EU citizens.

For practical information on employment in France, you might want to pick up Working in France by Carol Pineau and Maureen Kelly. Two other titles with extensive sections on France (including Paris) are Summer Jobs Abroad edited by David Woodworth, and Working Holidays, published by the Central Bureau for Educational Visits and Exchanges in London.

To work legally in France you must have a residence permit known as a carte de séjour. Getting one is almost automatic for EU nationals and almost impossible for anyone else except full-time students (see Visas in the Documents section, earlier in this chapter).

Non-EU nationals cannot work legally unless they obtain an autorisation de travail (work permit) before arriving in France. This is no easy matter, as a prospective employer has to convince the authorities that there is no French – and increasingly no EU – citizen who can do the job being offered to you.

The Agence Nationale pour l'Emploi (ANPE), France's national employment service, has lists of job openings. The ANPE has branches throughout the city; the one at 20bis Rue Sainte Croix de la Bretonnerie, 4e (☎ 01 42 71 24 68; metro Hôtel de Ville) deals with those people residing in arrondissements 1er, 2e and 12e, for example.

Centres Régionaux Information Jeunesse (CRIJ) offices have information on housing, jobs, professional training and educational options. The Paris headquarters (☎ 01 44 49 12 00; fax 01 40 65 02 61; metro Champ de Mars-Tour Eiffel) is at 101

Quai Branly (15e). These offices sometimes have noticeboards with work possibilities. But remember, these bodies are useless if you don't have a carte de séjour.

If you play an instrument or have some other talent you could try busking. Busking is a common sight in front of the Centre Pompidou, around Sacré Cœur and on the metro, where the RATP police are in charge. To avoid hassles, talk to other street artists.

Au Pair Work

Under the au pair system, single young people (aged 18 to about 27) who are studying in France live with a French family and receive lodging, full board and a bit of pocket money in exchange for taking care of the kids, babysitting, doing light housework and perhaps teaching English to the children. Most families prefer young women, but a few positions are also available for young men. Many families want au pairs who are native English speakers, but knowing at least some French may be a prerequisite.

For practical information, pick up *The Au Pair and Nanny's Guide to Working Abroad* by Susan Griffith and Sharon Legg.

By law, au pairs must have one full day off a week. In Paris, some families also provide weekly or monthly metro passes. The family must also pay for French social security, which covers about 70% of medical expenses (it's a good idea to get supplementary insurance).

Residents of the EU can easily arrange for an au pair job and a carte de séjour after arriving in France. Non-EU nationals who decide to try to find an au pair position after entering the country cannot do so legally and won't be covered by the protections provided for under French law.

Check the bulletin boards at the American Church and Saint Joseph's Church (see Cultural Centres) as well as the publication *France USA Contacts* (see Newspapers & Magazines) for job ads. The Paris tourist office has a list of au pair placement agencies.

The Architecture of Paris

At first glance, much of the architecture of Paris may appear to be the same – six or seven-storey apartment blocks in the Deuxième Empire style lining grand boulevards and interspersed with leafy squares. That is in effect what Baron Haussmann (see the boxed text) had in mind when, in the middle of the 19th century, he oversaw the construction of a new city. But Paris is a treasure trove of architectural styles – from Roman arenas and bathhouses to postmodernist cubes and glass pyramids which not only look great but serve a function.

Gallo-Roman

Classical architecture is characterised both by its elegance and its grandeur. The Romans adaptation and use of the classical Greek orders – Doric, Ionic and Corinthian – influenced western architecture for millennia. The Romans were the first to use bricks and cement to build vaults, arches and domes. The emphasis was on impressive public buildings, aqueducts, triumphal arches, temples, fortifications, marketplaces, amphitheatres and

Baron Haussmann

Few town planners anywhere in the world have had as great an impact on the city of their birth as Baron Georges-Eugène Haussmann (1809-91) did on Paris. As Prefect of the Seine department under Napoleon III between 1853 and 1870, Haussmann and his staff of engineers and architects completely rebuilt huge swathes of Paris. He is best known (and most bitterly attacked) for having demolished much of medieval Paris, replacing the chaotic narrow streets – easy to barricade in an uprising – with the handsome, arrow-straight thoroughfares for which the city is celebrated. He also revolutionised Paris' water supply and sewerage systems and laid out many of the city's loveliest parks, including Parc des Buttes-Chaumont (19e), Parc Montsouris (14e) and large areas of the Bois de Boulogne (16e) and Bois de Vincennes (12e).

Rue de Rivoli

RACHEL BLACK

bathhouses – examples of which can be found all over France and, to a much lesser degree, in Paris. The Romans also established regular street grids at many settlements.

From the mid-1st century BC, the Romans turned a small Gallic settlement of wattle and daub huts on the Île de la Cité into a provincial capital called Lutetia (Lutèce in French). A temple to Jupiter was erected on the site where Notre Dame now stands, and the Roman town spread to the south bank, with Rue Saint Jacques as the main thoroughfare. A forum stood at the corner of today's Rue Soufflot, near the Panthéon and the Jardin du Luxembourg.

Traces of Roman Paris can be seen in the residential foundations and dwellings in the Crypte Archéologique (Map 6) under the square in front of Notre Dame; in the partially reconstructed Arènes de Lutèce (Map 5); and in the frigidarium and other remains of Roman baths dating from around 200 AD at the Musée National du Moyen Age (Map 6), formerly known as the Musée de Cluny.

Merovingian & Carolingian

Although quite a few churches built during the Merovingian and Carolingian periods (5th to 10th century), very little remains of them in Paris.

After the Merovingian ruler Clovis I made Paris his seat in the early 6th century, he established an abbey dedicated to Sts Peter and Paul on the south bank of the Seine. All that remains of this once great abbey (later named in honour of Paris' patron saint, Geneviève, and demolished in 1802) is the Tour Clovis, a Romanesque tower within the grounds of the prestigious Lycée Henri IV (Map 6), just east of the Panthéon.

Clovis' son and successor, Childeric II, founded the Abbey of Saint Germain des Prés; the Merovingian kings were buried here during the 6th and 7th centuries, but their tombs disappeared during the Revolution. The dynasty's most productive ruler, Dagobert, established an abbey at Saint Denis north of Paris, which would soon become the richest and most important monastery in France. Archaeological excavations in the crypt of the 12th-century Basilique Saint Denis have uncovered extensive tombs from both the Merovingian and Carolingian periods. The oldest of these dates from around 570 AD.

Romanesque

A religious revival in the 11th century led to the construction of a large number of *roman* (Romanesque) churches, so-called

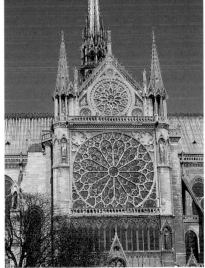

Top: I M Pei's glass pyramid, at the main entrance to the Louvre
Bottom Left: Hôtel de Ville
Bottom Right: The rose windows of Notre Dame

TONY WHEELER

SIMON BRACKEN

BETHUNE CARMICHAEL

SIMON BRACKEN

MARK HONAN

Top: The Panthéon
Middle Left: Marble interior of the Panthéon
Middle Right: Bas-relief sculpture, Notre Dame

Bottom Left: Carved stone, Notre Dame
Bottom Right: Notre Dame's stained
glass windows

TONY WHEELER

TONY WHEELER

TONY WHEELER

Top Left: Sculptures at La Défense
Top Right: Institut du Monde Arabe
Middle Right: External escalators of the Centre Pompidou

Bottom: The colonne de Juillet and Opéra Bastille

TONY WHEELER

SIMON BRACKEN

Top: Gare du Nord
Bottom: Palais du Luxembourg

because their architects adopted many architectural elements (eg vaulting) from Gallo-Roman buildings still standing at the time. Romanesque buildings typically have round arches, heavy walls whose few windows let in very little light, and a lack of ornamentation that borders on the austere. Châteaux built during this era tended to be massive, heavily fortified structures which afforded few luxuries to their inhabitants.

No churches in Paris are entirely Romanesque in style, but a few have important representative elements. The Église Saint Germain des Prés (Map 6), for example, built in the 11th century on the site of the Merovingian ruler Childeric's 6th-century abbey, has been altered many times over the centuries, but the Romanesque bell tower over the west entrance has changed little since 1000 AD. There are also some decorated capitals in the nave dating from this time. The choir and apse of the Église Saint Nicholas des Champs (Map 8) are Romanesque dating from about 1130 as is the truncated bell tower. The Église Saint Germain L'Auxerrois (Map 7) was built in a mixture of Gothic and Renaissance styles between the 13th and 16th centuries on a site used for Christian worship since about 500 AD. The square belfry rising from next to the south transept arm is Romanesque in style.

Several churches outside Paris also have important Romanesque elements. The choir and ambulatory of the Basilique Saint Denis have features illustrating the transition from Romanesque to Gothic while the magnificent 13th-century cathedral at Chartres is crowned by two soaring spires – one Gothic, the other Romanesque. The west entrance to the cathedral, known as the Portail Royal (Royal Portal), is adorned with statues whose features are elongated in the Romanesque style. The structure's other main Romanesque feature is the Clocher Vieux (Old Bell Tower), which was begun in the 1140s. At 105m, it is the tallest Romanesque steeple still standing. Also in Chartres is the empty shell of the Collégiale Saint André, a Romanesque collegiate church dating from the 12th century. The Église Saint Étienne in Beauvais, begun in the 12th century, has a Romanesque nave.

Gothic

The Gothic style originated in the mid-12th century in northern France, whose great wealth enabled it to attract the finest architects, engineers and artisans. Gothic structures are characterised by ribbed vaults carved with great precision, pointed arches, slender verticals, chapels (often built by rich people or guilds), galleries and arcades along the nave and chancel, refined decoration and large stained-glass windows. If you look closely at certain Gothic buildings, however, you'll notice that they're slightly asymmetrical. These elements were introduced to avoid monotony, in accordance with standard Gothic practice.

The first Gothic building to combine various late Romanesque elements to create a new kind of structural support in which each arch counteracted and complemented the next was the basilica at Saint Denis. Begun in around 1135, the basilica served as a model for many other 12th-century French cathedrals, including Notre Dame and the one at Chartres. Gothic technology and the width and height it made possible subsequently spread to the rest of western Europe.

Cathedrals built in the early Gothic style, which lasted until about 1230, were majestic but lacked the lightness and airiness of later works. Since the stained-glass windows could not support the roof, thick stone buttresses were placed between them. It was soon discovered that reducing the bulk of the buttresses and adding outer piers to carry the thrust created a lighter building without compromising structural integrity.

The flying buttresses of Notre Dame

TONY WHEELER

This discovery gave rise to flying buttresses, which helped lift the Gothic style to its greatest achievements between 1230 and 1300. During this period, when French architecture dominated the European scene for the first time, High Gothic masterpieces such as the seminal cathedral at Chartres were decorated with ornate tracery (the delicate stone ribwork on stained-glass windows) and huge, colourful rose windows.

Because of the fiascoes at Beauvais cathedral, whose 48m-high vaults collapsed in 1272 and again in 1284, it became clear that Gothic technology had reached its limits. Architects became less interested in sheer size and put more energy into ornamentation.

Rayonnant Gothic

In the 14th century, the Rayonnant (Radiant) Gothic style – named after the radiating tracery of the rose windows – developed, with interiors becoming even lighter thanks to broader windows and more translucent stained glass. One of the most influential Rayonnant buildings was the Sainte Chapelle in Paris, whose stained glass forms a sheer curtain of glazing. The two transept façades of Notre Dame and the Conciergerie's vaulted Salle des Gens d'Armes (Cavalrymen's Hall), the largest surviving medieval hall in Europe, are other fine examples of the Rayonnant Gothic style.

Flamboyant Gothic

By the 15th century, decorative extravagance led to Flamboyant Gothic, so named because its wavy stone carving was said to resemble flames. Beautifully lacy examples of Flamboyant architecture include the Clocher Neuf at Chartres, the Église Saint Séverin (Map 6) and the Tour Saint Jacques (Maps 6 and 8), a 52m-high tower which is all that remains of the Église Saint Jacques la Boucherie from the early 16th century. Inside the Église Saint Eustache (Map 7), there's some exceptional Flamboyant Gothic archwork holding up the ceiling of the chancel. Several *hôtels particuliers* were also built in this style, including the Hôtel de Cluny (now the Musée National du Moyen Age) and the Hôtel de Sens (Map 8) near Hôtel de Ville.

Renaissance

The Renaissance, which began in Italy in the early 1400s, set out to realise a 'rebirth' of classical Greek and Roman culture. It had its first impact on France at the end of the 15th century, when Charles VIII began a series of invasions of Italy. The French Renaissance introduced a variety of classical components and decorative motifs which were blended with the rich decoration of Flamboyant Gothic.

The French Renaissance is usually divided into two periods: early Renaissance and Mannerism.

Early Renaissance

During the first period, a variety of classical components and decorative motifs (columns, tunnel vaults, round arches, domes etc) were blended with the rich decoration of Flamboyant Gothic, a synthesis best exemplified in Paris by the churches of Saint Eustache on the Right Bank and Saint Étienne du Mont on the Left.

Mannerism

Mannerism began around 1530, when François I (who had been so deeply impressed by what he'd seen in Italy that he brought Leonardo da Vinci back with him in 1516) hired Italian architects and artists – many of them disciples of Michelangelo or Raphael – to design and decorate his new château at Fontainebleau. Over the following decades, French architects who had studied in Italy took over from their Italian colleagues.

In 1546 Pierre Lescot designed the richly decorated southwestern corner of the Louvre's Cour Carrée (Map 7). The Petit Château at Chantilly was built about a decade later. The Marais (Map 8) remains the best area for spotting reminders of Renaissance Paris, with some fine hôtels particuliers from this era such as the Hôtel Carnavalet and Hôtel Lamoignan.

Because French Renaissance architecture was very much the province of the aristocracy and designed by imported artists, the middle classes – resentful French artisans among them – remained loyal to the indigenous Gothic style, and Gothic churches continued to be built throughout the 1500s. The Mannerist style lasted until the early 17th century.

Baroque

During the baroque period, which lasted from the tail end of the 1500s to the late 1700s, painting, sculpture and classical architecture were integrated to create structures and interiors of great subtlety, refinement and elegance.

With the advent of the baroque, architecture became more pictorial, with the painted ceilings in churches illustrating infinity to the faithful, and palaces invoking the power and order of the state. Baroque architecture in France bears little resemblance to that in, say, Austria and the rest of Catholic central and southern Europe. Here, as in the Protestant countries of northern Europe, baroque architecture was meant to appeal to the intellect – not the senses. As a result it was more geometric, formal and precise.

Salomon de Brosse, who designed Paris' Palais du Luxembourg (Map 6) in 1615, set the stage for two of France's most prominent early baroque architects: François Mansart, designer of the church of Val-de-Grâce (Map 6), and his younger rival, Louis Le Vau, the architect of Vaux-le-Vicomte, which served as a model for Louis XIV's palace at Versailles. Baroque elements are particularly evident in Versailles' lavish interiors, such as the Galerie des Glaces (Hall of Mirrors). Jules Hardouin-Mansart, Le Vau's successor at Versailles,

Palais du Luxembourg

MARK HONAN

also designed the landmark Église du Dôme (Map 4; 1670s) at Invalides, considered the finest church built in France during the 17th century. Other fine examples of French baroque are the Église Saint Louis en l'Île (Map 8), built between 1656 and 1725; the Chapelle de la Sorbonne (Map 6); the Palais Royal (Map 7); the Val-de-Grâce; and the 17th-century Hôtel de Sully (Map 8), with its Cour d'Honneur decorated with allegorical figures. The Cathédrale Saint Louis in the town of Versailles fuses elements of baroque and neoclassicism.

Rococo

Rococo, a derivation of late baroque, was popular during the Enlightenment (1700-80). The word 'rococo' comes from the French *rocaille* for loose pebbles which, together with shells, were used to decorate inside walls and other surfaces in the 16th century. In France, rococo was confined almost exclusively to the interiors of private residences and had a minimal impact on churches, châteaux and façades, which continued to follow the conventional rules of baroque classicism. Rococo interiors, such as the oval rooms of the Archives Nationales building (Map 8), were lighter, smoother and airier than their 17th-century predecessors and favoured pastels over vivid colours.

Neoclassicism

Neoclassical architecture, which emerged in about 1740 and remained popular in Paris until well into the 19th century, had its roots in the renewed interest in classical forms. Although it was in part a reaction against baroque and rococo, with their emphasis on decoration and illusion, neoclassicism was more profoundly a search for order, reason and serenity through the adoption of the forms and conventions of Graeco-Roman antiquity: columns, simple geometric forms and traditional ornamentation.

Among the earliest examples in Paris of this reaction against baroque and rococo is the new Italianate façade for Église Saint Sulpice (Map 6) designed in 1733 by Giovanni Servandoni, which took inspiration from Chistopher Wren's Cathedral of Saint Paul in London, and the Petit Trianon at Versailles (1761-64), designed by Jacques-Ange Gabriel for Louis XV. The domed building housing the Institut de France (Map 6) is a masterpiece of early French neoclassical architecture, but France's greatest neoclassical architect of the 18th century was Jacques-Germain Soufflot, who designed the Panthéon (Map 6).

Neoclassicism really came into its own, however, under Napoleon, who used it extensively for monumental architecture intended to embody the grandeur of imperial France. Well known Paris sights designed (though not necessarily completed) during the First Empire (1804-14) include the Arc de Triomphe (Map 2), the Arc de Triomphe du Carrousel (Map 7), La Madeleine (Map 2), the Pont des Arts (Map 7), the Rue de Rivoli (Map 8), the Canal Saint Martin (Map 3), the Bourse (Map 7) and the Assemblée Nationale (Map 4).

Neoclassicism remained very much in vogue in Paris – though in slightly different forms – until late into the 19th century, spilling even into the 20th century in some cases, for

Arc de Triomphe

RACHEL BLACK

example the Palais de Chaillot (Map 4), which was built for the World Exhibition of 1937. Two architects associated with the École des Beaux-Arts, the most important centre of architectural education in Europe in the 19th century, who best exemplify this late period of classicism are Jacques-Ignace Hittorff, who designed the Gare du Nord (May 3; 1861–65), and Louis Duc, responsible for the Palais de Justice (Map 6; 1867-68). The work of both men influenced a generation of architects including Henri Deglane and Victor Laloux, who designed the Grand Palais (Map 2) and the Gare d'Orsay (Map 4; now Musée d'Orsay) for the World Exhibition in 1889, held to commemorate the centenary of the Revolution. The Eiffel Tower (Map 4), which at first faced massive opposition from Paris' artistic and literary élite, was also opened for the 1889 World Exhibition.

However, the climax of 19th-century classicism in Paris is thought to be the Opéra (Map 7), designed by Charles Garnier to showcase the splendour of Napoleon III's France and one of the most impressive monuments erected during the Second Empire (1852-70). It was one of the crowning glories of the urban redevelopment plans of Baron Haussmann (see boxed text).

Art Nouveau

Gothic Revival never caught on in Paris as it had in London; much of the style was confined to restorations (eg Viollet-le-Duc's work at Sainte Chapelle, Notre Dame and the Église Saint Germain L'Auxerrois). Art Nouveau, which emerged in Europe and the USA in the second half of the 19th century under various names (Jugendstil, Sezessionstil, Stile Liberty) but came to be seen as outdated by around 1910, was another story.

Art Nouveau was characterised by sinuous curves and flowing, asymmetrical forms reminiscent of tendrilous vines, water lilies, the patterns on insect wings and the flowering boughs of trees. Influenced by the arrival of *objets d'art* from Japan, its name came from a Paris gallery that featured works in the new style.

Art Nouveau had a profound impact on all of the applied arts, including interior design, glass work, wrought-iron work, furniture making and graphics. Art Nouveau combined a variety of materials – including iron, brick, glass and ceramics – in ways never seen before. Paris is still graced by Hector Guimard's Art Nouveau metro entrances. There are some fine Art Nouveau interiors in the Musée d'Orsay, an Art Nouveau

One of Hector Guimard's Art Nouveau metro entrances.

TONY WHEELER

glass roof over the Grand Palais and, on Rue Pavée in the Marais, a synagogue (Map 8) designed by Guimard. The city's three main department stores – Le Bon Marché (Map 4), Galeries Lafayette (Map 7) and Samaritaine (Map 7) – also have elements of this style throughout.

Modern Architecture

France's best known architect this century, Charles-Édouard Jeanneret (better known as Le Corbusier), was born in Switzerland but settled in Paris in 1917 at the age of 30. A radical modernist, he tried to adapt buildings to their functions in industrialised society without ignoring the human element. Not everyone thinks he was particularly successful in his endeavours.

Most of Le Corbusier's work was done outside Paris though he did design several private residences (eg Villa Savoye in the suburb of Poissy) and the Pavillon Suisse (a dormitory for Swiss students) at the Cité Universaire (Map 1). Perhaps most interesting – and frightening – was Corbusier's Projet Voisin (Neighbour Project), a plan for Paris that never left the drawing board. The project would have required bulldozing much of the Latin Quarter to create a wide, skyscraper-lined boulevard linking the Gare Montparnasse and the Seine.

Until 1968 French architects were still being trained almost exclusively at the conformist École de Beaux-Arts, which certainly shows in most of the early structures erected in the skyscraper district of La Défense (eg the CNIT building; see La Défense in the Things to See & Do chapter). Among some of the more forgettable buildings around is the UNESCO building (Map 4; 1958) south-west of the École Militaire in the 7e and the Tour Montparnasse (Map 4; 1974).

Thank goodness for pomposity. For centuries France's leaders have sought to immortalise themselves by erecting huge, public edifices, known as *grands projets*, in Paris. The recent past has been no different; the late President Georges Pompidou commissioned the once reviled but now much loved Centre Beaubourg (1977), which was later renamed the Centre Pompidou (Map 8), and his successor, Giscard d'Estaing, was instrumental in transforming a derelict train station into the glorious Musée d'Orsay, which opened in 1986. But François Mitterrand surpassed them both with his dozen or so monumental commissions in Paris alone.

Since the early 1980s, Paris has seen the construction of such projects as I M Pei's glass pyramid at the Louvre (Map 7), an architectural *cause célèbre* in the late 1980s; the city's second opera house, Opéra Bastille (Map 5); the Grande Arche at La Défense; the huge science museum and park at La Villette (Map 1); Parc André Citroën (Map 1) in the western corner of the 15e arrondissement; the Finance Ministry offices in Bercy (Map 1); and the controversial Bibliothèque Nationale de France François Mitterrand (Map 1). One of the most beautiful new buildings in Paris is Jean Nouvel's Institut du Monde Arabe (Maps 5 and 8), a highly praised structure (opened in 1987) that successfully mixes modern and traditional Arab and western elements.

The Grande Arche at La Défense

TONY WHEELER

It must be said that, while many of these projects have been huge successes, the initiatives have brought gentrification and soaring housing prices to central Paris. As a result, many working class and immigrant Parisians have been forced to relocate to dingy, postwar suburbs. The result – Paris proper has become more socio-economically homogeneous than ever before.

France's first new cathedral in more than a century was inaugurated in 1995 in Evry, a 'new town' 20km south of Paris. Designed by architect Mario Botta and built at a cost of 65FF million, the controversial Cathédrale de la Résurrection is a cylinder of red brick whose truncated, sloping roof has two dozen lime trees planted around its rim to symbolise Christ's crown of thorns.

Getting There & Away

For information on transport options between the city and the airports, see the Getting Around chapter.

AIR
Airports & Airlines

Paris has two airports: Aéroport d'Orly, 16km south of central Paris, and Aéroport Roissy Charles de Gaulle, which is 27km north of the city centre.

The following is a list of selected airlines. Airline offices can also be found in the Paris Yellow Pages under *Transports Aériens*.

Air France
(☎ 0802 802 802) for information and reservations and (☎ 08 36 68 10 48) for recorded information on arrivals and departures. By Minitel, dial 3615 or 3616 AF. Offices (generally open Monday to Saturday from 9 am to 6 pm) include the one at 40 Ave George V, 8e (Map 2; metro George V), just off the Ave des Champs Élysées.

Air Inter
(☎ 01 45 46 90 00) for information and reservations and (☎ 08 36 68 34 24) for flight information. By Minitel, dial 3615 AIRINTER. Offices include one at 119 Ave des Champs-Élysées, 8e (Map 2; metro George V).

Air Liberté
(☎ 01 49 79 09 09 or 08 03 80 58 05; Minitel 3615 AIR LIBERTE), 3 Rue Pont des Halles, Rungis 94656.

Air Littoral
(☎ 08 03 83 48 34; metro Vavin), 100 Blvd Montparnasse, 14e.

Air UK
(☎ 01 44 56 18 08; Minitel 3615 AIR UK; metro Madeleine), 2 Rue Chauveau Lagarde, 8e.

American Airlines
(☎ 01 69 32 73 07 or toll free 0801 872 872; metro Saint Philippe du Roule), 109 Rue du Faubourg Saint Honoré, 8e.

British Airways
(☎ 0802 802 902; metro Madeleine), 13 Blvd de la Madeleine, 1er.

Canadian Airlines International
(☎ 01 69 32 73 00; metro Miromesnil), 109 Rue du Faubourg Saint Honoré, 8e.

Continental
(☎ 01 42 99 09 09 or toll free 0800 25 31 81; Minitel 3615 CONTINENTAL; metro George V), 92 Ave des Champs-Élysées, 8e.

Corsair
(☎ 01 49 79 49 79), 24 Rue Saarinen, Rungis 94150.

El Al
(☎ 01 44 55 00 00; metro Madeleine), 35 Blvd des Capucines, 2e.

Northwest Airlines
(☎ 01 42 66 90 00; metro Madeleine), 16 Rue Chauveau Lagarde, 8e.

Qantas
(☎ 01 44 55 52 00, metro Madeleine), 13 Blvd de la Madeleine, 1er.

SAS
(☎ 01 53 43 25 25; Minitel 3615 FLYSAS; metro St Augustin), 18 Blvd Malesherbes, 8e.

Singapore Airlines
(☎ 01 45 53 90 90; metro Boissière), 43 Rue Boissière, 16e.

South African Airways (SAA)
(☎ 01 49 27 05 50; metro Tuileries), 350 Rue Saint Honoré, 1er.

TAT
(☎ 01 49 75 15 15 or 08 03 80 58 05; Minitel 3615 TAT; metro Opéra), 17 Rue de la Paix, 2e.

Thai
(☎ 01 44 20 70 80; metro Franklin D Roosevelt), 23 Ave des Champs-Élysées, 8e.

Tower Air
(☎ 01 55 04 80 80; metro Madeleine), 20 Rue Royale, 8e.

United
(☎ 01 41 40 30 30; Minitel 3615 UNITED; metro Opéra), 34 Ave de l'Opéra, 2e.

England

A straightforward fully flexible London-Paris ticket with British Airways, British Midland or Air France will cost £158/252 one way/return, although a seven-day excursion ticket taking in a Saturday night can cost somewhere around £90. With so many transport choices – the Eurostar train, Le Shuttle for cars, motorcycles and their passengers, cross-channel ferries and the airlines – there are often good deals going.

One-way fares as low as £49 are available on Air UK.

From Paris, the cheapest return ticket to London is currently around 800FF.

Continental Europe
Return discount charter fares from Paris include Athens (1500 to 1800FF), Belgrade (1750FF), Berlin (1400 to 1800FF), Budapest (1300 to 1900FF), Dublin (1500FF), Istanbul (1500 to 1800FF), Madrid (1200 to 1400FF) and Rome (1200 to 1300FF). The cheapest fares are available in early spring and late autumn.

North America
You should be able to fly New York-Paris return for US$400 to US$500 in the low season and US$550 to US$700 in the high season. Equivalent fares from the West Coast would be from US$600 in the low season and US$650 in the high. Check the travel pages of major city Sunday newspapers like the *New York Times*, *Los Angeles Times*, *San Francisco Chronicle* or *Boston Globe* for cheap flight ads or try travel agents like STA or Council Travel if all you're looking for is the lowest priced fare.

From Paris, one-way charter flights on the Paris-New York route usually cost about 1250 to 1500FF. Return fares from about 2000FF are sometimes available, but a more usual fare is 2500FF. Return fares to the West Coast are about 1200FF more.

Another option is a courier flight. A New York-Paris return ticket can be had from as low as US$350 to $400 (about $100 more from the West Coast). You can also fly one way. The drawbacks are that your stay in Europe may be limited to one or two weeks; your luggage is usually restricted to hand luggage (the courier company uses your checked luggage allowance to send its parcel) and you may have to be a local resident and apply for an interview before they'll take you on.

You can find out more about courier flights from Council Travel in New York (☎ 212-822 2700) and in Los Angeles (☎ 310-208 3551), as well as Discount Travel International in New York (☎ 212-362 3636). It is a good idea to call two or three months in advance, at the very beginning of the calendar month.

If you are travelling from Canada, Travel CUTS (☎ 888-838-CUTS) has offices in all major cities including Toronto (☎ 416-979 2406). You might also scan the budget travel agents' ads in Toronto's *Globe & Mail*, *Toronto Star* and the *Vancouver Province*.

From Paris, you may find that flights are a bit cheaper to Montreal than to Toronto, with one-way/return charter fares as low as 1200/2000FF, depending on the date.

Australia & New Zealand
Discounted return fares, on mainstream airlines through a reputable budget ticket agency like STA or Flight Centre, cost between A$1350 (October to mid-November and mid-January to late February) and A$2059 (mid-May to late August, and mid-December). Flights to/from Perth cost around A$1450.

London-Paris Fares & Travel Times
The opening of the Channel Tunnel in 1995 unleashed an all-out fare war among the airlines, the Eurostar and Le Shuttle train services, the bus services and the channel ferry operators. Though things have settled down quite a bit since then, fares between London and Paris – or simply those across the Channel – can vary tremendously according to the season and time of day you travel, so it's definitely worth shopping around to see what special deals are available. The costs we've indicated are strictly guidelines.

Flying London-Paris takes about an hour, while Eurostar takes about three hours, but there's not much in it, city centre to city centre, when getting to and from the airport, check-in times and waiting for baggage (sometimes a mysteriously long operation at Paris' Roissy Charles de Gaulle airport) are taken into account.

From Paris, return trips to Melbourne or Sydney start at about 6000 or 7000FF. Forum Voyages, Nouvelles Frontières and the student travel companies (see General Travel Agencies in the Facts for the Visitor chapter) have some of the best fares.

The cheapest fares to Paris from New Zealand (7000FF) are routed through Asia. A round-the-world (RTW) ticket could be cheaper than a return ticket.

Asia

Many of the cheapest fares from Asia to Europe are offered by eastern European or Middle Eastern carriers. STA has branches in Hong Kong, Tokyo, Singapore, Bangkok and Kuala Lumpur.

From Paris, sample discount return prices (low season) include: Bangkok (3300FF), Mumbai (3200FF), Hong Kong (3850FF), Jakarta (3300FF), Kuala Lumpur (3250FF) and Singapore (3400FF).

BUS

Eurolines runs buses from Paris to cities all over Europe. The company's Gare Routière Internationale Paris Gallieni (International bus terminal; Map 1; ☎ 01 49 72 51 51; metro Gallieni) is on the eastern edge of the 20e arrondissement in the inner suburb of Bagnolet.

Eurolines' ticket office (Map 6; ☎ 1 43 54 11 99; Minitel 3615 EUROLINES; euroline@imaginet.fr; www.eurolines.fr; metro Cluny-La Sorbonne) at 55 Rue Saint Jacques (5e) is open from 9.30 am to 1 pm and 2.30 to 7 pm (6 pm on Monday and Saturday, closed Sunday); from late June to August, there's no midday closure. In summer, it's not a bad idea to make a reservation a few days in advance.

England

Eurolines (London booking office ☎ 0171-730 8235 or, in Luton, 01582-404511), 52 Grosvenor Gardens SW1W 0AU, has bus services from London's Victoria Coach Station. Adult one-way/return fares to Paris are £31/44 in the low season; fares for those aged 13 to 26 are £28/39 and for children aged four to 12 years £16/22. In the peak season, the adult fares are £34/49 while the youth fares are £32/45 and children's fares £18/25. Bookings can be made through any office of National Express.

Continental Europe

Eurolines has representatives across Europe, including Eurolines (☎ 020-560 8787), Amstel Busstation, Julianaplein in Amsterdam; Deutsche Touring (☎ 089-591 824), at the Hauptbahnhof in Munich and in Frankfurt (☎ 069-790 350) at Am Römerhof 17; and Lazzi Express (☎ 06-44 23 39 28), Via Tagliamento 27 in Rome.

From Paris, Eurolines has direct services to Amsterdam, Athens, Berlin, Budapest, Istanbul, Madrid, Prague, Rome, Vienna and Warsaw.

TRAIN

Paris has six major train stations: Gare d'Austerlitz, Gare de l'Est, Gare de Lyon, Gare du Nord, Gare Montparnasse and Gare St Lazare. Each station handles passenger traffic to different parts of France and Europe. SNCF train information is available for mainline services on ☎ 08 36 35 35 35 (☎ 08 36 35 35 39 in English) and for suburban services on ☎ 01 53 90 20 20 or ☎ 08 36 67 68 69 (recording). By Minitel, key in 3615 SNCF.

England

There are two distinctly different services via the Channel Tunnel. Eurostar operates between London and Paris carrying passengers, while Le Shuttle goes only between Folkestone and just beyond Calais carrying cars, motorcycles and bicycles with their passengers or riders. Train-boat-train connections are possible but scarcely worth considering.

Eurostar The highly civilised Eurostar passenger train service through the Channel Tunnel takes three hours (not including the one-hour time change) to get from London's Waterloo Station to the Gare du Nord in Paris. Passport and customs checks take place on board or very cursorily on arrival.

The regular 2nd-class fare is £120/220 one way/return or £179/305 if you want to travel 1st class. A 2nd-class Leisure Return ticket costs £119 return (£199 in 1st) and requires that you stay away either three nights or a Saturday night. Changes to date and time of travel can be made before each departure, and full refunds are available before the outward trip. A 2nd-class Excursion return ticket must include a Saturday overnight; it costs £99 and although changes to date and time of travel can be made before departure of each train, it is nonrefundable. The 2nd-class Mid Week Travel ticket is the cheapest (£79) but carries a lot of restrictions: it must be purchased seven days in advance; it is valid for travel on Tuesday, Wednesday and Thursday only in each direction; your trip must include a Saturday night away; the ticket cannot be changed and is nonrefundable.

The Youth Return ticket (£85), available to those under 26, can be booked at any time. Changes can be made but, if you cancel your trip, a 50% refund is available only before departure of the outward trip. The same rules apply to Senior Return tickets (£99), available to those over 60.

Children's one-way/return fares, available for those aged four to 11 years, are £69/119 in 1st class and £37/65 in 2nd. There are often special deals on offer (eg day returns, weekend trips etc), so it pays to phone Eurostar or its agents for the latest information.

Eurostar tickets are available from some travel agents, at Waterloo Station, Victoria Station's Eurostar ticket office, international ticket offices at many of the UK's mainline train stations, from SNCF's French Railways House (☎ 0171-803 3030 or 0990-300003; tube Piccadilly Circus) at 179 Piccadilly, London W1V 0BA; it also sells all other SNCF tickets. To book by phone you can ring Eurostar on ☎ 0990-186186. The number to ring in Paris is ☎ 08 36 35 35 39. Tickets, for which you pay by credit card, can be either sent to you by post or picked up at Waterloo Station.

Bicycles can only be taken on Eurostar as registered baggage.

In France, the full 1st/2nd-class fares on Eurostar are 1455/820FF one way and 2450/1590FF return. The Loisir (Leisure Return) is 1590/990FF in 1st/2nd class and the 2nd-class Sourire (Excursion) is 790FF. Seniors/youths pay 850/650FF. Children aged four to 11 pay 590/990FF one way/return in 1st class and 290/490FF in 2nd.

Le Shuttle Le Shuttle, the train service through the Channel Tunnel between Folkestone and Coquelles (5km south-west of Calais), takes cars, motorcycles and, on some services, bicycles with their passengers or riders. Fares on Le Shuttle vary with the time of year, the day of the week, the time of the day and a variety of other competitive pressures! The normal one-way/return fare for a car with driver and all passengers is £95/120 but there are promotional fares as low as £12 (late departure and late return on the same day) and prices increase substantially in peak periods. A motorcycle and riders cost £45 for a same day return or £85 return for longer stays.

Bicycles can be taken on Le Shuttle but only on two trips per day, which must be booked 24 hours in advance on ☎ 01303-270111. The cost is £15 for bicycle and rider.

For information and reservations, contact a travel agent or call Le Shuttle in the UK (☎ 0990-353535) or in France (☎ 0800 12 71 27; Minitel 3615 LE SHUTTLE).

Le Shuttle runs 24 hours a day, every day of the year, with up to four departures an hour during peak periods. During the 35 minute crossing, passengers can sit in their cars or walk around the air-conditioned, soundproofed rail carriage. The entire process, including loading and unloading, should take about an hour.

Train-Boat-Train There are train-boat-train combos in association with Hoverspeed (☎ 0990-240241 or, in Dover, ☎ 01304-240241; ☎ 03 21 46 14 14 in Calais;

www.hoverspeed.co.uk) and others from London's Charing Cross Station to Paris' Gare du Nord which take between seven and eight hours and cost £44 one way for adults, £33 for children aged 12 to 15 and £22 for kids four to 11. The round-trip fares are £59/48/32. It's obviously cheaper than Eurostar but takes a lot longer, and you've got to mess around transferring by bus between the train station and the ferry terminal on both sides.

Continental Europe

Rail services link France with every country in Europe; schedules and tickets are available from major SNCF train stations. Because of different track gauges, you often have to change trains at the border (eg to Spain). There are TGV (trains á grande vitesse, ie high speed trains) services to Brussels and Amsterdam.

Fares One-way 2nd-class fares to destinations around France and abroad include:

Destination	Fare (FF)	Duration (hours)
Amsterdam	387	5
Annecy	335	3½
Berlin	879	11
Copenhagen	1133	16
Geneva	370	3½ *
Lille	269	1 *
Lyon	384	2 *
Madrid	631	16
Marseille	367	4¼ *
Nantes	345	2 *
Nice	438	6 *
Prague	974	16
Rome	644	12
Toulouse	433	5½ *
Strasbourg	210	4

* by TGV

CAR & MOTORCYCLE

Taking a car or motorcycle to Paris is quick and convenient if you want to brave the traffic. From the UK to France you can cross under the channel via Le Shuttle (see Train) or sail over via a variety of ferry routes (see Boat). Once in France, modern autoroutes will get you to Paris quickly if

rather expensively since tolls are charged on 'A'-designated roads (but not on ones beginning with 'N'). The Périphérique ring road encircles central Paris, and it's often quicker to skirt around Paris to the closest point on the Périphérique before diving into the city traffic.

HITCHING

Hitching is never entirely safe in any country, and we don't recommend it. Travellers who decide to hitch should understand that they are taking a small but potentially serious risk. People who do choose to hitch will be safer if they travel in pairs and let someone know where they are planning to go.

Le Shuttle motorists can take a car full of passengers through the Channel Tunnel free so you can hitch to France for nothing and at no cost to the driver. Channel ferry services also often include a number of passengers free with each car carried.

An organisation in Paris which matches travellers and drivers headed for the same destination is Allostop Provoya (☎ 01 53 20 42 42 or 01 53 20 42 44) at 8 Rue Rochambeau, 9e (Map 3; metro Cadet). It's open Monday to Friday from 9 am to 7.30 pm and on Saturday from 9 am to 1 pm and 2 to 6 pm.

BOAT

Tickets and reservations for ferry services across the Channel are available from the ferry operators themselves as well as travel agencies.

England

Fares vary widely according to seasonal demand and competitive pressures. Three or five-day excursion return fares cost about the same as regular one-way tickets.

The shortest Channel crossings are between Kent and the far-northern tip of France. The fastest way to cross the English Channel is to take one of the hovercraft operated by Hoverspeed, which ply the waters between Dover and Calais and Folkestone and Boulogne in less than an hour. The one-way standard fare (return times two) from Dover for a car and up to five passengers is from £79 to £109 or £95 to £135 for a five-day return, depending on the time of year. Adult/child foot passengers pay £25/13 year round. The standard one way from Folke-stone (return is double) for a car with up to five passengers is £74 to £99 or £85 to £125 for a five-day return. Adults/children on foot pay £25/13 all year. Note that the hov-ercrafts cannot operate in really rough weather.

Conventional car ferries are operated on the Dover-Calais route by P&O Stena (☎ 0990-980980) and Sea France (☎ 0990 711711 or, in Dover, ☎ 01304-212696; www.seafrance.com). They take around 1-1/2 hours. P&O Stena also runs ferries between Newhaven and Dieppe.

Return passage for passengers on the Dover-Calais route is typically £157 to £220 standard return for a car with four or more passengers, depending on when you travel; a single or five-day return is from £93 to £135. Adult/child foot passengers pay £22/12 for a standard return and £11/6 for a five-day one.

Other routes across the channel include Poole-Cherbourg, Portsmouth-Cherbourg, Portsmouth-Le Havre, Southampton-Cher-bourg, Plymouth-Roscoff, Poole-Saint Malo, Portsmouth-Saint Malo and Wey-mouth-Saint Malo. There are also ferry services linking the Channel Islands with Saint Malo.

Passengers can take bicycles free on hov-ercraft and ferry services. Although it's often more expensive than Le Shuttle train services, departures and routes may be more convenient.

Ireland

Eurail passes are valid for ferry crossings between Ireland and France. There is a charge to take along a bicycle.

Irish Ferries (☎ 01 42 66 90 90 for infor-mation in Paris; ☎ 01 44 94 20 40 for reservations; Minitel 3615 IRISH FERRIES)

sails to Rosslare from Roscoff and Cher-bourg (15 to 17 hours). There are usually three ferries a week from September to De-cember and again from April to mid-June; sailings are almost every second day in summer. Pedestrians pay 315 to 650FF one way; fares for students and people over 60 range from 270 to 550FF. From France, a re-served armchair costs 45FF; the cheapest couchette for two people is 210 to 305FF, de-pending on the season. A car with up to two passengers costs 900 to 2800FF, depending on the season; additional adult passengers (over age 15) cost 100 to 150FF extra. Transporting a bicycle is usually free but costs from 140 to 180FF in summer.

From mid-March to October, Brittany Ferries (☎ 0990 360360 in UK; ☎ 021-277801 in Cork; ☎ 08 03 82 88 28 in France; Minitel 3615 FERRY PLUS) has weekly car ferries linking Cork (Ringaskid-dy) with Roscoff (14 hours) and Cork with Saint Malo (18 hours). Foot passengers pay from 450 to 670FF one way; a car plus driver costs 1250 to 2000FF.

WARNING

This chapter is particularly vulnerable to change – prices for international travel are volatile, routes are introduced or cancelled, schedules change, special deals come and go, and rules and visa requirements are amended. Airlines seem to take a perverse pleasure in making price structures and reg-ulations as complicated as possible; you should check directly with the airline or travel agent to make sure you understand how a fare (and ticket you may buy) works. In addition, the travel industry is highly competitive, and there are many specials and bonuses.

The upshot of this is that you should get opinions, quotes and advice from as many airlines and travel agents as possible before you part with your hard-earned cash. The details given in this chapter should be re-garded as pointers; they are not a substitute for careful, up-to-date research.

Getting Around

TO/FROM THE AIRPORTS
Orly Airport
All six public transport options linking Orly with the city run daily every 15 minutes or so (less frequently late at night) from sometime between 5.30 and 6.30 am to 11 or 11.30 pm. Tickets are sold on board the buses.

Orlyval Links the airport with the city centre in 30 minutes flat, no matter what the traffic situation (57FF; 28FF for children aged four to 10). A completely automated (ie driverless) shuttle train connects both Orly terminals with the Antony RER station on RER line B in eight minutes; to get to Antony from the city, take line B4 toward Saint Rémy-lès-Chevreuse. Tickets are valid for 1st-class passage on the RER and metro travel within the city. Orlyval runs Monday to Saturday from 6 am to 10.30 pm and on Sunday from 7 am to 10.55 pm.

Orlyrail Links the airport with RER line C (30FF; 40 minutes to the city centre). An airport shuttle bus, which runs every 15 minutes from just before 6 am to 11.30 pm, takes you to/from the Pont de Rungis-Aéroport d'Orly RER station, to get there from the city, take a C2 train codenamed ROMI or MONA toward Pont de Rungis or Massy-Palaiseau. Tickets are valid for onward metro travel.

Orlybus An RATP-run bus to/from the Denfert Rochereau metro station, in the heart of the 14e, near Place Denfert Rochereau (Map 1; 30FF; 30 minutes; ☎ 01 40 02 32 94). In both directions, it makes several stops in the eastern 14e.

Jetbus One of the cheapest ways to get into the city (24FF; 20 minutes; ☎ 01 60 48 00 98). A bus, running every 12 to 15 minutes from about 6 am to about 10 pm, links both terminals with the Villejuif-Louis Aragon metro stop, which is a bit south of the 13e on the city's southern fringe. From there a regular metro ticket will get you into the city.

Air France Bus Air France bus No 1 (☎ 01 41 56 89 00) to/from Gare Montparnasse in the 15e (Map 4; metro Montparnasse Bienvenüe) and Aérogare des Invalides in the 7e (Map 4; metro Invalides). The trip costs 40FF (half-price for children aged five to 12), runs every 12 minutes from 5.50 am to 11 pm and takes 30 to 45 minutes. On your way into the city, you can request to get off at the Porte d'Orléans or Duroc metro stops.

RATP Bus No 183 A slow public bus that links Orly-Sud with the Porte de Choisy metro station (Map 1), at the southern edge of the 13e arrondissement. The cost is 24FF or three bus/metro tickets. It runs daily from 5.35 am to 12.40 am every 35 minutes. Not all buses with this number go all the way to Orly, however.

Taxi Taxis to/from central Paris cost between 110 and 150FF (plus 6FF per piece of luggage over 5kg) and take 15 or 20 minutes, depending on traffic conditions.

Roissy Charles de Gaulle Airport
The airport has two train stations: Aéroport Charles de Gaulle 1, linked to other parts of the airport complex by the free shuttle bus, and the sleek Aéroport Charles de Gaulle 2 at Aérogare 2. Both are served by commuter trains on RER line B3 (ie Roissyrail); the latter is on the TGV link that connects the TGV Nord line with the TGV Sud-Est line and is also connected with the TGV Atlantique line.

There are six public transport options for travel between Aéroport Charles de Gaulle and Paris. Unless otherwise indicated, they run from sometime between 5 and 6.30 am until 11 or 11.30 pm. Tickets are sold on board the buses.

Roissyrail Links the city with both of the airport's train stations (47FF; 35 minutes). To get to the airport, take any line B train whose four-letter destination code begins with E (eg EIRE). Regular metro ticket windows can't always sell these tickets, so you may have to buy one at the RER station where you board. The last train in both directions is sometime around midnight.

Roissybus An RATP-run bus (45FF; 45 minutes) which links all three aérogares with Place de l'Opéra, 9e (Map 7; ☎ 01 48 04 18 24; metro Opéra).

Air France Buses
Air France bus No 2 links the airport with two locations on the Right Bank: the end of Ave Carnot nearest the Arc de Triomphe (Map 2; metro Charles de Gaulle-Étoile) and the Palais des Congrès de Paris at Porte Maillots, 17e (Map 2; metro Porte Maillot). For information, ring ☎ 01 41 56 89 00. The cost is 55/28FF for adults/children aged five to 12. Buses run every 12 minutes from 5.50 am to 11 pm and take 35 to 50 minutes.

Air France bus No 4 links the airport with Gare Montparnasse in the 15e (Map 4; metro Montparnasse Bienvenüe). The ride costs 65/33FF for adults children and takes 45 to 55 minutes. Buses leave the airport every hour on the half-hour from 7.30 am to 7.30 pm; there are departures from the city every hour on the hour from 7 am to 9 pm.

RATP Bus No 350
Links both aérogares with Porte de la Chapelle (18e) and stops at Gare du Nord (at 184 Rue du Faubourg Saint Denis, 10e; Map 3) and Gare de l'Est (on Rue du 8 Mai 1945, 10e; Map 3). The trip takes 50 minutes (60 or 70 minutes during rush hour) and costs 48FF or six bus/metro tickets (five tickets or 40FF if you have a two-zone Carte Orange).

RATP Bus No 351
Goes to Ave du Trône (11e and 12e), on the eastern side of Place de la Nation (Map 1; metro Nation), and runs every half-hour or so until 8.20 pm (9.30 pm from the airport to the city). The

trip costs 48FF or six bus/metro tickets (five tickets or 40FF if you have a two-zone Carte Orange).

Taxi Taxis to the city centre should cost 185 to 225FF in the daytime (seven days a week) and 220 to 250FF at night (7 pm to 7 am), depending on the traffic. Luggage costs 6FF per bag weighing more than 5kg.

From Airport to Airport
Air France bus No 3 (☎ 01 41 56 89 00) runs between the two airports every 20 minutes from 6 am to 11 pm (70/35FF adults/children; free for Air France passengers with connecting flights). When traffic is not heavy, the ride takes 50 to 60 minutes.

Taking a combination of Roissyrail and Orlyval costs 103FF and takes about an hour. A taxi from one airport to the other should cost around 350FF.

BUS
Regular bus services operate Monday to Saturday from about 7 am to 8.30 pm. Bus service is drastically reduced on Sundays, holidays and after 8.30 pm. As your bus approaches, signal the driver by waving.

Bus Fares
Short bus rides (ie rides in one or two bus zones) cost one bus/metro ticket; longer rides within the city require two. Transfers to other buses or the metro are not allowed. Travel to the suburbs costs two to six tickets, depending on the distance. Special tickets valid only on the bus can be purchased from the driver.

Whatever kind of single-journey ticket you have, you must *oblitérer* (cancel) it in the *composteur* (cancelling machine) next to the driver. If you have a Carte Orange, Mobilis or Paris Visite pass, just flash it at the driver when you board. Do *not* cancel your magnetic *coupon*.

Noctambus
After the metro shuts down, the Noctambus network links the area just west of the Hôtel de Ville, 4e (Map 8), with lots of places on

the Right Bank (served by lines A to H) and a few destinations on the Left Bank (served by lines J and R). Look for the symbol of a little black owl silhouetted against a yellow moon. All 10 lines depart every hour on the half-hour from 1.30 to 5.30 am; line R also leaves at 1, 2, 3, 4 and 5 am.

Noctambus service is free if you have a Carte Orange, Mobilis or Paris Visite pass. Otherwise, a single ride costs three metro tickets (or four if you have to change/transfer to another bus at Châtelet).

METRO

There is always a metro station within 500m of wherever you are and want to go in Paris. Metro stations usually have a *plan du quartier* (map of the neighbourhood) hung on the wall near the exits.

Paris' underground network consists of two separate but linked systems: the Métropolitain, known as the *métro*, which has 13 lines and over 300 stations, and the RER, a network of suburban services that pass through the city centre. (A new high-speed line called the Météor and linking the Madeleine stop with the Bibliothèque Nationale de France (13e) and RER line C will probably have opened by the time you read this.) The term 'metro' is used in this book to refer to the Métropolitain as well as any part of the RER system within Paris proper.

For a list of the metro stations many Parisians try to avoid late at night, see Dangers & Annoyances in the Facts for the Visitor chapter.

Information

Metro maps are available for free at metro ticket windows. For information on the metro, RER and bus system, call the RATP's 24-hour enquiries number ☎ 08 36 68 77 14 if you speak French or ☎ 08 36 68 41 14 for English (2.23FF a minute). By Minitel, key in 3615 RATP.

Information on SNCF's suburban services (including certain RER lines) is available on ☎ 01 53 90 20 20 or ☎ 08 36 67 68 69 (recording). By Minitel, type 3615 SNCF.

Art in the Metro

There are more modern subway systems than the Paris metro, but few are as convenient, reasonably priced or, at the better stations, more elegant. Which is not to say that it can't be very tedious when the metro workers have one of their periodic *grèves* (strikes), or very sleazy at some of the more down and dirty stations late at night (see Dangers & Annoyances in the Facts for the Visitor chapter).

There are stations not to be missed, like the Louvre-Rivoli (a small taste of the nearby Musée du Louvre), Cluny-La Sorbonne (decorated with ceramic replicas of the signatures of intellectuals, artists and scientists from the quarter) or, best of all, Arts et Métier (looking like a brass-plated Jules Verne submarine).

Metro entrances are proclaimed by a variety of elegant signposts, and from Place de la Bastille you can spot all three standard signs. There are big yellow Ms beside the Opéra, standard red Art Nouveau signs on the Marais side of Place de la Bastille and, best of all, at the nearby Bréguet Sabin station, the writhing pale green metalwork of one of the Art Nouveau metro signs designed by Henri Guimard.

Guimard (1867-1942), the best known of French Art Nouveau architects, did other work, including the so-called Guimard synagogue in the Marais and the Castel Béranger apartment building on Rue La Fontaine (16e). But he'll always be remembered (and very fondly) for these bizarre metro signs, designed between 1898 and 1901, which look like escapees from a science fiction film.

Metro Network

Each Métropolitain train is known by the name of its end-of-the-line stop, which means that trains on the same line have different names depending on which direction they are travelling in.

Each line is also officially known by a number (1 to 13), but Parisians almost never use those and probably wouldn't understand you if you did.

In the stations, blue-on-white *direction* signs indicate how to get to the right platform. On metro lines which split into several branches the terminus served by each train is indicated on the cars with backlit panels.

Black-on-orange *correspondance* (change or transfer) signs show how to get to connecting trains. In general, the more lines that stop at a station, the longer your correspondances will be.

White-on-blue *sortie* signs indicate the station exits.

The last metro train on each line begins its final run of the night sometime between 12.25 and 12.45 am. After about midnight, metro travel is free. The metro starts up again around 5.30 am.

RER

The RER is faster than the Métropolitain, but the stops are more widely spaced. Some parts of the city, such as the Musée d'Orsay and the Eiffel Tower, can be reached far more conveniently by RER than by Métropolitain.

RER lines are known by an alphanumeric combination – the letter (A, B, C or D) refers to the line, the number to the spur it will follow somewhere out in the suburbs. Even-numbered lines head to Paris' southern or eastern suburbs, odd-numbered ones go north or west. All trains whose code begins with the same letter have the same end-of-run stop. Stations served are usually indicated on electric destination boards above the platform.

On the RER only 1st-class cars, which are located in the middle of the trains, can be identified by the yellow stripe across the upper part of the car and the numeral '1'.

Suburban Services

The RER and the SNCF's commuter lines serve destinations outside the city, ie in zones 2 to 8. Purchase a special ticket *before* you board the train or you won't be able to get out of the station when you arrive at your destination. You are not allowed to pay the additional fare when you get there.

If you are issued a full-sized SNCF ticket for travel to the suburbs, validate it in one of the orange time-stamp pillars before boarding the train. You may also be given a *contremarque magnétique* (magnetic ticket) to get through any metro/RER-type turnstiles you'll have to cross on the way to/from the platform. If you are travelling on a multizone Carte Orange, Paris Visite or Mobilis pass, do *not* punch the magnetic coupon in SNCF's orange time-stamp machines. Some – but not all – RER/SNCF tickets purchased in the suburbs for travel to the city allow you to continue your journey by metro; if in doubt, ask the person selling you the ticket.

For some destinations, tickets can be purchased at any metro ticket-window, but for others you'll have to get to an RER station on the line you need in order to buy a ticket. If you're trying to save every franc and have a Carte Orange, Paris Visite or Mobilis, you could get off the train at the last station covered by your coupon and then purchase a separate ticket for the rest of your trip.

Bus & Metro Tickets

The same 2nd-class tickets are valid on buses, trams (eg in the northern suburb of Saint Denis), the Montmartre funicular, the metro and – for travel within the Paris city limits – the RER. They cost 8FF if bought individually and 48FF for a *carnet* of 10. Children under four travel free; children under 10 for half the fare. Tickets are sold at every metro station, though not always at each and every entrance. At some stations, you can pay by credit card if the bill comes to at least 45FF.

One bus/metro ticket lets you travel between any two metro stations for a period of two hours, no matter how many transfers are required. You can also use it on the RER commuter rail system for travel within Paris (that is, within zone 1). However, a single ticket cannot be used to transfer from the metro to a bus, from a bus to the metro or between buses.

Always keep your ticket until you exit from the station.

Weekly & Monthly Tickets The cheapest and easiest way to travel the metro is to get a Carte Orange, a bus/metro/RER pass whose accompanying magnetic coupon comes in weekly and monthly versions. You can get tickets for travel within two to eight urban and suburban zones, but unless you'll be using the suburban commuter lines an awful lot, the basic ticket – valid for zones 1 and 2 – is probably sufficient.

The weekly ticket costs 75FF for zones 1 and 2 and is valid from Monday to Sunday. Even if you'll be in Paris for only three or four days, it may very well work out cheaper than purchasing a carnet – you'll break even at 16 rides – and it will certainly cost less than buying a daily Mobilis or Paris Visite pass. The monthly Carte Orange ticket (255FF for zones 1 and 2) begins on the first day of each calendar month. Both are on sale in metro and RER stations from 6.30 am to 10 pm and at certain bus terminals.

To get a Carte Orange, bring a small photograph of yourself to any metro or RER ticket counter (four photos for about 25FF are available from automatic booths in the train stations and certain metro stations). Request a Carte Orange (which is free) and the kind of coupon you'd like. To prevent tickets from being used by more than one person, you must write your *nom* (surname) and *prénom* (given name) on the Carte Orange, and the number of your Carte Orange on each weekly or monthly coupon you buy (next to the words *Carte No*).

Tourist Passes The rather pricey Mobilis and Paris Visite passes allow unlimited travel on the metro, the RER, SNCF's sub-

urban lines, buses, the Noctambus system, trams and the Montmartre funicular railway. They do not require a photo, though you should write your card number on the ticket.

The Mobilis card and its coupon allow unlimited travel for one day in two to eight zones (30 to 110FF). It's sold at all metro and RER ticket windows as well as SNCF stations in the Paris region, but you would have to make at least six metro trips in a day with a carnet of tickets to break even on this pass.

Paris Visite passes, which allow the holder discounts on entries to certain museums and activities as well as transport, are valid for one/two/three/five consecutive days of travel in either three, five or eight zones. The one to three-zone version costs 50/85/120/170FF for one/two/three/five days. Children aged four to 11 pay half price. They can be purchased at larger metro and RER stations, at SNCF bureaus in Paris and at the airports.

CAR & MOTORCYCLE
Driving in Paris is difficult but not impossible by any means – except for the nervy, faint-hearted or indecisive. The fastest way to get across Paris is usually the Périphérique (Map 1), the ring road or beltway that encircles the city.

In many parts of Paris you have to pay 10FF an hour to park your car on the street. Large municipal parking garages usually charge from 12 to 15FF an hour or, for periods of 12 to 24 hours, 80 to 130FF. Parking fines are usually 75 or 200FF. Parking attendants dispense them with great abandon (and some say glee), but Parisians appear simply to ignore them.

Car Rental
The easiest (if not cheapest) way to turn a stay in Paris into an uninterrupted series of hassles is to rent a car. If driving the car doesn't destroy your holiday-induced sense of carefree spontaneity, parking (or trying to park) the damn thing will. A small car (Peugeot 106) for one day with 400km, plus insurance and taxes, costs about 350FF but

TONY WHEELER
The meeting place of nosey women

TONY WHEELER
Street of bad boys

better deals – from as low as 199FF a day or 549FF for a three-day weekend with 800km – are available from smaller agencies.

Most of the larger companies have offices at the airports, and several are also represented at Aérogare des Invalides in the 7e (Map 4; metro Invalides). Higher rates may apply for airport rental, and you may have to return the car there.

To contact the major companies, ring their reservations centres:

Avis	☎ 01 46 10 60 60
Citer (Eurodollar)	☎ 01 44 38 61 61
Europcar	☎ 01 30 43 82 82
Hertz	☎ 01 39 38 38 38

For other rental operators check the Yellow Pages under *Location d'automobiles: tourisme et utilitaires*. A number of national and local companies offer relatively reasonable rates. It's a good idea to reserve

at least three days ahead, especially for holiday weekends and during summer.

ADA
(Map 2; ☎ 01 45 72 36 36 or 08 36 68 40 02 for general information and reservations; metro Porte Maillot), 271 Blvd Pereire, 17e. ADA has about a dozen other Paris bureaus, including those at 74 Rue de Rome, 8e (Map 2; ☎ 01 42 93 65 13; metro Rome); 49 Ave de Versailles, 16e (☎ 01 42 15 06 06; metro Mirabeau); and 34 Ave de la République, 11e (Map 3; ☎ 01 48 06 59 74; metro Parmentier).

OTU Voyages
(☎ 1 44 41 38 50 for rental information). The French student travel agency has very reasonable car-rental rates through Budget for anyone over 21 who has a student card or is under 26. See Student Travel Agencies in the Facts for the Visitor chapter.

Rent A Car 7
(Map 5; ☎ 01 43 45 15 15; Minitel 3615 RENTACAR; metro Bercy) at 9 Rue de Bercy (12e) has SEAT Marbellas with unlimited kilometres for around 300FF a day and is open Monday to Saturday from 8 am to 8 pm. It has 10 other branches in Paris, including one at 84 Ave de Versailles, 16e (☎ 01 42 88 40 04; metro Mirabeau).

TAXI

Parisian taxi drivers have a reputation for arrogance but, within reason, it's all part of the fun. They're often hair-raisingly bad drivers and not all of them know their way around Paris very well.

The *prise en charge* (flag fall fee) is 13FF. Within the city, it costs 3.45FF per kilometre for travel Monday to Saturday, 7 am to 7 pm (tariff A). At night, on Sundays and holidays (tariff B) it's 5.70FF per kilometre. It costs 130FF an hour to have a taxi wait for you.

There's an extra 8FF charge for taking a fourth passenger but always ask permission first, as many drivers are reluctant to take more than three people for insurance reasons. Each piece of baggage over 5kg costs 6FF and from certain train stations there's a 5FF supplement. A full list of surcharges is posted on the side window behind the driver. The usual tip is 2FF no matter what the fare, with the maximum about 5FF.

GETTING AROUND

Radio-dispatched taxi companies, on call 24 hours, include:

Alpha Taxis	☎ 01 45 85 85 85
Artaxi	☎ 01 42 41 50 50
G7 Radio	☎ 01 47 39 47 39
Taxis Bleus	☎ 01 49 36 10 10
Taxis-Radio 7000	☎ 01 42 70 00 42

BICYCLE

Paris now counts almost 100km of bicycle lanes – with another 50km planned by the year 2000 – running north-south and east-west through the city; for information ring ☎ 01 40 28 73 73. They're not particularly attractive or safe, but cyclists may be fined about 250FF for failing to use them. The tourist office distributes a free brochure-map called *100km pour Vivre Paris à Vélo*.

There's plenty of space for cyclists in the Bois de Boulogne (16e), the Bois de Vincennes (12e), along the Canal Saint Martin (10e) to Parc de la Villette (19e) and then along the south bank of the 108km-long Canal de l'Ourcq. The quays along the Seine on the Right Bank and the Quai d'Orsay on the Left Bank are closed to motor vehicles on Sunday between 10 am and 5 pm. For information on bicycle tours, see Organised Tours later in this chapter.

Bike rental (90 to 150FF a day) is possible in the Bois de Boulogne, at a number of RER/SNCF stations and at several locations in the city including:

Cycles Peugeot
  (☎ 01 45 27 91 39; metro La Muette), 7 Rue Duban, 16e.
Cyclic
  (☎ 01 43 25 63 67; metro Maubert Mutualité), 19 Rue Monge, 5e.
La Maison du Vélo
  (☎ 01 42 81 24 72; metro Gare du Nord), 11 Rue Fénelon, 10e.
Metro Bike
  (☎ 01 43 21 88 38; metro Edgar Quinet), 1 Blvd Edgar Quinet, 14e.
Paris à Vélo, C'est Sympa!
  (☎ 01 48 87 60 01: metro Bastille), 37 Blvd Bourdon, 4e.
Paris Vélo
  (☎ 01 43 37 59 22; metro Censier Daubenton), 2 Rue du Fer à Moulin, 5e.

Bikes are not allowed on the metro. You can take your bicycle for free on some RER lines out to the Paris suburbs on weekends and holidays (all day), and on weekdays before 6.30 am, between 9.30 am and 4.30 pm, and after 7.30 pm. More lenient rules apply to SNCF commuter services. For details, call the SNCF or the RATP or stop by one of their information offices.

ORGANISED TOURS

Sightseeing boats run by a number of companies ply the Seine between the Eiffel Tower and the Île Saint Louis.

Canal Cruises

From March to October, Canauxrama (Map 5; ☎ 01 42 39 15 00) barges travel between Port de Plaisance Paris-Arsenal (12e) and Parc de la Villette (19e) along charming Canal Saint Martin and Canal de l'Ourcq. Departures are at 9.45 am and 2.30 pm from the Parc de la Villette and 9.45 am and 2.30 pm from Port de Plaisance. The cost is 75FF (60FF for students; 45FF for kids aged six to 12, except on Sunday and holidays when everyone pays 75FF).

Paris Canal Croisières (☎ 01 42 40 96 97) has daily three-hour cruises from late March to mid-November from the Quai Anatole France just north-west of the Musée d'Orsay leaving at 9.30 am and returning from the Parc de la Villette at 2.30 pm. There are extra trips at 2.35 pm (from the museum) and 6.15 pm (from the park) from mid-July to August. The cost is 95FF for adults, 70FF for those aged 60 and over or between 12 and 25 (excluding Sunday afternoons and holidays) and 55FF for children aged four to 11.

Seine Shuttle

From late April to September, the Bateaux Parisiens Batobus river shuttle (Map 4; ☎ 01 44 11 33 99) docks at the following six stops:

Eiffel Tower (Port de la Bourdonnais next to the Pont d'Iéna, 7e; Map 4)
Musée d'Orsay (Port de Solférino, 7e; Map 4)
Saint Germain des Prés (Quai Malaquais, 6e; Map 6)

River shuttles and cruise boats ply the Seine

Notre Dame (Quai Montebello, 5e; Map 8)
Hôtel de Ville (Quai de l'Hôtel de Ville, 4e; Map 8)
Musée du Louvre (Quai du Louvre, 1er; Map 7)

The boats come by every 25 minutes from about 10 am to 7 pm (9 pm in July and August) and cost 20FF for the first journey between dockings and 10FF thereafter. Unlimited travel for the whole day costs 60FF (half-price for children under 12); two days is 90/45FF. Note that if you're travelling west (ie Hôtel de Ville to Eiffel Tower) you can travel the whole length of the trip for just 20FF (one stop); in the opposite direction it's three stops and will cost 40FF.

Seine Cruises

From its base just north of the Eiffel Tower at Port de la Bourdonnais (7e), Bateaux Parisiens (Map 4) also run one-hour river circuits (50FF, 25FF for under 12s) and lunch/dinner cruises (300/560FF) all year. From May to October, boats also depart from the dock (Map 8; ☎ 01 43 26 92 55; metro Maubert Mutualité) opposite Notre Dame, on Quai de Montebello (5e).

The Bateaux Mouches company (Map 2; ☎ 01 42 25 96 10 or 01 40 76 99 99 for an English-language recording; Minitel 3615 MOUCHES; metro Alma Marceau), based on the Right Bank just east of Pont de l'Alma (8e), runs 1000-seat tour boats, the biggest on the Seine. From mid-November to mid-March, there are sailings daily at 11 am, 2.30 and 3.15 pm, and hourly on the hour from 4 to 9 pm. Depending on demand, there are additional cruises at 1 and 9.30 pm. The rest of the year, boats depart every

half-hour from 10 am to 12.30 pm and 1.30 to 11.30 pm. A 1¼-hour cruise with commentary costs 40FF (20FF for those under 14). Lunch cruises are 200 to 300FF, dinner ones 500 to 650FF.

Vedettes du Pont Neuf (Map 6; ☎ 01 46 33 98 38; metro Pont Neuf), whose home dock is at the far western tip of the Île de la Cité (1er), offers one-hour boat excursions. Between April and November, boats generally leave every half-hour between 10 am and noon and 1.30 to 7 pm; night cruises depart every 30 minutes from 9 to 11 pm. From November to March there are about a dozen cruises from Monday to Thursday (when night services stop at 10 or 10.30 pm) and some seven on Friday, Saturday and Sunday. A ticket costs 50FF (25FF for children under 12).

Bus

On Sunday afternoons from mid-April to mid-September, RATP's Balabus follows a 50-minute route from Gare de Lyon to La Défense, passing many of central Paris' most famous sights. Details are available at metro counters.

Parisbus (☎ 01 42 88 69 15 or 01 42 88 98 88) runs red, London-style double-deckers in a 2¼-hour circuit that takes in Notre Dame, the Eiffel Tower and Musée d'Orsay as well as the usual list of Right Bank tourist sights. For 125FF (60FF for children aged four to 13) you can, over a period of two days, get on and off the company's buses wherever you like; their progress through the city is accompanied by commentary in English and French. Brochures showing the exact locations of Parisbus' stops are available at many hotels.

Cityrama (Map 7; ☎ 01 44 55 61 00; metro Tuileries) is based near the western end of the Louvre at 4 Place des Pyramides (1er) and runs two-hour tours of the city daily (150FF), accompanied by taped commentary in a dozen or so languages. The company also has trips to Chartres (270FF), Versailles (195FF) and other places around Paris.

Bicycle

Paris Vélo (Map 5; ☎ 01 43 37 59 22; metro Censier Daubenton) at 2 Rue du Fer à Moulin (5e) runs well reviewed bicycle tours of Paris and its major monuments for between 120 and 180FF. To reserve a place, phone a day ahead Monday to Saturday from 10 am to 12.30 pm and 2 to 6 pm (in summer from 10 am to 2 pm and 5 to 7 pm). It also rents bicycles for 90/420FF a day/week.

Things to See & Do

HIGHLIGHTS

Paris has a wealth of wonderful places to visit, but some features are so outstanding they deserve special mention. Here are the places not to miss in Paris:

Churches – La Madeleine, Notre Dame, Sainte Chapelle and Saint Eustache
Monuments – Arc de Triomphe, Eiffel Tower, Panthéon and Place de la Concorde
Museums and Art Galleries – Centre Pompidou (when renovated), Musée du Louvre, Musée d'Orsay, Musée Picasso and Musée Rodin
Neighbourhoods – Bastille, Île Saint Louis, Latin Quarter, the Marais and Montmartre
Odd Attractions – Catacombes and Musée des Égouts de Paris
Parks, Gardens and Cemeteries – Bois de Boulogne, Cimetière du Père Lachaise, Parc de la Villette, Jardin du Luxembourg and Jardin des Tuileries
Shopping – Blvd Montmartre arcades, the Marais, Rue du Faubourg Saint Honoré, Saint Germain des Prés and Triangle d'Or
Views – Eiffel Tower, Parc des Buttes-Chaumont, Sacré Cœur and Tour Montparnasse.

WALKING TOURS

Paris is a wonderful city to walk in and surprisingly pedestrian-friendly, in part because it's relatively compact. Metro stations are often so close you can see down the tunnel from one station to the next, so it's almost always just as fast (and much more enjoyable) to walk as to wait the minute or two for the next metro to turn up. Furthermore, it's a relatively level city, so apart from toiling up to Montmartre, there's no hill climbing involved. Traffic can be a problem, though; cars will only stop for pedestrians if they absolutely assert their rights on pedestrian crossings. And then there's those damn dogs (see the boxed text 'Remembrance of Dogs Passed and Present').

The sky's the limit on specialised and themed walking tours of Paris, whether

Remembrance of Dogs Passed

The Paris municipality spends vast sums of money to keep the city's pavements relatively passable, and the technology employed is undeniably impressive. But it would seem that repeated campaigns to get people to clean up after their pooches have been less than a howling success. Evidence to this effect takes the form of 'souvenirs' left by recently walked poodles and other breeds, often found smeared along the pavement – by daydreaming strollers, one assumes, or guidebook writers absorbed in jotting down something. Until that far-off day when Parisians – and their beloved canines – change their ways, the word on the streets remains the same: watch your step.

self-paced or led by a guide. The entertainment magazine *Pariscope* (3FF) lists different organised walks and tours each week in its 'Guide de Paris: Promenades' section as does *L'Officiel des Spectacles* (2FF) under 'À Travers Paris: Promenades'.

One outfit that gets good reports is Paris Walking Tours (☎ 01 48 09 21 49; fax 01 42 43 75 51; outword.compuserve.com/homepages/Paris Walking) based at 10 Rue Samson in Saint Denis, north of Paris. English-language tours (60FF) of Montmartre leave on Sunday and Thursday at 10.30 am from the Abbesses metro station; tours of Marais go from the Saint Paul metro station on Sunday at 2.30 pm and Wednesday at 10.30 am. Hemingway's Paris (60FF) takes place every Tuesday at 2 pm; starting point is the Cardinal Lemoine metro station.

The Bibliothèque Publique d'Information (BPI), the Centre Pompidou's huge, noncirculating library temporarily relocated at 11 Rue Brantôme, 3e (Map 8; metro Rambuteau), offers excellent literary tours (100FF; 80FF reduced tariff) of Paris that follow in the footsteps of such diverse writers as Céline, Rilke, Georges Simenon, Jean Cocteau and Henry Miller. Tours leave from the BPI on Wednesday and Sunday at 2.30 pm (also 10 am on Sunday) and last three hours. For information and reservations ring ☎ 01 44 78 45 73.

If you want to go on your own but need some direction (though aimless exploring is half the fun of Paris) consult any of the walking guides listed in the Books section of the Facts for the Visitor chapter.

The following list contains walking options from each area of sights contained in this chapter. The selections are neither exhaustive nor thematic but will lead you to backstreets, neighbourhoods, shops etc which you might otherwise miss.

Louvre Area

Strolling options to/from the Louvre (1er) are countless. The **Voie Triomphale** (Triumphal Way; Map 2), the axis of Ave des Champs-Élysées as it heads north-westward from the Louvre, has been a favourite venue for elegant promenades since its construction began in the 16th century. A stroll from the Louvre through the Jardin des Tuileries to the Arc de Triomphe involves about 3.5km of walking.

Opéra Garnier is 1km north of the Louvre along the prestigious Ave de l'Opéra, home to numerous airline offices and luxury goods shops.

Since Jardin des Tuileries is right across the Seine from the Musée d'Orsay, you can easily pop over to see the sights covered in the 7e Arrondissement section.

The eastern end of the Louvre is only 500m north-west of Île de la Cité and about the same distance south-west of the lively streets around Les Halles. It is linked with the area around Saint Germain des Prés (6e) by one of Paris' most romantic bridges, the pedestrians-only **Pont des Arts** (Map 7).

Les Halles Area

Rue Quincampoix (4e; metro Rambuteau or Châtelet), two blocks west of the Centre Pompidou, is home to quite a few art galleries, including **Galerie Zabriskie** (Map 8; ☎ 01 42 72 35 47) at No 37, open Tuesday to Saturday from 4 to 8 pm.

The Centre Pompidou is within easy walking distance of the Louvre (1km to the west) and Notre Dame (800m due south), though until renovations are completed you won't get to see much. The Marais, with its many museums, is only a few blocks to the east. Place de l'Hôtel de Ville (Map 8) is the perfect place to enjoy an ice cream on a sunny day. In winter you can even go ice-skating here.

Marais

Good streets for strolling include Rue des Rosiers (4e) and Rue des Francs Bourgeois as well as the Place des Vosges. Some of Paris' most interesting shops for cute little decorative items – the kind of expensive things with which a *branché* (trendy) young Parisian might enliven a chi-chi flat – can be found along Rue du Bourg Tibourg, Rue Sainte Croix de la Bretonnerie, Rue Saint Merri, Rue du Roi de Sicile, Rue François Miron and Rue du Pont Louis-Philippe (all are near metro stations Hôtel de Ville, Saint Paul or Pont Marie). The area also has quite a few small art galleries (eg along Rue Sainte Croix de la Bretonnerie).

The Marais is within easy walking distance of much of central Paris, including the Centre Pompidou, Place de la Bastille, Île Saint Louis, Notre Dame and – a bit over a kilometre to the west – the Louvre.

Bastille Area

There are a number of attractive **art galleries** along Rue de Charonne (11e), just north of Rue du Faubourg Saint Antoine.

On its south side, Place de la Bastille abuts the **Port de Plaisance de Paris-Arsenal**, the city's main port for pleasure boats. There's a **children's playground** (Map 5) just north of the footbridge over the port.

The Bastille area is a few blocks east of the Marais. Blvd Henri IV links Place de la Bastille with Île Saint Louis.

Latin Quarter

Almost every street in the Latin Quarter (5e) proper – the area bordered by Blvd Saint Germain, Rue Monge, Rue Claude Bernard and Blvd Saint Michel – has something unique to offer. Among the liveliest is **Rue Mouffetard** (Map 5), one of the oldest streets in Paris. The intense urbanity of the area is softened by the green expanses and pools of the Jardin du Luxembourg in the 6e.

The shop-lined **Blvd Saint Michel** (Map 6), popularly known as the 'Boul Mich' (pronounced 'bool mish'), runs along the border between the 5e and the 6e arrondissements. Bustling **Blvd Saint Germain** stretches over 3km from the Île Saint Louis westward past Saint Germain des Prés all the way to the Assemblée Nationale.

Right across the Seine from Notre Dame, along Rue Frédéric Sauton (Map 6), there's a cluster of small **galleries** with art objects from around the world. The area east of the Latin Quarter is covered in the section entitled Jardin des Plantes Area.

6e Arrondissement

A stroll along the streets between Église Saint Germain des Prés and the Institut de France is a good way to get a feel for the area. **Place de Furstemberg** (Map 6), a lovely, shaded square near the Église Saint Germain des Prés, is named after a former bishop of Strasbourg who laid out the area in 1699.

The most enjoyable way to walk from Saint Germain des Prés to the Latin Quarter is via Église Saint Sulpice and the Jardin du Luxembourg.

If you walk to the northern end of Rue Bonaparte, you'll find yourself at the Seine, from where it's a short stroll via the lovely, pedestrians-only **Pont des Arts** to the Louvre and the Forum des Halles. The Musée d'Orsay is 800m to the west along the river.

Eiffel Tower Area

The Musée d'Orsay (7e) is right across the river from the Jardin des Tuileries and the Louvre, but don't even *think* of visiting both museums in the same day. The Assemblée Nationale is linked to Place de la Concorde (8e) by Pont de la Concorde. The grassy expanse north of Invalides, the Esplanade des Invalides, is connected to the lovely eastern end of Ave des Champs-Élysées (8e) by **Pont Alexandre III** (Map 4), a richly ornamented bridge completed in 1900 and named in honour of Tsar Alexandre III of Russia.

An excellent way to approach the Eiffel Tower is from the north-west, starting at Place du Trocadéro et du 11 Novembre (Map 4; metro Trocadéro), known for its up-market cafés. After checking out the view from the terrace of the Palais de Chaillot, walk through the Jardins du Trocadéro and across Pont d'Iéna. After visiting the tower, you can continue south-eastward across the Champ de Mars to the École Militaire.

The Eiffel Tower and nearby sights are about 2km south of the Arc de Triomphe (8e), along some of the most fashionable avenues (including Ave Kléber) of the well-to-do 16e arrondissement.

Place de la Concorde Area

From Place de la Concorde, it's a short and elegant walk up Rue Royale – home to some of the most elegant boutiques in Paris – to La Madeleine. From there, you could continue on to the Opéra Garnier (Map 7) and the Grands Boulevards, and then loop back to the Louvre via Ave de l'Opéra.

Champs-Élysées Area

For details on the Voie Triomphale (Triumphal Way), see the Louvre Area earlier in this section. The most attractive part of Ave des Champs-Élysées is the shady, grass-covered stretch between Place de la Concorde and Rond Point des Champs-Élysées (Map 2).

The Petit Palais and Grand Palais (Map 2) are 1km north of the Invalides and the nearby Musée Rodin. The Eiffel Tower is separated from the Arc de Triomphe by about 2km of the fashionable 16e arrondissement.

Opéra Garnier Area

The area around Opéra Garnier (9e) makes for a stimulating (if congested) stroll. In addition to following the Grands Boulevards, you could walk south along Rue de la Paix, known for its jewellery shops, to Place Vendôme (Map 2; see the Louvre Area listing) or head south-east along the 1km-long Ave de l'Opéra to the Palais Royal and the Louvre. About 100m east of Opéra Garnier, you can explore Rue de la Chaussée d'Antin (Map 7), an enormously fashionable thoroughfare in the late 1700s.

Montmartre

The real attractions of Montmartre, apart from the great views, are the area's little parks and steep, winding, cobblestoned streets, many of whose houses seem about to be engulfed by creeping vines and ivy. On the corner of Rue Saint Vincent and Rue des Saules, there's even a small vineyard dating from 1933 called **Le Close du Montmartre** (Map 9) whose annual production in October – some 850 bottles of wine – is auctioned off for charity in the 18e.

Lovely streets to explore here include Rue de l'Abreuvoir, Rue Saint Vincent, Place Constantin Pecqueur and **Place Émile Goudeau**, where Kees Van Dongen, Max Jacob, Amedeo Modigliani and Pablo Picasso (among others) once lived in great poverty in an old piano factory and workshop at No 11b, dubbed by Jacob the **Bateau Lavoir** (Laundry Boat). It was rebuilt in 1978 after burning down eight years before and now houses some two dozen artists (closed to the public).

There's a **children's playground** and **carousel** (10FF) at the base of the stairs up to Sacré Cœur.

Place Pigalle and Blvd de Clichy, the lively heart of Pigalle, are 200m south of Place des Abbesses, with its particularly photogenic metro entrance and sign.

LOUVRE AREA

From the enormous Palais du Louvre (1er), you can walk in literally any direction and come upon some well known sights, including many of Paris' most famous public spaces. The Louvre area has long been a chic residential area for people of means.

Musée du Louvre

The vast Louvre (Map 7; ☎ 01 40 20 53 17 or, for a recording, ☎ 01 40 20 51 51; metro Palais Royal) was constructed around 1200 as a fortress and rebuilt in the mid-16th century for use as a royal palace. It began its career as a public museum in 1793. The paintings, sculptures and artefacts on display have been assembled by French governments over the past five centuries. Among them are works of art and artisanship from all over Europe and important collections of Assyrian, Etruscan, Greek, Coptic, and Islamic art and antiquities.

The Louvre may be the most actively avoided museum in Paris. Tourists and residents alike, daunted by the richness of the place and its sheer size (the side facing the Seine is almost 0.75km long), often find the prospect of an afternoon at a smaller museum far more inviting.

Eventually, most people do their duty and come, but many leave overwhelmed, unfulfilled, exhausted and frustrated at having gotten lost on their way to the *Mona Lisa*. Since it takes several serious visits to get anything more than the briefest glimpse of the works on offer, your best bet – after checking out a few things you really want to see (eg famous masterpieces such as the *Winged Victory of Samothrace* or *Venus de Milo*) – is probably to choose a period or section of the museum and pretend that the rest is somewhere across town.

The Louvre was one of the late President François Mitterrand's most ambitious and boldly conceived *grands projets*, and the French government has invested over US$1 billion in restoring, renovating and upgrading its exhibition halls and public spaces. The whole project, which was started in 1984, is slated to be completed around the

THINGS TO SEE & DO

TONY WHEELER

Pavillon Richelieu in the Musée de Louvre

turn of the century. If you haven't visited the Louvre for a few years, you'll hardly recognise the place: hundreds of masterpieces have come out of storage, old favourites have been moved, and grand new halls have been opened. Unfortunately, in recent years the Louvre has been plagued by thefts – some seven big ones since 1994 – and public access to many of its 500 rooms may have to be sacrificed to security.

Orientation The Louvre's main entrance and ticket windows in the Cour Napoléon are covered by a 21m-high **glass pyramid** (Map 7) designed by the China-born American architect IM Pei; on either side of it are two smaller glass pyramids. Commissioned by Mitterrand and completed in 1990, the design generated bitter controversy in the mid-1980s but is now generally acknowledged to be a brilliant success. You can avoid the queues outside the pyramid by entering the Louvre complex via the Carrousel du

Louvre shopping area (open daily from 8.30 am to 11 pm), with an entrance at 99 Rue de Rivoli (Map 7), or following the 'Louvre' exit from the Palais Royal metro stop.

The Louvre is divided into four sections. **Sully** forms the four sides of the Cour Carrée (Square Courtyard) at the eastern end of the building. **Denon** stretches for 500m along the Seine. **Richelieu**, the wing along the Rue de Rivoli, was occupied by the Ministry of Finance until the late 1980s and has some superb new halls. The underground **Carrousel du Louvre** shopping mall, where you'll find museum shops, a Virgin Megastore, a self-service restaurant (*Universal Resto*), a bunch of upmarket boutiques and the Comédie Française Studio Theatre, stretches from the pyramid to the Arc de Triomphe du Carrousel (see below). Its centrepiece is an **inverted glass pyramid** (Map 7), also by Pei.

The split-level public area under the pyramid is known as **Hall Napoléon**. It has an exhibit on the history of the Louvre, a bookshop, a restaurant, a café and auditoriums for concerts, lectures and films. Rudimentary maps of the museum complex *(Louvre Plan/Information)* are available at the round information desk in English. One of the best publications for a general overview is *Louvre First Visit* (20FF), which leads you past some 50 works of art including the Code of Hammurabi stele, Vermeer's *The Lacemaker* and the Apollo Gallery with the French crown jewels as well, of course, as the *Winged Victory of Samothrace*, the *Venus de Milo* and the *Mona Lisa*. The more comprehensive *Louvre: The Visit* (60FF) illustrates and describes more than 160 works of art. Both publications are available in the museum gift shop.

The Louvre's two courtyards, the Cour Napoléon and the Cour Carré, are beautifully illuminated at night and well worth a special visit just to marvel at the palace's architectural features.

Hours & Tickets The Louvre is open daily, except Tuesday and certain holidays. From Thursday to Sunday, hours are 9 am to 6 pm. On Monday and Wednesday, hours are 9 am to 9.45 pm, but on Monday only the Richelieu wing or other limited collections are open after 5.30 pm. Ticket sales end 45 minutes before closing time, and the guards begin clearing the halls 30 minutes before closing. The Hall Napoléon is open from 9 am to 9.45 pm, except Tuesday.

Entry to the permanent collections (but not temporary exhibitions) costs 45FF (26FF after 3 pm and all day Sunday); the first Sunday of every month is free. There are no discounts for students or senior citizens, but those under age 18 get in free. Tickets are valid all day long, so you can leave and re-enter as you please. A combination ticket for the permanent collections and Hall Napoléon costs 60/40FF before/after 3 pm.

Be prepared for queues throughout most of the year. The best times to come if you want to avoid the crowds are on Wednesday night and on Thursday and Friday afternoons. If possible, it's best to avoid the place entirely during the Christmas and Easter school holidays.

Guided Tours English-language guided tours (☎ 01 40 20 52 09) lasting 1½ hours are held three to five times a day (only one on Sunday at 11.30 am). The tours depart from the Accueil des Groupes area under the glass pyramid. Tickets cost 38FF (22FF for 13 to 18-year-olds; free for children under 13) in addition to the regular entry fee. Groups are limited to 30 people, so it's a good idea to sign up at least 30 minutes before departure time.

Recorded tours *(acoustiguides)* in six languages, available until 4.30 pm, can be rented for 30FF under the pyramid, at the entrances to each wing. The recording lasts 1½ hours as well.

Detailed explanations in a variety of languages, printed on heavy, plastic-coated *feuillets* (sheets), are stored on racks in each display room.

Église Saint Germain L'Auxerrois
Built between the 13th and 16th centuries in a mixture of Gothic and Renaissance styles, this parish church (Map 7; metro Louvre) stands on a site – facing the eastern side of the Louvre – that has been used for Christian worship since about 500 AD. After being mutilated by 18th-century churchmen intent on 'modernisation' and vandals during the Revolution, it was restored by the Gothic Revivalist architect Viollet-le-Duc in the mid-1800s. It is open daily from 8 am to 8 pm.

The square, Romanesque **belfry** that rises from next to the south transept arm contains the bell whose tolling served as a signal to begin the Saint Bartholomew's Day Massacre in August 1572, in which 3000 Protestants were slaughtered according to a plan devised by Catherine de Médecis and approved by her son, King Charles IX.

Jardin du Palais Royal
The **Palais Royal** (Map 7; metro Palais Royal), which briefly housed young Louis

XIV in the 1640s, is opposite Place du Palais Royal, north of the Louvre. Construction was begun in the 17th century by Cardinal Richelieu, though most of the present neo-classical complex dates from the latter part of the 18th century. It now contains the Conseil d'État (State Council) and is closed to the public. The colonnaded building facing Place André Malraux is the **Comédie Française** (Map 7), founded in 1680 and the world's oldest national theatre.

Just north of the main part of the palace is the Jardin du Palais Royal, a lovely park surrounded by arcades. During the late 1700s there was something of a permanent carnival here, and all sorts of things hard to find elsewhere in Paris (for example incendiary political tracts) were openly available since this was the private domain of the Duc d'Orléans and the police were unable to interfere. On 12 July 1789, the revolutionary Camille Desmoulins came to the gardens and made a fiery speech which helped push Paris toward open revolt.

The arcades on the eastern side of the garden, **Galerie de Valois**, shelter antiquarian bookshops; on the other side, in **Galerie de Montpensier**, you'll find art galleries, places which make colourful Legion of Honour-style medals (at Nos 3-4 and 7) and ones specialising in toy soldiers (at Nos 30, 34 and 37-38). Le Grand Véfour, one of Paris' oldest and most illustrious restaurants, is at the northern end. At the southern end there's a controversial **sculpture** of black-and-white striped columns of various heights by Daniel Buren, placed here in 1986.

The park is open daily from 7 am (7.30 am from October to March) to sometime between 8.30 pm in winter and 11 pm in summer.

Le Louvre des Antiquaires

This impressive building on the eastern side of Place du Palais Royal (Map 7; metro Palais Royal) houses about 250 elegant antique shops. Each is filled with precious objects from the past (*objets d'art*, furniture, clocks, classical antiquities) available

to shoppers with oodles of cash. It's open Tuesday to Sunday from 11 am to 7 pm. In July and August it closes on Sunday.

Galerie Véro Dodat

For a quick taste of 19th-century Paris, it's hard to beat this shopping arcade (Map 7) between 19 Rue Jean-Jacques Rousseau and 2 Rue du Bouloi, which opened in 1826 and retains its 19th-century skylights, ceiling murals and shop fronts. The stores specialise in antiques, objets d'art, art books and fashion accessories. *Café de l'Époque* at No 37 has drinks and light meals (quiche, boudin etc from 53 to 77FF). The more elaborate *Restaurant Véro Dodat* (☎ 01 45 08 92 86) at No 19 open for lunch and dinner from Monday to Saturday has a decent *menu* at 115FF.

Musée des Arts Décoratifs

The Museum of Decorative Arts (Map 7; ☎ 01 44 55 57 50; metro Palais Royal) on the 3rd floor at 107 Rue de Rivoli occupies the western tip of the Louvre's north wing. Displays include furniture, jewellery and objets d'art (such as ceramics and glassware) from the Middle Ages and the Renaissance through to the Art Nouveau and Art Deco periods. On the 1st and 2nd floors is the **Musée de la Mode et du Textile** (Museum of Fashion and Textile). The museums are open Tuesday to Friday from 11 am to 6 pm (to 9 pm on Wednesday) and Saturday and Sunday from 10 am to 6 pm. Entrance to both costs 30FF (20FF for those aged 18 to 25).

Place des Pyramides

The brightly gilded, 19th-century **statue of Joan of Arc** at Place des Pyramides next to 192 Rue de Rivoli (Map 7) is a favourite rallying point for royalists and parties of the extreme right.

Arc de Triomphe du Carrousel

Constructed by Napoleon to celebrate his battlefield triumphs of 1805, this triumphal arch (Map 7) set in the Jardin du Carrousel, at the eastern end of the Jardin des Tuileries, was once crowned by the Horses of

Montmartre street scene, near Sacré Cœur

Top: Museum of Evolution, Jardin des Plantes
Middle: Picasso Museum
Bottom: Sculptures and fountains, Centre Pompidou

Saint Mark's, stolen from Venice by Napoleon and taken back after Waterloo. The group of statues on top, added in 1828, celebrates the return of the Bourbons to the French throne after Napoleon's downfall. The sides are adorned with depictions of Napoleonic victories and eight pink marble columns, atop each of which stands a soldier of the emperor's Grande Armée.

Jardin des Tuileries
The formal Tuileries Gardens (Maps 2 and 7), which begin just west of the Louvre, were laid out in their present form (more or less) in the mid-1600s by André Le Nôtre, who also created the gardens at Versailles (see the Excursions chapter) and Vaux-le-Vicomte. The Tuileries soon became the most fashionable spot in Paris for parading about in one's finery. On 10 August 1792, after Louis XVI and his family had fled from the Louvre via the Tuileries palace, enraged revolutionaries attacked the Swiss Guards (responsible for palace security) and butchered 760 of them in the gardens.

Over the past few years, the gardens have been cleaned up and replanted. They are open daily from 7 am (7.30 am in winter) to between 7.30 and 9 pm, depending on the season.

The Voie Triomphale (also known as the **Grand Axe** or 'Great Axis'), the western continuation of the Tuileries' east-west axis, follows the Champs-Élysées to the Arc de Triomphe and, eventually, to the Grande Arche in the modern skyscraper district of La Défense.

Musée de l'Orangerie des Tuileries
The Orangerie Museum (Map 2; ☎ 01 42 97 48 16; metro Concorde), in the south-west corner of the Jardin des Tuileries at Place de la Concorde, has important impressionist works, including a series of Monet's *Décorations des Nymphéas* (Water Lilies) and paintings by Cézanne, Matisse, Picasso, Renoir and Soutine. It's open daily, except Tuesday from 9.45 am to 5.15 pm. Entrance costs 30FF (20FF for those aged 18 to 25); everyone pays 18FF on Sunday.

Jeu de Paume
The Galerie Nationale du Jeu de Paume (Map 2; ☎ 01 47 03 12 50; metro Concorde) is housed in a one-time *jeu de paume* (a court for playing real, or royal, tennis) built in 1861 during the reign of Napoleon III in the north-west corner of the Jardin des Tuileries. Once the home of a good part of France's national collection of impressionist works (now housed in the Musée d'Orsay), it reopened in 1992 as a gallery for innovative, two or three-month exhibitions of contemporary art (ie art from the last 20 or 30 years).

It's open Tuesday to Friday from noon to 7 pm (9.30 pm on Tuesday) and on weekends from 10 am to 7 pm. Admission is 38FF (28FF for people aged 13 to 18, students under 26 and people over 60). The Carte Musées et Monuments (see the boxed text 'Carte Musées et Monuments' later in this chapter) is not valid here.

Place Vendôme
Eight-sided Place Vendôme (Map 2) and the arcaded and colonnaded buildings around it were built between 1687 and 1721. In March 1796, Napoleon married Josephine in the building at No 3 (formerly the city hall of the 2e arrondissement). The Ministry of Justice has been at Nos 11-13 since 1815.

Today, the buildings around the square house the posh Hôtel Ritz (Map 2) and some of Paris' most fashionable and expensive boutiques, more of which can be found along nearby Rue de Castiglione, Rue Saint Honoré and Rue de la Paix (see the Shopping chapter).

Place Vendôme was originally built to showcase a giant statue of Louis XIV, which was destroyed during the Revolution. The 43.5m column now in the centre of the square, **Colonne Vendôme** (Map 2), consists of a stone core wrapped in a 160m-long bronze spiral made from 1250 Austrian and Russian cannons captured by Napoleon at the Battle of Austerlitz (1805). The bas-reliefs on the spiral depict Napoleon's victories of 1805-07. The statue on top, placed there in 1873, depicts Napoleon as a Roman emperor.

LES HALLES AREA

The huge pedestrian zone between the Centre Pompidou (1er) and the Forum des Halles is always filled with people, just as it was for the 850-odd years when the area served as Paris' main marketplace. During the day, the main attractions are museums, art galleries, shops and places to eat, while at night – and into the wee hours of the morning – restaurants, theatres and discos draw Parisians out for a night on the town.

Forum des Halles

Les Halles, Paris' main wholesale food market, occupied the area just south of Église Saint Eustache from around the early 12th century until 1969, when it was moved out to the suburb of Rungis. In its place, Forum des Halles (Map 7; metro Les Halles or Châtelet-Les Halles) – a huge and aesthetically controversial underground shopping mall – was constructed in the high-tech, glass-and-chrome style which was in vogue in the early 1970s. The complex's four levels of shops, built around an open courtyard, have proved highly popular with Parisian shoppers, especially those in search of reasonable prices.

Around Forum des Halles

Atop Forum des Halles is a popular **park** where you can picnic, people-watch and sunbathe on the lawn while gazing at the flying buttresses of Église Saint Eustache (Map 7). During the warmer months, street musicians, fire eaters and other performers display their talents throughout the area, especially at **Square des Innocents**, whose centre is adorned by a multitiered Renaissance fountain, **Fontaine des Innocents** (Map 7; 1549). The square and the fountain are named after the Cimetière des Innocents, a cemetery on this site from which two million skeletons were disinterred and transferred to the Catacombes (Map 1) in the 14e in the 1780s. One block south of the fountain is **Rue de la Ferronnerie** where in 1610, while passing house No 11 in his carriage, Henri IV was assassinated by a Catholic fanatic named François Ravaillac.

RICHARD NEBESKY
Men playing boules, Les Halles

Église Saint Eustache

This majestic church (Map 7; metro Les Halles), one of the most attractive in Paris, is just north of the grassy area on top of Forum des Halles. Constructed between 1532 and 1640, its general design is Gothic. The classical west façade was added in the mid-18th century.

Inside, there's some exceptional Flamboyant Gothic archwork holding up the ceiling of the chancel, though most of the interior ornamentation is Renaissance and classical, as you can see from the cornices and Corinthian columns. The gargantuan, 101-stop, 8000-pipe organ above the west entrance is used for concerts, a long tradition here; you can hear it played for 15 minutes on Sunday at 10.45 am and 12.15 and 5.30 pm as well as at High Mass at 11 am and 6 pm.

The nave and choir are lined with chapels, some containing tombs, including that of Louis XIV's finance minister, Jean-Baptise Colbert (1619-83). The church is open Monday to Saturday from 9 am to 7 pm (8 pm in summer); Sunday from 9 am to 12.30 pm and 2.30 to 7 pm (8 pm in summer).

La Samaritaine Rooftop Terrace

For an amazing 360° panoramic view of central Paris, head to the roof of building No 2 of La Samaritaine department store (Map 7; ☎ 01 40 41 20 20; metro Pont Neuf) on Rue de la Monnaie (1er), just north of Pont Neuf. The 11th-floor lookout and its viewpoint indicator are open Monday to Saturday from 9.30 am to 7 pm (10 pm on Thursday). You can have something to drink at the outdoor café on the 10th floor, reached by taking the lift to the 9th floor and then by a flight of stairs.

Centre Pompidou

The Centre Georges Pompidou (Maps 5 and 8; ☎ 01 44 78 12 33; Minitel 3615 BEAUBOURG; www.cnac-gp.fr; metro Rambuteau), also known as the Centre Beaubourg, is dedicated to displaying and promoting modern and contemporary art. Thanks in part to its vigorous schedule of outstanding temporary exhibitions in recent years, it has become the most visited cultural sight in Paris. Unfortunately, the Centre Pompidou is undergoing a massive renovation which will not be completed until late 1999 though the escalator with its spectacular views remains open and temporary exhibition spaces have been set up.

The design of the Centre Pompidou has not ceased to draw wide-eyed gazes and critical comment since its construction between 1972 and 1977. In order to keep the exhibition halls as spacious and uncluttered as possible, the architects – the Italian Renzo Piano and the Briton Richard Rogers – put the building's 'insides' on the outside. The purpose of each of the ducts, pipes and vents that enclose the centre's glass walls could then be divined from the paint job: escalators and lifts in red, electrical circuitry in yellow, the plumbing green and the air-conditioning system blue. Alas, the innovative structure has aged poorly, and thus the need for the overhaul, which will also enlarge and create new exhibition spaces.

Information & Tickets The Tipi (teepee; ☎ 01 44 78 14 63) set up in the Place Georges Pompidou (the plaza to the west) has multimedia information on the centre and its activities as well as updates on the works in progress. It is open daily, except Tuesday, from 12.30 pm (2 pm on Saturday and Sunday) to 6 pm. Entry is free.

Attractions Many of the 30,000-plus works of the **Musée National d'Art Moderne (MNAM)**, France's national collection of modern and contemporary (ie 20th century) art, are on loan to other museums in Paris, elsewhere in France or abroad, but one-man shows (Bruce Nauman, Max Ernst, David Hockney etc) continue at the **Galerie Sud** on the centre's southern side on Rue Saint Merri. The museum bookstore and gift shop (open to 8 pm) have also been moved here.

The **Atelier Brancusi**, the studio of the Romanian-born sculptor Constantin Brancusi (1876-1957), reconstructed on the plaza just north of the Tipi, contains almost 140 examples of his work as well as drawings, paintings and glass photographic plates. The Galerie Sud and the Atelier Brancusi are open daily, except Tuesday, from noon (10 am at the weekend) to 10 pm. Admission to the Atelier Brancusi is 20FF; to both the atelier and the Galerie Sud it's 30FF (20FF reduced price).

The free **Bibliothèque Publique d'Information** (BPI; ☎ 01 44 78 12 33), a huge, noncirculating library usually spread over three floors of the Centre Pompidou, has been relocated to 11 Rue Brantôme, 3e (Map 8; metro Rambuteau) until the renovation of the centre is completed. For information see Libraries in the Facts for the Visitor chapter. The BPI also offers excellent literary walking tours of Paris (see Walking Tours at the start of this chapter).

Around the Centre Pompidou

Place Georges Pompidou The west side of the centre and nearby pedestrianised streets attract buskers, mime artists, musicians, jugglers, and, so Parisians complain, pickpockets and drug dealers. The fanciful, colourful **mechanical fountains** – of skeletons, dragons, G-clefs and a big pair of ruby-red lips – at Place Igor Stravinsky, on the centre's south side were created by Jean Tinguely and Niki de Saint-Phalle. They are a delight.

Le Défenseur du Temps (Defender of Time; Map 8), a mechanical clock (1979) whose protagonist does hourly battle from 9 am to 10 pm with the elements (air, water and earth in the form of a phoenix, crab and dragon), is a block north of the Centre Pompidou along Rue Brantôme (3e), in a modern development known as Quartier de l'Horloge. Particularly lively combat takes place at noon and 6 and 10 pm when our hero is attacked by all three 'villains'.

Tour Saint Jacques

The 52m Flamboyant Gothic Tower of Saint James, 4e (Maps 6 and 8) is all that remains of the Église Saint Jacques la Boucherie, commissioned by the powerful butchers' guild in 1523. It is not open to the public.

Hôtel de Ville

Paris' city hall (Maps 5 and 8; ☎ 01 42 76 40 40; metro Hôtel de Ville) was rebuilt in the neo-Renaissance style between 1874 and 1882 after having been gutted during the Paris Commune (1871). The ornate façade is decorated with 108 statues of noteworthy Parisians. Free guided tours (☎ 01 42 76 50 49 for reservations) of the interior are held in French every first Monday of the month at 10.30 am, except on public holidays and during official functions. The visitors' entrance is at 29 Rue de Rivoli (4e), where there's a hall used for temporary exhibitions (open Monday to Saturday from 9.30 am to 6 pm).

The Hôtel de Ville faces majestic, fountain-and-lamp-adorned **Place de l'Hôtel de Ville**, used since the Middle Ages to stage many of Paris' celebrations, rebellions, book burnings and public executions. Known as Place de Grève (Strand Square) until 1830, it was in centuries past a favourite gathering place of the unemployed, which is why a strike is, to this day, called *une grève* in French. In winter the square is turned into an ice-skating rink.

MARAIS

The Marais (literally, 'marsh'; 4e and 3e), the area of the Right Bank directly north of Île Saint Louis, was in fact a swamp until the 13th century when it was converted to agricultural use. In the early 1600s, Henri IV built Place des Vosges, turning the area into Paris' most fashionable residential district and attracting wealthy aristocrats, who erected luxurious but subtle **hôtels particuliers** (private mansions). When the aristocracy moved to Versailles and Faubourg Saint Germain (7e) during the late 17th and 18th centuries, the Marais and its townhouses passed into the hands of ordinary Parisians. The 110-hectare area was given a major face-lift in the late 1960s and 70s.

Today, the Marais is one of the few neighbourhoods of Paris that still has almost all of its pre-Revolutionary architecture extant; indeed the house at 3 Rue Volta, 3e (Map 8), built in 1292, is thought to be the oldest in the city. In recent years the area has become trendy, but it's still home to a long-established Jewish community and is the centre of Paris' gay life. On Friday and Saturday nights, the Marais is crowded with people out dining, bar-hopping or just carousing.

A number of the 16th and 17th-century hôtels particuliers here, many built around enclosed garden courtyards, have been turned into museums.

Place des Vosges

Place des Vosges, 4e (Map 8; metro Bastille or Chemin Vert), inaugurated in 1612 as Place Royale, is a square ensemble of 36 symmetrical houses with ground-floor arcades, steep slate roofs and large dormer windows. Only the earliest houses were built of brick; to save time, the rest were given timber frames and faced with plaster, later painted to resemble brick. Duels were once fought in the elegant park in the centre. The square received its present name in 1800 to honour the Vosges département, the first in France to pay its taxes. Today, the arcades around Place des Vosges are occupied by upmarket art galleries, pricey antique shops and elegant places to sip tea.

Victor Hugo lived at 6 Place des Vosges from 1832 to 1848. **Maison de Victor Hugo** (Map 8; ☎ 01 42 72 10 16; metro Saint Paul or Chemin Vert) is now a municipal museum, and is open from 10 am to 5.40 pm (closed Monday and holidays). The entry fee is 27FF (19FF for students; free for under 18s).

Hôtel de Sully

While in the vicinity of Place des Vosges, it's well worth ducking into the Hôtel de Sully (Map 8; metro Saint Paul), a superb, early 17th-century aristocratic mansion at 62 Rue Saint Antoine (4e) that is now home to the Caisse Nationale des Monuments Historiques et des Sites (a body responsible for many of France's historical monuments). The two beautifully decorated, late Renaissance-style courtyards are adorned with bas-reliefs of the seasons and the elements. Revolving photographic exhibitions take place at the Hôtel de Sully (☎ 01 42 74 47 75) Tuesday to Sunday from 10 am to 10.30 pm.

Musée Carnavalet

Also known as the Musée de l'Histoire de Paris (Map 8; ☎ 01 42 72 21 13; metro Saint Paul or Chemin Vert), 23 Rue de Sévigné (3e), this museum of Parisian history is housed in two hôtels particuliers: the mid-16th century, Renaissance-style Hôtel Carnavalet, once home to the late 17th-century writer Madame de Sévigné, and the late 17th-century Hôtel Le Peletier de Saint Fargeau. The artefacts on display chart the history of Paris from the Gallo-Roman period to the 20th century. The museum has the country's most important collection of documents, paintings and other objects from the French Revolution. It also has *in situ* Fouquet's Art Nouveau jewellery shop from the Rue Royale and Proust's cork-lined bedroom from his apartment on Blvd Haussmann.

The Musée Carnavalet is open daily (except on Monday and public holidays)

from 10 am to 5.40 pm; from 11.50 am for the 19th and 20th century rooms. Entrance costs 27FF (14.50FF reduced price); the price goes up a bit during temporary exhibitions.

Musée Picasso

The Picasso Museum (Map 8; ☎ 01 42 71 25 21; metro Saint Paul or Chemin Vert), housed in the mid-17th century Hôtel Salé at 5 Rue de Thorigny (3e), is one of Paris' best loved art museums. Displays include more than 3500 engravings, paintings, ceramic works, drawings and an unparalleled collection of sculptures donated by heirs of Pablo Picasso (1881-1973) to the French government in lieu of inheritance taxes. You can also see part of Picasso's personal art collection, which includes works by Braque, Cézanne, Matisse and Degas. Inaugurated in 1985, the museum is open daily, except Tuesday, from 9.30 am to 6 pm (5.30 pm from October to March); ticket sales end 45 minutes earlier. The entry fee is 30FF (20FF reduced price and, on Sunday, for everyone). Special exhibits cost between 6 and 10FF extra.

Musée de la Serrure

The Lock Museum (Map 8; ☎ 01 42 77 79 62; metro Saint Paul or Chemin Vert) at 1 Rue de la Perle (3e), also known as the Musée Bricard, showcases a fine collection of locks, keys and door knockers. One lock, made around 1780, traps your hand in the jaws of a bronze lion if you try to use the wrong key. Another one, created in the 19th century, shoots anyone who inserts an incorrect key. The museum is open from 10 am to noon and 2 to 5 pm (closed on weekends, holidays, Monday mornings and in August). Entrance costs 30FF (15FF for students and seniors; free for under 18s).

Musée Cognacq-Jay

The Musée Cognacq-Jay (Map 8; ☎ 01 40 27 07 21; metro Saint Paul) at 8 Rue Elzévir (3e) brings together oil paintings, pastels, sculpture, objets d'art, jewellery, porcelain and furniture from the 18th century. The

The Museums of Paris

The following list contains the names of all the museums mentioned in this chapter. For easy reference, we've listed them by their English name first, followed by the French name (the reverse of what appears in the text).

Arab World Institute
Institut du Monde Arabe (Map 5; ☎ 01 40 51 38 38; metro Cardinal Lemoine or Jussieu), 1 Rue des Fossés Saint Bernard, 5e.

Army Museum
Musée de l'Armée (Map 4; ☎ 01 44 42 37 67; metro Varenne or La Tour Maubourg), Hôtel des Invalides, Esplanade des Invalides, 7e.

Baccarat Crystal Museum
Musée du Cristal Baccarat (Map 3; ☎ 01 47 70 64 30; metro Château d'Eau), CIAT Building, 30bis Rue de Paradis, 10e.

Bourdelle Museum
Musée Bourdelle (Map 4; ☎ 01 49 54 73 73; metro Falguière), 18 Rue Antoine Bourdelle, 15e.

Buddhist Pantheon
Panthéon Bouddhique (Map 2; ☎ 01 47 23 88 11; metro Iéna), 19 Ave d'Iéna, 16e.

Carnavalet Museum (History of Paris)
Musée Carnavalet – also known as the Musée de l'Histoire de Paris – (Map 8; ☎ 01 42 72 21 13; metro Saint Paul or Chemin Vert), 23 Rue de Sévigné, 3e.

Cernuschi Museum
Musée Cernuschi (Map 2; ☎ 01 45 63 50 75; metro Villiers), 7 Ave Vélasquez, 8e.

Cinema Museum
Musée du Cinéma Henri Langlois (Map 4; ☎ 01 45 53 74 39; metro Trocadéro), Palais de Chaillot, Place du Trocadéro, 16e.

City of Music
Cité de la Musique (Map 1; ☎ 01 44 84 44 84; metro Porte de Pantin), Parc de la Villette, 221 Ave Jean Jaurès, 19e.

City of Sciences & Industry
Cité des Sciences et de l'Industrie (Map 1; ☎ 01 40 05 12 12 or 08 36 68 29 30; metro Porte de la Villette), 30 Ave Corentin Cariou, 19e.

Cognacq-Jay Museum
Musée Cognacq-Jay (Map 8; ☎ 01 40 27 07 21; metro Saint Paul), 8 Rue Elzévir, 3e.

Coins & Medals Museum
Musée de la Monnaie (Map 6; ☎ 01 40 46 55 35 or 01 34 51 93 53; metro Pont Neuf), 11 Quai de Conti, 6e.

Dali Museum
Espace Montmartre Salvador Dali (Map 9; ☎ 01 42 64 40 10; metro Abbesses), 9-11 Rue Poulbot, 18e.

Decorative Arts Museum
Musée des Arts Décoratifs (Map 7; ☎ 01 44 55 57 50; metro Palais Royal), 107 Rue de Rivoli, 3rd floor, 1er.

Eugene Delacroix Museum
Musée National Eugène Delacroix (Map 6; ☎ 01 44 41 86 50; metro Mabillon or Saint Germain des Prés), 6 Place de Furstemberg, 6e.

Eroticism Museum
Musée de l'Érotisme (Map 9; ☎ 01 42 58 28 73; metro Blanche), 72 Blvd de Clichy, 18e.

Fashion & Clothing Museum
Musée de la Mode et du Costume (Map 2; ☎ 01 47 20 85 23; metro Iéna or Alma Marceau), Palais Galliera, 10 Ave Pierre 1er de Serbie, 16e.

Fashion & Textile Museum
Musée de la Mode et du Textile (Map 7; ☎ 01 44 55 57 50; metro Palais Royal), 107 Rue de Rivoli, 1st and 2nd floors, 1er.

Fine Arts Museum
Musée des Beaux-Arts de la Ville de Paris, (Map 2; ☎ 01 42 65 12 73; metro Champs-Élysées Clemenceau), Petit Palais, Ave Winston Churchill, 8e.

French History Museum
Musée de l'Histoire de France (Map 8; ☎ 01 40 27 60 96; metro Rambuteau), Hôtel de Soubise, 60 Rue des Francs Bourgeois, 3e.

French Monuments Museum
Musée des Monuments Français (Map 4; ☎ 01 44 05 39 10; metro Trocadéro), Palais de Chaillot, Place du Trocadéro, 16e.

Grand Palais National Galleries
Nationales Galeries du Grand Palais (Map 2; ☎ 01 44 13 17 17; metro Champs-Élysées Clemenceau), Ave Winston Churchill, 8e.

Grévin Museum
Musée Grévin (Map 7; ☎ 01 42 46 13 26; metro Rue Montmartre), 10-12 Blvd Montmartre, 9e.

Guimet Museum
Musée Guimet (Map 2; ☎ 01 47 23 88 11; metro Iéna), 6 Place d'Iéna, 16e.

Hôtel de Sully
Hôtel de Sully (Map 8; ☎ 01 42 74 47 75; metro Saint Paul), 62 Rue Saint Antoine, 4e.

Victor Hugo House
Maison de Victor Hugo (Map 8; ☎ 01 42 72 10 16; metro Chemin Vert), 6 Place des Vosges, 3e.

Jacquemart-André Museum
Musée Jacquemart-André (Map 2; ☎ 01 42 89 04 91; metro Miromesnil), 158 Blvd Haussmann, 8e.

Jeu de Paume National Gallery
Galerie Nationale du Jeu de Paume (Map 2; ☎ 01 47 03 12 50; metro Concorde), Place de la Concorde, 1er.

Jewish Art Museum
Musée d'Art Juif (Map 9; ☎ 01 42 57 84 15; metro Lamarck Caulaincourt), 42 Rue des Saules, 3rd floor, 18e; soon to move to Hôtel de Saint Aignan, 71 Rue du Temple, 3e (metro Rambuteau).

Lock Museum
Musée de la Serrure (Map 8; ☎ 01 42 77 79 62; metro Saint Paul or Chemin Vert), 1 Rue de la Perle, 3e.

Louvre
Musée du Louvre (Map 7; ☎ 01 40 20 53 17; metro Palais Royal), Cour Napoléon, 1er.

Luxembourg
Musée du Luxembourg (Map 6; ☎ 01 42 34 25 94; metro Luxembourg), 19 Rue de Vaugirard, 6e.

Mankind Museum
Musée de l'Homme (Map 4; ☎ 01 44 05 72 72; metro Trocadéro), Palais de Chaillot, Place du Trocadéro, 16e.

Maritime Museum
Musée de la Marine (Map 4; ☎ 01 53 65 65 69; metro Trocadéro), Palais de Chaillot, Place du Trocadéro, 16e.

Modern Art of the City of Paris
Musée d'Art Moderne de la Ville de Paris (Map 2; ☎ 01 53 67 40 00; metro Iéna or Alma Marceau), Palais de Tokyo, 11 Ave du Président Wilson, 16e.

Claude Monet Museum
Musée Marmottan-Claude Monet (Map 1; ☎ 01 42 24 07 02; metro La Muette), 2 Rue Louis Boilly, 16e.

Montmartre Museum
Musée de Montmartre (Map 9; ☎ 01 46 06 61 11; metro Lamarck Caulaincourt), 12 Rue Cortot, 18e.

Gustave Moreau Museum
Musée Gustave Moreau (Map 3; ☎ 01 48 74 38 50; metro Trinité), 14 Rue de La Rochefoucauld, 9e.

Naive Art
Musée d'Art Naïf Max Fourny (Map 9; ☎ 01 42 58 72 89; metro Anvers), Halle Saint Pierre, 2 Rue Ronsard, 18e.

National Museum of African & Oceanic Art
Musée National des Arts d'Afrique et d'Océanie (Map 1; ☎ 01 44 74 84 80; metro Porte Dorée), 293 Ave Daumesnil, 12e.

National Museum of the Middle Ages
Musée National du Moyen Âge-Thermes de Cluny (Map 6; ☎ 01 53 73 78 00; metro Cluny-La Sorbonne), 6 Place Paul Painlevé, 5e.

Natural History Museum
Musée National d'Histoire Naturelle (Map 5; ☎ 01 40 79 30 00; metro Censier Daubenton or Gare d'Austerlitz), Jardin des Plantes, 57 Rue Cuvier, 5e.

Nissim de Camondo Museum
Musée Nissim de Camondo (Map 2; ☎ 01 53 89 06 40; metro Monceau or Villiers), 63 Rue de Monceau, 8e.

Open Air Sculpture Museum
Musée de Sculpture en Plein Air (Map 5), Quai Saint Bernard, 5e.

Opera Museum
Musée de l'Opéra (Map 7; ☎ 01 47 42 07 02; metro Opéra), Opéra Garnier, Place de l'Opéra, 9e.

Orangerie Museum
Musée de l'Orangerie (Map 2; ☎ 01 42 97 48 16; metro Concorde), Place de la Concorde, 1er.

Orsay Museum
   Musée d'Orsay (Map 4; ☎ 01 40 49 48 14; metro Musée d'Orsay or Solférino), 1 Rue de Bellechasse, 7e.

Palace of Discovery
   Palais de la Découverte (Map 2; ☎ 01 40 74 80 00; metro Champs-Élysées Clemenceau), Ave Franklin D Roosevelt, 8e.

Petit Palais Museum
   Musée du Petit Palais (Map 2; ☎ 01 42 65 12 73; metro Champs-Élysées Clemenceau), Ave Winston Churchill, 8e.

Photography House
   Maison Européenne de la Photographie (Map 8; ☎ 01 44 78 75 00; metro Saint Paul or Pont Marie), 5-7 Rue de Fourcy, 4e.

Picasso Museum
   Musée Picasso (Map 8; ☎ 01 42 71 25 21; metro Saint Paul or Chemin Vert), 5 Rue de Thorigny, 3e.

Pompidou Centre (National Museum of Modern Art)
   Centre Pompidou-Musée National d'Art Moderne (Maps 5 and 8; ☎ 01 44 78 12 33; metro Châtelet-Les Halles or Rambuteau), Rue Beaubourg, 4e.

Popular Arts & Traditions Museum
   Musée National des Arts et Traditions Populaires (Map 1; ☎ 01 44 17 60 00; metro Les Sablons), 6 Ave du Mahatma Gandhi, 16e.

Postal Museum
   Musée de la Poste (Map 4; ☎ 01 42 79 23 45; metro Montparnasse Bienvenüe), 34 Blvd de Vaugirard, 5th floor, 15e.

Rodin Museum
   Musée Auguste Rodin (Map 4; ☎ 01 47 05 01 34; metro Varenne), 77 Rue de Varenne, 7e.

Sewers of Paris Museum
   Musée des Égouts de Paris (Map 4; ☎ 01 47 05 10 29; metro Pont de l'Alma), Quai d'Orsay, 7e.

Unknown Jewish Martyr Memorial & Museum
   Mémorial du Martyr Juif Inconnu (Map 8; ☎ 01 42 77 44 72; metro Pont Marie or Saint Paul), 17 Rue Geoffroy l'Asnier, 4e.

TONY WHEELER

Detail of the Palais de Tokyo façade, Musée d'Art Moderne.

objects on display, assembled by the founders of La Samaritaine department store, give a pretty good idea of upper-class tastes during the Age of Enlightenment. It is open from 10 am to 5.40 pm (closed Monday and holidays). Entry costs 17FF (9FF if you're aged 18 to 25; free for under 18s).

Maison Européenne de la Photographie

The Maison Européenne de la Photographie (Map 8; ☎ 01 44 78 75 00; metro Saint Paul or Pont Marie), housed in an 18th-century hôtel particulier at 5-7 Rue de Fourcy (4e), has permanent and temporary exhibits on the history of photography with particular connection to France. The museum is open Wednesday to Sunday from 11 am to 8 pm and entry is 30FF (15FF for those under 26 or over 60 and for everyone on Wednesday after 5 pm).

Archives Nationales

France's National Archives (☎ 01 40 27 60 96) are headquartered in the impressive, early 18th-century **Hôtel de Soubise** (Map 8; metro Rambuteau) at 60 Rue des Francs Bourgeois 3e. The complex also contains the **Musée de l'Histoire de France**, where you can view documents dating from the Middle Ages. The ceiling and walls of the early 18th-century interior are extravagantly painted and gilded in the rococo style. The museum is open weekdays, except Tuesday, from noon to 5.45 pm and on Saturday and Sunday from 1.45 pm. Entrance costs 15FF (10FF for teachers and people under 25 or over 60).

Jewish Neighbourhood

The area around **Rue des Rosiers** and **Rue des Écouffes**, known as the Pletzl (Map 8; metro Saint Paul), is one of Paris' liveliest Jewish neighbourhoods. Jewish cuisines from North Africa, central Europe and Israel are served at a variety of eateries.

When renovation of the Marais began in the 1960s, the area – long home to a poor but vibrant Jewish community – was pretty run-down. Now trendy and expensive boutiques coexist side-by-side with Jewish bookshops

and *cacher* (kosher) grocery shops, butcher shops and restaurants. The area is very quiet on the Sabbath (Saturday).

The **Guimard synagogue** (Map 8; 1914) at 10 Rue Pavée is renowned for its Art Nouveau architecture, which is the work of Hector Guimard, designer of the famous metro entrances. The interior is closed to the public. And the street's other claim to fame? Rue Pavée was the first 'Paved Street' in Paris.

There are Jewish neighbourhoods with a distinctly North African flair in Belleville and in the 9e along Rue Richer and Rue Cadet (Map 7; metro Cadet).

Mémorial du Martyr Juif Inconnu

The Memorial to the Unknown Jewish Martyr (Map 8; ☎ 01 42 77 44 72; metro Pont Marie or Saint Paul) at 17 Rue Geoffroy l'Asnier (4e), established in 1956, includes a memorial to the victims of the Holocaust, various temporary exhibits and small permanent exhibits on the 1st, 2nd and 3rd floors. It is open daily, except Saturday and on Jewish holidays, from 10 am to 1 pm and 2 to 6 pm (4.30 or 5 pm on Friday). Entry to the crypt and museum is 15FF.

BASTILLE AREA

After years as a run-down immigrant neighbourhood notorious for its high crime rate, the Bastille area, encompassing mostly the 11e and 12e but also the westernmost part of the 4e, has undergone a fair degree of gentrification, in large part because of the Opéra Bastille, which opened in 1989. The area east of Place de la Bastille retains its lively atmosphere and ethnic flair.

Bastille

The Bastille, built during the 14th century as a fortified royal residence, is the most famous monument in Paris that doesn't exist; the infamous prison – the quintessential symbol of monarchic despotism – was demolished shortly after a mob stormed it on 14 July 1789 and freed all seven prisoners. The site where it once stood, Place de la Bastille, is now a very busy traffic round-about.

In the centre of Place de la Bastille is the 52m **Colonne de Juillet** (July Column; Map 5), whose shaft of greenish bronze is topped by a gilded and winged figure of Liberty. It was erected in 1833 as a memorial to the people killed in the street battles that accompanied the July Revolution of 1830; they are buried in vaults under the column. It was later consecrated as a memorial to the victims of the February Revolution of 1848.

Opéra Bastille

Paris' giant 'second' opera house (Map 5; ☎ 01 44 73 13 99 or ☎ 08 36 69 78 68 for enquiries; metro Bastille) at 2-6 Place de la Bastille (12e), designed by the Canadian Carlos Ott, was inaugurated on 14 July 1989, the 200th anniversary of the storming of the Bastille. Conceived by the Socialist François Mitterrand as an opera house for the people, it was built in a resolutely working-class part of the city, but huge cost overruns have kept ticket prices out of the reach of the average Parisian. And there's been no end to its structural problems; in recent years the 2.75FF billion structure has been shrouded in 5000 sq metres of netting after cracked marble panels began falling into the building's courtyard. For details on the building's almost daily 1¼ hour guided tours (50FF; 30FF for children under 16, students and seniors), which usually take place in the afternoon, call ☎ 01 40 01 19 70. See the Entertainment chapter for information on tickets to performances.

Viaduc des Arts

The arches beneath this railway viaduct, which was taken out of service in 1969, along Ave Daumesnil (12e) have now been transformed into a showcase for trendy designers and artisans; if you need your Gobelins tapestry restored or a frame regilded, this is the place for you. The top of the viaduct has been turned into a leafy promenade called the **Promenade Plantée** and offers excellent views of the surrounding area. It's open from 8 am (9 am on Saturday and Sunday) to 5.30 pm (9.30 pm from May to August). Don't miss the spectacular Art Deco police station at No 85 (opposite Rue de Rambouillet) topped with a dozen huge marble torsos.

ÎLE DE LA CITÉ

The site of the first settlement around the 3rd century BC and later the centre of the Roman town of Lutetia (Lutèce in French), the Île de la Cité (1er and 4e) remained the centre of royal and ecclesiastical power even after the city spread to both banks of the Seine during the Middle Ages. The middle part of the island was demolished and rebuilt during Baron Haussmann's great urban renewal scheme of the late 19th century.

The Île de la Cité is well endowed with great spots for a picnic. They include **Square Jean XXIII** (Map 8), the park that runs along the south side of Notre Dame;

TONY WHEELER

Opéra Bastille

the shaded, triangular **Place Dauphine** (Map 6), created in 1607 near the island's western end; and **Square du Vert Galant** (Map 6), the little park next to Pont Neuf at the prow-shaped western tip of the island. You can picnic, walk or sunbathe on the stone walkways along the riverbanks.

Notre Dame

Notre Dame (Map 8; ☎ 01 42 34 56 10; metro Cité), Paris' cathedral, is one of the most magnificent achievements of Gothic architecture. Built on a site occupied by earlier churches – and, some two millennia ago, a Gallo-Roman temple – it was begun in 1163 and completed around 1345. Viollet-le-Duc carried out extensive renovations to the cathedral in the 19th century. The interior is 130m long, 48m wide and 35m high, and can accommodate over 6000 worshippers. Some 12 million people visit it each year.

Notre Dame is known for its sublime balance, although if you look closely you'll see all sorts of minor asymmetrical elements introduced to avoid monotony, in accordance with standard Gothic practice. These include the slightly different shapes of each of the three main entrances, whose statues were once brightly coloured to make them more effective as a *Biblia pauperum* – a 'Bible of the poor' to help the illiterate understand the Old Testament stories, the Passion of Christ and the lives of the saints. One of the best views of Notre Dame is from Square Jean XXIII, the lovely little park behind the cathedral, where you can see the mass of ornate **flying buttresses** that encircle the chancel and support its walls and roof.

The Hunchback of Notre Dame

The story of the Hunchback of Notre Dame as told by Victor Hugo in his romantic novel *Notre Dame de Paris* – and not the silly Disney cartoon version with the happy ending – goes something like this ... The setting is 15th-century Paris during the reign of Louis XI. Gypsy girl Esmeralda is in love with Captain Phoebus, but the evil and jealous archdeacon, Claude Frollo, denounces her as a witch. The hunchbacked bell-ringer, Quasimodo (the name comes from the Latin Mass on the first Sunday after Easter, which begins *Quasi modo geniti infantes*, meaning 'as newborn babes') is devoted to Esmeralda and saves her (for a while) when she seeks protection from the mob in the belfry of Notre Dame. We won't give the ending away but suffice to say that everyone comes to a tragic end – including Captain Phoebus, who gets married.

Was *Notre Dame de Paris*, which has no basis in historical fact except for the setting, just a good story, or was there more to it? Hugo began the book during the reign of the unpopular and reactionary Charles X who, with the guidance of his chief minister, had abolished freedom of the press and dissolved Parliament. The ascent of Louis-Philippe, a bourgeois king with liberal leanings, in the July Revolution of 1830 took place shortly before the book was published. *Notre Dame de Paris* can thus be seen as a condemnation of absolutism (ie Charles X) and of a society that allows the likes of people such as Frollo and Phoebus to heap scorn and misery on unfortunate characters like Esmeralda and Quasimodo.

But there is even more to the novel. Hugo's evocation of the colourful and intense life of the late 15th century is seen by some as a plea for the preservation of Gothic Paris and its decaying architecture. Indeed, the condition of Notre Dame in the early 19th century was so bad that artists, politicians and writers, including Hugo, beseeched Louis-Philippe to do something about it. Hugo was appointed to the new Commission for Monuments and the Arts, where he sat for 10 years. In 1845 the Gothic revivalist architect Viollet-le-Duc began his renovation of Notre Dame, in which he added the steeple and the gargoyles (among other things). The work continued for almost two decades.

Inside, exceptional features include three spectacular **rose windows**, the most renowned of which are the window over the west facade, which is a full 10m across, and the window on the north side of the transept, which has remained virtually unchanged since the 13th century. The 7800-pipe organ was restored in 1990-92 at a cost of US$2 million.

Notre Dame is open daily from 8 am to 6.45 pm (7.45 pm on weekends). The *trésor* (treasury), which contains sacred liturgical objects and works of art, is at the back of the cathedral and costs 15FF (10FF for students). It's open Monday to Saturday from 9.30 am to 6.30 pm. There are free **guided tours** of the cathedral in English on Wednesday and Thursday at noon and on Saturday at 2.30 pm (daily in August).

Distances from Paris throughout France are measured from **Place du Parvis Notre Dame**, the square in front of Notre Dame. A bronze star, set in the pavement across the street from the cathedral's main entrance, marks the exact location of *point zéro des routes de France* (Map 6).

North Tower The entrance to Notre Dame's north tower (Map 8; ☎ 01 43 29 50 40) is on Rue du Cloître Notre Dame – to the right and around the corner as you walk out of the main doorway. From the base, a long, spiral climb up 238 steps gets you to the top of the **west façade**, from where you can view many of the cathedral's most frightening gargoyles – not to mention a good part of Paris. Tickets are on sale daily from 9.30 am to 6.45 pm (10 am to 4.45 pm from October to March) and cost 32FF (21FF for those aged 12 to 25; free for children under 12).

Crypte Archéologique
Under the square in front of Notre Dame, the Archaeological Crypt (Map 6; ☎ 01 43 29 83 51), also known as the Crypte du Parvis, displays *in situ* the remains of structures from the Gallo-Roman and later periods. It is open daily from 10 am to 5 pm (6 pm from April to September); ticket sales

---

Notre Dame's Kestrels

Bird watchers estimate that about 40 pairs of kestrels *(Falcon tinnunculus)*, known as sparrow hawks in the US and windhovers in the UK, currently nest in Paris, preferring tall old structures like the towers at Notre Dame. Four or five pairs of kestrels regularly breed in convenient cavities high up in Notre Dame and once a year, usually in late June, local ornithologists set up a public kestrel-watching station behind the cathedral, with telescopes and even a video camera transmitting close-up pictures of one of the nesting sites. The birds form their partnerships in February and eggs are laid in April. Kestrel chicks hatch in May and are ready to depart by early July. In late June, bird watchers may spot the adult kestrels returning to their young with a tasty mouse or sparrow. Unfortunately, Paris' pigeons – those dirty flying rats – are too large for a kestrel chick to handle!

---

end 30 minutes earlier. Fees are the same as those for the cathedral's north tower. A *billet jumelé* (combination ticket) valid for both the crypt and the tower costs 40FF.

Sainte Chapelle
The gem-like Sainte Chapelle (Map 6; ☎ 01 53 73 78 51; metro Cité), whose upper chapel is illuminated by a veritable curtain of luminous 13th-century **stained glass** (the oldest and finest in Paris), is inside the **Palais de Justice** (Law Courts), which is on the west side of Blvd du Palais (1er). Consecrated in 1248, Sainte Chapelle was built in only 33 months to house what was believed to be Jesus' crown of thorns and other relics purchased by King Louis IX (Saint Louis) earlier in the 13th century. The chapel's exterior can be viewed from across the street from the law courts' magnificently gilded 18th-century gate, which faces Rue de Lutèce.

Sainte Chapelle is open daily from 9.30 or 10 am to 5 pm (6.30 pm from April to

September); ticket sales end 30 minutes before. Entry costs 32FF (21FF for people aged 12 to 25). A ticket valid for both Sainte Chapelle and the nearby Conciergerie costs 50FF. The visitors' entrance is directly opposite 7 Blvd du Palais. Be prepared for airport-type security, with x-ray machines, bag searches etc.

Conciergerie

The Conciergerie (Map 6; ☎ 01 53 73 78 50, metro Cité), whose entrance is at 1 Quai de l'Horloge, was a luxurious royal palace when it was built in the 14th century, but it later lost favour with the kings of France and was turned into a prison and torture chamber. During the Reign of Terror (1793-94), the Conciergerie was used to incarcerate alleged enemies of the Revolution before they were brought before the Revolutionary Tribunal, which met next door in the Palais de Justice. Among the 2600 prisoners held here before being sent in tumbrils to the guillotine were Queen Marie-Antoinette and, as the Revolution began to turn on its own, the Revolutionary radicals Danton, Robespierre and, finally, the judges of the Tribunal themselves.

The huge Gothic **Salle des Gens d'Armes** (Cavalrymen's Hall) dates from the 14th century and is a fine example of the Rayonnant Gothic style. It is the largest surviving medieval hall in Europe. **Tour de l'Horloge**, the tower on the corner of Blvd du Palais and Quai de l'Horloge, has held a public clock aloft since 1370. Opening hours and entry fees at the Conciergerie are the same as those at Sainte Chapelle; a combination ticket to both costs 50FF.

Flower Market

The Île de la Cité's famous **marché aux fleurs** (Map 6; metro Cité), Paris' oldest, has been at Place Louis Lépine, the square just north of the Préfecture de Police, since 1808. It is open Monday to Saturday (and when holidays fall on Sunday) from 8 am to about 7 pm.

On Sunday, the marché aux fleurs is transformed into a **marché aux oiseaux** (bird market) open from 9 am to 7 pm.

Mémorial des Martyrs de la Déportation

At the south-eastern tip of the Île de la Cité, behind Notre Dame, is the Deportation Memorial (Map 8) erected in 1962, a stark, haunting Nazi monument to the 200,000 residents of France – including 76,000 Jews – killed in concentration camps. A single barred 'window' separates the bleak, rough concrete courtyard from the waters of the Seine. The Tomb of the Unknown Deportee is flanked by 200,000 bits of backlit glass. The memorial is open daily from 10 am to noon and 2 to 5 pm (7 pm from April to September).

Pont Neuf

The now sparkling white stone spans of Paris' oldest bridge, Pont Neuf (literally, 'New Bridge'; Map 6), link the western end of the Île de la Cité with both banks of the Seine. Begun in 1578, it was completed in 1607, when Henri IV inaugurated it by crossing the bridge on a white stallion; the occasion is commemorated by an equestrian **statue of Henri IV**. The arches are decorated with humorous and grotesque figures of street dentists, pickpockets, loiterers and the like. The bridge has been an objet d'art at least twice in the recent past; the Japanese designer Kenzo covered it in flowers in 1984 and the Bulgarian-born 'environmental sculptor' Christo wrapped it in beige fabric the following year.

ÎLE SAINT LOUIS

The smaller of the Seine's two islands, the Île Saint Louis (4e) is just downstream from the Île de la Cité. It was actually two uninhabited islands – sometimes used for duels – until the early 17th century, when a building contractor and two financiers worked out a deal with Louis XIII to create one island out of the two and build two stone bridges to the mainland. In exchange they would receive the right to subdivide and sell the newly created real estate. This they did with great success, and between 1613 and 1664 the entire island was covered with fine new houses. Little has changed since then except that many of the buildings are now marked with plaques detailing when some person of note lived there.

The area around **Pont Saint Louis**, the bridge linking the island with the Île de la Cité, and **Pont Louis-Philippe**, the bridge to the Marais, is one of the most romantic spots in all of Paris. On warm summer days, lovers mingle with cello-playing buskers and teenage skateboarders. After nightfall, the Seine dances with the watery reflections of streetlights, headlamps, stop signals and the dim glow of curtained windows. Occasionally, tourist boats with super bright floodlamps cruise by.

The island's 17th-century, grey-stone houses and the small-town shops that line the streets and quays impart a village-like, provincial calm. Rue Saint Louis en l'Île is home to a number of upmarket art galleries.

Église Saint Louis en l'Île

This French baroque church at 19bis Rue Saint Louis en l'Île (Map 8; metro Pont Marie) was built between 1656 and 1725 and is open Tuesday to Sunday from 9 am to noon and 3 to 7 pm. It often has classical music concerts.

JARDIN DES PLANTES AREA

This area is just east of the Latin Quarter (5e).

Jardin des Plantes

Paris' botanical gardens (Map 5; ☎ 01 40 79 30 00; metro Gare d'Austerlitz or Jussieu) at 57 Rue Cuvier were founded in 1626 as a medicinal herb garden for Louis XIII. Today the gardens are endearingly informal, even unkempt; they look as though a group of dedicated but conservative, underfunded and slightly absent-minded professors had been running the place for a couple of centuries. The first greenhouse, constructed in 1714, was home to a coffee tree whose offspring helped establish coffee

production in South America. The gardens are open daily from 7.30 am until sometime between 5.30 pm (in the dead of winter) and 8 pm (in summer).

The **Serres Tropicales** (Tropical Greenhouses; Map 5), also known as the Jardin d'Hiver (Winter Garden), are open on weekdays, except Tuesday, from 1 to 5 pm; weekend hours are 10 am to 5 pm (6 pm from April to September). Admission costs 15FF (10FF for students aged 16 to 25 and people over 60; 5FF for children). The **Jardin Alpin** (Alpine Garden; Map 5) and the gardens of the **École de Botanique** (Botanical School), both of which are free, are open from April to September on Monday and from Wednesday to Friday.

Ménagerie The northern section of the Jardin des Plantes is taken up by the **Ménagerie** (Map 5; ☎ 01 40 79 37 94; metro Jussieu or Gare d'Austerliz), a medium-sized zoo founded in 1794. During the Prussian siege of Paris in 1870, most of the animals were eaten by starving Parisians. It is open daily from 9 am to 5 pm (6 pm from April to September, when closing time is 6.30 pm on Sunday and holidays). Entrance costs 30FF (20FF for students aged 16 to 25 and people over 60; 10FF for children).

There's a **children's playground** near the Ménagerie's western entrance.

Musée National d'Histoire Naturelle The National Museum of Natural History (☎ 01 40 79 30 00; metro Censier Daubenton or Gare d'Austerlitz), created by a decree of the Convention in 1793, was the site of important scientific research in the 19th century. It is housed in four buildings along the southern edge of the Jardin des Plantes.

The five-level **Grande Galerie de l'Évolution** (Map 5; ☎ 01 40 79 39 39), 36 Rue Geoffroy Saint Hillaire, has some imaginative exhibits on evolution and humankind's effect on the world's ecosystem, but unless you can read French it's pretty much a traditional natural history museum, with lots of imaginatively displayed stuffed animals and mounted insects. The African parade, as if Noah had lined up his cargo for the ark, is quite something. The Salle des Espèces Menacées et des Espèces Disparues, on level No 2, displays extremely rare specimens of 'endangered and extinct species' of animals. The Salles de Découverte (Discovery Rooms) house interactive exhibits for kids. They are all open daily, except Tuesday, from 10 am to 6 pm (10 pm on Thursday). Entry costs 40FF (30FF for students, those aged 16 to 25 and over 60; 10FF children).

The **Galerie de Minéralogie et Paléobotanie** (Map 5; 30FF; 20FF for students, those aged 16 to 25 and over 60; 10FF children) which covers mineralogy and paleobotany (ie fossilised plants), has an amazing exhibit of giant natural crystals and a basement display of precious objects made from minerals. Out the front there's a rose garden. The **Galerie d'Anatomie Comparée et de Paléontologie** (Map 5; 30FF; 20FF reduced and children 10FF) has displays on comparative anatomy and paleontology. Both are open daily, except Tuesday and holidays, from 10 am to 5 pm (6 pm on weekends). The **Galerie d'Entomologie** (Map 5; 15FF; 10FF reduced price and children 5FF) specialises in the study of insects. It's open Monday and Wednesday to Friday, 1 to 5 pm; Saturday and Sunday, 10 am to 6 pm.

Musée de Sculpture en Plein Air

The Open-Air Sculpture Museum (Map 5) is an imaginatively landscaped riverside promenade stretching for about 600m along the Seine from the Jardin des Plantes to the Institut du Monde Arabe, which is right across the river from the Île Saint Louis. Colourful riverboats are often moored along the pedestrian quay.

Mosquée de Paris

Paris' central mosque (Map 5; ☎ 01 45 35 97 33; metro Place Monge), whose entrance is at Place du Puits de l'Ermite (next to the square minaret), was built between 1922 and 1926 in an ornate Hispano-Moorish style. Islam forbids images of people or animals, so the two serene courtyards are elaborately decorated with verses from the Koran in Arabic calligraphy and coloured tiles in geometrical designs. Shoes must be removed at the entrance to the prayer hall. Guided tours (15FF; 10FF for children and students) take place from 9 am to noon and 2 to 6 pm, except on Friday; tickets are sold through the arch to the right as you enter. Visitors must be modestly and respectfully dressed (women should not wear shorts or sleeveless blouses).

The mosque complex includes a North African-style *salon de thé*, a restaurant (☎ 01 43 31 38 20) with excellent couscous and tajines (60 to 110FF) and a **hammam** (bathhouse; ☎ 01 43 31 18 14), both of whose entrances are at 39 Rue Geoffroy Saint Hilaire (across from the Grande Galerie de l'Évolution). The hammam (85FF) is open to men on Tuesday and Sunday only; on other days it is reserved for women.

Institut du Monde Arabe

The Arab World Institute (Maps 5 and 8; ☎ 01 40 51 38 38; metro Cardinal Lemoine or Jussieu) at 1 Rue des Fossés Saint Bernard, set up by France and 20 Arab countries to promote cultural contacts between the Arab world and the west, is housed in a highly praised building (1987) which successfully mixes modern and traditional Arab and western elements. The thousands of *mushrabiyah* (incredibly costly aperture-like mechanisms built into the glass walls), inspired by the traditional latticed wooden windows that let you see out without being seen, are opened and closed by electric motors in order to regulate the amount of light and heat that reaches the interior of the building.

The 7th-floor **museum** displays 9th to 19th-century art and artisanship from all over the Muslim world as well as astrolabes and instruments from other fields of scientific endeavour in which Arab technology once led the world. It is open Tuesday to Sunday from 10 am to 6 pm. Tickets cost 25FF (20FF for students, people under 25 and seniors). Temporary exhibitions (enter from Quai Saint Bernard) involve a separate fee.

Arènes de Lutèce

This heavily reconstructed, 2nd-century Roman amphitheatre (Map 5; metro Place Monge), discovered in 1869, could once seat around 10,000 people for gladiatorial combats and other events. Today, it is used by neighbourhood youth playing football and *boules* (bowls). There are entrances at 49 Rue Monge and opposite 7 Rue de Navarre. Entry is free.

LATIN QUARTER

Known as the Quartier Latin (5e) because all communication between students and professors here took place in Latin until the Revolution, this area has been the centre of Parisian higher education since the Middle Ages. It has become increasingly touristy in recent years, however, and its near monopoly on the city's academic life has waned as students have moved to other campuses, especially since 1968. The Latin Quarter does have a large population of students and academics affiliated with the Sorbonne, which is now part of the University of Paris system, the Collège de France, the École Normale Supérieure (all Map 6) and other institutions of higher learning.

Musée National du Moyen Âge

The National Museum of the Middle Ages (Map 6; ☎ 01 53 73 78 00; metro Cluny-La Sorbonne), also known as the Musée de Cluny, is housed in two structures: the frigidarium and other remains of **Gallo-Roman baths** dating from around 200 AD, and the late 15th-century **Hôtel de Cluny**, considered the finest example of medieval civil architecture in Paris. The spectacular displays include statuary, illuminated manuscripts, arms, furnishings and objects made of gold, ivory and enamel. A series of six late 15th-century tapestries from the southern Netherlands known as *La Dame à la Licorne* (Lady and the Unicorn) is hung in a round room on the 1st floor.

The museum, whose entrance is at 6 Place Paul Painlevé, is open from 9.15 am to 5.45 pm (closed Tuesday). The entrance fee is 30FF (20FF for people aged 18 to 25 and on Sunday for everyone over 18).

Sorbonne

Paris' most renowned university, the Sorbonne (Map 6), was founded in 1253 by Robert de Sorbon, confessor of King Louis IX, as a college for 16 poor theology students. Closed in 1792 by the Revolutionary government after operating for centuries as France's premier theological centre, it was reopened under Napoleon. Today, the Sorbonne's main complex (bounded by Rue de la Sorbonne, Rue des Écoles, Rue Saint Jacques and Rue Cujas) and other buildings in the vicinity house several of the 13 autonomous universities created when the University of Paris was reorganised following the violent student protests of 1968.

Place de la Sorbonne links Blvd Saint Michel with **Chapelle de la Sorbonne** (Map 6), the university's gold-domed church built between 1635 and 1642. The interior is open only when there are special exhibitions on.

Panthéon

The domed landmark now known as the Panthéon (Map 6; ☎ 01 43 54 34 51; metro Luxembourg) was commissioned around 1750 as an abbey church, but because of financial problems wasn't completed until 1789. Two years later, the Constituent Assembly converted it into a secular mausoleum for the *'grands hommes de l'époque de la liberté française'* (great men of the era of French liberty), removing all Christian symbols and references. After another stint as a church, the Panthéon once again became a secular necropolis. The Panthéon's ornate marble interior is gloomy in the extreme and much of it will be closed – including the colonnaded dome – for some time during a massive renovation.

Permanent residents of the Panthéon's crypt include Voltaire, Jean-Jacques Rousseau, Louis Braille, Victor Hugo, Émile Zola and Jean Moulin. Personages removed for reburial elsewhere after a reevaluation of their greatness include Mirabeau and Marat. The first woman to be interred in the Panthéon in recognition of her own achievements was the double

Nobel Prize-winner Marie Curie (1867-1934), who was reburied here (along with her husband Pierre) in 1995.

The Panthéon is open daily April to September from 9.30 am to 6.30 pm, and October to March from 10 am to 6.15 pm; ticket sales end 45 minutes before closing time. Tickets cost 32FF (21FF for those aged 12 to 25; free for children under 12).

Église Saint Étienne du Mont

This lovely church (Map 6; metro Cardinal Lemoine) at Place de l'Abbé Basset (behind the Panthéon) was built between 1492 and 1626. The most exceptional feature of the Gothic interior is its graceful **rood screen** (1535) separating the chancel from the nave. During the late Renaissance, all of Paris' rood screens except this one were removed because they prevented the faithful assembled in the nave from seeing the priest celebrate Mass. Also of interest is the carved **wooden pulpit** of 1650, held aloft by a figure of Samson, and the 16th and 17th-century **stained glass**. Just inside the entrance, a plaque in the floor marks the spot where a defrocked priest, armed with a knife, murdered an archbishop in 1857.

6e ARRONDISSEMENT

Centuries ago, Église Saint Germain des Prés (Map 6) and its affiliated abbey, founded by the Merovingian King Childeric in 542 AD, owned most of the 6e and 7e arrondissements. The neighbourhood around the church began to be built up in the late 1600s, and these days – under the name Saint Germain des Prés – it is celebrated for its 19th-century charm. Cafés such as Les Deux Magots and Café de Flore (see Pubs, Bars & Cafés – 6e Arrondissement in the Entertainment chapter), favourite hangouts of postwar, Left Bank intellectuals, are where existentialism was born.

These days, though, only *very* wealthy intellectuals can afford to buy flats in this area. The 6e arrondissement becomes increasingly hard-core bourgeois as you move west and north-west from the Jardin du Luxembourg, one of Paris' loveliest green spaces.

Jardin du Luxembourg

When the weather is warm – or even just slightly sunny – Parisians of all ages flock to the French-style formal terraces and chestnut groves of the 25-hectare Luxembourg Gardens (Map 6; metro Luxembourg) to read, write, relax and sunbathe. Ernest Hemingway claimed that as an impoverished young writer he would come to the gardens and, when the police were distracted with other matters, catch pigeons for his supper.

Activities for Children The Jardin du Luxembourg offers all of the delights of a Parisian childhood a century ago and is one of the best places in Paris to take kids. The atmosphere of bygone days is enhanced by the képi-topped Senate guards.

At the Grand Bassin (the octagonal pond, Map 6), **model sailboats** – many of them old enough to have been sailed by today's grandparents back when they were children – can be rented on Wednesday, Saturday and Sunday (daily during school holiday periods, including July and August) from 2 pm until sometime between 4.30 pm (in winter) and 7 pm (in summer).

About 200m south-west of the pond, at the pint-sized **Théâtre du Luxembourg** (Map 6; ☎ 01 43 26 46 47), visitors are treated to a complete theatre experience in miniature; in a hall filled with child-sized seats, **marionettes** put on shows whose antics can be enjoyed even if you don't understand French. The puppets put on one to five performances (23FF), at least one of which starts around 3.30 pm on Wednesday, Saturday, Sunday and holidays and daily during school vacation periods at 2.30, 3.30 and 4.30 pm (3 and 4 pm on Saturday and Sunday).

Next to the Théâtre du Luxembourg, the modern **playground** (Map 6) – one half for kids up to age seven, the other half for children aged seven to 12 – costs 14FF per child (7.50FF for adults). Not far away, the vintage **swings** cost 7FF per child, as does the old-time **carousel** (merry go round).

A hundred metres north of the theatre, kids of up to 35kg can ride Shetland ponies (13FF; carriage rides 10FF) daily – unless

꙰ ꙮ ꙰ ꙮ ꙰ ꙮ ꙰ ꙮ ꙰ ꙮ ꙰ ꙮ ꙰ ꙮ ꙰ ꙮ ꙰ ꙮ ꙰ ꙮ ꙰ ꙮ ꙰ ꙮ ꙰ ꙮ ꙰ ꙮ ꙰ ꙮ ꙰ ꙮ ꙰ ꙮ ꙰ ꙮ

Parks & Gardens

Though upwards of 90,000 trees (mostly plane and chestnut trees) line the streets of Paris, at times the city can feel excessively built-up. You don't have to escape all the way to the Bois de Boulogne, 16e (Map 1; metro Porte Dauphine), or the Bois de Vincennes, 12e (Map 1; metro Porte Dorée), the city's 'green lungs' to the west and south-east, to get a bit of grass under your feet and leaves over your head, though. The Jardin du Luxembourg, 6e (Map 6; metro Luxembourg) and Jardin des Tuileries, 1er (Map 2; metro Tuileries), while small formal affairs, can give you the illusion of countryside; and the Parc des Buttes-Chaumont, 19e (Maps 1 & 3; metro Buttes-Chaumont), and the Parc de Monceau, 8e (Map 2; metro Monceau), are fully fledged green and open spaces.

In recent years the city government has spent millions of francs transforming vacant lots and derelict industrial land into new parks. Some of the better ones are Parc de la Villette, 19e (Map 1; metro Porte de la Villette), Parc de Bercy, 12e (Map 1; metro Bercy), Jardin de l'Atlantique near Gare Montparnasse, 15e (Map 4; metro Montparnasse Bienvenüe), and the Promenade Plantée, the 'planted promenade' above the Viaduc des Arts, a disused railway viaduct along Ave Daumesnil, 12e (Map 5; metro Gare de Lyon or Daumesnil), that has been transformed into a showcase for trendy designers and artisans.

꙰ ꙮ ꙰ ꙮ ꙰ ꙮ ꙰ ꙮ ꙰ ꙮ ꙰ ꙮ ꙰ ꙮ ꙰ ꙮ ꙰ ꙮ ꙰ ꙮ ꙰ ꙮ ꙰ ꙮ ꙰ ꙮ ꙰ ꙮ ꙰ ꙮ ꙰ ꙮ ꙰ ꙮ ꙰ ꙮ ꙰ ꙮ

it's raining – starting at 11 am (2 pm on Monday, Tuesday, Thursday and Saturday).

In the south-west corner of the gardens, you can visit the *ruches* (**beehives**; Map 6), established here in 1856, where Parisians can take beekeeping courses (☎ 01 45 42 29 08). They are staffed all day on Wednesday and often on Saturday as well. There's an **orchard** just south of the beehives.

Activities for Adults In the north-west corner of the Jardin du Luxembourg, just north of the tennis courts, **chess and card games** (Map 6) – often a dozen at a time – are held every afternoon of the year, rain or shine. BYOB (bring your own board).

On the north side of the Théâtre du Luxembourg, there are **basketball** and **volleyball courts** – you could try to join in a game. **Boules courts**, sometimes used for tai chi practice in the morning, are located just north of the beehives.

Palais du Luxembourg The Luxembourg Palace (Map 6), at the northern end of the Jardin du Luxembourg along Rue de Vaugirard, was built for Marie de Médicis (queen of France from 1600 to 1610) to assuage her longing for the Pitti Palace in Florence, where she spent her childhood. Just east of the palace is the Italianate **Fontaine des Médicis**, a long, ornate goldfish pond built around 1630.

The palace was used as a prison during the Reign of Terror and, during WWII, as Luftwaffe headquarters, when fortified shelters were built under the gardens. Since 1958 it has housed the Sénat, the upper house of the French parliament. There are tours of the interior (☎ 01 42 34 20 60 for information, ☎ 01 44 61 21 66 for reservations) on the first Sunday of each month at 10 am.

Musée du Luxembourg The Luxembourg Museum (Map 6; ☎ 01 42 34 25 94; metro Luxembourg) at 19 Rue de Vaugirard, which opened at the turn of the century in the *orangerie* (greenhouse for tropical plants) of the Palais du Luxembourg and was dedicated to presenting the work of artists still living, hosts temporary art exhibits, often from different regions of France. It is open Tuesday to Sunday from 11 am to 6 pm (to 8 pm on Thursday). Entry is 31FF (21FF reduced price and for everyone on Tuesday).

Église Saint Sulpice

This church (Map 6; metro Saint Sulpice), its interior lined with chapels, is a block north of the Jardin du Luxembourg at Place Saint Sulpice and was built between 1646 and 1780 on the site of earlier churches dedicated to Saint Sulpicius, a 6th-century archbishop of Bourges. The Italianate façade, designed by a Florentine architect, has two rows of superimposed columns and is topped by two towers. The neoclassical décor of the vast interior reflects the influence of the Counter-Reformation. The **Chapelle des Saints Anges** (Chapel of the Holy Angels), the first to the right as you enter, was decorated by Eugène Delacroix. The monumental **organ loft** dates from 1781. Every Sunday, the 10.30 am Mass is accompanied by music, and there are regular recitals.

Place Saint Sulpice is adorned by a very energetic fountain, **Fontaine des Quatre Évêques** (Map 6; 1844). Nearby streets are known for their couture houses (see Clothes & Fashion Accessories in the Shopping chapter).

Église Saint Germain des Prés

The Romanesque-style Church of Saint Germanus of the Fields (Map 6), the oldest (though hardly the most interesting) church in Paris, was built in the 11th century on the site of a 6th-century abbey. It has since been altered many times, but the bell tower over the west entrance has changed little since 1000, apart from the addition of the spire in the 19th century.

France's Merovingian kings were buried here during the 6th and 7th centuries, but their tombs disappeared during the Revolution. The interior is disfigured by truly appalling polychrome paintings and frescoes from the 19th century. The church, which is often used for concerts, is open daily from 8 am to 7 pm.

In early September 1792, a group of priests was hacked to death by a Revolutionary mob in what is now **Square Félix Desruelles**, the park between the church and Blvd Saint Germain. The glazed arch at the park's west end was created for the World Fair of 1900 by Sèvres.

Musée National Eugène Delacroix

The Eugène Delacroix Museum (Map 6; ☎ 01 44 41 86 50; metro Mabillon or Saint Germain des Prés), just east of Église Saint Germain des Prés at 6 Place de Furstemberg, was the artist's home and studio at the time of his death in 1863. It is open daily, except Tuesday, from 9.30 am to 5.30 pm (last entry at 4.30 pm). Tickets cost 22FF (15FF reduced price and for all on Sunday).

Institut de France

The Institut de France was created in 1795 by bringing together five of France's academies of arts and sciences. The most famous of these is the **Académie Française**, founded in 1635, whose 40 members (known as the Immortels, ie *Immortals*) are charged with the Herculean task of safeguarding the purity of the French language (*Ouèbe* in favour of 'Web', for example). Over the centuries, many of France's greatest writers and philosophers have been denied membership in favour of now forgotten people fawned over by the establishment of their day. The first woman Immortal (Marguerite Yourcenar) was not admitted until 1980.

The domed building housing the Institut de France (Map 6; ☎ 01 44 41 44 41; metro Mabillon or Louvre-Rivoli), a masterpiece of French neoclassical architecture from the mid-17th century, is at 23 Quai de Conti, right across the Seine from the eastern end of the Louvre.

The only part of the complex that can be visited without joining a tour is the **Bibliothèque Mazarine** (Mazarine Library; ☎ 01 44 41 44 06), 25 Quai de Conti, the oldest public library in France (founded in 1643). You can visit the bust-lined, late 17th-century reading room or consult the library's collection of 500,000 items on weekdays from 10 am to 6 pm (closed during the first half of August). Entry is free but you must leave your ID at the office on the left-hand side of the entryway to secure a pass; a second piece of ID is needed to gain access to the books.

For information on tours (about 50FF) of the Institut de France, usually held on weekends at 1.30 or 3 pm, look under 'Conférences' in *Pariscope* or *L'Officiel des Spectacles* (see Listings in the Entertainment chapter).

Musée de la Monnaie

The Museum of Coins and Medals (Map 6; ☎ 01 40 46 55 35 or ☎ 01 34 51 93 53; metro Pont Neuf) at 11 Quai de Conti – just across Pont Neuf from Île de la Cité – traces the history of French coinage from antiquity to the present and includes coins and medals as well as presses and other minting equipment. It's open Tuesday to Friday from 11 am to 5.30 pm and from noon to 5.30 pm at the weekend. The entry fee is 20FF (15FF for students and people over 60; free for under 16s and, on Sunday, for everyone).

The Hôtel des Monnaies, which houses the museum, became a royal mint during the 18th century and is still used by the Ministry of Finance to produce commemorative medals. Except in August, French-language tours of the mint's workshops are held on Wednesday and Friday at 2.15 pm and cost 20FF.

MONTPARNASSE

After WWI, writers, poets and artists of the avant-garde abandoned Montmartre and crossed the Seine, shifting the centre of Paris' artistic ferment to the area around Blvd du Montparnasse (6e, 14e and 15e). Chagall, Modigliani, Léger, Soutine, Miró, Kandinsky, Picasso, Stravinsky, Hemingway, Henry Miller and Cocteau, as well as such political exiles as Lenin and Trotsky, all used to hang out here, talking endlessly in the cafés and restaurants for which the quarter became famous. Montparnasse remained a creative centre until the mid-1930s. Today, especially since the construction of the Gare Montparnasse complex, there is little to remind visitors of the area's bohemian past except those now touristy restaurants and cafés.

Although the trendy Latin Quarter crowd considers the area hopelessly nondescript, **Blvd du Montparnasse** (on the southern border of the 6e) and its many fashionable restaurants, cafés and cinemas attract large numbers of people in the evening. Rue d'Odessa and Rue de Montparnasse, known for their crêperies, were founded by Bretons who, after arriving in Paris by train, apparently ventured no farther than the area around the station.

Tour Montparnasse

The 209m-high Montparnasse Tower (Map 4; ☎ 01 45 38 52 56; metro Montparnasse Bienvenüe) at 33 Ave du Maine (15e), built in 1974 of steel and smoked glass, affords spectacular views of the city, especially around sunset when, if you stay long enough (the sun sets pretty slowly at this latitude), you can also see the city at night. The lift to the 56th-floor indoor observatory, with shops, an exhibition and a video about Paris, costs 32FF (27FF for those over 60; 24FF for students and those aged 15 to 20; 17FF for under 14s). If you want to combine the lift trip with a hike up the stairs to the 59th-floor open-air terrace, the cost is 42/36/33/26FF. From April to September, the tower is open daily from 9.30 am to 11.30 pm. The rest of the year, hours are 9.30 am to 10.30 pm (11 pm on Friday, Saturday and holidays). The last ascent up to the 56th floor is 30 minutes before closing.

Musée de la Poste

The Postal Museum (Map 4; ☎ 01 42 79 23 45; metro Montparnasse Bienvenüe, Gare Montparnasse exit), a few hundred metres south-west of Tour Montparnasse at 34 Blvd de Vaugirard (5th floor; 15e), was closed for renovation at the time of publication but will reopen soon. It illustrates the history of postal service – a matter of particular importance in a highly centralised state like France – from Roman times to the present. The exhibition rooms showcase the original designs of French stamps, antique postal and telecommunications equipment and models of postal conveyances. In the past the museum was open Monday to Saturday from 10 am to 6 pm.

Cimetière du Montparnasse

Montparnasse Cemetery (Map 1; ☎ 01 44 10 86 50; metro Edgar Quinet or Raspail), accessible from both Blvd Edgar Quinet and Rue Froidevaux (14e), was opened in 1824. It contains the tombs of such illustrious personages as Charles Baudelaire, Samuel Beckett, Guy de Maupassant, François Rude, Frédéric August Bartholdi, Constan-

tin Brancusi, Chaim Soutine, Man Ray, Camille Saint-Saëns, André Citroën, Alfred Dreyfus, Jean Seberg, Simone de Beauvoir and Jean-Paul Sartre. If Père Lachaise has Jim Morrison, the equivalent here is French singer Serge Gainsbourg (division No 1); fans leave metro tickets with their names inscribed on them in his memory. Maps showing the location of famous tombs are posted near most entrances and are available free from the Conservation office at 3 Blvd Edgar Quinet. The cemetery is open daily from 8 am weekdays (8.30 on Saturday and

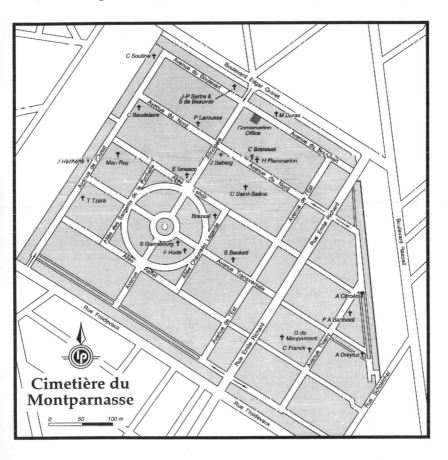

Cimetière du Montparnasse

9 am on Sunday) to 6 pm (5.30 pm from early November to mid-March).

Musée Bourdelle

The Bourdelle Museum (Map 4; ☎ 01 49 54 73 73; metro Falguière) due north of the Gare Montparnasse at 18 Rue Antoine Bourdelle (15e) contains monumental bronzes in the very house and workshop where the eponymous sculptor Antoine Bourdelle (1861-1929) lived and worked. The three sculpture gardens are particularly lovely. It is open Tuesday to Sunday, except on public holidays, from 11 am to 5.30 pm and entry costs 17.50FF (9FF for students and those over 60). Special exhibitions can bump the admission up by 10FF.

7e ARRRONDISSEMENT

The 7e arrondissement stretches along the Left Bank from Saint Germain des Prés (6e) to the Eiffel Tower (see Eiffel Tower Area) and includes, among other things, the Musée d'Orsay and the Invalides.

Musée d'Orsay

The Musée d'Orsay (Map 4; ☎ 01 40 49 48 14 or, for a recording, ☎ 01 45 49 11 11; Minitel 3615 ORSAY; metro Musée d'Orsay or Solférino), along the Seine at 1 Rue de Bellechasse, displays France's national collection of paintings, sculptures, objets d'art and other works produced between 1848 and 1914, including the fruits of the impressionist, postimpressionist and Art Nouveau movements. It thus fills the chronological gap between the Louvre and the Musée National d'Art Moderne at the Centre Pompidou (under renovation until the end of 1999). The Musée d'Orsay is spectacularly housed in a former railway station built in 1900 and reinaugurated in its present form in 1986.

Many visitors head straight to the upper level lit by skylight to see the famous **impressionists** (Monet, Renoir, Pissarro, Sisley, Degas, Manet, Van Gogh, Cézanne) and **postimpressionists** (Seurat, Matisse), but there's also a great deal to see on the ground floor, including some early works

by Manet, Monet, Renoir and Pissarro. The middle level has some magnificent **Art Nouveau rooms**.

The Musée d'Orsay is open daily, except Monday, from 10 am (9 am on Sunday and from mid-June to August) to 6 pm (9.45 pm on Thursday). Ticket sales stop 30 minutes before closing time. Tickets for the permanent exhibits cost 39FF (27FF for those aged 18 to 25 or over 60; free for under 18s) and are valid all day long (ie you can leave and re-enter the museum as you please). There are separate fees for temporary exhibitions.

English-language **tours** begin daily, except Sunday and Monday, at 11 am and on Thursday at 7 pm; tickets (40FF in addition to the entry fee; no discounts) are sold at the information desk to the left as you enter the building. **Audioguides** (1½ hour cassette tours), available in six languages, point out 30 major works – many of which had a revolutionary impact on 19th-century art – that the uninitiated might easily miss. They can be rented for 30FF (no discounts; ID deposit) on the right just past the ticket windows. An excellent full-colour museum guide, *Guide to the Musée d'Orsay* (95FF), is available in English.

Faubourg Saint Germain

Faubourg Saint Germain, the area between the Musée d'Orsay and, 1km to the south, Rue de Babylone, was Paris' most fashionable neighbourhood in the 18th century. Its luxurious homes, enclosed by high walls and ornate gates, were built by aristocrats and financiers, many of whom were later beheaded or exiled during the Revolution. Some of the most interesting mansions, many of which now serve as embassies or government ministries, are along three east-west oriented streets: Rue de Lille, Rue de Grenelle and Rue de Varenne. The **Hôtel Matignon** (Map 4), since 1958 the official residence of France's prime minister, is at 57 Rue de Varenne.

Assemblée Nationale

The National Assembly, the lower house of the French parliament, meets in the 18th-century Palais Bourbon (Map 4; ☎ 01 40 63 60 00; metro Assemblée Nationale) at 33 Quai d'Orsay right across the Seine from Place de la Concorde (8e). There are free guided tours (in French; ☎ 01 46 36 41 13) every Saturday at 10 or 11 am and 2 or 3 pm. Admission is on a first-come, first-served basis (each tour has only 30 places), so join the queue early. A national ID card or passport is required.

The Second Empire-style **Ministère des Affaires Étrangères** (Foreign Affairs Ministry; Map 4), built from 1845 to 1855 and popularly referred to as the Quai d'Orsay, is next door at 37 Quai d'Orsay.

Musée Rodin

The Musée Auguste Rodin (Map 4; ☎ 01 47 05 01 34; metro Varenne) at 77 Rue de Varenne, one of the most relaxing spots in the whole city, is some people's favourite Paris museum. Rooms on two floors display extraordinarily vital bronze and marble sculptures by Rodin and Camille Claudel, including casts of some of Rodin's most celebrated works: *The Hand of God*, *The Burghers of Calais*, *The Kiss*, *Cathedral* and, of course, that crowd-pleaser *The Thinker*. There's a delightful rear **garden** filled with sculptures and shade trees. The museum is housed in the Hôtel Biron, a private residence built in 1728 and bearing the name of a general who lived here before being guillotined in 1793.

The Musée Rodin is open daily, except Monday, from 9.30 am to 4.45 pm (5.45 pm from April to September). Entrance costs 28FF (18FF if you're 18 to 25 or over 60 and, on Sunday, for everyone; free for under 18s). The gardens cost 5FF to visit.

Hôtel des Invalides

The Hôtel des Invalides (Map 4; metro Varenne or La Tour Maubourg) was built in the 1670s by Louis XIV to provide housing for 4000 *invalides* (disabled veterans). On 14 July 1789, the Paris mob forced its way into the building and, after fierce fighting, seized 28,000 rifles before heading on to the Bastille prison. The 500m-long **Esplanade des Invalides** (Map 4; metro Invalides), which stretches from the main building to the Seine, was laid out between 1704 and 1720.

The **Église du Dôme** (Map 4), with its sparkling dome, was built between 1677 and 1735 and is considered one of the finest religious edifices erected under Louis XIV. The church's career as a mausoleum for military leaders began in 1800, and in 1861 it received the remains of Napoleon, encased in six concentric coffins. The buildings on either side of the **Cour d'Honneur**, the main courtyard, house the **Musée de l'Armée** (☎ 01 44 42 37 67), a huge military museum. The Musée de l'Armée and the extravagant **Tombeau de Napoléon 1er** (Napoleon's Tomb) in the Église du Dôme are open daily from 10 am to 4.45 pm (5.45 pm from April to September). Entrance to the whole show costs 37FF (27FF for children, students and seniors).

Musée des Égouts de Paris

A city cannot grow, prosper and become truly great unless some way is found to deal with the important question of sewerage. You can learn all about this aspect of Paris' greatness, if you so desire, by visiting the Paris Sewers Museum (Map 4; ☎ 01 47 05 10 29; metro Pont de l'Alma), a unique working museum whose entrance – a rectangular maintenance hole – is across the street from 93 Quai d'Orsay (7e). Raw sewage with all sorts of vaguely familiar objects floating in it flows beneath your feet as you walk through 480m of odoriferous tunnels, passing artefacts illustrating the development of Paris' wastewater disposal system. Signs are in French, English, German and Spanish.

The sewers are open Saturday to Wednesday (except, God forbid, when rain threatens to flood the tunnels) from 11 am to 5 pm (6 pm from May to September); the last entry is an hour earlier. Tickets cost 25FF (20FF for children, students and seniors).

EIFFEL TOWER AREA

Paris' most prominent and recognisable landmark, the Eiffel Tower is surrounded by open areas on both banks of the Seine (7e and 16e). Nearby parts of the Right Bank have several outstanding museums.

Eiffel Tower

The Tour Eiffel (Map 4; ☎ 01 44 11 23 23 or ☎ 01 45 50 34 565; metro Champ de Mars-Tour Eiffel or Bir Hakeim) faced massive opposition from Paris' artistic and literary élite when it was built for the 1889 Exposition Universelle (World Fair), held to commemorate the centenary of the Revolution. It was almost torn down in 1909 but was spared for purely practical reasons – it proved an ideal platform for the transmitting antennas needed for the new science of radiotelegraphy. It was the world's tallest structure until Manhattan's Chrysler Building was completed in 1930.

The Eiffel Tower, named after its designer, Gustave Eiffel, is 320m high, including the television antenna at the very tip. This figure can vary by as much as 15cm, as the tower's 7000 tonnes of iron, held together by 2.5 million rivets, expand in warm weather and contract when it's cold.

When you're done peering upwards through the girders, you can choose to visit any of the three levels open to the public. The lift (west and north pillars), which follows a curved trajectory, costs 20FF for the 1st platform (57m above the ground), 42FF for the 2nd (115m) and 57FF for the 3rd (276m). Children aged four to 12 pay 10/21/27FF respectively; there are no youth or student rates. You can avoid the lift queues by walking up the stairs in the south pillar to the 1st or 2nd platforms (14FF).

The tower is open every day from 9.30 am (9 am from late March to early September) to 11 pm (midnight from early July to early September). The stairs are open from 9 am to 6.30 pm (9 pm in the late spring, approximately May and June, 11 pm in July and August).

Champ de Mars

The grassy area south-east of the Eiffel Tower, whose name means 'Field of Mars' (Mars was the Roman god of war), was originally a parade ground for the cadets of the 18th-century **École Militaire** (Military Academy; Map 4), the vast, French classical-style building at the south-eastern end of the lawns whose graduates include Napoleon (class of 1785).

In 1783 the Champ de Mars (Map 4; metro École Militaire or Champ de Mars-Tour Eiffel) was the site of one of the world's first balloon flights. During the Revolutionary period, two important mass ceremonies were held here: the Fête de la Fédération (Federation Festival), held on 14 July 1790 to celebrate the first anniversary of the storming of the Bastille, and the Fête de l'Être Suprême (Festival of the Supreme Being) of 1794, at which Robespierre presided over a ceremony that established a Revolutionary state religion.

When the weather is good, young Parisians flock to the Champ de Mars to skateboard or roller-skate; it's also an excellent place for a picnic. For the young at heart, there are **marionette shows** (☎ 01 48 56 01 44; metro École Militaire; 16FF) on Wednesday, Saturday, Sunday and holidays and during school holiday periods (including July and August) daily at 3.15 and 4.15 pm.

Jardins du Trocadéro

The Trocadéro Gardens (Map 4; metro Trocadéro), whose fountains and statue garden are grandly illuminated at night, are across Pont d'Iéna from the Eiffel Tower in the posh 16e. They are named after the Trocadéro, a Spanish stronghold near Cadiz captured by the French in 1823.

Palais de Chaillot

The two curved, colonnaded wings of the Palais de Chaillot (Map 4; metro Trocadéro), which was built for the World Exhibition of 1937, and the terrace between them afford an exceptional panorama of the Jardins du Trocadéro, the Seine and the Eiffel Tower.

The Palais de Chaillot and Eiffel Tower

The vast complex normally houses four museums but two of them – the **Musée du Cinéma Henri Langlois** (Henri Langlois Cinema Museum; ☎ 01 45 53 74 39) and the **Musée des Monuments Français** (French Monuments Museum; ☎ 01 44 05 39 10) – were closed at the time of going to press, probably until late 1999. The other two, which are reached from the gap between the two wings and both closed on Tuesday, are the **Musée de l'Homme** (Museum of Mankind; ☎ 01 44 05 72 72; 30FF for adults; 20FF reduced price), with anthropological and ethnographic exhibits from Africa, Asia, Europe, the Arctic, the Pacific and the Americas, and the **Musée de la Marine** (Maritime Museum; ☎ 01 53 65 65 69; 38FF for adults; 25FF reduced price), known for its beautiful ships' models.

At the far eastern tip of the Palais de Chaillot, the **Cinémathèque Française**

(Map 4; ☎ 01 45 53 21 86 or, for a recording, ☎ 01 47 04 24 24) screens several nondubbed films (28FF; 17FF reduced price) almost every day (see Cinema in the Entertainment chapter for details).

Musée Guimet

The Guimet Museum (Map 2; ☎ 01 47 23 88 11; metro Iéna), also called the Musée des Arts Asiatiques (Museum of Asian Arts) at 6 Place d'Iéna (16e), which is about midway between the Eiffel Tower and the Arc de Triomphe, usually displays antiquities and works of art from Afghanistan, India, Nepal, Pakistan, Tibet, Cambodia, China, Japan and Korea. However, until massive renovations are completed sometime in 1999, part of the collection will be housed at the **Musée du Panthéon Bouddhique** (Buddhist Pantheon Museum; Map 2), the Guimet annexe a short distance to the north at 19 Ave d'Iéna with Chinese and Japanese Buddhist paintings and sculptures brought to Paris in 1876 by Émile Guimet. It is open daily, except Tuesday, from 9.45 am to 5.45 pm. Entrance costs 16FF (12FF reduced price; free for under 18).

Musée d'Art Moderne de la Ville de Paris

The **Palais de Tokyo** at 11 Ave du Président Wilson (16e), like the Palais de Chaillot built for the World Exhibition of 1937, houses the Modern Art Museum of the City of Paris (Map 2; ☎ 01 53 67 40 00; metro Iéna or Alma Marceau). Its collections include representatives of just about every major artistic movement of the 20th century: fauvism, cubism, the School of Paris, surrealism and expressionism. Artists with works on display include Matisse, Picasso, Braque, Soutine, Modigliani, Chagall and Dufy. Part of the museum is being rebuilt as the **Palais du Cinema**.

The museum is open Tuesday to Friday from 10 am to 5.30 pm and at the weekend from 10 am to 6.45 pm. Tickets cost 27FF (19FF reduced price) but more if there's a temporary exhibit.

Musée de la Mode et du Costume

The Fashion and Clothing Museum (Map 2; ☎ 01 47 20 85 23; metro Iéna or Alma Marceau) housed in the Palais Galliera just opposite the Musée d'Art Moderne de la Ville de Paris (enter from 10 Ave Pierre 1er de Serbie) contains some 10,000 outfits and accessories from the past three centuries. The lovely building and gardens are in themselves worth a visit. The museum is open Tuesday to Sunday from 10 am to 6.40 pm and costs 45FF (reduced price 32FF).

Place de l'Alma

South-west of the Palais Galliera is the Place de l'Alma, an insignificant square that would go unnoticed by most travellers if not for the tragic event that occurred in the underpass running parallel to the Seine shortly after midnight on 31 August 1997: Diana, Princess of Wales, her companion, Dodi Al Fayed, and their chauffeur, Henri Paul, were killed when the car in which they were travelling struck the 13th concrete pillar in the underpass. (Diana's bodyguard, Trevor Rees-Jones, the only one in the car to be wearing a seat belt at the time of the crash, survived but was badly disfigured and is still suffering from partial amnesia.) The tragedy unleashed a torrent of grief – unseen since the assassination of US President John F Kennedy in 1963 – in the UK and around the world.

Though there was some talk early on of renaming the square Place Diana, the only reminder of the tragedy is the bronze **Flame of Liberty** (Map 2; metro Alma Marceau), a replica of the one atop the torch of the State of Liberty in New York Harbour, placed here by American firms based in Paris in 1989 to honour the bicentennial of the French revolution. It has become something of a **memorial to Diana** – a mini Kensington Gardens – strewn with flowers, photographs and personal notes.

There were reports at the time of writing that the city government had approved Italian architect Gaetano Pesce's design for a more fitting memorial for the late princess but final say must come from the Royal

family. The Diana Memory Column is an above-ground extension of the infamous 13th pillar. The concrete base would recreate the pillar while the upper part, made of translucent resin, would glow at night. Pedestrians are barred from entering the underpass.

PLACE DE LA CONCORDE AREA

The cobblestone expanses of Place de la Concorde (8e) are sandwiched between the Jardin des Tuileries and the parks at the eastern end of Ave des Champs-Élysées.

Place de la Concorde

Place de la Concorde was laid out between 1755 and 1775. The 3300-year-old pink granite **obelisk** (Map 2) in the middle was given to France in 1831 by Muhammad Ali, viceroy and pasha of Egypt. Weighing 230 tonnes and towering 23m over the cobblestones, it once stood in the Temple of Ramses at Thebes (modern-day Luxor). The eight female statues adorning the four corners of the square represent France's largest cities.

In 1793, Louis XVI's head was lopped off by a guillotine set up in the north-west corner of the square near the statue representing the city of Brest. During the next two years, another guillotine – this one near the entrance to the Jardin des Tuileries – was used to behead 1343 more people, including Marie-Antoinette and, six months later, the Revolutionary leader Danton. Shortly thereafter, Robespierre lost his head here, too. The square was given its present name after the Reign of Terror had come to an end in the hope that it would be a place of peace and harmony.

The two imposing buildings on the north side of Place de la Concorde are the **Hôtel de la Marine** (Map 2), headquarters of the French Navy, and the **Hôtel de Crillon**, one of Paris' most luxurious and exclusive hotels (see the Places to Stay chapter). In 1778, the treaty by which France recognised the independence of the new USA was signed in the Hôtel de Crillon by Louis XVI and Benjamin Franklin.

Église de la Madeleine

The neoclassical Church of Saint Mary Magdalen (Map 2; metro Madeleine), known as La Madeleine, is 350m north of Place de la Concorde along Rue Royale. Built in the style of a Greek temple, it was consecrated in 1842 after almost a century of design changes and construction delays. It is surrounded by 52 Corinthian columns standing 20m tall. The marble and gilt interior, topped by three skylighted cupolas, is open Monday to Saturday from 7 am to 7 pm, and on Sunday from 7.30 am to 1 or 1.30 pm and 3.30 to 7 pm. You can hear the massive organ being played at Mass on Saturday at 6 pm and on Sunday at 11 am and 6 pm.

The **monumental staircase** on the south side affords one of Paris' quintessential panoramas: down Rue Royale to Place de la Concorde (and the obelisk) and on across the Seine to the Assemblée Nationale. The gold dome of the Invalides appears in the background, a bit to the right of the Assemblée Nationale.

Place de la Madeleine

Paris' cheapest *belle époque* attraction is the **public toilet** (Map 2) on the east side of La Madeleine, which dates from 1905 (2.20FF to sit down, 2FF for the urinals). There has been a **flower market** on the east side of the church since 1832; it's open daily, except Sunday, until 8.30 or 9 pm.

CHAMPS-ÉLYSÉES AREA

Ave des Champs-Élysées (8e), whose name means Elysian Fields (Elysium was where happy souls dwelt after death, according to Greek and Roman mythology), links Place de la Concorde (8e) with the Arc de Triomphe (8e). Since the Second Empire (1852-70), it has come to symbolise the style and *joie de vivre* of life in Paris.

Ave des Champs-Élysées

Popular with the aristocracy of the mid-19th century as a stage on which to parade their wealth, the 2km-long Ave des Champs-Élysées has, since WWII, been taken over by airline offices, cinemas, car showrooms and fast-food restaurants. The wealthy denizens of the Triangle d'Or (see the Triangle d'Or section on the next page) consider the Champs-Élysées to be completely – but not quite inexorably – degraded and popularised, by which they mean the same thing.

In recent years, the municipality invested US$48 million to regain some of the 72m-wide Champs-Élysées' former sparkle and prestige. The pavements have been widened to 21m (their original width) and paved with granite, street lights with emerald globes have been installed, and retro news kiosks have replaced the old aluminium and glass ones. Hundreds of 30-year-old plane trees, brought by truck from Germany, have increased the greenery.

The even-numbered side of Ave des Champs-Élysées between Rond Point des Champs-Élysées and Rue de Berri is perforated by a series of **shopping arcades** (Map 2).

Rue du Faubourg Saint Honoré

Rue du Faubourg Saint Honoré (the western extension of Rue Saint Honoré), 400m north of the Champs-Élysées, links Rue Royale (metro Concorde) with Place des Ternes (metro Ternes). It is home to some of Paris' most renowned couture houses (see Clothes & Fashion Accessories in the Shopping chapter). Other luxury items available here include jewellery and fine antiques.

The most noteworthy of the avenue's 18th-century mansions is the **Palais de l'Élysée** (Map 2) at the intersection of Rue du Faubourg Saint Honoré and Ave de Marigny. The official residence of the French president and symbol of his extensive powers, it was built in 1718 and has been home to 19 French presidents since 1873.

Musée du Petit Palais

The Petit Palais Museum (Map 2; ☎ 01 42 65 12 73; metro Champs-Élysées Clemenceau) on Ave Winston Churchill, built for the Exposition Universelle of 1900, houses the **Musée des Beaux-Arts de la Ville de Paris**, the Paris municipality's Museum of

Fine Arts. It specialises in medieval and Renaissance objets d'art (porcelain, clocks), tapestries, drawings and 19th-century French painting and sculpture. The Petit Palais is open Tuesday to Sunday from 10 am to 5.40 pm (last entry at 5 pm) and to 8 pm on Thursday. Tickets cost 27FF (14.50FF reduced price); if there's a temporary exhibition, they rise to 40 and 30FF.

Grand Palais
The Grand Palais (☎ 01 44 13 17 17; metro Champs-Élysées Clemenceau), across Ave Winston Churchill from the Petit Palais (the main entrance faces Ave des Champs-Élysées), houses the **Nationales Galeries du Grand Palais** (Map 2), which hosts special exhibitions lasting three or four months. Built for the 1900 Exposition Universelle, it has an iron frame and an Art Nouveau-style glass roof.

It is open daily, except Tuesday, from 10 am to 8 pm (last entry at 7.15 pm) and on Wednesday to 10 pm (last entry 9.15 pm).

Palais de la Découverte
The Palace of Discovery (Map 2; ☎ 01 40 74 80 00 or ☎ 01 40 74 81 82 for a recording; Minitel 3615 DECOUVERTE; metro Champs-Élysées Clemenceau), a fascinating science museum on Ave Franklin D Roosevelt, has interactive exhibits on astronomy, biology and medicine, chemistry, mathematics and computer science, physics and earth sciences Although the signs, explanations and excellent public demonstrations (great for kids) are in French, much of the material is self-explanatory if you still remember a bit of high-school physics and biology. The two **Euréka rooms** have exhibits for young children.

The Palais de la Découverte is open Tuesday to Saturday from 9.30 am to 6 pm and 10 am to 7 pm on Sunday and holidays. Entrance costs 27FF (17FF for students and people under 18 or over 60; free for half an hour before closing time). The **planetarium** (☎ 01 40 74 81 73), which has four shows a day in French (usually at 11.30 am and 2,

3.15 and 4.30 pm with an additional one on weekends at 5.45 pm), costs an extra 13FF.

Triangle d'Or
Many of Paris' richest residents, finest hotels and most fashionable couture houses can be found in the Triangle d'Or (Golden Triangle), an ultra-exclusive neighbourhood whose corners are at Place de la Concorde, the Arc de Triomphe and Place de l'Alma. Ave Montaigne, home of *haute couture* (see Clothes & Fashion Accessories in the Shopping chapter), is a good place from which to start exploring the area.

Arc de Triomphe
The Arc de Triomphe (Map 2; ☎ 01 43 80 31 31; metro Charles de Gaulle-Étoile) is 2.2km north-west of Place de la Concorde in the middle of Place Charles de Gaulle (or Place de l'Étoile), the world's largest traffic roundabout and the meeting point of 12 avenues (and three arrondissements – the 8e, 16e and 17e). It was commissioned in 1806 by Napoleon to commemorate his imperial victories but remained unfinished when he started losing – first battles and then whole wars. It was finally completed in 1836.

Among the armies to march triumphantly through the Arc de Triomphe were the Germans in 1871, the Allies in 1919, the Germans in 1940 and the Allies in 1944. Since 1920, the body of an Unknown Soldier from WWI taken from Verdun in Lorraine has lain beneath the arch, his fate and that of countless others like him commemorated by a memorial flame rekindled each evening around 6.30 pm. France's national remembrance service is held here annually at 11 am on 11 November.

The most famous of the four high-relief panels is to the right as you face the arch from the Ave des Champs-Élysées side. Entitled *Départ des Volontaires de 1792* and also known as *La Marseillaise*, it is the work of François Rude. Higher up, a frieze running around the whole monument depicts hundreds of figures, each one measuring 2m high.

From the viewing platform on top of the arch (284 steps) you can see the 12 avenues – many of them named after Napoleonic victories and illustrious generals – radiating toward every part of Paris. Ave de la Grande Armée heads north-west to the sky-scraper district of **La Défense** (see later in this chapter), where the **Grande Arche**, a hollow cube 112m on each side, defines the western end of the Grand Axe (the Louvre–Arc de Triomphe axis). From April to September, the Arc de Triomphe platform can be visited daily, except on major holidays, from 9.30 am to 11 pm; during the rest of the year the hours are 10 am to 10 pm. Tickets cost 35FF (23FF if you're 12 to 25; free for children) and are sold in the underground passageway.

The only sane way to get to the base of the arch is via the underground passageway – *not* linked to nearby metro tunnels – that surfaces on the even-numbered side of Ave des Champs-Élysées. The similar northern passage to the Ave de la Grande Armée has been closed for security reasons. Driving around the roundabout is Paris' ultimate driving challenge, especially during rush hour.

Ave Foch

Ultra-exclusive Ave Foch (pronounced 'fosh') in the 16e is Paris' widest boulevard, linking the Arc de Triomphe with the Bois de Boulogne. Grassy areas with shaded paths – perfect for walking neurotic little dogs – separate the main lanes of traffic from the stately (and *very* expensive) apartment buildings along either side. Laid out in 1854, Ave Foch is named after Maréchal Ferdinand Foch (1851-1929), commander of the Allied forces during the last few difficult months of WWI.

PARC DE MONCEAU AREA

The elegant residential districts that surround the Parc de Monceau (8e) are a bastion of Paris' haute bourgeoisie.

Parc de Monceau

Pass through one of the gates in the elaborate wrought-iron fence around the Parc de Monceau (Map 2; metro Monceau) and you find yourself amid Paris' most immaculately tended lawns, flowerbeds, trees and pseudo-classical statues. From the many benches, you can observe the city's best dressed children out with their nannies or on their way home from expensive private schools. Nearby streets are lined with opulent mansions and grand apartment buildings from the mid-19th century. The world's first parachute jump – from a balloon – was made here in 1797. The park is open daily until 8 pm (10 pm from April to October).

Musée Cernuschi

The Cernuschi Museum (Map 2; ☎ 01 45 63 50 75; metro Villiers) at 7 Ave Vélasquez houses a collection of ancient Chinese art (funerary statues, bronzes, ceramics) and works from Japan assembled during the 19th century by the banker Henri Cernuschi. It is open from 10 am to 5.40 pm (closed Monday and holidays). Entry costs 30FF (20FF reduced price).

Musée Nissim de Camondo

The Nissim de Camondo Museum (Map 2; ☎ 01 53 89 06 40; metro Monceau or Villiers) at 63 Rue de Monceau displays 18th-century furniture, wood panelling, tapestries, porcelain and other objets d'art collected by Count Moïse de Camondo, who established this museum in memory of his son Nissim, who died in WWI. It is open Wednesday to Sunday from 10 am to 5 pm. Tickets cost 27FF (18FF for people under 25 or over 60).

Musée Jacquemart-André

The Jacquemart-André Museum (Map 2; ☎ 01 42 89 04 91; metro Miromesnil) at 158 Blvd Haussmann is housed in an opulent residence built during the mid-19th century. The collection includes furniture, tapestries and enamels but is most noted for its paintings by Rembrandt and Van Dyck and some Italian Renaissance works of Bernini, Botticelli, Carpaccio, Donatello, Mantegna, Tintoretto, Titian and Uccello. The museum

Carte Musées et Monuments

The Museums and Monuments Card is valid for entry to around 70 venues in Paris and the Île de France, including the Louvre and the Musée d'Orsay. The cost for one/three/five days is 80/160/240FF. There is no reduced rate for students or senior travellers. The pass is available from the participating venues, tourist offices, FNAC outlets and some metro stations in Paris.

Note that most museums in Paris are free for those under 18, give a reduced rate for those 18 to 25 and over 60, and are closed on Monday or Tuesday.

is open daily, from 10 am to 6 pm, and entry is 46FF (33FF reduced price) including an audioguide in one of six languages.

OPÉRA GARNIER AREA

Opéra Garnier (9e), Paris' world-famous opera house, abuts the Grands Boulevards, broad thoroughfares whose *belle époque* elegance has only partially been compromised by the traffic and pedestrian tumult of a modern city.

Opéra Garnier

Paris' renowned opera house (Map 7; ☎ 01 40 01 22 63; metro Opéra) at Place de l'Opéra (9e), designed in 1860 by Charles Garnier to showcase the splendour of Napoleon III's France, is one of the most impressive monuments erected during the Second Empire. The extravagant **entrance hall**, with its **Grand Escalier** (Great Staircase), is decorated with multicoloured, imported marble and a gigantic chandelier. The **ceiling** of the auditorium was painted by Marc Chagall in 1964. Other parts of the building are likely to undergo repairs until the end of the century.

Known as Opéra Garnier since the opening of the Opéra Bastille in 1989, it contains the **Musée de l'Opéra** (☎ 01 47 42 07 02), which is open daily from 10 am

to 5 pm (ticket sales end a half-hour before). The entrance fee is 30FF (20FF for children, students and seniors; free for under 10s) and includes a visit to the opera house unless there's a daytime rehearsal or performance going on; operas and concerts are staged both here and at the Opéra Bastille (see the Entertainment chapter for details).

Blvd Haussmann

Blvd Haussmann (8e and 9e), just north of Opéra Garnier, is the heart of a commercial and banking district and is known for having some of Paris' most famous department stores, including **Galeries Lafayette** (Map 7) at No 40 and **Printemps** (Map 2) at No 64 (see the Shopping chapter).

Grands Boulevards

The eight contiguous Grands Boulevards (Maps 2, 3 and 7) – Madeleine, Capucines, Italiens, Montmartre, Poissonière, Bonne Nouvelle, Saint Denis and Saint Martin – stretch from elegant Place de la Madeleine (8e) eastward to the less-than-luxurious Place de la République (3e and 10e), a distance of just under 3km. Lined with the kind of grand 19th-century buildings for which Paris is famous, they were established in the 1600s on the site of obsolete fortifications. The Grands Boulevards served as a centre of café and theatre life in the 18th and 19th centuries, reaching the height of fashion during the belle époque.

The Grands Boulevards pass by the following sights: Place de l'Opéra, designed by Haussmann; the lively nightlife district along Blvd Montmartre and nearby parts of Rue du Faubourg Montmartre (2e and 10e); a number of 19th-century arcades; and two small triumphal arches, Porte Saint Denis and Porte Saint Martin (see 10e Arrondissement).

19th-Century Arcades

Stepping into the covered shopping arcades off Blvd Montmartre is the best way to visit early 19th-century Paris. The **Passage des Panoramas** (Map 7; metro Rue Montmartre) at 11 Blvd Montmartre (2e), which was opened in 1800 and received Paris' first gas lighting in 1817, was expanded in 1834 with the addition of four other interconnecting passages: Feydeau, Montmartre, Saint Marc and Variétés. The arcades are open daily from 6.30 am to midnight.

On the other side of Blvd Montmartre (9e), between Nos 10 and 12, is **Passage Jouffroy** (Map 7; metro Rue Montmartre), which leads across Rue de la Grange Batelière to **Passage Verdeau**. Both contain shops selling antiques, old postcards, used and antiquarian books, gifts, pet toys, imports from Asia and the like. The arcades are open until 10 pm. A bit to the west at 97 Rue de Richelieu (2e) is the sky-lighted **Passage des Princes** (Map 7; metro Richelieu Drouot).

Musée Grévin

This waxworks museum (Map 7; ☎ 01 42 46 13 26; metro Rue Montmartre) is most notable for its location – it's inside the Passage Jouffroy at 10-12 Blvd Montmartre. The collection is not up to that of Madame Tussaud's but would you get to see the death masks of French Revolutionary leaders in London? It's open seven days a week from 10 to 7 pm (from 10 am during school holiday periods), and the ticket counter closes one hour before. Entry is an outrageous 55FF (36FF for children aged 6 to 14).

10e ARRONDISSEMENT

The lively, ethnically mixed working-class area (metro Château d'Eau and Gare de l'Est) around Blvd de Strasbourg and Rue du Faubourg Saint Denis (especially south of Blvd de Magenta) is home to large communities of Indians, Pakistanis, west Indians, Africans, Turks and Kurds. Strolling through **Passage Brady** (Map 3; metro Château d'Eau) is almost like stepping into a back alley in Bombay.

Tranquil Canal Saint Martin links the 10e with Parc de la Villette (19e). Rue de Paradis (metro Château d'Eau) is famed for its crystal, glass and tableware shops (see the Shopping chapter).

Porte Saint Denis & Porte Saint Martin

Porte Saint Denis (Map 3; metro Strasbourg Saint Denis), the 24m-high triumphal arch at the intersection of Rue du Faubourg Saint Denis and Blvd Saint Denis, was built in 1672 to commemorate Louis XIV's campaign along the Rhine. On the north side, carvings represent the fall of Maastricht in 1673.

Two blocks to the east, at the intersection of Rue du Faubourg Saint Martin and Blvd Saint Denis, is another triumphal arch, 17m-high Porte Saint Martin (Map 3), erected in 1674 to commemorate the capture of Besançon and the Franche-Comté region by Louis XIV's armies.

Baccarat Crystal Museum

The glittering, incredibly pricey Baccarat showroom (Map 3; ☎ 01 47 70 64 30; metro Château d'Eau) in the CIAT (Centre International des Arts de la Table) building at 30bis Rue de Paradis is a fine example of Napoleon III-era industrial architecture. The attached museum is filled with stunning pieces of crystal, many of them custom made for princes and dictators of desperately poor ex-colonies. It is open weekdays from 9 am to 6 pm, and on Saturday from 10 am to noon and 2 to 5 pm; entry is 15FF.

Canal Saint Martin

The little-touristed, 4.5km-long Saint Martin Canal (Map 3; metro République, Jaurès and others) is one of Paris' hidden delights. Its shaded towpaths – speckled with sunlight filtering through the plane trees – are a wonderful place for a romantic stroll or bike ride past nine **locks**, metal bridges and ordinary Parisian neighbourhoods. Parts of the waterway – built in 1806 to link the Seine with the 108km-long Canal de l'Ourcq – are higher than the surrounding land.

Between the Port de Plaisance de Paris-Arsenal (the pleasure-boat marina next to Place de la Bastille) and Square Frédéric Lemaître (10e), Canal Saint Martin disappears under reinforced concrete vaults for over 2km. The northern, open-air half of the canal, which links Square Frédéric

Lemaître with Parc de la Villette (19e), was saved thanks to the failure of a plan – mooted in the early 1970s – to pave it over and turn it into an autoroute. For information on barge rides, see Organised Tours in the Getting Around chapter.

BERCY
The area along the Seine between Gare de Lyon and Porte de Bercy (12e) spent most of the 1980s as a huge construction site for several of former President Mitterrand's imposing grands projets. These days, Bercy – long cut off from the rest of the city by railway tracks and the Seine but now joined with the left bank by the new 240FF million Pont Charles de Gaulle – has some of Paris' most important new buildings, including the octagonal **Palais Omnisports de Paris-Bercy** (Map 1) on Blvd de Bercy, designed to serve as both an indoor sports arena and a concert, ballet and theatre venue, and the giant **Ministry of Finance** on Blvd de Bercy, whose minions and economists were dragged here, kicking and screaming, from the beautiful north wing of the Louvre.

13e ARRONDISSEMENT
The generally nondescript 13e arrondissement begins a few blocks south of the Jardin des Plantes (5e).

Bibliothèque Nationale de France François Mitterrand
Right across the river from Bercy is the controversial, US$2 billion National Library of France (Map 1; ☎ 01 53 79 59 59; metro Quai de la Gare) at 11 Quai FrancMauriac, sarcastically known – recalling the TGV train – as the TGB (Très Grande Bibliothèque, meaning 'very large library').

Conceived by Mitterrand as a 'wonder of the modern world', no expense was spared to carry out a plan that many people said defied logic. While many of the more than 10 million books and historical documents were shelved in the four sun-drenched, 80m-high towers – shaped like half-open books – patrons sit in artifi-

cially lit basement halls built around a forest of 126 50-year-old pines, trucked here from Normandy at a cost of US$22,000 each. The towers have since been fitted with an expensive and complex shutter system and the basement is prone to flooding from the Seine, but the library has at last been opened to readers. See Libraries in the Facts for the Visitor chapter for details.

Chinatown
In the triangle bounded by Ave de Choisy, Ave d'Ivry and Blvd Masséna, Paris' highrise Chinatown (Map 1; metro Tolbiac, Porte d'Ivry or Porte de Choisy) has a distinctly Franco-Chinese ambience, thanks to scores of east Asian restaurants, shops and travel agencies.

14e ARRONDISSEMENT
The less-than-thrilling 14e is best known for Cimetière du Montparnasse (see Montparnasse Area); **Parc Montsouris** (Map 1; metro Cité Universitaire), a beautiful park across Blvd Jourdan from the lawns and university dorms of the **Cité Internationale Universitaire** (Map 1); and the discount clothing outlets along Rue d'Alésia (Map 1; see Clothes & Fashion Accessories in the Shopping chapter).

Catacombes
In 1785, it was decided to solve the hygienic and aesthetic problems posed by Paris' overflowing cemeteries (especially the Cimetière des Innocents, just south of modern-day Forum des Halles) by exhuming the bones and storing them in the tunnels of three disused quarries. One ossuary created during this period is the Catacombes (Map 1; ☎ 01 43 22 47 63; metro Denfert Rochereau), without a doubt the most macabre place to visit in Paris. After descending 20m from street level, visitors follow 1.6km of underground corridors in which the bones and skulls of millions of Parisians from centuries past are neatly stacked along the walls. During WWII, these tunnels were used by the Résistance as a headquarters.

SIMON BRACKEN

RICHARD NEBESKY

MARK HONAN

Top: Place des Vosges
Bottom Left: Église Saint Eustache, seen from Les Halles
Bottom Right: Palais de Chaillot from the Eiffel Tower

TONY WHEELER

TONY WHEELER

BRENDA TURNNIDGE

MARK HONAN

JAMES LYON

TONY WHEELER

Top Left: Mosaic façade of a Marais boulangerie
Top Right: Cafe, Pont Saint Louis
Bottom: Les meilleurs! Parisian food

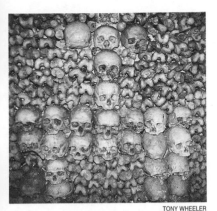

TONY WHEELER

Bones and skulls lining a tunnel
in Paris' Catacombes

The route through the Catacombes begins from the small green building at 1 Place Denfert Rochereau. The site is open Tuesday to Friday from 2 to 4 pm and on weekends from 9 to 11 am and 2 to 4 pm. Tickets cost 27FF (19FF for students and children). Flash photography is no problem, but tripods are forbidden. It's a good idea to bring along a torch (flashlight).

The exit (metro Mouton Duvernet), where a guard will check your bag for stolen bones, is on Rue Remy Dumoncel, 700m south-west of Place Denfert Rochereau.

MONTMARTRE

During the 19th century – especially after the Communard uprising of 1871, which began in this district – the bohemian lifestyle of Montmartre (18e) attracted artists and writers whose presence turned the area into Paris' most important centre of creativity. Although such activity shifted to Montparnasse after WWI, Montmartre retains an upbeat, leafy ambience that all the tourists in the world couldn't spoil.

In English-speaking countries, Montmartre's mystique of unconventionality has been magnified by the supposed notoriety of the **Moulin Rouge** (Map 9; see also Cabaret in the Entertainment chapter), a

nightclub on the edge of the Pigalle district that was founded in 1889 and is known for its scantily clad chorus girls.

Getting Around

The RATP's sleek funicular (Map 9) up Montmartre's southern slope – really just a slightly horizontal lift – whisks visitors from Square Willette (metro Anvers) to Sacré Cœur. It runs until 12.40 am and costs one metro/bus ticket each way. Weekly and monthly Carte Orange coupons as well as Paris Visite and Mobilis passes are valid here.

Montmartrobus, run by the RATP, takes a circuitous route all over Montmartre; maps are posted at bus stops.

Basilique du Sacré Cœur

The Basilica of the Sacred Heart (Map 9; ☎ 01 53 41 89 00; metro Lamarck Caulaincourt), perched at the very top of Butte de Montmartre (Montmartre Hill), was built from contributions taken from Parisian Catholics as an act of contrition after the humiliating Franco-Prussian War of 1870-71. Construction began in 1873, but the basilica was not consecrated until 1919.

On warm evenings, groups of young people gather on the steps below the church to contemplate the view, play guitars and sing. Although the basilica's domes are a well loved part of the Parisian skyline, the architecture of most of the building, which is typical of the style of the late 19th century, is not very graceful. It's always dark in the nave and the enormous mosaic of a plainly angry Christ over the main altar does little to dispel the gloom.

A 234-step climb up narrow spiral staircases takes you up to the **dome** (15FF; 8FF for children and students under 25), which affords one of Paris' most spectacular panoramas; you can see as far away as 30km on a clear day. The chapel-lined **crypt** (15FF; 8FF reduced price) is huge but not very interesting.

The basilica is open daily from 7 am to 11 pm. The dome and the crypt, down the stairs to the right as you exit the basilica, are open daily from 9 am to 6 pm (7 pm from April to September).

Place du Tertre

Half a block west of the **Église Saint Pierre de Montmartre** (Map 9), parts of which date from the 12th century (it's the only building left from the great Benedictine abbey of Montmartre, 1147-1680), is Place du Tertre (metro Abbesses), once the main square of the village of Montmartre. These days, it's filled with cafés, restaurants, portrait artists and tourists and is always animated. Look for the two **windmills** to the west on Rue Lepic.

Espace Montmartre Salvador Dalí

Over 300 works by Salvador Dalí (1904-89), the flamboyant Catalan surrealist printmaker, painter, sculptor and self-promoter, are on display at this museum (Map 9; ☎ 01 42 64 40 10; metro Abbesses) at 9-11 Rue Poulbot, around the corner from Place du Tertre. It is open daily from 10 am to 6 pm, and entry is 35FF (25FF reduced rate).

Musée de Montmartre

The Montmartre Museum (Map 9; ☎ 01 46 06 61 11; metro Lamarck Caulaincourt) at 12 Rue Cortot displays paintings, lithographs and documents mostly relating to the area's rebellious and bohemian/artistic past. It's hard to appreciate what the big deal is (and to justify the admission fee) unless you care about Montmartre's mythology – and can read French. There's a lush little garden out the back. The museum is open Tuesday to Sunday from 11 am to 6 pm. Tickets cost 25FF (20FF for students and seniors).

Musée d'Art Naïf Max Fourny

The Museum of Naive Art, founded in 1986, is housed in Halle Saint Pierre (Map 9; ☎ 01 42 58 72 89; metro Anvers) at 2 Rue Ronsard, across from Square Willette and the base of the funicular. The colourful, vivid paintings – gathered from around the world – are immediately appealing, thanks in part to their whimsical and generally optimistic perspective on life. The museum, whose themed exhibitions change frequently, is open daily from 10 am to 6 pm. Tickets cost a pricey 40FF (30FF for students, seniors and teachers; 20FF for children). Workshops for children are open on Wednesday and at the weekend from 3 to 4 pm.

The **gallery** on the ground floor hosts temporary exhibitions and there's a very pleasant café.

Musée d'Art Juif

The small Museum of Jewish Art (Map 9; ☎ 01 42 57 84 15; metro Lamarck Caulaincourt), on the 3rd floor of the Jewish community centre at 42 Rue des Saules, has a modest collection of synagogue models, paintings and ritual objects from Eastern Europe and North Africa. It is open Sunday to Thursday from 3 to 6 pm (closed on Jewish holidays and in August). Entrance costs 30FF (20FF for students; 10FF for children). There are plans for the museum's collections to be combined with medieval Jewish artefacts from the Musée National du Moyen Age to create the **Musée d'Art et d'Histoire du Judaïsme**, to be housed in the Hôtel de Saint Aignan at 71 Rue du Temple (3e) in the Marais (metro Rambuteau).

Cimetière de Montmartre

Montmartre Cemetery (Maps 1 and 9; ☎ 01 43 87 64 24; metro Place de Clichy), established in 1798 is, after Père Lachaise, the most famous cemetery in Paris. It contains the graves of the writers Émile Zola, Stendahl, Alexandre Dumas the younger and Heinrich Heine; composers Jacques Offenbach and Hector Berlioz; painter Edgar Degas; director François Truffaut; and the dancer Vaslav Nijinsky.

The entrance nearest the Butte de Montmartre is at 20 Ave Rachel, down the stairs from 10 Rue Caulaincourt. From mid-March to early November, it is open weekdays from 8 am (8.30 am on Saturday, 9 am on Sunday and holidays) to 6 pm (last entry at 5.45 pm). The rest of the year, it's open from 8.30 am to 5.30 pm.

Pigalle

Only a few blocks south-west of the tranquil, residential streets of Montmartre is lively, neon-lit Pigalle (Maps 3 and 9), one of Paris' two main sex districts (the other, near Forum des Halles, is along Rue Saint Denis). But Pigalle is more than simply a sleazy red-light district; while the area around Blvd de Clichy between the Pigalle and Blanche metro stops is lined with erotica shops and striptease parlours and, appropriately enough, the new Musée de l'Érotisme (see below), there are also plenty of trendy night spots, including La Locomotive disco and the Moulin Rouge (see the Entertainment chapter for more information).

Despite the prostitutes, the peep shows and the blatant but controlled seediness, Pigalle is so filled with people of all sorts (including whole busloads of fascinated middle-aged tourists from the USA and Japan) that even late at night it's not unsafe, especially if you're with other people. However, after nightfall the Abbesses metro stop is considered a more prudent bet than the Blanche, Pigalle and, in particular, the Château Rouge stations.

The new **Musée de l'Érotisme** (Museum of Eroticism; Map 9; ☎ 01 42 58 28 73; metro Blanche) at 72 Blvd de Clichy tries to put titillating statuary and sexual aids from days gone by on a loftier plane – with erotic art both antique and new from four continents spread over seven levels. But we know why we've come here. The museum is open daily from 10 am to 2 am. Entry is 40FF (30FF reduced tariff).

Musée Gustave Moreau (Map 3; ☎ 01 48 74 38 50; metro Trinité), about 500m south-west of Place Pigalle at 14 Rue de La Rochefoucauld (9e), is dedicated to the eponymous symbolist painter's work, and the two storey museum (housed in what was once Moreau's studio) is crammed with paintings, drawings and sketches. It is open Monday and Wednesday from 11 am to 5.15 pm and Thursday to Sunday from 10 am to 12.45 pm and 2 to 5.15 pm. Admission costs 22FF (15FF for students and those over 60; free for those under 18).

19e ARRONDISSEMENT

The 19e is of interest to visitors mainly because of the Canal Saint Martin (see 10e Arrondissement) and its eastern continuation, Canal de l'Ourcq, and two large parks: Parc de la Villette, next to Paris' largest science museum, and hilly Parc des Buttes-Chaumont.

Parc de la Villette

This whimsical, 30-hectare park (Map 1), which opened in 1993 in the city's far north-eastern corner, stretches 600m from the Cité des Sciences et de l'Industrie (metro Porte de la Villette) southward to the Cité de la Musique (metro Porte de Pantin). Split into two sections by Canal de l'Ourcq, its lawns are enlivened by shaded walkways, imaginative public furniture, a series of themed gardens and whimsical, bright red building-sculptures known as *folies* (follies). Check out the giant sculpture entitled *Bicyclette Ensevelie*, which is just that, a huge 'Buried Bicycle'.

For kids, there's a **merry-go-round** near the Cinaxe, a **playground** between the Géode and the nearest bridge, and two large play areas: the **Jardin des Vents** (Garden of Winds, Map 1) and the adjacent **Jardin des Dunes** (Garden of Dunes). Divided into three areas for children of different ages, they are across Galerie de la Villette (the covered walkway) from the **Grande Halle** (Map 1), a wonderful old slaughterhouse of wrought iron and glass now used for concerts, theatre performances, expositions and conventions.

For information on barge rides to Parc de la Villette from the Port de Plaisance de Paris-Arsenal and Quai Anatole France near the Musée d'Orsay, see Organised Tours in the Getting Around chapter.

Cité des Sciences et de l'Industrie

The enormous City of Sciences and Industry (Map 1; ☎ 01 40 05 12 12 or ☎ 08 36 68 29 30; Minitel 3615 VILLETTE; www.cite-sciences.fr; metro Porte de la Villette), at the northern end of Parc de la Villette at 30 Ave Corentin Cariou, has all sorts of high-tech exhibits on matters scientific. The

Statues & Sculptures

Paris is dotted with outdoor statuary and beautiful fountains, such as the romantic Fontaine des Médicis (Map 6; metro Luxembourg) which combines fountain, pond and statuary in one elegant group in the Jardin du Luxembourg. Like the Tuileries on the Right Bank, the Jardin du Luxembourg is dotted with sculptures and statuary. The Fontaine de l'Observatoire, at the southern point of the gardens (Map 6; metro Port Royal), is a favourite.

Not far away on foot, but on the other side of the universe in concept, is the very modern *Statue of Centaur* at the junction of Rue du Cherche Midi and Rue du Sèvres (Map 4; metro Saint Sulpice). A much-loved modern piece of sculpture is the giant head, looking like it's just rolled away from an equally gigantic guillotine, beside Église Saint Eustache at the Forum des Halles (Map 7; metro Les Halles). Equally striking is Claes Oldenburg's huge *Buried Bicycle*, protruding from the grass in the Parc de la Villette (Map 1; metro Porte de la Villette).

It was the French who gave New York City its Statue of Liberty, so it's fitting that they kept a smaller one for Paris. It's right in the middle of the Seine, a short distance downstream from the Eiffel Tower (Map 1; metro Ave du President Kennedy, Maison de Radio France). The *Flame of Liberty*, a replica of the one atop the torch of the State of Liberty in New York Harbour, was placed in the Place de l'Alma (Map 2; metro Alma Marceau) by US firms based in Paris in 1989 to honour the bicentennial of the French revolution. It has become a memorial to Diana, Princess of Wales, since August 1997 when she was killed in a car accident in the underpass beneath it.

dazzle-'em-with-gadgets presentation reflects France's traditionally deferential approach to technology and white lab-coated scientists, whom the public – with the encouragement of the government technocracy – always seems to think know best.

Musée Explora The huge, rather confusing main museum of the City of Sciences and Industry is open daily, except Monday, from 10 am to 6 pm (7 pm on Sunday). A ticket good for Explora, the planetarium, a 3-D film and the French Navy submarine *Argonaute* (commissioned in 1957) costs 50FF (35FF for those aged eight to 25, seniors and teachers and everyone on Saturday; free for children) and allows you to enter and exit up to four times during the day. Various combo tickets valid for the Cité des Sciences, the Géode and Cinaxe are available.

A free map-brochure in English and the detailed 80-page *Guide to the Permanent Exhibitions* (20FF) are available from the round information counter at the Cité des Sciences' main entrance. According to one reader, the best sections of the museum are

Sons (Sounds) on level No 1, *Expression et Comportement* (Expression and Behaviour) on level No 2 and *Jeux de Lumière* (Light Tricks), whose exhibits are based on those at the Exploratorium in San Francisco.

Cité des Enfants The highlight of the Cité des Sciences is the brilliant Cité des Enfants, whose colourful and imaginative hands-on demonstrations of basic scientific principles are divided into two sections, one for three to five-year-olds, the other for five to 12-year-olds. Younger kids can explore, among other things, the conduct of water (waterproof lab ponchos provided), while older children can build toy houses with industrial robots and stage news broadcasts in a TV studio equipped with real video cameras.

The 90-minute visits begin four times a day at two-hour intervals from 9.30 or 10.30 am. Each child is charged 25FF and must be accompanied by an adult. During school holiday periods, it's a good idea to make reservations two or three days in advance (☎ 08 36 68 29 30 or Minitel 3615 VILLETTE).

Géode Just south of the Cité des Sciences at 26 Ave Corentin Cariou is the Géode (Map 1; ☎ 01 40 05 12 12), a 36m-high sphere whose mirror-like surface made up of thousands of highly polished, stainless-steel triangles has made it one of the architectural calling cards of modern Paris. Inside, high-resolution, 70mm films – virtual reality, special effects, nature etc – lasting 45 minutes are projected onto a spherical, 180° screen which gives viewers a sense of being surrounded by the action. Films begin every hour on the hour from 10 am to 9 pm (closed Monday except during school holiday periods). Headsets which pick up an English soundtrack are available for no extra charge.

Tickets to the Géode cost 57FF (44FF for under 25s, seniors and teachers; not available on weekends and holidays from 2 to 5 pm). For afternoon shows during school holiday periods and on Tuesday and Thursday from March to June, make advance reservations.

Cinaxe The Cinaxe (☎ 01 42 09 34 00), a hydraulic cinema with seating for 60 people that moves in synchronisation with the action on the screen, is right across the walkway from the south-western side of the Cité des Sciences. This example of proto-virtual reality technology is open from 11 am to 6 pm (closed Monday) and costs 33FF (29FF for children, students and seniors). Shows begin every 15 minutes.

Cité de la Musique
On the southern edge of Parc de la Villette, the City of Music (Map 1; ☎ 01 44 84 44 84; Minitel 3615 CITEMUSIQUE; www.cite-musique.fr; metro Porte de Pantin), 221 Ave Jean Jaurès, which opened in 1995, is a striking triangular concert hall whose brief is to bring non-elitist music from around the world to Paris' multi-ethnic masses. Some 900 rare musical instruments are on display in its **Musée de la Musique** (Music Museum), which is open Tuesday to Thursday from noon to 6 pm, Friday and Saturday to 7.30 pm and Sunday from 10

am to 6 pm. Entry costs 35FF (25FF for students and seniors; 10FF for those aged six to 18). The **Centre d'Information Musique et Danse** (☎ 01 44 84 46 09; Minitel 3615 MUSIQUE or 3615 DANSE) lets you try out interactive CD-ROMs (many of them in English) connected to music – subjects range from Beethoven to techno. It is open Tuesday to Saturday from noon to 6 pm (Sunday from 10 am); entry is free. For details on concerts (some of them free) at the Cité de la Musique, see Opera & Classical Music in the Entertainment chapter.

Parc des Buttes-Chaumont
Encircled by tall apartment blocks, the 25-hectare Buttes-Chaumont Park (Maps 1 and 3; metro Buttes-Chaumont or Botzaris) is the closest thing in Paris to Manhattan's Central Park. Great for jogging, cycling or tanning, its lush, forested slopes hide grottoes and artificial waterfalls. The romantic **lake** is dominated by a temple-topped **island** linked to the mainland by two bridges. Once a quarry and rubbish tip, the park – encircled by Rue Manin and Rue Botzaris – was given its present form by Haussmann in the 1860s. Except in icy conditions, it's open daily from 7 am to 9 pm (11 pm from May to September).

20e ARRONDISSEMENT
The multicultural, working-class 20e, last stronghold of the Commune of 1871 and long a bastion of proletarian radicalism, is a lively, untouristed corner of the city.

Cimetière du Père Lachaise
Founded in 1805, Père Lachaise Cemetery (see Map 1 for location; ☎ 01 43 70 70 33; metro Philippe Auguste, Père Lachaise or Gambetta), whose 70,000 ornate (and at times ostentatious) tombs of the rich and/or famous form a verdant, open-air sculpture garden, is the most visited necropolis in the world. Among the one million people buried here are the composer Chopin; the writers Molière, Apollinaire, Oscar Wilde, Balzac, Marcel Proust, Gertrude Stein and Colette; artists

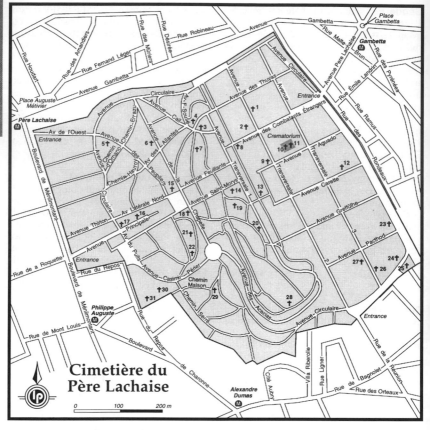

Cimetière du
Père Lachaise

0   100   200 m

David, Delacroix, Pissarro, Seurat and Modigliani; actors Sarah Bernhardt, Simone Signoret and Yves Montand; singer Édith Piaf; dancer Isadora Duncan; and even those immortal 12th-century lovers, Abélard and Héloïse. The only tomb most young visitors seem to be interested in is the grave (in Division 6) of 1960s rock star **Jim Morrison**, lead singer of the Doors, who died in an apartment on Rue Beautreillis (4e) in the Marais in 1971.

On 27 May 1871, the last of the Communard insurgents, cornered by government forces, fought a hopeless, all-night battle among the tombstones. In the morning, the 147 survivors were lined up against the **Mur des Fédérés** (Wall of the Federalists) and shot. They were buried where they fell in a mass grave.

The cemetery, which has four entrances (two of them on Blvd de Ménilmontant), is open weekdays from 8 am to 5.30 pm (Saturday from 8.30 am,

1 Marcel Proust
2 Guillaume Apollinaire
3 Eugène Delacroix
4 Honoré de Balzac
5 Georges Seurat
6 Georges Bizet
7 Hilaire Belloc
8 Hippolyte Kardec
9 Yves Montand & Simone Signoret
10 Isadora Duncan
11 Max Ernst
12 Oscar Wilde
13 Sarah Bernhardt
14 Dominique Ingres
15 Jacques Louis David
16 Georges Haussmann
17 Sidonie Colette
18 Théodore Géricault
19 Jean-Baptiste Corot
20 Molière
21 Vincenzo Bellini
22 Frédéric Chopin
23 Gertrude Stein
24 Paul Éluard
25 Mur des Fédérés
26 Edith Piaf & Théo Sarapo
27 Amedeo Modigliani
28 Beaumarchais
29 Jim Morrison
30 Héloïse & Abélard
31 Camille Pissarro

SIMON BRACKEN

Chopin's grave

Sunday from 9 am). From mid-March to early November, the cemetery closes at 6 pm. Maps indicating the location of noteworthy graves are posted around the cemetery and can be obtained free from the Conservation office at 16 Rue du Repos. Newsstands and kiosks in the area sell the more detailed *Plan Illustré du Père Lachaise* (Illustrated Map of Père Lachaise) for 10FF. Two-hour tours (☎ 01 40 71 75 23) of the cemetery in French leave every Saturday (and on certain Tuesdays and Sundays as well) from the Conservation office at 2.30 pm. They cost 37FF (26FF reduced rate) and can be either general tours or themed ones.

Belleville
This buoyant and utterly unpretentious working-class 'village' around Blvd de Belleville (Maps 1 and 3; metro Belleville) is home to large numbers of immigrants, especially Muslims and Jews from North Africa and Vietnamese and Chinese from Indochina. In recent years, its none-too-solid, late 19th-century workers' flats have become a trendy address for avant-garde artists in search of cheap housing and the cachet that comes with slumming it. This is one of the best places in Paris to dine on couscous, the meat available either kosher or halal. See Oberkampf, Ménilmontant & Belleville Areas in the Places to Eat chapter.

The **Parc de Belleville** (Map 1; metro Couronnes), which opened in 1992 a few blocks east of Blvd de Belleville, occupies a hill almost 200m above sea level. It offers superb views of the city.

BOIS DE BOULOGNE

The 8.65-sq-km Boulogne Woods (16e; Map 1), on the western edge of the city, are endowed with lakes, lawns, forested areas, flower gardens, meandering paths, cycling trails and belle époque cafés. The park owes its informal layout to its designer, Baron Haussmann, who took his inspiration from London's Hyde Park rather than the more formal and geometric French models.

The southern reaches of the woods take in **Stade Roland Garros** (Map 1), home of the French Open tennis tournament, and two horse-racing tracks, the Hippodrome de Longchamp (for flat races) and the Hippodrome d'Auteuil (for steeplechase). For details, see Horse Racing under Spectator Sports in the Entertainment chapter.

Gardens

The enclosed **Parc de Bagatelle**, in the north-western corner of the Bois de Boulogne, is renowned for its beautiful gardens; they surround the **Château de Bagatelle**, built in 1775. There are areas dedicated to irises (which bloom in May), roses (June to October) and water lilies (August).

The **Pré Catelan** (Map 1) includes a garden in which you can see the plants, flowers and trees mentioned in Shakespeare's plays.

Rowboats & Bicycles

Rowboats can be hired at Lac Inférieur (Map 1; metro Ave Henri Martin), the largest of the park's lakes and ponds. Paris Cycles (☎ 01 47 47 76 50 for a recorded message or, for bookings, ☎ 01 47 47 22 37) rents bicycles at two locations: on Ave du Mahatma Gandhi (metro Les Sablons) across from the Porte Sablons entrance to the Jardin d'Acclimatation amusement park, and near the Pavillon Royal (metro Avenue Foch) at the northern end of Lac Inférieur. Except when it rains, bicycles are available daily mid-April to mid-October from 10 am to sundown and the same hours on Wednesday, Saturday and Sunday during the rest of the year. The rental cost is 80FF per day.

Night-time in the Bois de Boulogne

Each night after about 10 pm, especially on weekends, little sections of the Bois de Boulogne are taken over by all manner of prostitutes (the great majority of whom have AIDS or are HIV positive, according to a recent study). They are joined by professionals and amateurs with certain sexual preferences and interests: *échangistes* (people interested in partner-swapping), voyeurs, flashers, people who arrange orgies etc. In recent years, the police have cracked down on the park's sex trade, but locals still advise both men and women not to walk through the area alone at night. The areas around the Parc de Bagatelle and the Pré Catelan are also popular gay cruising grounds but, as the *Spartacus International Gay Guide* correctly points out, they are AYOR (at your own risk).

Musée National des Arts et Traditions Populaires

The National Museum of Popular Arts and Traditions (Map 1; ☎ 01 44 17 60 00; metro Les Sablons), near the Jardin d'Acclimatation at 6 Ave du Mahatma Gandhi, has displays illustrating life in rural France before and during the Industrial Revolution. It is open from 9.45 am to 5.15 pm (closed Tuesday). Tickets cost 25FF (17FF reduced price, available to everyone on Sunday).

Jardin d'Acclimatation

This kids-orientated amusement park (Map 1; ☎ 01 40 67 90 82; metro Les Sablons) on Ave du Mahatma Gandhi (at the northern edge of the Bois de Boulogne) is open every day, all year long from 10 am to 6 pm. Entrance costs 12FF (6FF reduced price).

To the south-west of the Jardin d'Acclimatation is Bowling de Paris (☎ 01 40 67 94 00), a bowling alley open weekdays from 11 am to 2 am (from 10 am at weekends) where games cost 20 to 32FF per person. The highest tariffs are in force after 8 pm and on weekends. This place also has French and American billiards and snooker.

Musée Marmottan-Claude Monet
Two blocks east of the Bois de Boulogne, between Porte de la Muette and Porte de Passy, the Marmottan-Claude Monet Museum (Map 1; ☎ 01 42 24 07 02; metro La Muette) at 2 Rue Louis Boilly (16e) has the world's largest collection of works by the impressionist Monet, as well as paintings by Gauguin and Renoir. It is open Tuesday to Sunday from 10 am to 5.30 pm (last entry 5 pm). Entrance costs 40FF (25FF reduced price).

BOIS DE VINCENNES
Paris' other large English-style park, the 9.3-sq-km Bois de Vincennes (12e), is in the far south-eastern corner of the city. The **Parc Floral** (Floral Park; Map 1; metro Château de Vincennes), just south of the Château de Vincennes, is on Route de la Pyramide. The **Jardin Tropical** (Tropical Garden; RER stop Nogent-sur-Marne) is at the park's eastern edge on Ave de la Belle Gabrielle.

Every year from the end of March to early May, a huge amusement park known as the **Foire du Trône** installs itself on the Pelouse de Reuilly at the Bois de Vincennes.

Musée National des Arts d'Afrique et d'Océanie
The National Museum of African and Oceanic Art (Map 1; ☎ 01 44 74 84 80) at 293 Ave Daumesnil is devoted to the art of the south Pacific, North Africa and western and central Africa. The residents of the **tropical aquarium** include Nile crocodiles. The museum is open on weekdays, except Tuesday, from 10 am to noon and 1.30 to 5.30 pm (no midday closure during special exhibitions), and on weekends from 12.30 pm (10 am for the aquarium) to 6 pm.

The entry fee is 30FF (20FF if you're 18 to 24 or over 60; free for under 18s).

Zoo
The Parc Zoologique de Paris (Map 1; ☎ 01 44 75 20 10; metro Porte Dorée), founded in 1934, is at 53 Ave de Saint Maurice, just east of the Blvd Périphérique (the ring road around Paris). The park is open daily from 9 am to 6 pm (6.30 pm on Sunday) in summer and from 9 am to 5 pm (5.30 pm on Sunday) in winter; the last entry is 30 minutes before closing. The entrance fee is 40FF (30FF reduced tariff, 10FF for students).

Château de Vincennes
The Château de Vincennes (☎ 01 48 08 31 20; metro Château de Vincennes) at the northern edge of the Bois de Vincennes is a bona fide royal château complete with massive fortifications and a moat. Louis XIV spent his honeymoon in the mid-17th century **Pavillon du Roi**, the westernmost of the two royal pavilions flanking the **Cour Royale** (Royal Courtyard). The 52m-high **Donjon**, completed in 1369, was used as a prison during the 17th and 18th centuries. It will be closed for repairs until the end of 1999.

You can walk around the grounds for free, but the only way to see the Gothic **Chapelle Royale**, built between the 14th and 16th centuries, is to take a guided tour (in French, with an information booklet in English). Tickets cost 32FF (reduced price 21FF) for a long tour and 25FF (15FF) for a short one. There are five long and five short tours a day from May to September when the château is open from 10 am to 6 pm and four of each the rest of the year from 10 am to 5 pm.

LA DÉFENSE
La Défense (metro La Défense), Paris' skyscraper district, is 3km west of the 17e arrondissement. Set on the sloping west bank of the Seine, its ultramodern architecture and multi-storey office blocks are so radically different from the

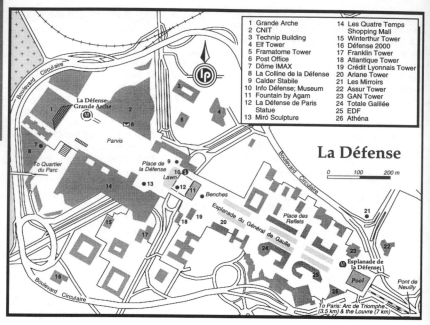

1	Grande Arche	14	Les Quatre Temps
2	CNIT		Shopping Mall
3	Technip Building	15	Winterthur Tower
4	Elf Tower	16	Défense 2000
5	Framatome Tower	17	Franklin Tower
6	Post Office	18	Atlantique Tower
7	Dôme IMAX	19	Crédit Lyonnais Tower
8	La Colline de la Défense	20	Ariane Tower
9	Calder Stabile	21	Les Mirroirs
10	Info Défense; Museum	22	Assur Tower
11	Fountain by Agam	23	GAN Tower
12	La Défense de Paris	24	Totale Galilée
	Statue	25	EDF
13	Miró Sculpture	26	Athéna

La Défense

rest of centuries-old Paris that it's well worth a brief visit. Some of the towering buildings are examples of modern architecture at its best, and the public areas are adorned with giant works of contemporary art.

One of the world's most ambitious urban construction projects, La Défense was begun in the late 1950s. Its first major structure was the Centre des Nouvelles Industries et Technologies (Centre for New Industries and Technologies), better known as **CNIT**, inaugurated in 1958 and renovated in 1989. During the mid-1970s, when skyscrapers fell out of fashion, office space in La Défense became hard to sell or lease. Whole buildings stood empty and the entire project appeared in jeopardy. But things picked up in the 1980s and 1990s, and today La Défense has some 60 buildings, the tallest of which is the 45-storey, 178m-high **Framatome**.

La Défense houses the head offices of

more than half of France's 20 largest corporations, and a total of 1200 companies of all sizes employ some 140,000 people. Most of the district's 30,000 residents live in high-rise apartment blocks.

Information

Info Défense (☎ 01 47 74 84 24; fax 01 47 78 17 93), a bit north-west of the Agam fountain at 15 Place de la Défense, is open daily from 9.30 or 10 am to 6 or 6.30 pm. There's a guide to the area's monumental art (15FF), a *Guide to Architecture* (35FF) and details on cultural activities. It also contains a museum of the development of La Défense through the years with drawings, architectural plans and scale models, including one of the planned 400m skyscraper nicknamed the Tour sans Fin. This 'Endless Tower' was to be built next to the Grande Arche, but the project has now been scrapped.

La Défense de Paris

La Défense, one of the world's most ambitious urban construction projects, is named after *La Défense de Paris*, a sculpture erected here in 1883 to commemorate the defence of Paris during the Franco-Prussian War of 1870-71. Removed in 1971 to facilitate construction work, it was placed on a round pedestal just west of the Agam fountain in 1983.

Many people don't like the name La Défense, which sounds rather militaristic, and EPAD (Établissement Public pour l'Aménagement de La Défense, the project management authority) did consider changing it. But it didn't, of course, causing some peculiar misunderstandings over the years. A high-ranking EPAD executive was once denied entry to Egypt because his passport indicated he was the 'managing director of La Défense', which Egyptian officials apparently assumed was part of France's military-industrial complex. Another time, a visiting Soviet general expressed admiration at how well the area's military installations had been camouflaged!

Grande Arche

The remarkable Grande Arche (☎ 01 49 07 27 27), designed by Danish architect Otto von Spreckelsen, is a hollow cube of white marble and glass measuring 112m on each side. Inaugurated on 14 July 1989, it forms the current western terminus of the 8km-long **Grand Axe** (Great Axis), which stretches from the Louvre's glass pyramid through the Jardin des Tuileries and along the Ave des Champs-Élysées to the Arc de Triomphe, Porte Maillot and finally the fountains, shaded squares and plazas of La Défense's Esplanade du Général de Gaulle. The structure, which symbolises a window open to the world, is ever so slightly out of alignment with the Grand Axe. Also known as the Tête Défense, it houses government and business offices.

Neither the view from the rooftop nor the temporary exhibitions housed in the top storey justify the ticket price of 40FF (30FF for students, those aged six to 18 and seniors). Both are open daily May to September from 10 am to 6 pm. During the rest of the year the weekday hours are 11 am to 5 pm, the weekend ones 10 am to 5 pm.

Le Parvis & Esplanade

In a largely successful attempt to humanise the district's somewhat harsh mixture of glass, steel and concrete, the Parvis, Place de La Défense and Esplanade du Général de Gaulle, which together form a 1km-long pedestrian precinct, have been turned into a **garden of contemporary art**. The nearly 70 monumental sculptures and murals here – and west of the Grande Arche in the **Quartier du Parc** and **Jardins de l'Arche**, a 2km-long westward extension of the Grand Axe – include colourful and imaginative works by Calder, Miró and Agam. The tourist office's *Guide to Works of Art* (15FF) provides details on the works and their creators. In the south-west corner of Place de la Défense and opposite the Info Défense office is something much older – a statue entitled **La Défense de Paris** (1883), which solemnises the Franco-Prussian War of 1870-71 and from which the district's name is derived (see the boxed text).

La Colline de La Défense

This complex, on top of Les Quatre Temps shopping mall just south of the Grande Arche, houses the huge **Dôme IMAX** (☎ 08 36 67 06 06), a 460-seat, 180° cinema that gives you the feeling of being inside the films on screen. Tickets cost 57FF (44FF for children under 16, students and seniors) and 40FF for the second film. On Saturday a double feature costs 80/70FF. Screenings start every hour from 12.30 to 6.45 pm (8 pm on Saturday).

Of more conventional interest is the **Musée de l'Automobile** (☎ 01 46 92 46 00), whose outstanding collection of vintage motorcars includes lots of very early French models. Many of the signs are in English.

It's open daily from 12.15 to 7.30 pm. Entry is 35FF (20FF reduced price).

MUSÉE DE L'AIR ET DE L'ESPACE

The Aeronautics and Space Museum (☎ 01 49 92 71 99 or, for a recording, ☎ 01 49 92 71 71) in Paris' northern suburb of Le Bourget has some 180 military and civilian aircraft, dozens of rockets and spacecraft and other displays which chart the history of flight and space exploration. It's open daily, except Monday, from 10 am to 5 pm (6 pm from May to October). Entry costs 30FF (22FF for students and those aged eight to 16).

To get to the museum, take RATP bus No 350 (every 10 to 20 minutes until at least 10 pm) from Gare de l'Est (right out front) or the Gare du Nord bus terminal (behind the station, just off Rue du Faubourg Saint Denis). You can also catch bus No 152 from near the Porte de la Villette metro station (19e).

ACTIVITIES

Paris' weekly entertainment pamphlets, *Pariscope* and *L'Officiel des Spectacles* (see Listings in the Entertainment chapter), have up-to-date information in French on every imaginable sort of activity.

Entries entitled 'Sports-Loisirs', 'Activités Sportives' or 'Promenades' have details on *randonnées pédestres* (hiking in groups), *cyclisme* (cycling, including group rides), *escalade* (rock-climbing excursions), *parachutisme* (parachuting), *piscines* (swimming pools), *patinoires* (ice-skating rinks), *canoë-kayak* (canoeing/kayaking), squash, tennis, golf etc.

Sports Facilities

For information (in French) on Paris' sporting activities and facilities (including its three dozen swimming pools), call Allô Sports on ☎ 01 42 76 54 54 (Minitel 3615 PARIS). It is staffed on weekdays from 10.30 am to 5 pm (4.30 pm on Friday).

Canal Boating

The Paris area's three rivers – the Seine, Marne and Oise – and its canals (Saint Martin and Ourcq) offer a unique vantage point from which to enjoy the delights of Paris. A one or two-week rental – less expensive than many hotels if there are four or more of you – can easily be split between quiet canal/river cruises and days spent moored in the city. Within Paris proper, the only places you can stay overnight are Bassin de la Villette, 19e (Map 1) and the Port de Plaisance de Paris-Arsenal (Map 5; see Houseboats under Places to Stay), but it's possible to stop for an hour or two at a number of quays along the Seine. Heavy traffic and currents make navigating the Seine pretty tricky, but foreigners are not required to have a special permit.

Europ' Yachting (Map 5; ☎ 01 43 44 66 77; fax 01 43 44 74 18; metro Bastille) at 11 Blvd de la Bastille (12e), on the ground floor of the Capitainerie of the Port de Plaisance de Paris-Arsenal, rents out boats for four to seven people. From mid-March to mid-October, you can rent by the week (6000 to 10,000FF). On weekends and holidays year round, boats are available for 945 to 1900FF a day, depending on the boat and the period. Reservations should be made three weeks ahead, though boats are sometimes available at the last minute. The office is open Monday to Saturday from 10 am to 1 pm and 2.30 to 7 pm.

COURSES

Language Courses

All manner of French-language courses, lasting from two weeks to nine months, are available in Paris. A number of language schools begin new courses every month or so. Many of the organisations detailed below can also arrange homestays or other accommodation.

The French Cultural Service (see Cultural Centres in the Facts for the Visitor chapter) has reams of information on studying in France, as do French government tourist offices and consulates. You might also contact the Ministry of Tourism-sponsored International Cultural Organisation

(ICO; ☎ 01 42 36 47 18; fax 01 40 26 34 45; metro Châtelet) at 55 Rue de Rivoli (1er).

The many French-language schools in the capital include:

Accord Language School
(Map 7; ☎ 01 42 36 24 95; fax 01 42 21 17 91; accordel@easynet.fr; metro Les Halles), 52 Rue Montmartre, 75002. A dynamic language school whose classes get high marks from students. Four-week classes on five levels with a maximum of 14 students (and often less) start at the beginning of each month of the year. They cost 1800FF for the *cours semi-intensif* in winter (eight hours a week) and, in summer, 2700FF (15 hours a week over three weeks). The *cours intensif* classes (20 hours a week over four weeks in winter, 25 hours a week over three weeks in summer) cost 3800FF and are held in the morning. The *cours extensif* (three hours a week for three months), which meets at night, costs 1800FF. Another option is the four-week grammar workshop (three hours a week) for 750FF. The school's office is open weekdays from 9 am to 6 pm. If there's space, you can sign up until the first day of class.

Alliance Française
(Map 4; ☎ 01 45 44 38 28; fax 01 45 44 89 42; info@paris.alliancefrancaise.fr; metro Saint Placide), 101 Blvd Raspail, 75006. This is the Paris headquarters of a venerable institution whose brief is to promote French language and civilisation around the world. Month-long French courses at all levels – but of variable quality, according to readers – begin during the first week of each month; registration takes place during the five business days before the start of each session. If there's space, it's possible to enrol for just two weeks. *Intensif* courses, which meet for four hours a day, cost 3050FF a month; *extensif* courses, which involve two hours of class a day, cost 1525FF a month. The enrolment fee is 250FF. The registration office is open Monday to Friday from 9 am to 5 pm. Bring your passport and a passport-sized photo. Payment, which must be made in advance, can be done with travellers cheques or credit cards. The mailing address of the Alliance Française is 101 Blvd Raspail, 75270 Paris CEDEX 06.

Cours de Langue et Civilisation Françaises de la Sorbonne
(☎ 01 40 46 22 11; fax 01 40 46 32 29), 47 Rue des Écoles, 75005. The Sorbonne's famous French Civilisation Course, from which one of the authors graduated sometime in the late Dark Ages, has courses in French language and civilisation for students of all levels. Costs vary but a four-week summer course should cost about 3250FF while 16 to 20 hours a week of lectures and tutorials costs between 6350 and 7400FF per semester. The instructors take a very academic and stilted (though solid) approach to language teaching; don't expect to learn how to haggle in a market or cuss about road hogs even after a year here.

Eurocentre
(☎ 01 40 46 72 00; fax 01 40 46 72 06; parinfi@eurocentres.com; metro Odéon), 13 Passage Dauphine, 75006. This is the Paris branch of the Zürich-based, nonprofit Eurocentre chain, which has schools in 10 countries. Two/four-week intensive courses with 12 to 15 participants, well reviewed by Lonely Planet readers, cost 3750/7150FF, including – each week – 25 50-minute lessons, three lectures and five to 10 hours in the multimedia learning centre. New courses begin every two, three or four weeks.

Institut Parisien de Langue et de Civilisation Françaises
(Map 4; ☎ 01 40 56 09 53; fax 01 43 06 46 30; institut.parisien@dial.oleane.com; metro Dupleix), 87 Blvd de Grenelle, 75015. Four-week courses with a maximum of 12 students per class cost 2440/3600/6040FF for 10/15/25 hours a week; six-week courses are 3620/5340/8960FF. The office is open on weekdays from 8.30 am to 5 pm.

Langue Onze
(Map 3; ☎ 01 43 38 22 87; fax 01 43 38 36 01; metro Parmentier), 15 Rue Gambey, 11e. This small, independent language school gets good reports. Four/two week intensive courses are 3300/1900FF, evening classes start at 2000FF a trimester and individual lessons are 120FF an hour. Classes have a maximum of nine students.

Cooking Courses

The major cooking schools in Paris include École Le Cordon Bleu (☎ 01 53 68 22 50; fax 01 48 56 03 96; metro Vaugirard) at 8 Rue Léon Delhomme, 75015; École Ritz Escoffier (☎ 01 43 16 30 50; fax 01 43 16 31 50; metro Concorde) at 38 Rue Cambon, 75001; and La Toque d'Or (☎ 01 45 44 86 51; fax 01 45 44 86 81; metro Varenne) at 55 Rue de Varenne, 75007. Tuition varies widely but count on paying US$200 to US$500 a day.

Places to Stay

To determine where any form of accommodation is located, turn to the map indicated before the venue's telephone number. Also remember that in budget hotel rooms without a private shower or bath, you may be charged from 10FF to as much as 30FF each time you use the hall shower. Even in the middle category not all places will come with a bath or shower.

ACCOMMODATION SERVICES
Accueil des Jeunes en France (AJF)

No matter what age you are, the AJF (Map 8; ☎ 01 42 77 87 80; metro Rambuteau), at 119 Rue Saint Martin (4e) across the square from the Centre Pompidou, can *always* find you accommodation, even in summer. It works like this: you come in on the day (or the day before) you need a place to stay and pay the AJF for the accommodation (plus a 10FF fee). The staff then give you a voucher to take to the hostel or hotel. Prices for doubles start at about 250FF and, thanks to special AJF discounts, are often less than the price you'd pay if you contacted the hotel yourself. The earlier in the day you come, the better; the conveniently located and cheap places always go first. AJF is open Monday to Friday from 10 am to 6.45 pm and on Saturday to 5.45 pm. Be prepared for long queues in summer.

Tourist Office

The main Paris tourist office (Map 2; ☎ 01 49 52 53 54; metro George V) at 127 Ave des Champs-Élysées (8e) and its three annexes (in the Gare du Nord and Gare de Lyon and, in summer, at the base of the Eiffel Tower) can find you a place to stay for the night of the day you stop by. They also have a number of brochures on homestays, including one on *pensions de famille*, which are similar to B&Bs. Pensions de famille in Paris include the following:

Pension Bairi (☎ 01 47 70 78 72; metro Poissonière), 62 Rue du Faubourg Poissonière, 10e. Singles/doubles 150/220FF or 240/400FF half-pension.
Pension Les Gravières (☎ 01 47 27 64 48; metro Trocadéro), 5 Rue des Sablons, 16e. Singles with breakfast 140FF.
Pension Ladagnous (☎ 01 43 26 79 32; metro Vavin or Notre Dame des Champs), 78 Rue d'Assas, 6e. Singles/doubles 265/380FF half-pension.
Pension Les Marroniers (☎ 01 43 26 37 71; fax 01 43 26 07 72; metro Vavin or Notre Dame des Champs), 78 Rue d'Assas, 6e. Half-pension singles 190 to 395FF, doubles 398 to 444FF.
Pension Au Palais Gourmand (☎ 01 45 48 24 15; fax 01 42 22 33 41; metro Vavin or Notre Dame des Champs), 120 Blvd Raspail, 6e. Half-pension singles 297 to 342FF, doubles 397 to 444FF.
Residence Cardinal (☎ 01 48 74 16 16; metro Liège or Place de Clichy), 4 Rue Cardinal Mercier, 9e. Singles with breakfast 160 to 190FF, doubles 220 to 270FF.

FAMILY STAYS

Under an arrangement known as *hôtes payants* (literally, 'paying guests') or *hébergement chez l'habitant* (lodging with the occupants of private homes), students, young people and tourists can stay with French families. In general you rent a room and have access (sometimes limited) to the family's kitchen and telephone. Many language schools (see Courses in the Things to See & Do chapter) arrange homestays for their students.

For details on each agency's prices and conditions, it's a good idea to call, write or fax at least six weeks in advance, though last-minute arrangements are sometimes possible.

Students and tourists alike should count on paying 3000 to 5200FF a month, 1200 to 1500FF a week or 130 to 300FF a day for a single room, including breakfast.

Accueil Familial des Jeunes Étrangers (☎ 01 45 49 15 57; fax 01 45 44 60 48; metro Sèvres Babylone), 23 Rue du Cherche Midi, 75006. This organisation can find you a room with a family for 3000 to 3500FF a month, including breakfast. For stays of less than a month, expect to pay about 140FF a day. There's a subscription fee of 500FF for stays of less than a month. Longer stays incur a 100FF fee per month.

Amicale Culturelle Internationale (☎ 01 47 42 94 21; fax 01 49 24 02 67; metro Havre Caumartin), 27 Rue Godot de Mauroy, 75009. This agency can arrange stays in French homes in Paris (1500FF a week for B&B, 1800FF for half-board) and elsewhere in France. The minimum stay is two weeks.

France Lodge (☎ 01 53 20 09 09; fax 01 53 20 01 25; metro Le Peletier), 41 Rue La Fayette, 75009. This nonprofit organisation arranges accommodation in private homes and apartments. In Paris, prices start at about 130FF a night per person (cheaper by the month). Annual membership costs 85FF, and payment must be made in French francs.

SHORT-TERM FLATS

Allô Logement Temporaire (Map 8; ☎ 01 42 72 00 06; fax 01 42 72 03 11; metro Rambuteau) at 64 Rue du Temple (3e) is a nonprofit organisation that acts as a liaison between flat owners and foreigners looking for furnished apartments for periods of one week to one year. Small studios of about 20 sq metres cost 1000 to 3000FF a week. October, when university classes resume, is the hardest month to find a place, but over the summer it's usually possible to find something within a matter of days. Before any deals are signed, the company will arrange for you to talk to the owner by phone, assisted by an interpreter if necessary. There is a 300FF annual membership fee and, in addition to the rent and one month deposit (paid directly to the owner), a charge of 200FF for each month you rent. The office is open Monday to Friday from noon to 8 pm.

Another outfit with short-term furnished apartments available is AES (☎ 01 45 35 02 50 or ☎ 01 45 35 01 01; fax 01 45 35 01 00; asiacenter@aol.com; metro Glacière) at 8 Rue des Tanneries (13e).

SERVICED FLATS

Serviced flats – like staying in a hotel without all the extras – are an excellent option for those on a budget, particularly those in small groups. There are several locations around Paris.

Citadines Apparthôtels This hotel chain with apartment-style rooms has 10 properties in Paris including one on the Blvd du Montparnasse (see Hotels – 6e Arrondissement), in Montmartre (see Hotels – Montmartre & Pigalle), near the Opéra Garnier (see Hotels – Gare Saint Lazarre & Grands Boulevards Areas) and east of the Gare de Lyon (see Hotels – Bastille Area). Rates are substantially cheaper if you stay longer than seven days in any season.

Flatotel International (Map 4; ☎ 01 45 75 62 20; fax 01 45 79 73 30; metro Charles Michels), 14 Rue du Théâtre, 15e. Studios measuring 35 sq metres cost 680 to 750FF a day and two to five-room apartments are 1200 to 2900FF. All are equipped with kitchen facilities. The minimum stay is one day.

Hôtel et Résidence Trousseau (Map 5; ☎ 01 48 05 55 55; fax 01 48 05 83 97; metro Ledru Rollin), 13 Rue Trousseau, 11e. This hotel is perfect for families or groups of friends. The kitchenette-equipped rooms or apartments for two/three/four/six people are large and modern and cost 540/830/1100/1450FF (including weekly maid service) if you stay at least three nights.

RENTING A FLAT

The hardest time to find an apartment – especially a cheap one – in Paris is October, when everyone is back from their summer holidays and students are searching for digs for the academic year. Moderately priced places are easiest to come by toward the end of university semesters, ie between Christmas and early February and over the summer (July to September).

About 2000FF a month will get you a tiny garret room (9 sq metre minimum) with a washbasin but with no telephone, no proper place to cook and no private toilet. There may not even be a communal shower. These rooms, often occupied by students, are frequently converted *chambres de bonne* (maids' quarters) on the 6th or 7th floor of old apartment buildings without lifts but in decent neighbourhoods.

Small (15 to 30 sq metre), unfurnished/furnished studios with attached toilet start at about 90/100FF per sq metre a month. The per-metre cost theoretically goes down the larger the place is and the farther away it is from the city centre.

If you've exhausted your word-of-mouth sources (expats, students, compatriots living temporarily in Paris), it's a good idea to check out the bulletin boards at the American Church (see Cultural Centres in the Facts for the Visitor chapter). People who advertise there are unlikely to fear renting to foreigners, will probably speak some English and might be willing to sign a relatively short-term contract. *France USA Contacts – FUSAC*, a free periodical issued every two weeks and available at English-language bookshops, Anglophone embassies and the American Church as well as the bulletin board at Shakespeare & Co (see Bookshops in the Shopping chapter) might also have a few leads.

If you know a bit of French (or someone who does), you'll be able to consult several periodicals available from newsagents: *De Particulier à Particulier* (15F) and *La Centrale des Particuliers* (17F), both issued each Thursday, and *À Vendre à Louer* (7FF). You might also try the daily newspaper *Le Figaro*'s publication *Locations Ventes* (9FF). You'll have to do your calling in French though. If you have access to a telephone, you could place an apartment-wanted ad in *De Particulier à Particulier* and have people call you.

HOUSEBOATS

For groups of four or more, it can be cheaper – and a lot more fun – to stay on a rented canal boat than in a mid-range hotel: count on about 1500FF per person a week, including mooring fees. For details on rentals, see Canal Boating under Activities in the Things to See & Do chapter.

If you arrive by pleasure boat (or rent one), you can anchor it quite cheaply at the Port de Plaisance de Paris-Arsenal, 4e and 12e (Map 5), which stretches for 500m from the Seine (metro Quai de la Rapée) to Place de la Bastille (metro Bastille). About 200 moorings for vessels up to 25m long are available by the day, month or year. The daily rates for a 6m to 8m boat up to 2.5m wide are between 45FF (October to March) and 87FF (June to August); monthly rates are quite a bit cheaper. Larger boats (10m to 12m) range from 87 to 163FF. Electricity and water link-ups are included in the daily rates. Showers, mail service, fuel and laundry facilities are also available; long-term renters can have telephones installed. About 75% of the people staying here are foreigners.

The *Capitainerie* (harbour master's office; Map 5; ☎ 01 43 41 39 32; fax 01 44 74 02 66; metro Quai de la Rapée) at 11 Blvd de la Bastille (12e), open daily from 9 am (8 am in July and August) to 6, 7 or 8 pm, has details on fees and regulations. Reservations are not necessary for short-term stays.

CAMPING

Camping du Bois de Boulogne (☎ 01 45 24 30 00; fax 01 42 24 42 95) on Allée du Bord de l'Eau (16e), the only camping ground within the Paris city limits, is along the Seine at the far western edge of the Bois de Boulogne. Two people with a tent are charged 60 to 77FF (89 to 118FF with a vehicle) depending on the season, and reception at this 7 hectare site is staffed 24 hours a day. It's very crowded in summer, but there's always space for a small tent (though not necessarily for a car). There are also fully equipped caravans accommodating four people available for between 256 and 461FF, depending on the type and the season. The Porte Maillot metro stop, 4.5km to the east, is linked to the camping ground by RATP bus No 244 (runs 6 am to 8.30 pm) and, from around Easter to September, by a privately operated shuttle bus (11FF).

Paris' main tourist office has a sheet listing dozens of other camping grounds in the Île de France.

HOSTELS & FOYERS

Paris' hostels and *foyers* (student residence halls) don't come cheaply. Beds under 100FF are pretty few and far between, so two people who don't mind sleeping in the same bed may find basic rooms in budget hotels a less expensive proposition. Groups of three or four willing to share two or three beds will save even more.

Some hostels allow guests to stay for a maximum of three nights, particularly in summer, though places which have upper age limits (30, for example) tend not to enforce them. Only official *auberges de jeunesse* (youth hostels) require guests to present Hostelling International (HI) cards.

Curfews at Paris hostels are generally at 1 or 2 am. Few hostels accept telephone reservations from individuals, but those which do are noted in the text.

Louvre & Les Halles Areas

You can't get any more central than the 1er arrondissement between the Louvre and the Forum des Halles.

Centre International BVJ Louvre (Map 7; ☎ 01 53 00 90 90; fax 01 53 00 90 91; metro Louvre-Rivoli), 20 Rue Jean-Jacques Rousseau, 1er. This modern, 200-bed BVJ hostel charges 120FF (including breakfast) for a bunk in a single-sex room for two to 10 people. Guests should be aged under 35. Rooms are accessible

---

Budget Accommodation & Bookings

A veritable plague of renovations, redecorations and other improvements has turned many of Paris' finest flea-bag hotels into bright, spotless two-star places where sheets are changed every day and receptionists aren't rude. With a little shower cubicle in each room, guests no longer meet each other on the landing for a chat while waiting, towel-clad, for the shower to be free. Another little bit of Paris romance gone forever ...

But all is not lost. Outside the inner ring of arrondissements, quite a few budget hotels – places whose showerless, toiletless doubles cost less than two hostel beds – have so far been spared the onslaught of investment and upgrading. There are clusters of such places in the Marais (4e) and Montmartre (18e) as well as in the 10e, 11e, 13e and 14e arrondissements.

Most cheap hotels – especially the well run ones in desirable or central neighbourhoods – fill up quickly, even in winter, and in July and August almost all of them are completely booked out. It's a good idea to make reservations as many weeks ahead as possible. A three-minute international phone call to reserve a room (followed, if necessary, by written confirmation and/or deposit) is a lot cheaper than wasting your first day in Paris looking for a place to stay.

If you will be looking for cheap accommodation after arriving in Paris, your best bet, if possible, is to arrive early in the morning and begin your quest immediately. The best time to phone hotels (or drop by) is when yesterday's guests are liable to be checking out (ie from about 9 am). Shoestring travellers who arrive in the late afternoon or evening without reserved accommodation risk having to choose between a night in the train station or on a park bench or, worse, budgetary blowout.

One tip: hotels that cater to domestic businesspeople, often located in the less touristed arrondissements (ie 11e, 13e, 14e and 20e), tend to have plenty of space on weekends and during August when everyone in Paris seems to go on holiday, and they often offer special discounts at those times. However, they are often booked out from Monday to Thursday and – like hotels all over town – during Paris' convention season (September and October).

Many places listed under 'budget' in this chapter also have rooms in the middle range with shower and toilet. The prices in this chapter do not include the *taxe de séjour* (city tourist tax). At camping grounds and hotels with no stars it comes to 1FF per person per night. The tax on hotels with one/two/three/four stars is 3/5/6/7FF.

from 2.30 pm on the day you arrive and all day long after that. Kitchen facilities are not available. There is almost always space in the morning, even in summer. If you're on your way over, you can call and request that they hold a spot for a few hours. Be warned that this hostel is often booked out by groups.

Marais

The Marais (4e) is one of the liveliest sections of the city centre and its hostels are among the city's finest.

The Maison Internationale de la Jeunesse et des Étudiants runs three *hôtels de jeunes* (young people's hostels) in attractively renovated 17th and 18th-century residences in the Marais. Make reservations for all three MIJE hostels by calling the switchboard – they'll hold a bed for you until 3 pm, and the maximum stay is seven nights. During summer and other busy periods, there may not be space after about mid-morning. There's a 10FF annual membership fee.

MIJE Fauconnier (Map 8; metro Saint Paul or Pont Marie), 11 Rue du Fauconnier is a 118-bed hostel one block south of MIJE Fourcy. A bed in a shower-equipped, single-sex dorm room for four to eight people costs 125FF (137FF in a triple, 152F in a double, 198FF in a single), including breakfast. Rooms are closed from noon to 3 pm; curfew is from 1 to 7 am. Costs and phone number details are the same for the other two.

MIJE Fourcy (Map 8; ☎ 01 42 74 23 45; fax 01 40 27 81 64; metro Saint Paul), 6 Rue de Fourcy, 4e. This 207-bed place is the largest of the three hostels. There's also a cheap restaurant here with a three-course *menu* with a drink for 52FF and a *plat du jour* plus drink for 40FF.

MIJE Maubuisson (Map 8; metro Hôtel de Ville), 12 Rue des Barres, with 114 beds, is half a block south of the *mairie* (town hall) of the 4e.

Latin Quarter

The lively, student-filled Latin Quarter in the western part of the 5e arrondissement is ideal for young people.

Centre International BVJ Quartier Latin (Map 8; ☎ 01 43 29 34 80; fax 01 42 33 40 53; metro Maubert Mutualité), 44 Rue des Bernardins, 5e. This hostel, which welcomes individual

travellers over groups, has the same tariffs and rules as the Centre International BVJ Louvre (see Louvre & Les Halles Areas). Long-term singles/doubles with use of kitchen are also available for 3900/7200FF a month.

Y & H Hostel (Map 5; ☎ 01 45 35 09 53; fax 01 47 07 22 24; young@youngandhappy.fr; metro Place Monge), 80 Rue Mouffetard, 5e. This clean, very friendly, English-speaking place – the name is short for 'young and happy' – is in the hopping, happening centre of the Latin Quarter and is very popular with a younger crowd. The rooms are closed from 11 am to 5 pm but reception is always open. A bed in a cramped room with washbasin for two to four people costs 97FF, including breakfast; showers are free. The 2 am curfew is strictly enforced. The TV in the lounge area receives CNN and MTV. Reservations can be made if you pay a deposit for the first night. In summer, the best way to get a place is to stop by at about 9 am. There is a Franprix supermarket next door at 82 Rue Mouffetard.

Bastille Area

The relatively untouristed 11e and 12e (the areas north-east, east and south-east of Place de la Bastille) are unpretentious, working-class areas.

Auberge de Jeunesse Jules Ferry (Map 3; ☎ 01 43 57 55 60; fax 01 40 21 79 92; auberge@micronet.fr; metro République or Oberkampf), 8 Blvd Jules Ferry, 11e. This official hostel, a few blocks east of Place de la République, is a bit institutional, but the atmosphere is fairly relaxed and – an added bonus – they don't accept groups. Beds cost 113FF in a four or six-person room and 118FF in a double, including breakfast. Rooms are locked from 10.30 am to 2 pm. You have to have an HI card to stay here (available for 114FF) or pay an extra 19FF per night. You can send/receive emails and surf the Internet from the computer in the reception area (connection 5FF). There is a Franprix supermarket down the block at 28 Blvd Jules Ferry. The only other official hostel in central Paris is near the Porte de Bagnolet in the 20e (see 20e Arrondissement).

Auberge Internationale des Jeunes (Map 5; ☎ 01 47 00 62 00; fax 01 47 00 33 16; aij@aijparis .com; metro Ledru Rollin), 10 Rue Trousseau,

11e. This clean and very friendly hostel, 700m east of Place de la Bastille, attracts a young, international crowd and is very full in summer. Beds in dorms for two to six people cost just 81FF from November to February, 91FF from March to October, including breakfast. Rooms are closed for cleaning between 10 am and 3 pm. You can book in advance, and they'll hold a bed for you if you call from the train station.

Centre International de Séjour de Paris Ravel (Map 1; ☎ 01 44 75 60 00; metro Porte de Vincennes), 4-6 Ave Maurice Ravel, 12e. The 230-bed CISP Ravel, on the south-eastern edge of the city, charges 113FF per bed in a 12-person dormitory, 138FF in a two to five-person room and 181FF in a single, including breakfast. There are no upper age limits. Reception is open from 6.30 am to 1.30 am. Individuals (as opposed to groups, which predominate) can make telephone reservations up to two days ahead. To get there from the Porte de Vincennes metro station, walk south on Blvd Soult, turn left onto Rue Jules Lemaître and then go right onto Rue Maurice Ravel.

Maison Internationale des Jeunes pour la Culture et pour la Paix (MIJCP; Map 1; ☎ 01 43 71 99 21; fax 01 43 71 78 58; metro Faidherbe Chaligny), 4 Rue Titon, 11e. This MIJPC, 1.3km east of Place de la Bastille, charges 110FF for a bed in a spartan dorm room for up to eight people, including breakfast. Curfew is from 2 to 6 am. The upper age limit of 30 is not strictly enforced. Telephone reservations are accepted – your chance of finding a place is greatest if you call (or stop by) between 8 and 10 am. The maximum stay is theoretically three days, but you can usually stay for a week.

Résidence Bastille (Map 5; ☎ 01 43 79 53 86; metro Voltaire), 151 Ave Ledru Rollin, 11e. This 150-bed hostel, open year round, is about 900m north-east of Place de la Bastille. Beds in rooms for two to four people cost 120FF (110FF from November to February), including breakfast, and there are singles for 171FF (160FF in the low season). Reception is open for check-in from 7 am to 12.30 pm and 2 to 10 pm. Curfew is at 1 am – if you'll be coming back later, inform them in advance. Lockers are available between 9 am and 6 pm for 20FF a day.

Chinatown & Montparnasse Areas

The southern 13e, 14e and 15e arrondissements are not particularly exciting places, but neither are they very far from the Left Bank's major sights.

Aloha Hostel (Map 4; ☎ 01 42 73 03 03; fax 01 42 73 14 14; metro Volontaires), 1 Rue Borromée, 15e. Run by the same people (and with the same prices) as the Three Ducks (see later in this section) but much more laid-back and quiet, this place is about 1km west of Gare Montparnasse. Rooms, which have two to six beds and some with showers, are closed from 11 am to 5 pm but reception is always open. Curfew is at 2 am. Kitchen facilities and safe-deposit boxes are available.

Centre International de Séjour de Paris Kellermann (Map 1; ☎ 01 44 16 37 38; metro Porte d'Italie), 17 Blvd Kellermann, 13e. The 350-bed CISP Kellermann has beds in dorms accommodating two to four people for 138FF, and 113FF in those with eight beds. Basic singles are 156FF or 186FF with shower and WC. A double with facilities costs 312FF. Except on Friday and Saturday nights, curfew is at 1.30 am. The maximum stay is five or six nights. Kitchen facilities are not available. Telephone reservations can be made up to 48 hours before you arrive. Facilities for disabled people are available.

Foyer International d'Accueil de Paris Jean Monnet (Map 1; ☎ 01 45 89 89 15; fax 01 45 81 63 91; metro Glacière), 30 Rue Cabanis, 14e. FIAP Jean Monnet, a few blocks south-east of Place Denfert Rochereau, has modern, carpeted rooms for eight/four/two people – pretty luxurious by hostel standards – for 131/161/184FF per person (including breakfast); singles are 281FF. Rooms specially outfitted for *handicapés* (disabled people) are available. Curfew is from 2 to 6 am. Telephone reservations are accepted up to 15 days ahead, but priority is given to groups.

Foyer des Jeunes Filles (Map 1; ☎ 01 44 16 22 22; fax 01 45 65 46 20; metro Glacière), 234 Rue de Tolbiac, 13e. Also known as Foyer Tolbiac, this friendly, Protestant-run dormitory accepts women only, with no minimum or maximum stay and no upper age limit from mid-June to mid-September (and, if there's space, during the rest of the year). A single room costs 120FF (including breakfast except on Sunday) plus an annual fee of 30FF. There are kitchens on each floor. Reservations can be made by phone or fax, and reception is open 24 hours a day. There's no curfew. The *foyer* is about 600m south of the nearest metro stop so you might want to take bus No 21 or 62. Orlybus stops nearby.

Maison des Clubs UNESCO (Map 1; ☎ 01 43 36 00 63; fax 01 45 35 05 96; girardin@fiap. asso .fr; metro Glacière), 43 Rue de la Glacière, 13e. This rather institutional place charges 125FF for a bed in a large, unsurprising room for three or four people; singles/doubles are 165/145FF per person. In the multi-bed rooms, priority is given to 18 to 30-year-olds, but older travellers are accepted if there's space. Beds booked by telephone are usually held until 2 pm – if you'll be arriving later, ring them on the day of your arrival.

Three Ducks Hostel (Map 4; ☎ 01 48 42 04 05; metro Félix Faure or Commerce), 6 Place Étienne Pernet, 15e. Named after three ducks who used to live in the courtyard, the friendly, down-to-earth Trois Canards, at the southern end of Rue du Commerce, is a favourite with young backpackers, whose more exuberant exponents apparently get very noisy at night; we have had a litany of complaints from readers about loud music, drunken parties, tiny kitchens and ice-cold showers. A bunk bed in a basic room for two to eight people costs 97FF (87FF from November to April), including breakfast. Telephone reservations are accepted on the day of arrival. Kitchen facilities are available. Rooms are closed between 11 am and 5 pm and there's a 2 am curfew.

Montmartre & Pigalle

Both the 9e and 18e arrondissements have fine hostels, one them brand new.

Le Village Hostel (Map 9; ☎ 01 42 64 22 02; fax 01 42 64 22 04; village@levillage-hostel.fr; metro Anvers), 20 Rue d'Orsel, 18e. This fine new 26-room hostel with beamed ceilings and views of Sacré Cœur has beds in rooms for two to six people for 117FF (97FF from November to March) and doubles/triples/quads for 147/137/127FF per person (137/117/107FF in winter). Singles are 180FF. All rooms have showers and WC, prices include breakfast and kitchen facilities are available. There's also a bar here and a lovely terrace for sitting outside.

Woodstock Hostel (Map 3; ☎ 01 48 78 87 76; fax 01 48 78 01 63; metro Anvers), 48 Rue Rodier, 9e. This hostel is just down the hill from rowdy Pigalle in a quiet, residential quarter. A dorm bed in a room for four to six people costs 77FF in the off-season, and in a double room a bed is 87FF; both includ e breakfast. In summer prices rise to 87FF and 97FF respectively. There's a 2 am curfew and rooms are shut from 11.30 am to 5 pm.

20e Arrondissement

Auberge de Jeunesse D'Artagnan (Map 1; ☎ 01 40 32 34 56; fax 01 40 32 34 55; 101717. 3452@compuserve.com; metro Porte de Bagnolet), 80 Rue Vitruve. This official hostel, away from the centre of the action but just one metro stop from the Paris-Gallieni international bus station, has rooms with two to eight beds, big lockers, laundry facilities, Internet access and even a cinema! It has the same rules and rates as the Auberge de Jeunesse Jules Ferry (see Bastille Area).

STUDENT ACCOMMODATION

The Union Nationale des Étudiants Locataires (National Union of Student Renters; Map 1; ☎ 01 45 41 58 18; Minitel 3615 UNEL; metro Pernety) at 2 Rue Pernety (14e) will let anyone with a student card who pays the 120FF annual fee (photo required) consult its lists of available apartments and chambres de bonne. The usual rental period is 12 months, though six-month or one-semester leases do exist. The office is open on weekdays from 10 am to noon and 2 to 6 pm (open afternoons only from about January to April); year round; Wednesday hours are 10 am to 8 pm.

The Paris tourist office's sheet entitled *Logements pour Étudiants* lists other organisations which can help find accommodation for students who'll be in Paris for at least a semester. The so-called *foyers d'étudiants à Paris* are reserved for students aged 18 to 25.

HOTELS – LOUVRE & LES HALLES AREAS

This area – for the most part the 1er with bits of the western 4e and eastern 8e – may be very central, but don't expect to find tranquillity or many bargains; in fact, this is the area to come if you really want to blow the budget. Both airports are linked to the Châtelet-Les Halles metro/RER station by Roissyrail and Orlyval.

Budget

Hôtel de Lille (Map 7; ☎ 01 42 33 33 42; metro Palais Royal), 8 Rue du Pélican, 1er. Clean singles/doubles (200/230FF) come with washbasin, bidet and cheap ceiling tiles at this 13-room place. Doubles with shower are 280FF. A token for a 15-minute shower costs an appalling 30FF.

Middle

Hôtel Saint Honoré (Map 7; ☎ 01 42 36 20 38; fax 01 42 21 44 08; metro Châtelet), 85 Rue Saint Honoré, 1er. This upgraded but cramped one-star place offers doubles/quads from 280/450FF; more spacious doubles are 320 to 350FF.

Top End

Grand Hôtel de Champagne (Map 7; ☎ 01 42 36 60 00; fax 01 45 08 43 33; metro Châtelet), 17 Rue Jean Lantier, 1er. This very comfortable, three-star hotel has 42 rooms costing from 596 to 721FF (in July and August) up to 652 to 812FF (in June and from September to November).

Hôtel Brighton (Map 2; ☎ 01 47 03 61 61; fax 01 42 60 41 78; metro Tuileries), 218 Rue de Rivoli, 1er. This is a three-star, 70-room establishment with lovely singles/doubles/triples starting at 545/580/1025FF and climbing to 915/950/1125FF, depending on the season and the room. The rooms that overlook the Jardin des Tuileries are the most popular; those on the 4th and 5th floors afford views over the trees to the Seine.

Hôtel de Crillon (Map 2; ☎ 01 44 71 15 00; fax 01 44 71 15 02; metro Concorde), 10 Place de la Concorde, 8e. The colonnaded, two-centuries-old Crillon has sparkling public areas (including Les Ambassadeurs restaurant with two Michelin stars) sumptuously decorated with chandeliers, original sculptures, gilt mouldings, tapestries and inlaid furniture. This is the epitome of French luxury. Spacious

singles/doubles with pink marble bathrooms start at 2600/3250FF or from 2950/3550 in May-June and September-October. The cheapest suites are 4900FF, larger ones go for 6800 to 8500FF. Breakfast is another 170FF (continental) or 230FF (American).

Hôtel Meurice (Map 2; ☎ 01 44 58 10 10; fax 01 44 58 10 15; metro Tuileries), 228 Rue de Rivoli, 1er. The Meurice's stunning public spaces, modelled on Versailles, positively ooze elegance: designed at the turn of the century, they are decorated with gilded furniture, chandeliers and trompe l'œil paintings. Singles/doubles start at 2450/2800FF and reach 2800/3300FF, depending on the room and season. Junior suites go for 5500FF, apartments for 6500 to 9000FF. Continental/American breakfasts are 150/195FF.

Hôtel Ritz (Map 2; ☎ 01 43 16 30 30; fax 01 43 16 36 68; metro Opéra), 15 Place Vendôme, 1er. As one of the world's most celebrated and expensive hotels, the 142-room, 45-suite Ritz has sparkling singles/doubles starting at 2900/3500FF (3300/3900FF in May-June and September-October). Junior suites begin at 4700FF (5200FF); regular suites are 6000FF and up. Facilities include a deluxe health club, a swimming pool and squash courts. The hotel restaurant, L'Espadon, has two Michelin stars, and the renovated Hemingway Bar is where Papa imbibed.

HOTELS – MARAIS

Despite gentrification, the Marais (4e) still has a few cheapies left. There's also a good choice of middle-range places, as well as some top-end hotels in the vicinity of the elegant Place des Vosges.

Budget

Hôtel de la Herse d'Or (Map 8; ☎ 01 48 87 84 09; fax 01 48 87 94 01; metro Bastille), 20 Rue Saint Antoine, 4e. This is a friendly place with unsurprising, serviceable singles with washbasin for 160FF and with basin and toilet for 200FF; doubles with toilet and a small shower are 260 to 295FF. Hall showers are 10FF.

Hôtel Moderne (Map 8; ☎ 01 48 87 97 05; metro Saint Paul), 3 Rue Caron, 4e. The basic singles/doubles come with washbasin and start at 130/160FF; doubles with shower are 190FF

(220FF with toilet). There's a toilet and shower (15FF) on the stairs halfway between each floor. Telephone reservations are accepted up to a week before your scheduled arrival.

Hôtel Le Palais de Fès (Map 8; ☎ 01 42 72 03 68; fax 01 42 60 49 33; metro Hôtel de Ville), 41 Rue du Roi de Sicile, 4e. Fairly large, modern doubles cost 200FF with washbasin, 250FF with shower and 280FF with shower and toilet. Singles start at 150FF. Hall showers are 15FF. Reception is in the Moroccan restaurant on the ground floor.

Hôtel Pratic (Map 8; ☎ 01 48 87 80 47; fax 01 48 87 40 04; metro Saint Paul), 9 Rue d'Ormesson, 4e. This is a 23-room hotel with nondescript singles/doubles from 180/245FF (2450/290FF with shower). Doubles with bath and toilet are 340FF.

Hôtel Rivoli (Map 8; ☎ 01 42 72 08 41; metro Hôtel de Ville), 44 Rue de Rivoli, 4e. This hotel on the corner of Rue des Mauvais Garçons is one of the best deals in town. Basic and somewhat noisy rooms with washbasin start at 160FF. Singles with shower are 180FF; doubles with bath but no toilet are 190 to 220FF and a double with bath and toilet is 250FF. The hall shower (20FF) is sometimes lukewarm. The front door is locked from 2 to 6.30 am.

Hôtel Sully (Map 8; ☎ 01 42 78 49 32; metro Bastille), 48 Rue Saint Antoine, 4e. You'll find one-star doubles for 200FF with washbasin, 250FF with shower and 270FF with shower and toilet at this hotel, only one block south of Place des Vosges. A two-bed triple with shower and toilet costs 300FF. The hall shower is free.

Middle

Hôtel Castex (Map 8; ☎ 01 42 72 31 52; fax 01 42 72 57 91; metro Bastille), 5 Rue Castex, 4e. This cheery, 27-room establishment has been run by the same family since 1919. Quiet, old-fashioned (but immaculate) singles/doubles with shower cost 240/320FF (290 to 360FF with toilet, too). Triples/quads are 460/530FF. If possible, reserve at least four weeks ahead.

Hôtel Le Compostelle (Map 8; ☎ 01 42 78 59 99; fax 01 40 29 05 18; metro Hôtel de Ville), 31 Rue du Roi de Sicile, 4e. This three-star place is tasteful but not fancy. It has 26 singles/doubles which come with TV (from 300/400FF). Rooms with bath start at 490FF.

Hôtel de Nice (Map 8; ☎ 01 42 78 55 29; fax 01 42 78 36 07; metro Hôtel de Ville), 42bis Rue

de Rivoli, 4e. The English-speaking owner of this especially warm, family-run place has 23 comfortable singles/doubles/triples/quads for 380/450/550/650FF. Many rooms have balconies on which guests have been known to sunbathe.

Hôtel de la Place des Vosges (Map 8; ☎ 01 42 72 60 46; fax 01 42 72 02 64; metro Bastille), 12 Rue de Birague, 4e. Superbly situated right next to Place des Vosges, this 16-room, two-star place has rather average singles from 330FF (448FF in summer) and doubles with bathrooms from 475 to 664FF. There's a tiny lift from the 1st floor.

Top End

Grand Hôtel Malher (Map 8; ☎ 01 42 72 60 92; fax 01 42 72 25 37; metro Saint Paul), 5 Rue Malher, 4e. The 31 nicely appointed singles/doubles at this family-run, two-star establishment start from 475/605FF (580/730FF during high-season periods).

Hôtel Axial Beaubourg (Map 8; ☎ 01 42 72 72 22; fax 01 42 72 03 53; metro Hôtel de Ville), 11 Rue du Temple, 4e. The name of this three-star place says it all: modern mixed with historic. It's in the heart of the Marais and charges from 450FF for singles and 530FF for doubles.

Hôtel Central Marais (Map 8; ☎ 01 48 87 56 08; fax 01 42 77 06 27; metro Hôtel de Ville), 2 Rue Sainte Croix de la Bretonnerie, 4e. This seven-room, mostly gay male hotel also welcomes lesbians. Singles/doubles with one bathroom for every two rooms are 400/485FF; suites for two/three people are 595/720FF. After 3 pm, reception is around the corner in the bar (33 Rue Vieille du Temple). Reservations should be made four to six weeks ahead – they'll hold a room if you give them a Visa or MasterCard number.

HOTELS – ÎLE DE LA CITÉ & ÎLE SAINT LOUIS

The islands in the Seine are an easy walk from all of central Paris. Believe it or not, the only hotel on the Île de la Cité (1er) is a cheapie. The chi-chi Île de Saint Louis (4e) remains as pricey as ever.

Budget

Hôtel Henri IV (Map 6; ☎ 01 43 54 44 53; metro Cité or Saint Michel), 25 Place Dauphine, 1er. This old-fashioned, very popular hotel is a bit tattered and worn but has 21 adequate rooms with one bed from 116 to 260FF, two beds from 200 to 270FF (breakfast is included). Showers in the hall cost 15FF. The three rooms with their own showers cost 230 to 270FF. Reception is open until 8 pm but make reservations a month in advance. Credit cards are not accepted.

Top End

Hôtel des Deux Îles (Map 8; ☎ 01 43 26 13 35; fax 01 43 29 60 25; metro Pont Marie), 59 Rue Saint Louis en l'Île, 4e. This excellent 17-room hotel has singles from 710FF, doubles from 840FF.

Hôtel Saint Louis (Map 8; ☎ 01 46 34 04 80; fax 01 46 34 02 13; metro Pont Marie), 75 Rue Saint Louis en l'Île, 4e. The 21 doubles (695/895FF with one/two beds) at this three-star establishment are appealing but unspectacular though the public areas are lovely. The basement breakfast room dates from the early 1600s; breakfast costs 49FF.

HOTELS – LATIN QUARTER

Real cheapies have gone the way of the dodo in the Latin Quarter (5e), but there are dozens of two and three-star hotels, including a cluster near the Sorbonne and another grouping along lively Rue des Écoles. For top-end hotels the Latin Quarter generally offers better value than the nearby 6e.

Budget

Hôtel du Centre (Map 6; ☎ 01 43 26 13 07; metro Saint Michel), 5 Rue Saint Jacques, 5e. This is a run-down establishment with only basic singles/doubles which start at 100/150FF; doubles with shower are 180FF, triples 300FF. Hall showers are 20FF. Reservations are not accepted.

Hôtel de Médicis (Map 6; ☎ 01 43 54 14 66 for reception, ☎ 01 43 29 53 64 for the public phone in the hall; metro Luxembourg), 214 Rue Saint Jacques, 5e. This is exactly what a dilapidated Latin Quarter dive for impoverished students should be like. Very basic singles start at 85FF, but they're usually occupied; doubles/triples are 160/230FF. Reservations are not accepted.

Port Royal Hôtel (Map 1; ☎ 01 43 31 70 06; fax 01 43 31 33 67; metro Les Gobelins), 8 Blvd de Port Royal, 5e. The clean, quiet and well kept 46 singles/doubles at this older, one-star place start at 175/218FF (325FF with shower and toilet). Hall showers are 15FF.

Middle

Familia Hôtel (Map 5; ☎ 01 43 54 55 27; fax 01 43 29 61 77; metro Cardinal Lemoine), 11 Rue des Écoles, 5e. This is a welcoming, well situated, two-star establishment with 30 attractively decorated rooms. Eight rooms have balconies from which you can catch a glimpse of Notre Dame. Doubles go for 370 to 520FF, triples are 585 to 620 FF and quads 720FF.

Grand Hôtel du Progrès (Map 6; ☎ 01 43 54 53 18; metro Luxembourg), 50 Rue Gay Lussac, 5e. Washbasin-equipped singles at this older, 36-room hotel start at 150FF; large, old-fashioned doubles with a view and morning sunlight are 240FF (330FF with shower and toilet), including breakfast. Hall showers are free. Credit cards are not accepted. The hotel is closed in August.

Hôtel Cluny Sorbonne (Map 6; ☎ 01 43 54 66 66; fax 01 43 29 68 07; metro Luxembourg), 8 Rue Victor Cousin, 5e. This two-star hotel has pleasant, well kept singles/doubles/twins for 375/380/400FF, but its lift is the size of a telephone booth. If you'll be checking in before 1 pm, you can usually reserve a room by telephone without sending a deposit.

Hôtel Esmeralda (Map 6; ☎ 01 43 54 19 20; fax 01 40 51 00 68; metro Saint Michel), 4 Rue Saint Julien le Pauvre, 5e. This 19-room hotel, tucked away in a quiet street with full views of Notre Dame, has been everyone's secret 'find' for years now; book well in advance. A simple single with washbasin is 160FF; doubles with shower and toilet are 320FF and with bath and toilet from 450 to 490FF. Triples start at 500FF.

Hôtel Gay Lussac (Map 6; ☎ 01 43 54 23 96; fax 01 40 51 79 49; metro Luxembourg), 29 Rue Gay Lussac, 5e. This family-run, one-star place with a bit of character and a lift has small rooms starting as low as 160FF but averaging 200FF, rooms with toilet for 240 to 260FF and rooms with shower or bath and toilet for 310 to 340FF. Fairly large doubles/quads with shower, toilet and high ceilings are 360/500FF.

Hôtel Marignan (Map 6; ☎ 01 43 25 31 03; metro Maubert Mutualité), 13 Rue du Sommerard, 5e. This friendly, 30-room place has pleasant, old-fashioned singles/doubles triples/quads with washbasin for 190/270/340/410FF, with shower for 330/360/470/520FF; prices include breakfast. About half of the rooms have toilets. Guests have free use of a fridge, microwave, a washing machine and a clothes dryer.

Hôtel Saint Jacques (Map 6; ☎ 01 44 07 45 45; fax 01 43 25 65 50; metro Maubert Mutualité),

35 Rue des Écoles, 5e. This two-star hotel hasn't lost its old-time charm in the slightest. Spacious singles/doubles/triples, many with ornamented ceilings and balconies, start at 360/420/560FF.

Top End

Grand Hôtel Saint Michel (Map 6; ☎ 01 46 33 33 02; fax 01 40 46 96 33; metro Luxembourg), 19 Rue Cujas, 5e. This one-time two-star hotel has been given an extra étoile after a complete renovation and has raised its prices accordingly: singles/doubles (some with balconies) now cost 690/790FF while triples are 1090FF. The attached salon de thé is quite pleasant.

Hôtel de L'Espérance (Map 1; ☎ 01 47 07 10 99; fax 01 43 37 56 19; metro Censier Daubenton), 15 Rue Pascal, 5e. Just a couple of minutes walk south of lively Rue Mouffetard, this quiet and pleasantly elegant 38-room hotel has singles/doubles with shower and toilet for 360/390FF, with bath for 390/430FF, or larger rooms with two beds at 450FF. Triples are 500FF. Breakfast is 35FF.

Hôtel des Grandes Écoles (Map 5; ☎ 01 43 26 79 23; fax 01 43 25 28 15; metro Cardinal Lemoine), 65 Rue du Cardinal Lemoine, 5e. This three-star place with 47 rooms just down from the Place de la Contrescarpe has one of the loveliest positions in the Latin Quarter. Tucked away in a courtyard off a medieval street with its own garden, singles are 320 to 550FF, doubles 350 to 600FF.

Résidence Monge (Map 5; ☎ 01 43 26 87 90; 01 43 54 47 25; metro Place Monge), 55 Rue Monge, 5e. This clean, well managed hotel with 36 rooms right in the thick of things is an expensive choice if you're alone (singles 380 to 480FF) but a good deal if you've got a companion or two; doubles and triples start at 450FF.

Hôtel Au Royal Cardinal (Map 5; ☎ 01 43 26 83 64; fax 01 44 07 22 32; metro Cardinal Lemoine), 1 Rue des Écoles, 5e. We've heard good things about this very central, 37-room hotel near the Sorbonne. Singles are 300 to 435FF, doubles 310 to 495FF and triples 550 to 640FF.

Hôtel Saint Christophe (Map 5; ☎ 01 43 31 81 54; fax 01 43 31 12 54; metro Place Monge), 17 Rue Lacépède, 5e. A classy small hotel with 31 well equipped singles/doubles at 500/650FF, although discounts are often available.

HOTELS – 6e ARRONDISSEMENT

The middle range places listed below are the least expensive hotels the 6e has to offer. The pricey three-star hotels are located around Saint Germain des Prés.

Middle

Delhy's Hôtel (Map 6; ☎ 01 43 26 58 25; fax 01 43 26 51 06; metro Saint Michel), 22 Rue de l'Hirondelle. This 21-room, one-star hotel, through the arch from 6 Place Saint Michel, has neat, simple washbasin-equipped singles/doubles for as low as 180/290FF; with toilet they're 250/290FF, while a double with shower is 380FF. Hall showers cost 25FF. Breakfast (30FF) is usually obligatory during summer and holiday periods.

Hôtel des Académies (Map 4; ☎ 01 43 26 66 44; fax 01 43 26 03 72; metro Vavin), 15 Rue de la Grande Chaumière. This truly charming 21-room hotel has been run by the same friendly family since 1920 and has singles with washbasin for 210FF. Shower-equipped doubles are 285FF or 325 to 340FF with shower and toilet.

Hôtel de Nesle (Map 6; ☎ 01 43 54 62 41; metro Odéon or Mabillon), 7 Rue de Nesle. The Nesle is a spirited – often too jolly – hostelry that's been a favourite with young travellers since it was established in 1971. It remains a good place to meet other travellers. A bed in a simple double is 150FF, if you come alone they'll find you a roommate. Singles with shower are 250FF; doubles with toilet and shower or bath are 400FF. Reservations are not accepted – the only way to get a place is to stop by in the morning.

Hôtel Petit Trianon (Map 6; ☎ 01 43 54 94 64; metro Odéon), 2 Rue de l'Ancienne Comédie. Plain singles/doubles with washbasin and bidet at this 15-room hotel are 170/260FF; doubles with shower begin at 350FF. Doubles/triples with shower and toilet are 400/450FF. Showers in the hall are free.

Hôtel Saint André des Arts (Map 6; ☎ 01 43 26 96 16; fax 01 43 29 73 34; metro Odéon), 66 Rue Saint André des Arts. Rooms at this 31-room hotel, situated on a lively, restaurant-lined thoroughfare, start at 360/460/570/620FF for one/two/three/four people, including breakfast.

Hôtel Saint Michel (Map 6; ☎ 01 43 26 98 70; metro Saint Michel), 17 Rue Gît le Cœur. Comfortable but pretty standard, soundproofed rooms start from 190FF with nothing, from 285FF for rooms with shower but no toilet, and from 325 to 370FF for rooms with shower and toilet. The hall shower costs 12FF.

Top End

Citadines Apparthôtel Raspail Montparnasse (Map 6; ☎ 01 43 35 46 35; fax 01 40 47 43 01; metro Vavin), 121 Blvd du Montparnasse. At the southern boundary of the 6e near Gare Montparnasse, the apartment-style rooms feature kitchen areas. Prices vary during the year from 610 to 670FF for a small 'studette', 710 to 775FF for a two-person studio or 1230 to 1375FF for a two-bedroom apartment. Rates are cheaper if you stay longer than seven days.

Hôtel des Deux Continents (Map 6; ☎ 01 43 26 72 46; fax 01 43 25 67 80; metro Saint Germain des Prés), 25 Rue Jacob. This 41-room establishment has spacious, flowery singles for 695FF, doubles from 765 to 815FF and triples for 1020FF; breakfast is 45FF.

Hôtel du Globe (Map 6; ☎ 01 43 26 35 50; fax 01 46 33 62 69; metro Odéon), 15 Rue des Quatre Vents. The 15 singles/doubles in this eclectic two-star hotel – each with their own theme – cost from 350 to 450FF.

Hôtel des Marronniers (Map 6; ☎ 01 43 25 30 60; fax 01 40 46 83 56; metro Saint Germain des Prés), 21 Rue Jacob. This 37-room place has less-than-huge singles/doubles/triples from 540/735/1060FF. It also has a charming garden out the back.

Hôtel Michelet Odéon (Map 6; ☎ 01 46 34 27 80; fax 01 46 34 55 35; metro Odéon), 6 Place de l'Odéon. Only a minute's walk from the Jardin du Luxembourg, this 42-room place has tasteful, generously proportioned singles for 420FF, doubles for 480 to 540FF, triples from 645FF and quads from 700FF. Rooms with bath rather than shower are 50 to 60FF more expensive.

HOTELS – GARE SAINT LAZARRE & GRANDS BOULEVARDS AREAS

The better deals are away from Gare Saint Lazare (8e), but there are several budget places as well as two and three-star hotels along Rue d'Amsterdam (9e), which runs along the eastern side of Gare Saint Lazare.

Budget

Hôtel Du Calvados (Map 2; ☎ 01 48 74 39 31; fax 01 48 74 33 75; metro Saint Lazare), 20 Rue d'Amsterdam, 9e. Singles at this 24-room hotel start at 180FF while doubles with washbasin and toilet are 220FF and 300FF with toilet and shower.

Middle

Hôtel Britannia (Map 2; ☎ 01 42 85 36 36; fax 01 42 85 16 93; metro Saint Lazare), 24 Rue d'Amsterdam, 9e. The Hôtel Britannia is a two-star, 46-room place with narrow hallways and pleasant, clean doubles with shower/bath for 445/490FF. Triples are a bit on the small side and cost 565/610FF.

Hôtel Chopin (Map 7; ☎ 01 47 70 58 10; fax 01 42 47 00 70; metro Rue Montmartre), 46 Passage Jouffroy, 9e. This 36-room, two-star hotel near 10 Blvd Montmartre is down one of Paris' most delightful 19th-century covered shopping arcades. Basic singles start at 355FF; shower-equipped singles/doubles/triples cost from 405/450/565FF. After the arcade closes at 10 pm, ring the illuminated sonnette de nuit (night doorbell).

Top End

Atlantic Hôtel (Map 2; ☎ 01 43 87 45 40; fax 01 42 93 06 26; metro Europe), 44 Rue de Londres, 8e. On the northern side of the station, this stylishly renovated three-star hotel has 87 rooms with singles at 530FF, doubles from 705 to 805FF and triples for 910FF.

Citadines Apparthôtel Opéra (Map 7; ☎ 01 44 50 23 23; fax 01 44 50 23 50; metro Richelieu Drouot), 18 Rue Favart, 2e. Almost opposite the Opéra Comique, this branch of the apartment-style chain has small studios accommodating one person for 675 to 755FF, two-person studios for 755 to 845FF and two-bedroom apartments from 1230 to 1380FF. Rates are lower if you stay more than a week.

Hôtel Peletier-Haussmann (Map 7; ☎ 01 42 46 79 53; fax 01 48 24 12 01; metro Richelieu Drouot), 15 Rue Le Peletier, 9e. This friendly, 24-room hotel just off the Blvd Haussmann has shower-equipped singles/doubles/triples/quads for 330/410/475/500FF.

HOTELS – GARE DU NORD AREA

The area around the Gare du Nord (10e) has a lot of two-star hotels.

Budget

Grand Hôtel Magenta (Map 3; ☎ 01 48 78 03 65; fax 01 48 78 41 64; metro Gare du Nord), 129 Blvd de Magenta, 10e. Clean, spacious rooms are available with washbasin and bidet for 130 to 145FF, with shower from 220FF or with shower and toilet from 260FF. Larger rooms for three to five people are 320 to 450FF. Hall showers are 20FF.

Hôtel Bonne Nouvelle (Map 3; ☎ 01 48 74 99 90; metro Gare du Nord), 125 Blvd de Magenta, 10e. The 'Good News' is a modest hotel with simple, clean, shower-equipped doubles for 150 to 220FF. Hall toilets are on the landing.

Hôtel de Milan (Map 3; ☎ 01 40 37 88 50; fax 01 46 07 89 48; metro Gare du Nord), 17-19 Rue de Saint Quentin, 10e. This friendly, old-fashioned one-star establishment is equipped with an ancient (and temperamental) lift. Clean, quiet but basic singles and doubles are available from 153 and 186FF. Doubles with toilet and shower are 266 to 346FF, triples cost from 429FF. Hall showers cost 18FF, breakfast 20FF.

Hôtel La Vieille France (Map 3; ☎ 01 45 26 42 37; fax 01 45 26 99 07; metro Gare du Nord), 151 Rue La Fayette, 10e. A 34-room place with spacious, pleasant and soundproofed doubles with washbasin and bidet for 195FF and with bath or shower and toilet for 265 to 295FF. Triples are 320 to 360FF. Hall showers cost 15FF.

Middle

Nord Hôtel (Map 3; ☎ 01 45 26 43 40; fax 01 42 82 90 23; metro Gare du Nord), 37 Rue de Saint Quentin, 10e. This 46-room hotel, right across from Gare du Nord, has clean, quiet singles for 275 to 330FF or doubles for 330 to 360FF. An extra person costs 95FF. Breakfast is 25FF.

HOTELS – GARE DE L'EST AREA

The 10e around the Gare de l'Est has some of Paris' grungiest flophouses, but the few diamonds in the rough offer some real bargains. There are also quite a few two and three-star places nearby.

Budget

Hôtel d'Alsace (Map 3; ☎ 01 40 37 75 41; 85 Blvd de Strasbourg, 10e; metro Gare de l'Est). An old but well maintained 32-room hostelry with bright, clean singles/doubles/quads with washbasin for 134/187/247FF. Doubles with shower are 227FF. Hall showers cost 10FF. The fireplaces give the rooms a bit of old-time charm. The entrance is on the left-hand side of the passageway.

Hôtel Château d'Eau (Map 3; ☎ 01 48 24 67 09; metro Château d'Eau), 61 Rue du Château d'Eau, 1st floor, 10e. If you like your linoleum with cigarette burns, this run-down, partly residential hotel is for you. Large, basic singles/ doubles cost 120/150FF (220FF with shower). Hall showers are 15FF.

Hôtel Liberty (Map 3, ☎ 01 42 08 60 58; fax 01 42 40 12 59; metro Château d'Eau), 16 Rue de Nancy, 1st floor, 10e. Clean, plain singles/ doubles start at 150/160FF (160/185FF with shower, 180/210FF with shower and toilet). A bed for a third person costs 40FF. Hall showers are 10FF.

Hôtel Pacific (Map 3; ☎ 01 47 70 07 91; fax 01 47 70 98 43; metro Château d'Eau), 70 Rue du Château d'Eau, 10e. An older one-star place, the Pacific has 24 spacious, unpretentious and clean doubles/triples for 130/220FF (250FF with shower). Hall showers are 15FF.

Sibour Hôtel (Map 3; ☎ 01 46 07 20 74; fax 01 46 07 37 17; metro Gare de l'Est), 4 Rue Sibour, 10e. This friendly, one-star place has 45 well kept rooms, including old-fashioned singles/doubles from 175/195FF (285FF with shower, toilet and TV). Hall showers cost 15FF.

Middle

Grand Hôtel de Paris (Map 3; ☎ 01 46 07 40 56; fax 01 42 05 99 18; metro Gare de l'Est), 72 Blvd de Strasbourg, 10e. This well run (though extravagantly named) establishment has 49 pleasant, soundproofed singles/doubles/triples/ quads (300/350/450/500FF) and a tiny lift. If you stay at least four days in the off-season, they may throw in breakfast (30FF) for free.

Hôtel Français (Map 3; ☎ 01 40 35 94 14; fax 01 40 35 55 40; metro Gare de l'Est), 13 Rue du 8 Mai 1945, 10e. A 71-room place with attractive, almost luxurious, singles/doubles/triples – some with balconies – for 385/430/530FF. Children accompanied by parents are free. It costs 30FF to park.

HOTELS – BASTILLE AREA

The area just east of Place de la Bastille (ie around Rue de Lappe, 11e) has become one of Paris' more lively nightlife areas since the construction of the Opéra Bastille a decade ago. Farther east and south-east (12e) is an ungentrified, typically Parisian working-class neighbourhood whose respectable, old-style hotels cater mainly to French businesspeople of modest means.

Two-star comfort is less expensive in the 11e than in the inner arrondissements. For information about kitchenette-equipped rooms or apartments at the Hôtel et Résidence Trousseau, see the Serviced Flats section of this chapter.

Budget

Hôtel des Alliés (Map 5; ☎ 01 44 73 01 17; metro Ledru Rollin), 90 Rue du Faubourg Saint Antoine, 12e. This uninspiring 37-room place offers one of the better deals in the Bastille area with singles/doubles/triples/quads from 90/150/195/240FF rising to 130/180/ 210/280FF in the high season. All rooms have showers (four with bath).

Hôtel Bastille Opéra (Map 5; ☎ 01 43 55 16 06; metro Bastille), 6 Rue de la Roquette, 11e. This ageing, 20-room place, just off Place de la Bastille, has basic singles/doubles starting at 130/180FF. Showers are free. Reception, open 24 hours, is on the 1st floor – push the intercom button to get in. Telephone reservations are not accepted, but if you call from the train station they'll hold a room for an hour or two. There are other hotels along Rue de la Roquette.

Hôtel Baudin (Map 5; ☎ 01 47 00 18 91; fax 01 48 07 04 66; metro Ledru Rollin), 113 Ave Ledru Rollin, 11e. This once grand, old-fashioned, one-star hostelry has 17 mercifully unmodernised singles/doubles from 120/220FF (220/270FF with bath and toilet); triples are 80FF more. Hall showers are free.

Hôtel Camélia (Map 1; ☎ 01 43 73 67 50; metro Nation), 6 Ave Philippe Auguste, 11e. This family-run, one-star establishment has 30 pleasant, well kept rooms from 150FF, 210FF with shower and 220 to 250FF with shower and toilet. Hall showers cost 20FF. The hotel is closed late July to late August.

Hôtel Central (Map 1; ☎ 01 43 73 73 53; metro Nation), 16 Ave Philippe Auguste, 11e. This quiet and clean place just north of Place de la Nation has singles/doubles/quads with washbasin and bidet for 128/155/260FF. Hall showers cost 20FF (less if you stay for a few days).

Hôtel Familial (Map 1; ☎ 01 43 67 48 24; metro Voltaire), 33 Rue Richard Lenoir, 11e. This family-run, old-time cheapie has basic, slightly run-down singles/doubles with washbasin starting from 100/120FF. Hall showers are 15FF.

Hôtel de France (Map 5; ☎ 01 43 79 53 22; metro Voltaire), 159 Ave Ledru Rollin, 11e. At this one-star establishment, decent, well maintained singles/doubles/triples with shower go for 150/220/280FF. All the toilets are off the hall.

Hôtel Saint Amand (Map 5; ☎ 01 47 00 90 55; metro Ledru Rollin), 6 Rue Trousseau, 11e. The linoleum-floored, washbasin-equipped singles/doubles spread over six lift-less floors are nothing fancy, but the prices begin at only 100/120FF (from 170FF with shower). Hall showers are 20FF.

Hôtel de Savoie (Map 1; ☎ 01 43 72 96 47; metro Voltaire), 27 Rue Richard Lenoir, 11e. Nondescript but serviceable singles/doubles at this hotel start at 120/150FF; showers are free. Rooms with shower are 150/220FF.

Vix Hôtel (Map 5; ☎ 01 48 05 12 58; metro Bastille or Ledru Rollin), 19 Rue de Charonne, 11e. This place is a bit dreary and not exactly spotless, but it has plenty of basic singles/doubles from 100/120FF; hall showers are 15FF. Doubles with shower cost 150FF. Telephone reservations are not usually accepted.

Middle

Hôtel Bastille (Map 5; ☎ 01 47 00 06 71; fax 01 43 38 54 27; metro Bastille), 24 Rue de la Roquette, 11e. The youthful staff at this friendly two-star establishment offer neat, modern singles/doubles/triples for 320/380/430FF, including breakfast. From June to September and around Christmas, a bed in a single-sex shared triple room with shower and toilet costs 121FF, including breakfast.

Hôtel Lyon Mulhouse (Map 5; ☎ 01 47 00 91 50; fax 01 47 00 06 31; metro Bastille), 8 Blvd Beaumarchais, 11e. This renovated two-star hotel with 40 rooms offers quiet, predictable singles at 330 to 355FF, and doubles with shower and toilet at 480FF; there are also triples (530 to 560FF) and quads (580 to 620FF) available.

Hôtel Pax (Map 5; ☎ 01 47 00 40 98; fax 01 43 38 57 81; metro Bastille or Ledru Rollin), 12 Rue de Charonne, 11e. Large, spotless rooms start at 200 to 250FF and continue from 250 to 380FF with toilets and showers.

Top End

Citadines Apparthôtel Bastille (Map 1; ☎ 01 40 01 15 15; fax 01 40 01 15 20; metro Reuilly Diderot), 14-18 Rue de Chaligny, 12e. Just south of the landmark Hôpital Saint Antoine, the apartment-style rooms in this chain hotel feature kitchen areas. Prices vary during the year from 460 to 515FF for a small 'studette' for one person, 545 to 600FF for a two-person studio or 760 to 1035FF for a two-bedroom apartment. Staying longer than a week allows cheaper rates.

HOTELS – CHINATOWN AREA

Paris' Chinatown is south of Place d'Italie along Ave d'Ivry and Ave de Choisy. The 13e may not be electrifying, but it has some good deals and there are plenty of restaurants nearby.

Budget

Hôtel Arian (Map 1; ☎ 01 45 70 76 00; fax 01 45 70 85 53; metro Tolbiac), 102 Ave de Choisy, 13e. This motel-ish, one-star place has simple singles for 160FF, with shower for 230FF. Doubles and triples with shower and toilet are 230 to 290FF.

Hôtel des Beaux-Arts (Map 1; ☎ 01 44 24 22 60; metro Tolbiac), 2 Rue Toussaint Féron, 13e. Singles/doubles start at 160/180FF and go up to 210 to 290FF with shower or bath and toilet.

Hôtel Tolbiac (Map 1; ☎ 01 44 24 25 54; fax 01 45 85 43 47; metro Tolbiac), 122 Rue de Tolbiac, 13e. Well lit, quiet and spot lessly clean singles/doubles go for 130/155FF with washbasin, 160FF with shower or 200FF with shower and toilet. Hall showers are free.

HOTELS – MONTPARNASSE AREA

Though untouristed and less than thrilling, the 14e and easternmost corner of the 15e do have a number of good deals. Just east of Gare Montparnasse, there are two and three-star places on Rue Vandamme and Rue de la Gaîté; the latter street is dotted with sex shops.

Budget

Celtic Hôtel (Map 4; ☎ 01 43 20 93 53; fax 01 43 20 66 07; metro Edgar Quinet), 15 Rue d'Odessa, 14e. The Celtic is an old-fashioned, one-star place that has undergone only partial modernisation. It has bare singles/doubles at 210/240FF, doubles/triples with shower at 280/370FF and with shower and toilet at 300/390FF.

Hôtel Aviatic (Map 1; ☎ 01 45 40 59 75; fax 01 45 40 67 48; metro Mouton Duvernet), 10 Rue de Brézin, 14e. The clean, basic singles/doubles, which at this family-run hotel-bar come equipped with steel-frame beds and linoleum floors, start at 110/130FF (210 to 230FF with shower and toilet). Hall showers are 10FF.

Hôtel de l'Espérance (Map 1; ☎ 01 43 21 63 84; metro Gaîté), 45 Rue de la Gaîté, 14e. This is a 14-room place whose doubles (175FF with washbasin, 185 to 195FF with shower) are a bit frayed and dreary. A bed for a third person is 50FF. Hall showers cost 15FF.

Hôtel L'Espérance (Map 1; ☎ 01 43 21 41 04; fax 01 43 22 06 02; metro Denfert Rochereau), 1 Rue de Grancey, 14e. This 14-room place has basic singles/doubles from 155/190FF (260 to 325FF with shower but no toilet).

Middle

Hôtel de Blois (Map 1; ☎ 01 45 40 99 48; fax 01 45 40 45 62; metro Mouton Duvernet), 5 Rue des Plantes, 14e. This one-star establishment offers smallish singles/doubles with washbasin and bidet for 230/280FF. Doubles with shower are 250FF and 270FF with shower and toilet. Fully equipped triples are 360FF.

Hôtel Floridor (Map 1; ☎ 01 43 21 35 53; fax 01 43 27 65 81; metro Denfert Rochereau), 28 Place Denfert Rochereau, 14e. Shower-equipped singles/doubles go for 279/307FF (297/325FF with toilet as well), including breakfast served in your room.

Petit Palace Hôtel (Map 1; ☎ 01 43 22 05 25; fax 01 43 21 79 01; metro Gaîté), 131 Ave du Maine, 14e. The same family has run this friendly, ambitiously named, two-star place since 1952. It has smallish but spotless doubles/triples for 250/310FF with washbasin and bidet and 310/400FF with shower and toilet. Hall showers are 20FF.

Top End

Hôtel Miramar (Map 4; ☎ 01 45 48 62 94; fax 01 45 48 68 73; metro Montparnasse Bienvenüe), 6 Place Bienvenüe, 15e. Soundproofed, small-ish and typically three-star singles/doubles/triples cost 456/512/818FF.

HOTELS – 15e ARRONDISSEMENT

Although the 15e is not particularly exciting it's conveniently close to the Eiffel Tower and the other attractions of the Left Bank. There are a number of mid-range hotels along Blvd de Grenelle, particularly around metro La Motte Picquet Grenelle.

Middle

Hôtel Saphir Grenelle (Map 4; ☎ 01 45 75 12 23; fax 01 45 75 62 49; metro La Motte Picquet

Grenelle), 10 Rue du Commerce. Conveniently close to restaurants and metro lines, this small hotel has modern singles/doubles at 390/460FF. Discount packages are available, including a three-night weekend for 990FF.

HOTELS – MONTMARTRE & PIGALLE

Montmartre, encompassing the 18e and the northern part of the 9e, is one of the most charming neighbourhoods in Paris. The flat area around the base of the hill has some surprisingly good deals. The lively, ethnically mixed area east of Sacré Cœur can be a bit rough – some people say its prudent to avoid the Château Rouge metro stop at night. The attractive two-star places on Rue Aristide Bruant are usually less full in July and August than in spring and autumn. There are several larger hotels near the entrance to the Cimetière de Montmartre.

Budget

Hôtel Audran (Map 9; ☎ 01 42 58 79 59; fax 01 42 58 39 11; metro Abbesses), 7 Rue Audran, 18e. Basic singles/doubles start at 120/160FF; doubles with shower are 180FF and 250FF for ones with shower and toilet. Each floor has a toilet; the 1st and 3rd floors have showers (10FF).

Hôtel de Carthage (Map 9; ☎/fax 01 46 06 27 03; metro Château Rouge), 10 Rue Poulet, 18e. This 40-room cheapie with basic but serviceable singles costs 90 to 110FF; doubles are 140 to 160FF. Hall showers cost 15FF. Doubles with shower and toilet cost 190 to 230FF. Curfew is at 1 am.

Hôtel de Rohan (Map 9; ☎ 01 46 06 82 74; metro Château Rouge), 90 Rue Myrha, 18e. Basic, tidy singles/doubles at this one-star establishment go for 110/140FF. Doubles/triples with shower are 170/200FF. Showers in the hall cost 20FF.

Hôtel Saint Pierre (Map 9; ☎ 01 46 06 20 73; metro Anvers), 3 Rue Seveste, 18e. This friendly, family-run establishment is in a renovated, older building with 36 simple but serviceable rooms. Singles/doubles cost from 120/180FF (170/190FF with shower and toilet, 230FF with bath and toilet). With Blvd Rochechouart so close, though, it can be a bit noisy here.

Idéal Hôtel (Map 9; ☎ 01 46 06 63 63; fax 01 42 64 97 01; metro Abbesses), 3 Rue des Trois Frères, 18e. This is an older place whose 45 simple but adequate rooms cost from 125 to 140FF for singles and 180FF for doubles. Rooms with shower, but no toilet, are 250FF. If you ring from the station, they'll hold a room for a few hours.

Middle

Hôtel des Arts (Map 9; ☎ 01 46 06 30 52; fax 01 46 06 10 83; metro Abbesses), 5 Rue Tholozé, 18e. This is a friendly, attractive 50-room place with singles/doubles from 340/430FF (460FF with two twin beds). Breakfast costs 30FF.

Hôtel Avenir (Map 9; ☎ 01 48 78 21 37; 01 40 16 92 62; metro Anvers), 39 Blvd Rochechouart, 9e. This two-star, 42-room place on noisy Blvd Rochechouart has singles/doubles/triples/quads from 240/280/310/400FF. All rooms have bath or shower and the rates include breakfast.

Hôtel des Capucines Montmartre (Map 9; ☎ 01 42 52 89 80; fax 01 42 52 29 57; metro Abbesses or Blanche), 5 Rue Aristide Bruant, 18e. Singles with TV and minibar cost 250 to 325, doubles 300 to 350FF and triples 350 to 420FF in this hotel at the foot of the Sacré Cœur. A bed for a third person is 80FF.

Hôtel Luxia (Map 9; ☎ 01 46 06 84 24; fax 01 46 06 10 14; metro Anvers), 8 Rue Seveste, 18e. This 45-room hotel takes mainly groups, but at least a few rooms are almost always left for independent travellers. Plain, clean singles/doubles/triples with shower, toilet and TV are 280/300/390FF.

Hôtel du Moulin (Map 9; ☎ 01 42 64 33 33; fax 01 46 06 42 66; metro Abbesses), 3 Rue Aristide Bruant, 18e. This is the third of this useful cluster of hotels and has 27 rooms with toilet and bath or shower at 250/300FF in winter and 290/380FF in summer.

Hôtel Utrillo (Map 9; ☎ 01 42 58 13 44; fax 01 42 23 93 88; metro Abbesses), 7 Rue Aristide Bruant, 18e. The 30 singles/doubles here start at 305/380FF. A double with bath and toilet is 420FF. Buffet breakfast costs 40FF.

Timhôtel Montmartre (Map 9; ☎ 01 42 55 74 79; fax 01 42 55 71 01; metro Abbesses), 11 Rue Ravignan and Place Émile Goudeau, 18e. This is a good choice if you place more value on location than room size. The 60 neat, modern singles/doubles cost 460/560FF. Some of the rooms on the 4th and 5th floors have stunning views of the city (110FF extra). Buffet breakfast is 49FF.

PLACES TO STAY

Top End

Citadines Apparthôtel Montmartre (Map 9; ☎ 01 53 42 43 44; fax 01 45 22 59 10; metro Blanche), 16 Ave Rachel, 18e. Right by the entrance to the Cimetière de Montmartre, and on a quiet street, this branch of the apartment-style hotel chain has small 'studettes' from 480 to 535FF, larger studios for two people from 570 to 630FF and two-bedroom apartments from 800 to 1065FF. Stays of longer than a week are cheaper.

Résidence Hôtel des Trois Poussins (Map 3; ☎ 01 53 32 81 81; fax 01 53 32 81 82; metro Saint Georges), 15 Rue Clauzel, 9e. This two-star hotel due south of Place Pigalle has singles/doubles from 350/450FF, but more than half of its 40 rooms are small studios (from 380/450) with their own cooking facilities.

HOTELS – AIRPORTS

Both airports have a wide selection of places including mid-range Ibis hotels and a rather unusual form of accommodation if you just need to rest.

Cocoon (☎ 01 48 62 06 16; fax 01 48 62 56 97), below departure level (Hall 36) at Aéroport Charles de Gaulle 1. This strange place has 60 'cabins' where you can sleep for up to 16 hours – but no longer than that. The single/double day rates (check in any time between 8 am to 6 pm) is 150/200FF, overnight they're 250/300FF. All cabins have TVs, telephones with fax and, most important, alarm clocks.

Hôtel Ibis (☎ 01 49 19 19 19; fax 01 49 19 19 21), next to the Aéroport Charles de Gaulle 1 train station. This large, modern chain hotel with two stars and 556 rooms has doubles and triples for 415FF (320FF at the weekend). The hotel is linked to all three terminals by shuttle bus.

Hôtel Ibis (☎ 01 46 87 33 50; fax 01 46 87 29 92), Orly Airport. This 299-room chain hotel is linked to both terminals by the airport shuttle bus. Doubles cost 395FF.

Places to Eat

FOOD

The cuisine of France is remarkably varied, with a great many regional differences based on the produce and gastronomy of each region. Eating well is still of prime importance to most Parisians, who spend an amazing amount of time thinking about, talking about and consuming food.

Many of the pubs, bars and clubs listed in the Entertainment chapter also serve snacks and light meals.

Ethnic Cuisines

Paris has a considerable population of immigrants from France's former colonies and protectorates in north and west Africa, Indochina, the Middle East, India, the Caribbean and the South Pacific, as well as refugees from every corner of the globe, so an exceptional variety of reasonably priced ethnic food is available.

Vegetarian Food

Vegetarians form only a small minority in France and are not very well catered for; specialised vegetarian restaurants are few and far between. Some restaurants have at least one vegetarian dish on the menu. Unfortunately, very few set *menus* include vegetarian options.

Meals in France

The French start the day with a *petit déjeuner* (breakfast; see the boxed text 'The Very Petit Déjeuner'), usually consisting of a croissant and a light bread roll or half a baguette (often left over from dinner the night before) with butter and jam, followed

BRENDA TURNNIDGE

Everywhere in Paris you'll find café tables spilling out onto the pavement.

by a *café au lait* (coffee with lots of hot milk), a small black coffee or hot chocolate.

For many people, lunch is still the main meal of the day. Dinner usually begins around 8.30 pm.

Eating Out

Restaurants & Brasseries Restaurants usually specialise in a particular variety of food (eg regional, traditional, North African etc), whereas brasseries serve more standard French fare.

Restaurants are usually open only for lunch and dinner, while brasseries stay open from morning until night and serve meals at all times of the day.

Most restaurants offer you the choice of ordering *à la carte* (from the menu) or ordering one fixed-price, multicourse meal known in French as a *menu* or a *formule*. The latter usually has fewer choices but allows you to pick two out of three courses (eg starter and main course or main course and dessert). A *menu* almost always costs much less than ordering à la carte. Note, however, that the word *menu* is one of the 'false friends' between English and French. If you really want a menu, ie a complete list of the dishes available, you must ask for *la carte*.

Cafés The café is an important focal point for social life, and sitting in one to read, write, talk with friends, watch the world go by or just daydream is an integral part of many Parisians' day-to-day existence. Only basic food is available in most cafés. A baguette filled with Camembert or pâté is a common option.

Salons de Thé Tearooms are trendy and somewhat pricey establishments which usually offer quiches, salads, cakes, tarts, pies and pastries in addition to tea and coffee.

Fast-Food & Chain Restaurants American fast-food companies, including McDonald's, Pizza Hut and KFC as well as the Haagen-Däzs ice-cream chain, have busy branches all over Paris, which must mean that the average French person is a lot more open to Anglo-Saxon culinary ideas than some defenders of French civilisation seem to think. There's a local hamburger chain called Quick.

A number of restaurants have several outlets around Paris with standard menus. They're a definite step up from the fast-food companies and can be good value in areas like the Ave des Champs-Élysées, where restaurants tend to be expensive or bad value or both.

Hippopotamus There are about 18 branches in Paris of this hugely popular national chain which specialises in solid, steak-based meals. *Menus* are available at 65 to 143FF and branches are typically open daily from 11.30 am to 1 am (1.30 am on Friday and Saturday). Five branches, however, are open till 5 am daily, including those at: 1 Blvd Capucines, 2e (☎ 01 47 42 75 70; metro Opéra); 1 Blvd Beaumarchais, 4e (☎ 01 44 61 90 40; metro Bastille); 42 Ave des Champs-Élysées, 8e (☎ 01 53 83 94 50; metro Franklin Roosevelt); 5 Blvd des Batignolles, 8e (☎ 01 43 87 85 15; metro Villiers); and 68 Blvd du Montparnasse, 14e (☎ 01 40 64 14 94; metro Vavin).

Batifol There are a dozen branches in Paris of these attractive and popular 1930s-style bistros with their jazz-theme décor. Specialities include *pot au feu* (stewed beef and vegetables) and *moëlle* (beef marrow on bread). The generous *plats du jour* (dishes of the day) cost 60 to 70FF and *menus* from 67 to 143FF (the 78FF one includes wine). Meals are served daily from noon to midnight.

Bistrot Romain This increasingly popular chain, also with a dozen branches around the city, has *menus* available from 59 to 99FF. They are usually open from 11.30 am to 1 am but the branch at 122 Ave des Champs-Élysées, 8e (Map 2; ☎ 01 42 56 88 45; metro George V) is open later.

Léon de Bruxelles The 12 branches of this restaurant are dedicated to only one thing: the preparation of *moules* (mussels).

RACHEL BLACK

TONY WHEELER

Top: Inside Galeries Lafayette
Bottom: Shakespeare & Company bookshop

SIMON BRACKEN

BRENDA TURNNIDGE

JAMES LYON

Top: Merry-go-round with Sacré Cœur in the background
Bottom left: A boutique, once a butcher shop specialising in horse meat, in the Marais
Bottom right: The *colonne Morris,* a hallmark of Paris

Meal-size bowls of the bivalves, served with chips and fresh bread, start at 59FF; there are *menus* available at 65FF, 69FF and 99FF. They're open daily from 11.30 am to 1 am (2 am on Saturday).

Other Chains There are three *Indiana Cafés* serving bland Tex-Mex food in popular tourist areas. They're open daily from 7 am to midnight or later, and apart from the Ave des Champs-Élysées branch they all have a 5 to 8 pm happy hour. *Pizza Pino* is open from 11.30 am until 5 am at three of their four Paris branches. The pizzas aren't bad and again they provide reasonably priced food (56 to 79FF for pizza, 32 to 45FF for salads, 55 to 83FF for pasta) in often expensive districts.

Self-Catering

One of Paris' culinary delights is stocking up on fresh breads, pastries, cheese, fruit, vegetables and prepared dishes and sitting down for a gourmet *pique-nique*. Many food shops are closed on Sunday afternoon and Monday, and almost all supermarkets close all day Sunday.

Fresh bread is baked and sold at *boulangeries* (see the boxed text below); mouth-watering pastries are available at

---

The Staff of Life

Nothing is more French than bread, and it comes in an infinite variety. Don't worry about buying too much; most *boulangeries* (bakeries) will sell you half a loaf. But you'll probably be able to eat a whole one in any case.

All Parisian boulangeries have 250g baguettes, which are long and thin, and 400g, wider loaves of *pain* (bread), both of which are at their best if eaten within four hours of baking. You can store them for longer in a plastic bag, but the crust becomes soft and chewy; if you leave them out, they'll soon be hard – which is the way many French people like them at breakfast. The pain is softer on the inside, has a less crispy crust than the baguette, and is slightly cheaper by weight. If you're not very hungry, ask for a *demi baguette* or *demi pain*. *Ficelles* are thinner, crustier versions of the baguette – really like very thick breadsticks.

Many boulangeries also have heavier, more expensive breads made with all sorts of grains and cereals, and some of these are so scrumptious they can be eaten plain. You will also find loaves flavoured with nuts, raisins or herbs. Other types of bread, which come in a wide range of sizes and shapes, vary from shop to shop, but since they are all on display, making a selection is easy.

Signs you're likely to see in boulangeries include: *pain cuit au feu de bois* (bread baked in a wood-fired oven), *pain de seigle* (rye bread), *pain complet* (wholemeal bread), *pain au son* (bread with bran), *pain de campagne* (country loaf) and *pain au levain* (traditionally made yeast bread that's usually a bit chewy). These heavier breads keep much longer than the baguettes and standard white flour breads.

To facilitate carrying it to your hotel or the park, you can ask for your baguette or loaf of bread to be *coupé en deux* (cut in two). If you ask for the bread to be sliced, there's a small charge (usually less than 1FF).

Bread is baked at various times of day, so it's available fresh as early as 6 am and also in the afternoon. Most boulangeries close for one day a week, but the days are staggered so that a town or neighbourhood is never left without a place to buy bread (except, perhaps, on Sunday afternoon). Places that sell bread but don't bake it on the premises are know as *dépôts de pain*.

pâtisseries; a *fromagerie* can supply you with cheese that is *fait* (ripe) to the exact degree that you request; a *charcuterie* offers sliced meats, pâtés etc; and fresh fruits and vegetables are sold at *épiceries* (greengrocers), supermarkets and open-air markets.

A general butcher is a *boucherie*, but for specialised poultry you have to go to a *marchand de volaille*. A *boucherie chevaline*, easily identifiable by the gilded horse's head above the entrance, sells horse meat, which some people prefer to beef or mutton. Fresh fish and seafood are available from a *poissonnerie*.

Paris' neighbourhood food markets offer the freshest and best-quality fruits, vegetables, cheeses, prepared salads etc at the lowest prices in town. The *marchés découverts* (open-air markets) – 60 of which pop up in public squares around the city two or three times a week – are usually open from 7 am to 1 pm. The dozen *marchés couverts* (covered markets) are open from 8 am to sometime between 12.30 and 1.30 pm and from 3.30 or 4 to 7.30 pm (closed Sunday afternoon and Monday). To find out when there's a market near your hotel, ask anyone who lives in the neighbourhood.

DRINKS
Nonalcoholic Drinks
Soft Drinks Soft drinks can be hideously expensive at Parisian cafés. One relatively inexpensive café drink is *sirop* (squash), served either *à l'eau* (mixed with water), with *soda* or Perrier. Restaurants will supply tap water if you ask for it, although touristy places may try to push mineral water. Ask for a *carafe d'eau* or raise a smile by asking for *Château Tiberi* (Jean Tiberi is the mayor of Paris).

Coffee A cup of coffee can take various forms, but the most ubiquitous is espresso. A small, black espresso is called *un café noir*, *un express* or simply *un café*. You can also ask for a *grand* (large) version.

Un café crème is espresso with steamed milk or cream. A small café crème is a *petit crème*. *Un café au lait* is lots of hot milk with a little coffee served in a large cup or even a small bowl. A *noisette* (literally, 'hazelnut') is an espresso with just a dash of milk. A coffee in a café can be as little as 6FF if you drink it standing up at the counter. Sit down and the price will double – or even triple on the Ave des Champs-Élysées.

Tea & Hot Chocolate *Thé* (tea) is unlikely to be up to the English standard but will be served with milk if you ask for *un peu de lait frais*. Herbal tea is popular and is called a *tisane* or *infusion*. *Chocolat chaud* (hot chocolate) can be excellent.

Wine
Two regions produce the most celebrated wines in France: Bordeaux and Burgundy. Burgundy of the right vintage can be extraordinary, but Bordeaux is more reliable. Beaujolais, a light Burgundy, is generally drunk very young (about two months old).

Other Alcoholic Drinks
Apéritifs Meals are often preceded by an appetite-stirring apéritif such as *kir* (white wine sweetened with a syrup such as cassis, ie blackcurrant syrup). Port is generally drunk as an apéritif rather than after the meal in France.

Digestifs France's most famous brandies are Cognac and Armagnac. The various other sorts of brandies are known collectively as *eaux de vie* (literally, 'waters of life'). Calvados is an apple brandy which ages beautifully. Well known liqueurs include Cointreau, Bénédictine and Chartreuse.

Beer *Bière*, which is usually served by the *demi* (about 33 mL), is either Alsatian (like Kronenbourg from Strasbourg, 33 or Pelforth) or imported from Germany or Belgium. A draught beer is a *bière à la pression*.

LOUVRE & LES HALLES AREAS
The area between the Forum des Halles and the Centre Pompidou (1er and western 4e)

is filled with scores of *branché* (plugged-in or trendy) restaurants, but few of them (except the many fast-food joints) are inexpensive. Streets with places to eat include Rue des Lombards, bar and bistro-lined Rue Montorgueil, and the narrow streets north and east of Forum des Halles.

French

The 1er and 4e have a diverse selection of French eating establishments.

L'Amazonial (Map 7; ☎ 01 42 33 53 13; metro Châtelet), 3 Rue Sainte Opportune, 1er. The food is nothing to write home about but the *formules* are only 65 and 85FF (including a kir, drink and coffee) at this gay restaurant. So if your franc is *rose* ... It's open daily for lunch and dinner to 1.30 am.

Aux Crus de Bourgogne (Map 7; ☎ 01 42 33 48 24; metro Châtelet Les Halles), 3 Rue de Bachaumont, 2e. This excellent bistro on a pedestrianised street serves excellent seafood (fresh lobster with mayonnaise, pike quenelles in Nantua sauce etc) as well as an excellent filet of beef in a morelle sauce. Expect to pay from 180FF per person. It's open weekdays only until 10.30 pm.

L'Épi d'Or (Map 7; ☎ 01 42 36 38 12; metro Châtelet-Les Halles), 25 Rue Jean-Jacques Rousseau, 1er. This oh-so-Parisian bistro serves classic, well prepared dishes like rabbit terrine and gigot d'agneau (leg of lamb), cooked for seven hours, to a suprisingly well heeled crowd. There's a *menu* for 105FF. It's open for lunch and dinner except midday Saturday and all day Sunday.

French Chain Restaurants There are branches of the following chain restaurants at Les Halles: *Batifol* (Map 7; ☎ 01 42 36 85 50; metro Les Halles), 14 Rue Mondétour, 1er; *Léon de Bruxelles* (Map 7; ☎ 01 42 36 18 50; metro Les Halles), 120 Rue Rambuteau, 1er; *Hippopotamus* (Map 7, ☎ 01 45 08 00 29; metro Les Halles), 29 Rue Berger, 1er; and *Bistrot Romain* (Map 7; metro Châtelet) at 32 Rue Saint Denis,1er.

Le Grand Véfour (Map 7; ☎ 01 42 96 56 27; fax 01 42 86 80 71; metro Pyramides), 17 Rue de Beaujolais, at the northern edge of the Jardin du Palais Royal, 1er. A dining favourite of the Paris élite since 1784, the traditional French

and Savoyard cuisine and 18th-century elegance have earned this lovely restaurant two Michelin stars. Count on spending around 800 to 1000FF per person for dinner. A lunch *menu* is available for 345FF, not including wine. Closed on Saturday and Sunday and during August. Reservations for dinner should be made about 10 days ahead; for lunch, one or two days should suffice.

Le Petit Mâchon (Map 7; ☎ 01 42 60 08 06; metro Palais Royal), 158 Rue Saint Honoré, 1er. This new bistro has Lyon-inspired specialities like snails in garlic butter and andouillette in mustard sauce. Starters are 38 to 70FF, main courses 72 to 108FF and there's a 98FF *menu*. It's open for lunch and dinner Tuesday to Sunday to 11.30pm.

Au P'tit Rémouleur (Map 8; ☎ 01 48 04 79 24; metro Hôtel de Ville), 2 Rue de la Coutellerie, just west of the Hôtel de Ville, 4e. This small, typically French fish restaurant includes bouillabaisse (60FF), mussels and a 65FF *menu* among its specialities. Main dishes cost 49 to 74FF; *menus* cost 65FF at lunch and 119FF at dinner. It is open Monday to Saturday from noon to 3 pm and 7 to 11 pm.

Au Pied de Cochon (Map 7; ☎ 01 40 13 77 00; metro Les Halles), 6 Rue Coquillère, 1er. Onion soup, pied de cochon (pig's trotter; from 82FF) and other pork dishes (eg tripe, 75FF) from this venerable establishment long satisfied the appetites of both market porters and theatre-goers. The clientele has become more uniformly upmarket and touristy since Les Halles was moved to the suburbs, but Au Pied de Cochon is still open 24 hours a day, seven days a week. The same block has a number of other restaurants in the same price bracket.

Willi's Wine Bar (Map 7; ☎ 01 42 61 05 09; metro Bourse), 13 Rue des Petits Champs, 1er. A civilised yet convivial wine bar run by two British expats who introduced the wine-bar concept to Paris in the mid-1980s. The lunch *menu* is 148FF, dinner is 189FF. À la carte starters average 60FF, main courses 90FF and desserts 45FF. It is open Monday to Saturday from noon to 11 pm.

Japanese

Businesspeople from Japan in search of real Japanese food flock to Rue Sainte Anne and other streets of Paris' 'Japantown', which is just west of the Jardin du Palais Royal.

Many of the restaurants offer surprisingly good value.

Higuma (Map 7; ☎ 01 47 03 38 59; metro Pyramides), 32bis Rue Sainte Anne, 1er. Stepping into this place is like ducking into a corner noodle shop in Shinjuku. To the delight of the almost exclusively Japanese clientele, the high-temperature woks are forever filled with furiously bubbling soups and simmering vegetables. A meal-sized bowl of soup noodles costs 40 to 48FF. It is open daily from 11.30 am straight through to 10 pm. The *menus* (63 to 70FF) are not served from 3 to 5 pm.

Matsuri Sushi (Map 7; ☎ 01 42 61 05 73; metro Pyramides), 36 Rue de Richelieu, 1er. Plates of sushi (21FF at lunch, 25 to 30FF in the evening) make their way around this sushi bar on a little conveyor belt. It is open weekdays from noon to 2.30 pm and 7 to 10 pm (11.30 pm on Friday and Saturday).

Other Cuisines

This part of Paris is a fast-food lovers' paradise, with a variety of chain outlets close to the Centre Pompidou and Les Halles.

Chicago Meatpackers (Map 7; ☎ 01 40 28 01 83; metro Châtelet-Les Halles), 8 Rue Coquillère, 1er. The décor and ambience of this huge place is about as American as any place with English bartenders could be. Culinary specialities include American-style hamburgers (73 to 80FF), ribs (77FF) and Haagen-Däzs ice cream. The restaurant section is open every day of the year from 11.45 am to 1 am. The bar at the back charges 29FF for a pint of beer. Happy hour runs daily from 6 to 9 pm (to 1 am on Thursday).

Au Clair de Lune (Map 7; ☎ 01 40 26 12 39 or 01 42 33 59 10; metro Étienne Marcel), 13 Rue Française, 2e. This Moroccan restaurant has decent couscous (54 to 70FF), tajine (a meat and vegetable 'stew' cooked in a domed earthenware pot; 65FF) and grills (56 to 86FF). The *menu* is 62FF.

Joe Allen (Map 7; ☎ 01 42 36 70 13; metro Étienne Marcel), 30 Rue Pierre Lescot, 1er. A very American bar-restaurant with great atmosphere and a good selection of Californian wines. Two/three-course menus are 140/170FF. It is open daily from noon to 1.30 am. Sunday brunch is from noon to 4 pm.

Lina's (Map 7; metro Pyramides), 9 Ave de l'Opéra, 1er. Another branch of the small chain serving upmarket sandwiches (21 to 45FF) and soups (from 27FF).

Le Loup Blanc (Map 7; ☎ 01 40 13 08 35; metro Étienne Marcel), 42 Rue Tiquetonne, 2e. Now we've heard everything – a techno restaurant (though it's hard to see or hear exactly why). It does do some decent main courses, though, like Thai-style prawns and squid with anise (57 to 85FF). It's open daily from 8 pm to 12.30 am and brunch is available on Sunday from noon to 5 pm. The area around Rue Tiquetonne is becoming very trendy.

La Maison Savoureuse (Map 7; ☎ 01 42 60 03 22; metro Quatre Septembre), 62 Rue Sainte Anne, 2e. This cheap and cheerful little place serves excellent value Vietnamese food (lunch *menus* at 36 and 48FF) à table or you can take your spring rolls (from 9FF) and vermicelli noodles and head for Square Louvois, a pretty little park a short distance to the south-east.

Mélodine Cafeteria (Map 8; ☎ 01 40 29 09 78; metro Rambuteau), 2 Rue Brantôme, across from the north side of the Centre Pompidou, 4e. The food at this huge, self-service cafeteria is better than you might expect, and it may satisfy finicky kids. Main dishes cost only 27 to 40FF, pizzas are 27 to 36FF and salads are available. Food is served daily from 11 am to 10 pm.

Pizza Pino (Map 7; ☎ 01 40 26 39 07; metro Châtelet-Les Halles), 43 Rue Saint Denis, 1er. A nicely located outlet of the pizza chain.

Self-Catering

There are a number of options along Ave de l'Opéra and Rue de Richelieu, as well as around Forum des Halles, including **supermarkets** *Monoprix* at 21 Ave de l'Opéra (Map 7), *Franprix* at 35 Rue Berger (Map 7), open Monday to Saturday from 8.30 am to 8 pm, and a bargain-priced *Ed l'Épicier* (Map 8) inside the courtyard at 80 Rue de Rivoli and open Monday to Saturday from 9 am to 8 pm. **Fine food shops** can be found on the Rue de Richelieu (Map 7; metro Pyramides) including a fromagerie at No 38 (closed from 2 to 4 pm, on Sunday and Monday, and in July and August) and *Evrard*, a *traiteur* (delicatessen or caterer) across the street at No 41 (open Monday to

⟨⟨ decorative border ⟩⟩

The Very Petit Déjeuner

French breakfasts are not every Anglo-Saxon's cup of tea. To many, a croissant, a bit of leftover baguette with butter and jam and a cup of over-milked coffee do not a breakfast make. Masters of the kitchen throughout most of the rest of the day, French chefs don't seem up to it in the morning.

The following are some decent choices for breakfast or brunch in Paris. Be advised, though, that you're here for the atmosphere and/or scenery (be it a park or on two legs) and not necessarily the *petit déjeuner* as such.

Café Beaubourg (Map 8; ☎ 01 48 87 63 96; metro Châtelet-Les Halles), 100 Rue Saint Martin, just opposite the Centre Pompidou, 1er. This minimalist café attracts an arty crowd, and there's always free entertainment on the large square in front. Sunday brunch (110FF) on the terrace is above average. It's open daily from 8 am to 1 am (2 am on Friday and Saturday).

Le Viaduc Café (Map 5; ☎ 01 44 74 70 70; metro Gare de Lyon), 43 Ave Daumesnil, 12e. The terrace of this very trendy café in one of the glassed-in arches of the Viaduc des Arts (see Bastille Area in the Things to See & Do chapter) is an excellent spot to while away the hours, but most people seem to come here for the jazz brunch on Sundays from noon to 4 pm with *menus* at 95, 125 and 135FF. The Viaduc Café is open seven days a week until 4 am.

Ma Bourgogne (Map 8; ☎ 01 42 78 44 64; metro Bastille), 19 Place des Vosges, 4e. Overlooking the restful Place des Vosges, this is one of the most glorious places in Paris for a late breakfast (available daily from 8 am till noon).

⟨⟨ decorative border ⟩⟩

Friday until 7.30 pm, closed in August). The latter has ready-to-eat delicacies.

Americans – or anyone else – who have cravings for things like bagels, cheesecake, carrot cake and brownies should head for *The Bagel Place* (☎ 01 40 28 96 40; metro Châtelet) at 6 Place Sainte Opportune, 1er (Map 7).

MARAIS

The Marais (4e and southern 3e), filled with small eateries of every imaginable kind, is one of Paris' premier neighbourhoods for eating out. The pretty little Place du Marché Sainte Catherine (Map 8; metro Saint Paul) is a square surrounded by small restaurants. They're all a bit pricey, but you're paying for the pleasant outdoor location.

French

Amadeo (Map 8; ☎ 01 48 87 01 02; metro Saint Paul or Hôtel de Ville), 19 Rue François Miron, 4e. This restaurant is decidedly gay, although straight diners are very welcome, and it produces delicious and stylish food at a set price of 165FF (85FF at lunch) for almost any starter, main course and dessert on their menu. On Tuesday evening, the *menu* is only 100FF and includes a kir. Amadeo is closed Saturday lunch and all day Sunday.

Le Gai Moulin (Map 8; ☎ 01 48 87 47 59; metro Rambuteau), 4 Rue Saint Merri, 4c. Traditional French cuisine, including a 100FF *menu*, is served daily from 7 pm to midnight at this small, modern place with a mainly (but not exclusively) gay clientele.

L'Impasse (Map 8; ☎ 01 42 72 08 45; metro Bastille), 4 Impasse Guéménée, 4e. This warm restaurant, with its beamed ceiling and stone walls, serves quality dishes 'just like grandma made': fresh cod with lentils, duck leg in wine with fruit, veal with chives. The 135FF fixed *menu* is excellent value for money and includes some fabulous desserts (eg gourmandise au chocolat). It's open for lunch and dinner except all day Sunday and midday on Monday and Saturday.

Madame Sans Gêne (Map 8; ☎ 01 42 71 31 71; metro Temple or Filles du Calvaire), 19 Rue de Picardie, 3e. Named after the buxom protagonist of the play of that name by Victorien Sardo (1831-1908), a statue of whom greets you on

PLACES TO EAT

arrival, this carefree restaurant run by a couple of young people offers average bistro food but the draw here is that the *menus* (95FF at lunch, 135FF at dinner) include endless carafes of wine drawn from a cask. Watch out for the narrow staircase to the main dining area on the 1st floor – especially coming down. It's open for dinner daily till 10.30 or 11.30 pm but for at lunchtime Monday to Friday only.

Marais Plus (Map 8; ☎ 01 48 87 01 40; metro Saint Paul), corner of Rue des Francs Bourgeois and Rue Payenne, 3e. This mellow salon de thé specialises in tartes salées (quiches; from 50FF) and tartes (pies; from 30FF). It is open daily from 10 am to Friday pm.

Le Petit Gavroche (Map 8; ☎ 01 48 87 74 26; metro Hôtel de Ville), 15 Rue Sainte Croix de la Brettonerie, 4e. This bar/restaurant attracts tables of raucous working-class regulars; it isn't the place for a quiet date. Solid, basic meals are served from noon to 2.30 pm and 7 pm to midnight (closed Saturday at noon and on Sunday). The bar is open from 8 am to 2 am. The *menus*, available until about 10 pm (or whenever they run out), cost 48 to 70FF (45FF at lunch). Main dishes are around 50FF; a small carafe of wine is 12FF.

Le Petit Picard (Map 8; ☎ 01 42 78 54 03; metro Hôtel de Ville), 42 Rue Sainte Croix de la Bretonnerie, 4e. Mainly gay and very popular, this restaurant serves traditional French cuisine. The *menus* cost 64FF (lunch only) and 84FF and there's one at 129FF of Picardie specialities. Closed for lunch on the weekends and all day Monday.

Robert et Louise (Map 8; ☎ 01 42 78 55 89; metro Saint Sébastien Froissart), 64 Rue Vieille du Temple, 3e. Delightful, unfussy and inexpensive French food prepared by a husband and wife team, including côte de bœuf cooked on an open fire with a country kitchen atmosphere. Those who know this place consistently give it rave reviews. Starters are 25 to 35FF, main courses 80 to 90FF, with a plat du jour at 75FF. It's open for lunch and dinner till 10 pm except Sunday.

Le Valet de Carreau (Map 8; ☎ 01 42 72 72 60; metro Temple), 2 Rue Dupetit Thouars, 3e. While this restaurant justifiably attracts its diners with such dishes as charlotte of salmon and duck galette (described by one wag as 'nouvelle cuisine with quantity'), the main draw here is the wonderful terrace under the

chestnut trees and facing the old Carreau du Temple market (open Tuesday to Saturday from 9 am to 12.30 pm and Sunday to 1 pm). The lunch *formule* is 85FF, the dinner *menus* 130 and 180FF. Expect to pay 180 to 200FF à la carte with wine. It's open daily for lunch and dinner to 10.30 pm except midday Saturday and all day Sunday.

Vins des Pyrénées (Map 8; ☎ 01 42 72 64 94; metro Bastille), 25 Rue Beautreillis, 4e. This restaurant is always busy. It's located in a former wine warehouse and is almost opposite the apartment block where American rock singer Jim Morrison of the Doors died in 1971. It's a good place to splurge on a French meal in the Marais, with starters from 35 to 60FF and main courses around 70 to 110FF. It's open daily for lunch and dinner to 11.30 pm except Sunday.

Jewish

The kosher and kosher-style restaurants along Rue des Rosiers serve specialities from North Africa, central Europe and Israel. Many are closed on Friday evening, Saturday and Jewish holidays.

Café des Psaumes (Map 8; ☎ 01 48 04 74 77; metro Saint Paul), 14-16 Rue des Rosiers, 4e. This is a strictly kosher brasserie with dishes (from 59 to 90FF) from Tunisia, central Europe and Israel. The meat/vegetarian *menus* are 49/75FF at lunch and 95/115FF at dinner. It is open from noon to midnight (closed Saturday, Jewish holidays and from mid- afternoon on Friday).

Chez Marianne (Map 8; ☎ 01 42 72 18 86; metro Saint Paul), 2 Rue des Hospitalières Saint Gervais, 4e. A kind of Sephardic (Middle Eastern/North African Jewish) alternative to the Ashkenazic (Eastern European Jewish) Jo Goldenberg, with an adjoining delicatessen. Plates with four/five/six different meze (felafel, hummus etc) cost 55/65/75FF. The window at the deli dispenses takeaway felafel sandwiches for 20FF.

Chez Rami et Hanna (Map 8; ☎ 01 42 78 23 09; metro Saint Paul), 54 Rue des Rosiers, 4e. Israeli dishes, including the assiette royale (a plate of seven salads; 60FF), are served daily from 11 am to 2 am.

Finkelsztajn Bakeries – Florence Finkelsztajn (Map 8; ☎ 01 48 87 92 85; metro Saint Paul) is at 24 Rue des Écouffes (4e), and *Sacha Finkelsztajn* (Map 8; ☎ 01 42 72 78 91; metro Saint Paul) is at 27 Rue des Rosiers. These places have scrumptious Jewish-style central European breads and pastries, including apple strudel and poppy-seed cakes. Florence's is also a deli. At least one of the two is open daily except Tuesday from 10 am to 2 pm and 3 to 7 pm.

Jo Goldenberg (Map 8; ☎ 01 48 87 20 16; metro Saint Paul), 7 Rue des Rosiers, 4e. Founded in 1920, this kosher-style restaurant-delicatessen has become Paris' most famous Jewish eatery. The mixed starters (30FF) and apple strudel (29FF) are excellent, but the plats du jour (80FF) don't measure up to New York deli standards by a long shot. Still, it's a very convivial, almost festive place for a meal. It's open 364 days a year (closed Yom Kippur) from 8.30 am until midnight or 1 am.

Vegetarian

The Marais is one of the few neighbourhoods in Paris that actually offers a choice of meatless restaurants.

Aquarius (Map 8; ☎ 01 48 87 48 71; metro Rambuteau), 54 Rue Sainte Croix de la Bretonnerie, 4e. The calming, airy atmosphere of this healthy restaurant makes you think of fresh bean sprouts – great if you're in the mood for something as light as that. The two-course *menu* (lunch only) costs 62FF; for 92FF you get three courses. It is open Monday to Saturday from noon to 10.30 pm; the plat du jour is available from noon to 2 pm and 7 to 10 pm.

Piccolo Teatro (Map 8; ☎ 01 42 72 17 79; metro Saint Paul), 6 Rue des Écouffes, 4e. The *menus* at this intimate place with stone walls, beamed ceiling and cosy little tables cost 53 and 75FF for lunch and 90 and 115FF for dinner; the tasty assiette végétarienne (vegetarian plate) is 65FF. It is open from noon to 3 pm and 7 to 11 pm (closed Monday) and often busy in the evening, especially on Friday and Saturday.

La Truffe (Map 8; ☎ 01 42 71 08 39; metro Hôtel de Ville), 31 Rue Vieille du Temple, 4e. This organic, vegetarian restaurant specialises in dishes made with mushrooms. The poêlée champignons (99FF as a starter, 129FF as a main course) and vegetable lasagne (69/79FF) are superb. A savoury tarte served with veg-

etables is 59 to 89FF. There's a lunchtime *menu* for 59FF. It is open daily from noon to 4 pm and 7 to 11 pm.

Other Cuisines

The area has a good selection of ethnic restaurants. If you're looking for authentic Chinese but can't be bothered to go all the way to the 13e, check out any of the small **Chinese noodle shops and restaurants** along Rue Au Maire, 3e (Map 8; metro Arts et Métiers), which is south-east of the Conservatoire des Arts et Métiers.

Takeaway falafel and *chawarma* (ie shwarma) are available all along Rue des Rosiers.

Au Bascou (Map 8; ☎ 01 42 72 69 25; metro Arts et Métiers), 38 Rue Réaumur, 3e. Basque cuisine might sound a little far-fetched but try it, you'll like it. Classics include pipérade basquaise (a kind of omelette with peppers, garlic, tomatoes and ham), crispy baby squid, milk-fed lamb and Bayonne ham in all its guises. The lunch *menu* is good value at 90FF. At dinner, expect to pay from 180 to 250FF à la carte. Au Bascou is open for lunch and dinner except midday Saturday and all day Sunday.

Caves Saint Gilles (Map 8; ☎ 01 48 87 22 62; metro Chemin Vert), 4 Rue Saint Gilles, 3e. This trendy Spanish wine bar north-east of Place des Vosges is where to come for tapas (80FF for a platter of them) and sangria. The red banquettes are always packed with people, and it's open daily until 2 am.

Chez Omar (Map 8; ☎ 01 42 72 36 26; metro Arts et Métiers), 47 Rue de Bretagne, 3e. Though hardly as refined as the 404, this place – long a favourite of showbiz and fashion types – is another excellent choice for couscous (eg couscous royal at 110FF) and tajines. It's an old converted café and an excellent place for people watching. It also offers one of the warmest welcomes in Paris. It's open daily for lunch and dinner to 10 pm except midday Sunday.

L'Enoteca (Map 8; ☎ 01 42 78 91 44; metro Pont Marie), 25 Rue Charles V, 4e. If you feel like splashing out on an Italian meal in Paris, do it here. Risotto with gorgonzola and pears, tagliatelle with prawns and asparagus, carpaccio

PLACES TO EAT

with rocket – this is haute cuisine à l'italienne and there's an excellent list of Italian wines. The weekday lunch *menu* is good value at 95FF (including wine). À la carte expect to pay between 200 and 250FF.

Minh Chau (Map 8; ☎ 01 42 71 13 30; metro Hôtel de Ville), 10 Rue de la Verrerie, 4e. For only 26 to 32FF you can enjoy tasty main dishes (grilled chicken with lemon grass, roast duck) at this tiny but welcoming Vietnamese place. It is open Monday to Saturday from 11.30 am to 3 pm and 5.30 to 11 pm.

La Perla (Map 8; ☎ 01 42 77 59 40; metro Saint Paul or Hôtel de Ville), 26 Rue François Miron, 4e. A favourite with younger Parisians, this trendy California-style Mexican place is more bar than restaurant. Specialities include guacamole (29FF), nachos (30FF) and burritos (from 46FF). Meals are served Monday to Friday from noon to 3 pm and 7 to 11 pm, and on weekends nonstop from noon to 11 pm. Monday to Friday happy hour (cocktails, tequila and mezcal only) is 6 to 8 pm.

404 (Map 8; ☎ 01 42 74 57 81; metro Arts et Métiers), 69 Rue des Gravilliers, 3e. The 404 has some of the best couscous and tajine in Paris (both 90 to 105FF). It also has excellent grills from 90FF, aniseed bread and *menus* at 59FF, 79FF and 119FF, which are great value. The restaurant, done up like the inside of an old Moroccan home, is owned by the French-Arab comedian Smaïn, so the atmosphere is always upbeat. It's open for Monday to Saturday for lunch and dinner; the *brunch berbère* (Berber brunch; 100FF) is available on Sunday from noon to 5 pm.

Restaurant China (Map 8; ☎ 01 42 71 78 82; metro Hôtel de Ville), 70 Rue de la Verrerie, 4e. The all-you-can-eat buffet for 59FF (66FF at night) at this friendly Chinese restaurant is one of the Right Bank's great bargains. It is open daily from noon to 3.30 pm and 6 to 11 pm.

Le Studio (Map 8; ☎ 01 42 74 10 38; metro Rambuteau), 41 Rue du Temple, 4e. This popular and trendy place is Texas as only the French could imagine it. Tacos, enchiladas and chimichangas go for 74 to 89FF, combination platters average 94FF and there's a lunchtime *menu* for 69FF. While dining you can watch – and hear – flamenco, tap and jazz lessons at the dance school opposite in the courtyard. It is open Tuesday to Sunday from noon to midnight.

Woolloomooloo (Map 8; ☎ 01 42 72 32 11; metro Bastille), 36 Blvd Henri IV, 4e. Paris' one and only Australian restaurant opened in 1994. The dishes, served in a bright, open dining area, bring together the culinary traditions of South-East Asia and the Mediterranean. Three-course *menus* are 155FF. The extensive Australian wine list generally costs 100 to 300FF a bottle. It is open from noon to 2.30 pm and 7.30 to 11.30 pm (till midnight on Friday and Saturday; closed all day Monday). Brunch (110 to 130FF) is served on Sunday from noon to 3 pm.

Self-Catering

There's a whole bunch of **food shops** on the odd-numbered side of Rue Saint Antoine (Map 8) between the *Monoprix* supermarket (open Monday to Saturday from 9 am to 9 pm) at No 71 and the *Supermarché G20* at No 117 (open Monday to Saturday from 9 am to 8.30 pm). There's a *Franprix* supermarket at No 133 of the same street (open Monday to Saturday from 8.30 am to 7.45 pm and on Sunday from 9 am to 12.45 pm).

Flo Prestige (Map 8; ☎ 01 53 01 91 91; metro Bastille), 10 Rue Saint Antoine, on the corner with Rue des Tournelles, 4e. This branch of the famous traiteur, with some 10 outlets around town, has picnic supplies and, more importantly, some of the most delectable pastries and baked goods in Paris. It's open daily from 8 am to 11 pm.

Gourmaud (Map 8; metro Saint Paul), 91 Rue Saint Antoine, 4e. This is one of the few gourmet shops in Paris where you can assemble an entire picnic – everything from herrings, quiches and quenelles to eclairs – in one place. It's open 365 days a year from 9 am to 10 pm.

G Millet Fromager (Map 8; metro Saint Paul), 77 Rue Saint Antoine, 4e. This store, next door to one of the few boucheries chevalines (horse meat butchers) left in Paris, sells Poilâne sourdough bread as well as cheeses (closed from 1 to 4 pm, on Sunday afternoon and on Monday).

ÎLE SAINT LOUIS

Famed for its ice cream as much as anything else, the Île Saint Louis (4e) is generally an expensive place to eat. It's best suited to those looking for a light snack or the finest ingredients for lunch beside the Seine. Rue Saint Louis en l'Île has several salons de thé, and there are lots of restaurants along this street, but they tend to be touristy and either disappointing or expensive (or both).

Berthillon (Map 8; ☎ 01 43 54 31 61; metro Pont Marie), 31 Rue Saint Louis en l'Île, 4e. This ice-cream parlour is reputed to have Paris' most delicious frozen delicacies. While the fruit flavours are justifiably renowned, the chocolate, coffee, marrons glacés, Agenaise (Armagnac and prunes) and nougat au miel (honey nougat) are incomparably richer. The takeaway counter is open from 10 am to 8 pm (closed Monday, Tuesday and during school holiday periods); one/two/three small scoops cost 9/16/20FF. The *salon dégustation* (sit-down area) is open the same days from 1 pm (2 pm on weekends) to 8 pm. Other places on the Île Saint Louis also feature Berthillon ice cream but without the long queues.

Brasserie de l'Île Saint Louis (Map 8; ☎ 01 43 54 02 59; metro Pont Marie), 55 Quai de Bourbon, 4e. Founded in 1870, this spectacularly situated brasserie features choucroute garnie (sauerkraut with assorted prepared meats) and other Alsatian dishes for under 100FF, but you can enjoy the location by just ordering coffee/beer (6/15FF at the bar, 14/20FF at a table or on the terrace). It is open from 11.30 am (6 pm on Thursday) to 1 am (closed Wednesday and in August).

Les Fous de L'Île (Map 8; ☎ 01 43 25 76 67; metro Pont Marie), 33 Rue des Deux Ponts, 4e. An exception to the touristy nature of the Île Saint Louis, this friendly and down-to-earth establishment serves meals for between 120 and 150FF per person. It's open Tuesday to Friday from noon to 11 pm, Saturday from 3 to 11 pm and Sunday from noon to 7 pm.

Self-Catering
The Île Saint Louis, home to some of Paris' finest and priciest food shops, is a great place to assemble a gourmet picnic. Along Rue Saint Louis en l'Île (Map 8; metro Pont Marie) there are a number of fromageries and groceries that are usually closed on Sunday afternoon and Monday. There are more **food shops** on Rue des Deux Ponts.

Le Moule à Gâteau (Map 8; metro Pont Marie), 47 Rue Saint Louis en l'Île, 4e. This store has some of the most delicious fancy breads in all of Paris as well as fantastic brownies and chocolate cake (10FF). It is open from 8.30 am to 8 pm (closed Monday).

LATIN QUARTER
Rue Mouffetard, 5e (Map 6), is filled with scores of places to eat. It's especially popular with students, in part because of the unparalleled selection of stands selling baguette sandwiches, *panini* (Italian toasted bread with fillings) and crêpes. Rue Soufflot (metro Luxembourg) is lined with cafés.

Avoid Rue de la Huchette (see boxed text 'Bacteria Alley') unless you're after chawarma, available at several places around No 14.

French
L'Arbre à Cannelle (Map 5; ☎ 01 43 31 68 31; metro Jussieu), 14 Rue Linné, 5e. A bright, upbeat salon de thé known for its brunches (90 to 120FF) and its plats du jour (70FF). It is open daily from noon to 6.30 pm.

Les Bouchons de François Clerc (Map 6; ☎ 01 43 54 15 34; metro Maubert Mutualité), 12 Rue de l'Hôtel Colbert, 5e. Along with excellently prepared dishes like a black-pudding tart cooked with apples and crispy cod (*menus* at 117 and 219FF), the draw cards here are very affordable wines (almost wholesale prices) and an excellent cheese selection. It's open for lunch and dinner except midday Saturday and all day Sunday.

Castor et Pollux (Map 6; ☎ 01 43 31 15 00; metro Censier Daubenton), 8 Rue Tournefort, 5e. This totally untouristed place is a perfect example of a restaurant du quartier, an intimate little place frequented by local residents who appreciate the high quality of the cooking and the amicable welcome. The lunch *menu* is 62FF; there are dinner *menus* at 78 and 120FF. The plat du jour is 48FF.

Chez Léna et Mimille (Map 6; ☎ 01 47 07 72 47; metro Censier Daubenton), 32 Rue Tournefort, a block west of Rue Mouffetard, 5e. The three-course lunch/dinner *menus* at this elegant French restaurant cost 98/185F; wines are in the 100 to 165FF range. It closes on Saturday at noon and in winter on Sunday. The terrace overlooks a lovely little park.

Crêpes Stand (Map 5; metro Place Monge), 61 Rue Mouffetard, 5e. This sidewalk stand serves some of the best discount crêpes in Paris. Savoury crêpes are only 12 to 25FF; sweet crêpes are 7 to 23FF. It is open daily from 11 am to 12.30 am (2 am on Friday and Saturday nights).

L'Étoile de Berger (Map 6; ☎ 01 43 26 38 87; metro Maubert Mutualité), 42 Rue de la Montagne Sainte Geneviève, 5e. This Savoyard restaurant, decorated like a mountain chalet, specialises in raclette and fondue (85 to 105FF).

Moissonnier (Map 5; ☎ 01 43 29 87 65; metro Cardinal Lemoine), 28 Rue des Fossés Saint Bernard, 5e. Excellent Lyon-inspired cuisine has been served at this elegant restaurant since 1960. There's a *menu* at 150FF; if ordering à la carte, count on a full meal costing about 250FF (starters from 60FF, main courses from 95FF). It is open from noon to 1.30 pm and 7 pm to 9.30 pm (closed on Sunday night and all day Monday).

Le Navigator (Map 6; ☎ 01 43 54 35 86; metro Maubert Mutualité), 63 Rue Galande, two blocks from Notre Dame, 5e. This restaurant serves traditional French cuisine from 11.45 am to 2.30 pm and 6.45 to 11 pm (closed Monday). *Menus*, including wine, are available for 120, 140, 160 and 220FF.

Perraudin (Map 6; ☎ 01 46 33 15 75; metro Luxembourg), 157 Rue Saint Jacques, 5e. If you fancy bœuf Bourguignon (59FF), gigot d'agneau (leg of lamb; 59FF) or confit de canard (potted duck; 59FF), try this reasonably priced traditional French restaurant that hasn't changed much since the turn of the century. At lunchtime, there's a *menu* for 63FF and a quarter litre of wine is 10FF. It is open from noon to 2.15 pm and 7 to 11.15 pm (closed Saturday at noon and all day Sunday).

Tea Caddy (Map 6; ☎ 01 43 54 15 56; metro Saint Michel), 14 Rue Saint Julien le Pauvre, 5e, a half-block from the Seine. A fine place to enjoy English tea (from 27FF); light meals run from 35 to 45FF and salads from 30 to 35FF. It is open from noon to 7 pm (closed Wednesday).

La Tour d'Argent (Map 8; ☎ 01 43 54 23 31; fax 01 44 07 12 04; metro Cardinal Lemoine), 15 Quai de la Tournelle, 5e. Famous for its canard (duck), La Tour d'Argent was the shock story in the Michelin *Guide Rouge* a few years ago when it was downgraded from three to two stars. You can still expect to pay over 1000FF per person for dinner (though there's a set lunch at 395FF). Lunch reservations should be made eight to 10 days in advance; for dinner, reserve three weeks ahead. It's open Tuesday to Sunday.

La Truffière (Map 6; ☎ 01 46 33 29 82; metro Place Monge), 4 Rue Blainville, 5e. A lovely little restaurant off the Rue Mouffetard with an ancient fireplace, low ceilings and pink tablecloths. The winning dish here is the suprême de volaille with truffles. *Menus* are available for 90 and 110FF at lunch, 140FF till 8 pm and 198FF. At night all starters are 70FF, mains 100FF and desserts 40FF. It's open for lunch and dinner Tuesday to Sunday to 10.30.

Le Vigneron (Map 6; ☎ 01 47 07 29 99; metro Place Monge), 18-20 Rue du Pot de Fer, 5e. Just off the lively Rue Mouffetard, the 'Wine Grower' specialises in south-west cuisine (including their award-winning joue de bœuf) with *menus* at 108 and 148FF. À la carte prices are 80 to 110FF for starters, 90 to 120FF for main dishes and 50 to 65FF for desserts. Wines range from 80 to 150FF, with the average around 110FF. The ambiance here is intimate, the service superb.

North African & Middle Eastern

Founti Agadir (Map 5; ☎ 01 43 37 85 10; metro Censier Daubenton), 117 Rue Monge, 5e. This Moroccan restaurant has some of the best couscous, grills and tajines (70 to 85FF) on the Left Bank. There's a *menu* – with or without couscous – for 84FF. It's open daily except Monday.

Al Dar (Map 6; ☎ 01 43 25 35 62; metro Maubert Mutualité), 8-10 Rue Frédéric Sauton, 5e. This Lebanese restaurant has a great deli section on the corner. The latter, open daily from 7 am to midnight, serves delicious dishes of the highest quality, including little pizzas (15FF) and stuffed grape leaves (4FF each). The restaurant, open daily from noon to 3 pm and 7 pm to midnight, has lunch *menus* for 89 and 150FF; à la carte main courses are 64 to 75FF. The plat du jour is 70FF.

Koutchi (Map 5; ☎ 01 44 07 20 56; metro Cardinal Lemoine), 40 Rue du Cardinal Lemoine,

5e. The décor of this Afghan restaurant is reminiscent of a Central Asian caravanserai. Specialities include Afghan salads (25 to 30FF), meat dishes (65 to 85FF) and desserts (25 to 30FF). The evening *menu* costs 98FF; the lunchtime one is 55FF. It is open from noon to 2.30 pm and 7 to 11 pm (closed Saturday at noon and on Sunday).

La Voie Lactée (Map 5; ☎ 01 46 34 02 35; metro Cardinal Lemoine), 34 Rue du Cardinal Lemoine, 5e. The 'Milky Way' is a Turkish place with modern and traditional Anatolean cuisine, including a buffet of Turkish salads. Starters range from 32 to 55FF, main courses from 52 to 70FF. The 60FF 'lunch' *menu* is available till 9 pm; evening *menus* cost 85, 100 and 120FF. It is open from noon to 3 pm and 7 to 11 pm (closed on Sunday). Come Thursday night for some specially prepared dishes.

Asian

Chez Maï (Map 6; ☎ 01 43 54 05 33; metro Maubert Mutualité), 65 Rue Galande, 5e. This hole-in-the-wall Vietnamese place is open daily from noon to 3 pm and 7 to 11 pm. Main dishes (including excellent shrimp ones) cost only 25 to 30FF; soup is 20FF and salads and omelettes from 20FF.

Au Coin des Gourmets (Map 6; ☎ 01 43 26 12 92; metro Maubert Mutualité), 5 Rue Dante, 5e. This place serves decent (if not particularly memorable) hybrid Indochinese food. *Menus* cost 69FF at lunchtime and 85 and 97FF at dinner. It's open from noon to 2.30 pm and 7 to 10.30 pm (closed Tuesday).

Restaurant A (Map 8; ☎ 01 46 33 85 54; metro Maubert Mutualité), 5 Rue de Poissy, 5e. This place serves standard Chinese favourites (spring rolls, sweet and sour fish, Peking duck) at affordable prices; *menus* are 68 and 88FF at lunch and 108FF at dinner. Check out the artist-owner's sculpted vegetables and ice. Open daily except Monday lunch until 11 pm.

Tao (Map 6; ☎ 01 43 26 75 92; metro Luxembourg), 248 Rue Saint Jacques, 5e. Decidedly more upmarket than Chez Maï, this place serves some of the best Vietnamese cuisine in the Latin Quarter; try the warm beef noodle salad or grilled minced prawns. It's not cheap (150 to 200FF per person), but the portions are huge. Open daily except Sunday to 10.30 pm.

Tashi Delek (Map 6; ☎ 01 43 26 55 55; metro Luxembourg), 4 Rue des Fossés Saint Jacques,

5e. The lunch *menu* at this intimate Tibetan restaurant (whose name means 'bonjour' in Tibetan) costs 65FF; the 105FF dinner *menu* includes wine. There are about seven vegetarian choices on the menu ranging in price from 36 to 45FF. It is open Monday to Saturday from noon to 2.30 pm and 7 to 10.30 pm.

Vegetarian

Jardin des Pâtes (Map 5; ☎ 01 43 31 50 71; metro Cardinal Lemoine), 4 Rue Lacépède, 5e. OK, not *strictly* vegetarian but 100% *biologique* (natural), the cosy 'Garden of Pastas' has as many types of pasta as you care to name (wholewheat, buckwheat, chestnut etc) for 55 to 80FF. It's open for lunch and dinner to 11 pm except midday Monday.

Le Petit Légume (Map 5; ☎ 01 40 46 06 85; metro Cardinal Lemoine), 36 Rue des Boulangers, 5e. A good place for a quick vegetarian lunch. Dinner *menus* are 50, 64 and 75FF.

Other Cuisines

Machu Picchu (Map 6; ☎ 01 43 26 13 13; metro Luxembourg), 9 Rue Royer Collard, 5e. This small Peruvian restaurant, with main dishes from 60 to 80FF and a 48FF lunch *menu*, is open from noon to 2 pm and 7.30 to 11 pm (closed Saturday at noon and on Sunday).

Savannah Café (Map 5; ☎ 01 43 29 45 77; metro Cardinal Lemoine), 27 Rue Descartes, 5e. The food served at this charming little restaurant just north of the Place de la Contrescarpe is as eclectic as the carnival-like decorations strewn around the place. Tabouli mixes with tortellini and fromage blanc with baklava – in short, food from the south. *Menus* cost 75FF (at lunch) and 134FF. À la carte entrées are 37 to 60FF, main courses 76 to 84FF and pasta dishes from 72 to 76FF. It's open for lunch and dinner till 11.30 pm except all day Sunday and Monday at midday.

Self-Catering

Barbecued publishers are no longer available on Place Maubert (this is where Rabelais' publisher, Étienne Dolet, was hanged and then burned in 1546), but on Tuesday, Thursday and Saturday from 7 am to 1 pm, the square (Map 6; metro Maubert Mutualité) is transformed into a lively **food**

Bacteria Alley

Paris' largest concentration of tourist restaurants is squeezed into a labyrinth of narrow streets in the 5e arrondissement across the Seine from Notre Dame. The Greek, North African and Middle Eastern restaurants between Rue Saint Jacques, Blvd Saint Germain, and Blvd Saint Michel attract mainly foreigners, unaware that some people refer to Rue de la Huchette (and nearby streets like Rue Saint Séverin and Rue de la Harpe) as 'bacteria alley'. To add insult to injury, many of the poor souls who eat here are under the impression that this little maze is the famous Latin Quarter.

Although you'll probably be better off if you avoid the establishments that ripen their meat and seafood in the front window, it's still possible to get a cheap, decent meal in the northern 5e. For details see the Latin Quarter section in this chapter.

market. **Food shops** are also found here and along nearby Rue Lagrange.

There's another **food market** on Rue Mouffetard, at the bottom end, around Rue de l'Arbalète (Map 5; metro Censier Daubenton). The stalls tend to close on Sunday afternoons and Mondays. This is one of Paris' oldest and liveliest market areas, with many interesting shops along the street. There is a *Franprix* supermarket at 82 Rue Mouffetard (Map 5; metro Censier Daubenton) open Monday to Saturday from 9 am to 8 pm and on Sunday to 1 pm.

Rue Saint Jacques, just south of Rue Soufflot (Map 6; metro Luxembourg), also has a variety of food shops and another **food market** can be found at Place Monge (Map 5; metro Place Monge). It's open Wednesday, Friday and Sunday mornings until 1 pm. Nearby at 37 Rue Lacépède (Map 5) is a cheap *Ed l'Épicier* supermarket open Monday to Saturday from 9 am to 7.30 pm. There's a *Shopi* supermarket at 34 Rue Monge (Map 5) open Monday to Saturday from 8.30 am to 9 pm.

For sandwiches, try the popular hole-in-the-wall *Douce France* (Map 6; metro Luxembourg) at 7 Rue Royer Collard, where the lunchtime line of Sorbonne students confirms the quality of the sandwiches (including vegetarian options, 13.50FF), coffee (3FF) and fruit juices (6FF). There are no tables inside but you can take your mini-picnic over to the Jardin du Luxembourg. It's open weekdays from 11 am to 4 pm.

6e ARRONDISSEMENT

Rue Saint André des Arts (Map 6; metro Saint Michel or Odéon) is lined with restaurants, including a few down the covered passage between Nos 59 and 61. There are lots of places between Église Saint Sulpice and Église Saint Germain des Prés, especially along Rue des Canettes, Rue Princesse and Rue Guisarde. Place Carrefour de l'Odéon (Map 6; metro Odéon) has a cluster of lively bars, cafés and restaurants.

French

Place Saint Germain des Prés is home to three famous cafés. Brasserie Lipp is listed below; Les Deux Magots and Café de Flore are covered in the Entertainment chapter under 6e Arrondissement.

L'Arbuci (Map 6; ☎ 01 44 32 16 00; metro Mabillon), 25 Rue de Buci. This large, animated retro-style restaurant's specialities include seafood and spit-roasted beef, chicken, pork, salmon and – of all things – bananas. *Menus* cost 83, 133 and 139FF. All-you-can-eat access to oysters of modest size costs 146FF. It is open daily from noon to 1 or 2 am. From Wednesday to Saturday there's live jazz in the basement from 10.30 pm (not during July and August).

Brasserie Lipp (Map 6; ☎ 01 45 48 53 91; metro Saint Germain des Prés), 151 Blvd Saint Germain. Politicians rub shoulders with intellectuals and editors here, while tuxedoed waiters serve pricey à la carte dishes (choucroute, 102FF; plats du jour, 120FF) at this old-time, wood-panelled café-brasserie. The *menu* costs 196FF (including 0.25L of wine). Many people make a big fuss about sitting downstairs rather than upstairs, which is the nonsmoking section and considered 'nowheresville'. Brasserie Lipp is open daily from 8.30 am to 1 am.

Lina's (Map 6; ☎ 01 43 29 14 14; metro Odéon), 27 Rue Saint Sulpice. A conveniently situated and comfortable member of a small chain with classy sandwiches in the 21 to 45FF range and soups from 27FF.

Le Mâcon d'Henri (Map 6; ☎ 01 43 29 08 70; metro Saint Sulpice), 8-10 Rue Guisarde. This very Parisian bistro in a street awash with bars serves up Lyon-inspired dishes like lentil salad, various charcuteries, saucisson chaud (hot Lyon sausage) and tarte aux pommes (apple pie). Starters are 35 to 40FF, main courses 60 to 80FF. It's open daily for lunch and dinner until 11.30 pm.

Les Mouettes (Map 6; ☎ 01 45 48 22 31; metro Saint Placide), 27 Rue de Vaugirard. Traditional, family-style French cuisine is served at this neighbourhood restaurant from noon to 3 pm and 7 to 11 pm (closed on Sunday). The *menus* cost from 85FF (for lunch) and 95FF (for dinner).

Le Petit Zinc (Map 6; ☎ 01 42 61 20 60; metro Saint Germain des Prés), 11 Rue Saint Benoît. This wonderful and expensive (entrées from 52 to 110FF, main courses 110 to 160FF) place serves regional specialities from the south-west of France in true Art Nouveau splendour. There's a *menu* at 168FF. Try to get a table on the raised level in order to enjoy all the goings-on. It's open daily from noon to 2 am.

Polidor (Map 6; ☎ 01 43 26 95 34; metro Odéon), 41 Rue Monsieur le Prince. A meal at this *crêmerie-restaurant* is like a quick trip back to Victor Hugo's Paris – the restaurant and its décor date from 1845 – but everyone knows about it, and the place has become pretty touristy. Guests are seated together at tables of six, 10 or 16. *Menus* of tasty, family-style French cuisine are available for 55FF (lunch only) and 100FF. Specialities include bœuf Bourguignon (50FF), blanquette de veau (veal in white sauce; 68FF) and the most famous tarte tatin (caramelised apple pie; 25FF) in Paris. It is open daily from noon to 2.30 pm and 7 to 12.30 am (11 pm on Sunday). Neither reservations nor credit cards are accepted.

Rôtisserie d'En Face (Map 6; ☎ 01 43 26 40 98; metro Odéon), 2 Rue Christine. This modern but traditional place, a short walk south-east of the Pont Neuf, is a good choice if you're looking for simple but well prepared French food. The lunch *menu* is 139FF; at dinner there's one at 159FF and another at 210FF. It's open for lunch and dinner to 11 pm except midday Saturday and all day Sunday.

Italian

Le Golfe de Naples (Map 6; ☎ 01 43 26 98 11; metro Mabillon), 5 Rue de Montfaucon. Italian residents of Paris say this restaurant/pizzeria has the best pizza and home-made pasta in a city not generally celebrated for its Italian food (many Parisians don't consider it 'serious' enough). Pizzas range from 49 to 59FF, and don't forget to try the grilled fresh vegetables (85FF).

Osteria del Passe-Partout (Map 6; ☎ 01 46 34 14 54; metro Saint Michel), 20 Rue de l'Hirondelle, through the arch from 6 Place Saint Michel. Pasta (49 to 77FF), meat dishes (60 to 71FF) and tiramisu (28FF) with an excellent reputation are served at this modern Italian place with medieval touches. Open from noon to 2.15 pm and 7.15 to 11 pm (closed Saturday at noon and on Sunday). The *menus* start at 65FF; the plat du jour is 52FF.

Vegetarian

Guenmaï (Map 6; ☎ 01 43 26 03 24; metro Saint Germain des Prés or Mabillon), 2bis Rue de l'Abbaye. Macrobiotic, organically grown meals are served from Monday to Saturday from 11.45 am to 3.30 pm. The plat du jour is 64FF; soups are around 27FF and main courses in the 50 to 57FF range.

Other Cuisines

Chez Albert (Map 6; ☎ 01 46 33 22 57; metro Odéon), 43 Rue Mazarine. Authentic Portuguese food is not easy to come by in Paris, but this place has it in spades; pork with clams, numerous bacalhau (dried cod) dishes and prawns sautéed in lots of garlic. The *menus* are 80 and 135FF, and it's open for lunch and dinner except all day Sunday and midday on Monday.

Indonesia (Map 6; ☎ 01 43 25 70 22; metro Luxembourg), 12 Rue de Vaugirard. This 'embassy of Indonesian cooking', run as a non-profit cooperative, has all the standards – from an elaborate, multi-course rijstafel to nasi goreng, rendang and gado-gado. *Menus* are available at 89, 99 and 129FF. It's open daily for lunch and dinner to 10.30 or 11 pm except Sunday at midday.

Self-Catering

With the Jardin du Luxembourg nearby, this is the perfect area for a picnic lunch. See the Latin Quarter section for more picnic suggestions.

Champion (Map 6; metro Mabillon), 79 Rue de Seine. This supermarket is open Monday to Saturday from 8.40 am to 9 pm.

Chez Jean-Mi (Map 6; metro Odéon), 10 Rue de l'Ancienne Comédie. This boulangerie and restaurant is open 24 hours a day, 365 days a year.

Food shops (Map 6; metro Mabillon), Rue de Seine and Rue de Buci. This is the largest cluster of shops in the 6e.

Marché Saint Germain (Map 6; metro Mabillon), Rue Lobineau, just north of the eastern end of Église Saint Germain. This covered market has a huge array of produce and prepared foods.

Monoprix (Map 6; metro Saint Germain des Prés), 52 Rue de Rennes. This store's supermarket, at the back of the basement level, is open Monday to Saturday from 9 am to 9 pm.

Pâtisserie Viennoise (Map 6; ☎ 01 43 26 60 48; metro Odéon), 8 Rue de l'École de Médicine. This shop has a delightful selection of tourtes (quiche-like pies; 25FF), salads (from 18FF), apple-cinnamon strudel (15FF) and Sachertorte (17FF). Light plats du jour are about 35FF. It's open Monday to Friday from 9 am to 7.15 pm.

Poilâne (Map 4; ☎ 01 45 48 42 59; metro Sèvres Babylone), 8 Rue du Cherche Midi. This is the most famous boulangerie in Paris. Its delicious sourdough bread, baked in wood-fired ovens every two hours, has a crunchy, slightly burned crust (19FF for a small round loaf). Open from 7 am to 8.15 pm (closed on Sunday).

CHAMPS-ÉLYSÉES AREA

Few places along touristy Ave des Champs-Élysées offer good value, but some of the restaurants in the surrounding areas are excellent.

French

L'Ardoise (Map 2; ☎ 01 42 96 28 18; metro Concorde or Tuilleries), 28 Rue du Mont Thabor, 1er. The incomparable American food writer Patricia Wells raved about this place with no menu (*ardoise* means 'blackboard', which is all there is) so who are we to argue? The rabbit and hazelnut terrine and the beef fillet with morels, prepared so dexterously by chef Pierre Jay (ex Tour d'Argent), are superb and the 165FF *menu* offers excellent value. It's open for lunch and dinner until 11.30 pm except all day Monday and midday on Tuesday.

L'Étoile Verte (Map 2; ☎ 01 43 80 69 34; metro Charles de Gaulle-Étoile), 13 Rue Brey, 17e. When one of us was a student in Paris, this was the place for a splurge and it still feels like it did way back then. All the old classics remain – the onion soup, the snails, the rabbit – and there are *menus* for 74FF (available 11.30 am till 9 pm daily except Saturday and Sunday), 100FF (with wine) and 145FF (with apéritif, wine and coffee). À la carte entrées start at 39FF, main courses at 59FF.

Fauchon (Map 2; ☎ 01 47 62 60 11; metro Madeleine), 26-30 Place de la Madeleine, 8e. Paris' most famous luxury food store (see Food & Wine in the Shopping chapter) also has five eat-in areas, including a *cafeteria*, in the basement at No 30 – where you can purchase hot drinks, cold dishes, sandwiches and exquisite pastries. It is open Monday to Saturday from 9.40 am to 7 pm. After that, and until midnight, the cafeteria turns into a *brasserie*. *La Trattoria* (☎ 01 47 42 90 30), an Italian restaurant on the 1st floor at No 26, is open from noon to 3 pm and 7 to 11 pm (closed on Sunday and holidays).

French Chain Restaurants – There are branches of a number of the French chains along the Ave des Champs-Élysées (8e), including *Hippopotamus Citroën* at No 42 (Map 2; ☎ 01 53 83 94 50; metro Franklin D Roosevelt); *Bistrot Romain* at No 73 (Map 2; ☎ 01 42 56 88 45; metro Champs-Élysées Clemenceau); and *Pizza Pino* at No 33 (Map 2; ☎ 01 43 59 23 89; metro Franklin D Roosevelt.

Hédiard (Map 2; metro Madeleine), 21 Place de la Madeleine, 8e. Another luxury food shop (see the Shopping chapter), Hédiard has an adjoining *café-restaurant* (☎ 01 43 88 99), with starters priced at 65FF and main courses at 120FF. It is open for lunch and dinner Monday to Saturday to 10.30 pm.

La Maison d'Alsace (Map 2; ☎ 01 53 93 97 00; metro Franklin D Roosevelt), 39 Ave des Champs-Élysées, 8e. A pricey, Alsatian-style brasserie where you can dine 24 hours a day, 365 days a year. Specialities include seafood (oysters are 120 to 180FF a dozen), choucroute Strasbourgeoise (Strasbourg-style sauerkraut with garnishes; 83FF) and fish and meat dishes (81 to 154FF). Beer is 25FF for a demi.

Maison Prunier (Map 2; ☎ 01 44 17 35 85; fax 01 44 17 90 10; metro Charles de Gaulle-Étoile), 16 Ave Victor Hugo, 16e. This venerable fish and seafood restaurant, founded in 1925, is famed for its Art Deco interior. First courses generally cost 90 to 250FF, mains are 160 to 280FF. It is open from noon to 2.30 pm and 7 to 11 pm (closed on Sunday and at lunch on Monday). Make reservations at least two days ahead.

Le Petit Champerret (Map 2; ☎ 01 43 80 01 39; metro Porte de Champerret), 40 Rue Vernier, 17e. This little bistro north of Place Charles de Gaulle serves hearty home cooking in an intimate, friendly atmosphere. Try the stuffed rabbit with wild mushrooms or the tête de veau (calf's head cooked in a white court-bouillon). There's a lunch *menu* at 90FF; an à la carte meal will set you back about 180FF. It's open weekdays only.

American

Chicago Pizza Pie Factory (Map 2; ☎ 01 45 62 50 23; metro George V), 5 Rue de Berri (8e) just off Ave des Champs-Élysées. A vastly popular eatery that specialises in Chicago-style deep-dish pizzas (88 to 149FF for the two person size). Weekday lunch *menus* are available for 51, 62 and 71FF. It is open daily from 11.45 am to 1 am. Happy hour at the bar is from 4 to 7 pm.

Planet Hollywood (Map 2; ☎ 01 53 83 78 27; metro George V), 78 Ave des Champs-Élysées, 8e. The Paris version of this show-biz hamburger chain offers pizzas at 70 to 87FF, burgers at 72 to 79FF, desserts at 40 to 47FF, beers at 30 to 40FF and wine by the glass at 25FF. It's open daily from 11.30 am to 1 am.

Self-Catering

Place de la Madeleine, 8e (Map 2; metro Madeleine) is the luxury food centre of one of the world's food capitals. The delicacies on offer don't come cheap, but even travellers on a modest budget can turn a walk around La Madeleine into a gastronomic odyssey. Most places are open from Monday to Saturday.

Prisunic (Map 2; metro Franklin D Roosevelt), 62 Blvd des Champs-Élysées, 8e. This store's supermarket section is in the basement. It is open Monday to Saturday from 9 am to midnight.

GARE SAINT LAZARRE & GRANDS BOULEVARDS AREAS

This area, encompassing part of the 2e and 9e, has a number of fine restaurants worth trying. Neon-lit Blvd du Montmartre (Map 7; metro Rue Montmartre or Richelieu Drouot) and nearby parts of Rue du Faubourg Montmartre (neither of which are anywhere near the neighbourhood of Montmartre) form one of Paris' most animated café and dining districts.

French

Chartier (Map 7; ☎ 01 47 70 86 29; metro Rue Montmartre), 7 Rue du Faubourg Montmartre, 9e. A real gem that is justifiably famous for its 330-seat, *belle époque* dining room, virtually unaltered since 1896. The prices and fare are similar to those at Le Drouot (the management is the same) and among the cheapest for a sit-down meal in Paris. It is open every day of the year from 11.30 am to 3 pm and 6 to 10 pm. Reservations are not accepted, so don't be surprised if there's a queue.

Le Drouot (Map 7; ☎ 01 42 96 68 23; metro Richelieu Drouot), 103 Rue de Richelieu (1st floor), 2e. The décor and ambience of this inexpensive restaurant haven't changed since the late 1930s; dining is like a trip back to prewar Paris. A three-course traditional French meal with wine should cost less than 100FF: fish and meat main courses are 35 to 60FF, a demi of cider or beer is 13FF. *Menus* cost 55, 62 and 79FF. It is open 365 days a year from 11.45 am to 3 pm and 6.30 to 10 pm. Reservations are not accepted.

Vegetarian

Country Life (Map 7; ☎ 01 42 97 48 51; metro Opéra), 6 Rue Daunou, 2e. A food shop/restau-

PLACES TO EAT

rant that serves an all-you-can-eat buffet (65FF) from 11.30 am to 2.30 pm and 6.30 to 10 pm (closed on Friday night, Saturday and Sunday).

Other Cuisines

Hard Rock Café (Map 7; ☎ 01 42 46 10 00; metro Rue Montmartre), 14 Blvd du Montmartre, 9e. Housed in the theatre where Maurice Chevalier made his debut, Paris' hopping Hard Rock Café attracts businesspeople for lunch and a mix of tourists and young, trendy Parisians at night. Salads are 50 to 78FF, burgers 62 to 75FF, and main courses 78 to 105FF. It is open every day of the year, except Christmas Day, from 11.30 am to 2 am. Beer is 24FF, 0.5L of wine 46FF, and cocktails start at 52FF. Happy hour is between 6 and 8 pm. The boutique (open daily from 10 am to 12.30 am) does a roaring business selling T-shirts, bomber jackets and other fashion items.

North African Jewish Restaurants (all 9e; Map 7), Rue Richer, Rue Cadet and Rue Geoffroy Marie. These kosher places are just south of the Cadet metro stop. The pick of the crop is said to be *Les Ailes*, next door to the Folies Bergères at 34 Rue Richer (Map 7; ☎ 01 47 70 62 53; metro Cadet). It's a kosher Tunisian place serving superb couscous with meat or fish starting at 105FF and has a good selection of North African salads. Les Ailes is open daily except Friday night and Saturday (open on Saturday night in winter).

GARE DU NORD & GARE DE L'EST AREAS
French

There's a cluster of brasseries and bistros opposite the façade of Gare du Nord.

Brasserie Terminus Nord (Map 3; ☎ 01 42 85 05 15; metro Gare du Nord), 23 Rue de Dunkerque, 10e. The copper bar, white tablecloths and brass fixtures – reflected brightly in the mirrored walls – look much as they did between the wars. Also known as Brasserie 1925, this Art Deco palace is a decent spot for a last, nostalgically Parisian meal before boarding the Eurostar back to Old Blighty and for that reason has become rather touristy. Breakfast (45FF) is available daily from 7 to 11 am; full meals are served from 11 am

straight through to 12.30 am. The 123FF *menu du garçon* is not available from 6 to 10 pm; the late-night (after 10 pm) *faim de nuit menu* costs 121FF.

Le Chalet Maya (Map 3; ☎ 01 47 70 52 78; metro Poissonière or Gare de l'Est), 5 Rue des Petits Hôtels, 10e. A nice little unpretentious restaurant whose food (seafood cassoulet, tête de veau) is not about to change the world but for a 60FF *menu* at lunch and 95FF at dinner, you shouldn't expect much more. It's open for lunch and dinner except Sunday and midday on Monday.

French Chain Restaurants – Branches include *Hippopotamus* (Map 3; ☎ 01 48 78 29 26; metro Gare du Nord), 27 Rue de Dunkerque, 10e, and *Batifol* (Map 3; ☎ 01 42 80 34 74; metro Gare du Nord), 9 Blvd de Denain, 10e. *Menus* range from 65 to 143FF.

Au Gigot Fin (Map 3; ☎ 01 42 08 38 81; metro Jacques Bonsergent), 56 Rue de Lancry, 10e. This very meaty restaurant serves specialities from Périgord, including cassoulet, duck confit and gigot d'agneau (leg of lamb) in many different ways. It has lovely décor (we liked the wrought-iron circular staircase), but it feels somewhat like a hotel restaurant. There's a lunch *menu* for 85FF and dinner ones at 100 and 175FF. It's open for lunch and dinner except midday Saturday and all day Sunday.

Other Cuisines

Paris-Dakar (Map 3; ☎ 01 42 08 16 64; metro Gare de l'Est), 95 Rue du Faubourg Saint Martin, 10e. *Menus* at this Senegalese restaurant cost 59FF (lunch only), 129 and 179FF. Specialities include tiéboudienne (rice, fish and vegetables; 98FF), yassa (chicken or fish marinated in lime juice and onion sauce; 70FF) and mafé (beef sautéed in peanut sauce; 69FF). There are *menus* at 59FF (lunch only), 99FF and 149FF (including wine). It is open from noon to 3 pm and 7 pm to midnight (closed on Monday and Friday at lunchtime). The popular bar here is open to 2 am.

Passage Brady (Map 3; metro Château d'Eau). Running between Blvd de Strasbourg and Rue du Faubourg Saint Denis, the tiny Passage Brady is a covered arcade that could easily be in Mumbai or Karachi. The incredibly cheap (and usually crowded) Indian and Pakistani places are generally open for one of the best lunch deals in Paris (meat curry, rice and a tiny salad from 30FF) and for dinner, with *menus* at 49 to 55FF. They include *Palais des Rajpout, La Reine du Kashmir, Shalimar, Bhai Bhai, Kashmir Express* and *Pooja*, perhaps the best of the lot.

Self-Catering

Rue du Faubourg Saint Denis, 10e (Map 3; metro Strasbourg Saint Denis), north of Blvd Saint Denis, is one of the cheapest places in Paris to buy food. It has a distinctively Middle Eastern air, and quite a few of the groceries offer Turkish and North African specialities. Many of the food shops, including the fromagerie at No 54, are closed on Sunday afternoon and Monday.

Franprix (Map 3; Gare de l'Est), 57 Blvd de Magenta, 10e. Open Monday to Saturday from 9 am to 7.30 pm. The Franprix opposite 6 Rue des Petites Écuries, 10e (Map 3; metro Château d'Eau) is open the same hours.

Marché Saint Quentin (Map 3; metro Gare de l'Est), opposite 92 Blvd de Magenta at the start of Rue de Chabrol, 10e. This huge covered market is open from 8 am to 1 pm and 3.30 to 7.30 pm (closed on Sunday afternoon and Monday).

BASTILLE AREA

This area, mostly the 11e and 12e but also the westernmost part of the 4e, is chock-a-block with restaurants. Narrow, scruffy Rue de Lappe (Map 5) may not look like much during the day, but it's one of the trendiest café and nightlife streets in Paris, attracting a young, alternative crowd. Many of the places speak with a Spanish accent – Tex-Mex, tapas and Cuban food can all be found here. Things really start to pick up late at night.

French

Traditional French food in all price ranges can be found in the Bastille Area.

Le Bistrot du Dôme (Map 8; ☎ 01 48 04 88 44; metro Bastille), 2 Rue de la Bastille, 4e. Opposite Bofinger, this superb restaurant, a distant cousin of the better known Le Dôme

Brasserie (Map 4) in Montparnasse, specialises in superbly prepared (and pricey) fish dishes. The blackboard menu has starters at 45 to 65FF, main courses at 90 to 130FF.

Brasserie Bofinger (Map 8; ☎ 01 42 72 87 82; metro Bastille), 5-7 Rue de la Bastille, 4e. This is reputedly the oldest brasserie in Paris (founded in 1864), with Art Deco-style brass, glass and mirrors. Specialities include choucroute (90 to 120FF) and seafood dishes (from 126FF). The 169FF *menu* includes half a bottle of wine. It is open daily from noon to 3 pm and 6.30 pm to 1 am (no afternoon closure on weekends and holidays). Reservations are necessary for dinner, especially on the weekend, and for Sunday lunch. Ask for a seat downstairs, under the *coupole* (stained-glass dome) if possible.

Café de l'Industrie (Map 5; ☎ 01 47 00 13 53; metro Bréguet Sabin), 16 Rue Saint Sabin, 11e. At this very popular restaurant with neocolonial décor main courses are in the 50 to 85FF bracket and the desserts – every imaginable kind of tarte – are from 24 to 34FF. It's open until 1 am every night except Saturday and it's wise to book.

Chez Paul (Map 5; ☎ 01 47 00 34 57; metro Ledru Rollin), 13 Rue de Charonne, at the end of Rue de Lappe, 11e. This is a convivial and extremely popular bistro with traditional French cuisine. Mains cost 62 to 95FF, so count on paying about 170FF for a meal with wine. It is open daily from noon to 3 pm and 7.30 pm to 12.30 am.

Crêpes Show (Map 5; ☎ 01 47 00 36 46; metro Ledru Rollin), 51 Rue de Lappe, 11e. This small restaurant specialises in sweet and savoury Breton crêpes and buckwheat galettes (18 to 43FF) and has *menus* at 43FF (lunch) and 59FF. Quite a few vegetarian dishes are also available, including salads (from 39FF). It is open from noon to 3 pm and 7 pm to 1 or 2 am (closed for lunch on weekends and, in winter, all day Sunday).

L'Encrier (Map 5; ☎ 01 44 68 08 16; metro Ledru Rollin), 55 Rue Traversière, 12e. If you're looking for lunch in the Bastille area, you couldn't do better than at the 'Inkwell', which serves an excellent value three-course *menu* for 58FF. It's open for lunch and dinner Monday to Friday.

French Chain Restaurants – Hippopotamus (Map 5; ☎ 01 42 72 98 37; metro Bastille), 1 Blvd

Beaumarchais, 4e, and *Léon de Bruxelles* (Map 5; ☎ 01 42 71 75 55; metro Bastille), 3 Blvd Beaumarchais, 4e.

Les Galopins (Map 5; ☎ 01 47 00 45 35; metro Bastille), 24 Rue des Taillandiers, 11e. This little neighbourhood bistro serves simple but high quality starters and main courses (60 to 80FF) like rabbit with mustard and green salad with foie gras. The reception is warm here; diners are offered a little glass of beer at the bar.

Jacques Melac (Map 5; ☎ 01 40 09 93 37; metro Charonne), 42 Rue Léon Frot, 11e. Farther east from the Bastille, Melac's regional specialities include a plat du jour at 60FF. It's open for lunch and dinner on weekdays except Monday evening.

Relais du Massif Central (Map 5; ☎ 01 47 00 46 55; metro Bastille), 16 Rue Daval, 11e. The culinary inspiration of this small, family-run French restaurant comes from the Massif Central of south-central France. The *menus* cost 67, 99 and 124FF, and the food is very conservative and traditional. It is open Monday to Saturday from noon to 3 pm and 7.30 to midnight.

Le Square Trousseau (Map 5; ☎ 01 43 43 06 00; metro Ledru Rollin), 1 Rue Antoine Vollon, 12e. This vintage bistro, with its etched glass, zinc bar and polished wood panelling, is comfortable rather than trendy and attracts a jolly and very mixed clientele. The food is of high quality and the standards high, but we suspect that most people come to enjoy the lovely terrace overlooking a small park. The lunch *menu* is 135FF; à la carte dinner with wine should cost between 180 and 250FF. Diners are received at the bar with a complimentary glass of wine. It's open daily till 11.30 pm.

Le Tabarin (Map 5; ☎ 01 48 07 15 22; metro Bréguet Sabin), 3 Rue du Pasteur-Wagner, corner of Rue Amelot, 11e. On the Marais-Bastille border, this friendly café-restaurant manages to combine tradition with a modern approach. Excellent and reasonably priced food like grilled salmon costs from 66 to 96FF. Open daily until midnight.

Other Cuisines

Cuisines from all over the world are found along Rue de la Roquette and Rue de Lappe, just east of Place de la Bastille, but Tex-Mex (usually rather bland in Paris) is the major attraction.

Babylon (Map 5; ☎ 01 47 00 55 02; metro Bastille), 21 Rue Daval, 11e. This small Middle Eastern grill has excellent chawarma (23FF takeaway, 25FF eat in) and falafel. The tables are round and very tiny. It is open Monday to Saturday from 11 am to 1 am.

Café Le Serail (Map 5; ☎ 01 43 38 17 01; metro Bastille), 10 Rue Sedaine, 11e. This trendy North African café-restaurant is a lounge lizard's paradise, with deep over-stuffed sofas where you can sit and sip mint tea before or after a meal. There's a lunch *menu* for 100FF; expect to pay about 200FF à la carte at dinner.

Chez Heang (Map 5; ☎ 01 48 07 80 98; metro Bastille), 5 Rue de la Roquette, 11e. You cook your food on a gas grill in the middle of your table at this Korean barbecue restaurant. *Menus* are 58FF at lunch and 68 to 148FF at dinner; the *fondue maison* – a kind of spicy hotpot in which you dip and cook your food – is 125FF per person (minimum two). It is open daily from noon to 2.30 pm and 6.30 to midnight.

Havanita Café (Map 5; ☎ 01 43 55 96 42; metro Bastille), 11 Rue de Lappe, 11e. A bar-restaurant decorated with posters and murals inspired, like the food and drinks, by Cuba. Not as trendy as it used to be but still worth a look. Draught beers are 20 to 24FF, cocktails 40 to 48FF, starters 34 to 78FF and the excellent main courses 58 to 160FF. It's open daily from noon to 3 pm and 5 pm to 2 am. Happy hour – when cocktails are 15 to 20FF cheaper – is from 5 to 8 pm.

Le Kiosque (Map 1; ☎ 01 43 79 74 80; metro Philippe Auguste), 26 Rue de la Folie Régnault, 11e. A culinary adventure along the Silk Road, this restaurant serves an amalgamation of Turkish, Indian, Chinese and Lebanese – and it works. The lovely décor (Turkish ceramics, carpets on the walls) sets the tone. Try the mixed meze, the lamb curry Madras-style or the chicken biryani. There's a *menu* at 82FF; ordering à la carte should cost around 160FF per person. It's open until 2 am, weekdays only.

La Pirada Bar Tapas (Map 5; ☎ 01 47 00 73 61; metro Bastille), 7 Rue de Lappe, 11e. This popular place has live music at night. Other nearby Tex-Mex options are *Café 66* (named after US Route 66) at No 8 and *Del Rio Café* at No 26.

Suds (Map 5; ☎ 01 43 14 06 36; metro Ledru Rollin), 55 Rue de Charonne, 11e. No, not a trendy laundrette but a very branché bar-restaurant with a name that means 'Souths', and with jazz in the basement. The cuisine here is anything and everything from the south – from Mexican and Peruvian to Portuguese and North African. Suds packs them in daily for lunch and dinner till 1 am (midnight on Sunday and Monday), but neither the food nor the mainstream music impressed us. Lunch *menus* are available for 59 to 88FF. À la carte starters at dinner range from 29 to 45FF, main courses from 59 to 88FF and desserts from 32 to 39FF; expect to pay about 200FF per person with wine at dinner. The vegetarian plate is 52FF.

Self-Catering

There are lots of **food shops and supermarkets** along Rue de la Roquette up toward Place Léon Blum (metro Voltaire). There's a *Monoprix* (Map 5; metro Ledru Rollin) at 97 Rue du Faubourg Saint Antoine, 11e, open Monday to Saturday from 9 am to 9 pm.

OBERKAMPF, MÉNILMONTANT & BELLEVILLE AREAS

In the northern part of the 11e, east of Place de la République, and into the 20e, Rue Oberkampf and its extension, Rue de Ménilmontant, are increasingly popular with diners and denizens of the night. Rue de Belleville is dotted with Chinese, Vietnamese and Turkish places and Blvd de Belleville has loads of kosher couscous restaurants (closed on Saturday).

French

Le Baratin (Map 1; ☎ 01 43 49 39 70; metro Pyrénées), 3 Rue Jouye-Rouve, 20e. This wine bistro offers some of the best food in the 20e with a choice of two or three starters and the same number of main courses. There's a lunch *menu* for 60FF; à la carte at dinner shouldn't set you back more than 160FF. Thankfully there's not canned music here as seems to be standard in most *bars à vin* in Paris. It's open for lunch and dinner except all day Sunday and Monday and at midday on Saturday.

Le Camelot (Map 5; ☎ 01 43 55 54 04; metro Saint Sébastien Froissart), 50 Rue Amelot, 11e. The *menu* here (120FF at lunch, 140FF at dinner) includes such delicacies as crab lasagne and honey-roasted duck. It's open weekdays only till 10.30 pm

Le Charbon (Map 3; ☎ 01 43 57 55 13; metro Parmentier), 109 Rue Oberkampf, 11e. More of a café than a restaurant, the Charbon serves a Saturday or Sunday brunch (75FF; 11 am to 5 pm) which is just right at a place that's not too chic, not too trendy, not too young and not too conservative. The plat du jour is 68FF. It's open daily from 9 am to 2 am.

Le Clown Bar (Map 8; ☎ 01 43 55 87 35; metro Filles du Calvaire), 114 Rue Amelot, 11e. This wonderful wine bar next to the Cirque d'Hiver is like a museum with painted ceilings, mosaics on the wall and a lovely round zinc bar. The food is simple and unpretentious; we loved the rabbit rillettes with onion compote and parmentier (black pudding mixed with mashed potatoes and baked). Starters are 30 to 58FF, main courses around 75FF; expect to pay from 150FF per person. It's open daily for lunch and dinner to 11.30 except Sunday from October to April.

Le Repaire de Cartouche (Map 8; ☎ 01 47 00 25 86, metro Saint Sébastien Froissart), 8 Blvd des Filles du Calvaire or 99 Rue Amelot, 11e. This old-fashioned place with a distinctly modern approach (rissole of black pudding cooked with figs, cod roasted with leeks) has taken a new direction with the arrival of a young and energetic chef. Starters are 35 to 45FF, main courses 65 to 90FF and desserts 30 to 40FF. Wines average about 160FF a bottle. It's open for lunch and dinner till 11 pm except all day Sunday and Monday evening.

Au Trou Normand (Map 8; ☎ 01 48 05 80 23; metro Oberkampf), 9 Rue Jean-Pierre Timbaud, 11e. Hosted by several grannies, this very French and cosy little restaurant has some of the lowest prices in Paris. Starters are 10 to 25FF (the vegetable soup is particularly good), main courses are from 29 to 39FF, desserts are under 10FF. Diners sit at shared tables covered with plastic tablecloths. It's open from noon to 2.30 pm and 7.30 to 11 pm except Saturday lunch and all day Sunday.

Le Villaret (Map 3; ☎ 01 43 57 89 76; metro Parmentier), 13 Rue Ternaux, 11e. This excellent neighbourhood restaurant, a stone's throw from the Cirque d'Hiver and the great food market on Blvd Richard Lenoir (Map 5; metro Richard Lenoir), has diners coming from across Paris till late to sample such specialities as artichoke and foie gras salad, calf's liver with truffled mashed potatoes and cod cooked with creamed mussels. Starters are 40 to 50FF, main courses 80 to 135FF and desserts 40FF. Wines range from 85 to 320FF but average around 150FF. It's open for dinner only, Monday to Saturday to 1 am.

Other Cuisines

Café Florentin (Map 3; ☎ 01 43 55 57 00; metro Parmentier), 40 Rue Jean-Pierre Timbaud, 11e. Superb Italian fare in cosy surroundings. The lunch *menu* is 65FF (including wine); à la carte starters are 21 to 55FF and main courses 58 to 90FF. The two dozen pasta dishes range in price from 56 to 78FF. It's open for lunch and dinner until 11.45 pm except Saturday midday and all day Sunday.

Chez Lalou (Map 3; ☎ 01 43 58 35 28; metro Couronnes), 78 Blvd de Belleville, 20e. The pick of the kosher couscous crop on the Blvd de Belleville, this place has killer couscous from 60 to 80FF, grills from 60FF, brick à l'oeuf for 20FF and salads from 25FF. The terrace is a lovely – and lively – place to dine in the warm weather.

Chez Vincent (Map 1; ☎ 01 42 02 22 45; metro Botzaris), 5 Rue du Tunnel, 19e. This restaurant on the southern boundary of the Parc des Buttes-Chaumont offers refined (and rather expensive) Italian cuisine in a lively, smoky environment. There's a *menu* at 180FF but ordering à la carte won't leave you with much change from 300FF. It's open for lunch and dinner until 10.30 pm except on Sunday and at midday on Saturday.

Aux Délices du Cameroun (Map 3; ☎ 01 43 55 50 51; metro Parmentier), 69 Rue Jean-Pierre Timbaud, 11e. For an interesting change, here's African food with main courses from 70 to 90FF. There's live music Thursday to Saturday from 9 pm to 2 am. It's closed Saturday lunchtime and on Sunday.

Favela Chic (Map 3; ☎ 01 43 57 15 47; metro Ménilmontant), 131 Rue Oberkampf, 11e. Very branché Brazilian is the story at this small place with main courses at 50 to 70FF including a massive feijoada (65FF). It's open daily from noon to 2 am (from 7 pm on Saturday).

Felafel Ely Gel (Map 3; ☎ 01 47 97 09 73; metro Belleville), 142 Blvd de Belleville, 20e. The takeaway felafel along Rue des Rosiers in the Marais is decent enough but this place has them just that much more authentic for under 20FF.

Krung Thep (Map 1; ☎ 01 43 66 83 74; metro Pyrénées), 93 Rue Julien Lacroix, 20e. Considered by many to be the most authentic Thai restaurant in Paris, the 'Bangkok' is a small place with all our favourites: green curries, tom yam gung and fish steamed in banana leaves. Expect to pay about 120FF per person. It's open daily to 11 pm.

Le Montagnard (Map 1; ☎ 01 43 49 42 38; metro Ménilmontant), 132 Blvd Ménilmontant, 20e. Don't be fooled by the name – the 'Mountaineer' doesn't serve fondue and raclette but couscous and has a 55FF *menu*. There's a decent bar here too.

Naouri (Map 3; ☎ 01 47 97 16 70; metro Belleville), 122 Blvd de Belleville, 20e. This pâtisserie is positively groaning with kosher sweetmeats – both North African and Central European.

Le Pavillon Puebla (Map 3; ☎ 01 42 08 92 62; metro Buttes-Chaumont), in the Parc des Buttes-Chaumont (19e) near the entrance where Ave Simon Bolivar and Rue Botzaris meet. No, not Mexican but Catalan, this exquisite restaurant, housed in a Second Empire-style pavilion in the hilly Buttes-Chaumont, attracts not so much for its wonderful seafood and fish dishes like anchovy tarte, bouillabaisse and cod stuffed with snails, but for the wonderful terrace open in summer. *Menus* are 180 and 240FF. For dessert, don't miss the mille-feuille aux fraises (strawberries in layers of flaky pastry). It's open for lunch and dinner Tuesday to Saturday to 10.30 pm.

La Piragua (Map 5; ☎ 01 40 21 35 98; metro Saint Ambroise), 6 Rue Rochebrune, 11e. Colombian food and good Latino music feature at this small and friendly restaurant. There are *menus* at 96 and 110FF; à la carte starters like empañadas and fried plantains are 22 to 35FF, main courses are 59 to 98FF (try the marinated chicken Piragua cooked with smoked bacon and raisins, 60FF). La Piragua is open daily except Sunday.

Self-Catering
There's a *Franprix* supermarket at 23 Rue Jean-Pierre Timbaud, 11e (Map 3; metro Oberkampf) open Monday to Saturday from 8 am to 8 pm.

PLACE DE LA NATION
There are lots of decent restaurants on the roads fanning out from Place de la Nation.

French
Les Amognes (Map 1, ☎ 01 43 72 73 05; metro Faidherbe Chaligny), 243 Rue du Faubourg Saint Antoine, 11e. A meal at Les Amognes is a quintessentially French – rather than Parisian – experience: haute cuisine at a reasonable 190FF set price, discreet service, an atmosphere that is *correcte*, even a little provincial. Superb dishes include a tarte of marinated sardines, the lightly pan-fried scallops and the stuffed endives. The wines aren't cheap though (from 200FF for a bottle of Burgundy). It's open for lunch and dinner daily except all day Sunday and on Monday at midday until 10.30 pm.

Other Cuisines
À la Banane Ivoirienne (Map 1; ☎ 01 43 70 49 90; metro Ledru Rollin), 10 Rue de la Forge Royale, 11e. This friendly place serves West African specialities at dinner only from Tuesday to Saturday. Entrées are 20 to 35FF, main courses in the 60-to-85FF region. There's African music on Thursday from 10 pm.

Café Canelle (Map 5; ☎ 01 43 70 48 25; metro Ledru Rollin), 1bis Rue de la Forge Royale, 11e. This festive Moroccan restaurant just down the road from the Casbah club (see Discos & Clubs in the Entertainment chapter) is run by two Algerian brothers who do couscous with a twist – flavoured with cinnamon, orange flowers and dates. It's open daily from 7 pm to 2 am.

Khun Akorn (Map 1; ☎ 01 43 56 20 03; metro Nation), 8 Ave de Taillebourg, 11e. In this airy Thai restaurant most starters are 40 to 60FF, main courses 70 to 90FF. It's open for lunch from noon to 2 pm and dinner from 7.30 to 11 pm daily except Monday.

Mansouria (Map 1; ☎ 01 43 71 00 16; metro Faidherbe Chaligny), 11 Rue Faidherbe, 11e. We didn't eat the best couscous of our lives at this trendy Moroccan restaurant, but the milk-fed steamed lamb, the lovely décor and the excellent service impressed. The lunch *menu* is 135FF, dinner ones are 168 and 280FF (including wine). It's open daily for lunch and dinner till 11.30 except Sunday and Monday at midday.

Le Réservoir (Map 1; ☎ 01 43 56 39 60; metro Ledru Rollin), 16 Rue de la Forge Royale, 11e. This warehouse turned Italian-ish restaurant done up in modern kitsch is popular with punters and celebrities headed for the even more kitsch Casbah club next door. Count on spending from 200FF a head. It's open daily till 1 am.

CHINATOWN AREA
Dozens of East Asian restaurants line the main streets of Paris' Chinatown (13e), including Ave de Choisy, Ave d'Ivry and Rue Baudricourt. The cheapest *menus*, which go for about 50FF, are usually available only at lunch on weekdays. But there are a couple of French options too.

French
L'Avant-Goût (Map 1; ☎ 01 53 80 24 00; metro Place d'Italie), 26 Rue Bobillot, 13e. A prototype of the Parisian 'neo-bistro', this restaurant serves some of the most inventive modern cuisine around (cream of carrot soup with green cumin; lamb confit with rosemary and polenta) at an affordable 59FF for the lunch *menu* and 135FF for the dinner one. It's open Tuesday to Saturday for lunch and dinner until 10.30 pm.

La Fondue (Map 1; ☎ 01 45 81 15 67; metro Corvisart), 43 Rue des Cinq Diamants, 13e. This little place with a scant half-dozen tables and artsy B&W photos on the walls serves up fondue Savoyarde (cheese) or fondue Bourguignonne (meat) for 85FF.

Le Temps des Cérises (Map 1; ☎ 01 45 89 69 48; metro Corvisart), 18-20 Rue de la Buttes aux Cailles, 13e. The relaxed, easygoing feeling of this 'anarchistic' restaurant run by a workers' cooperative, the good solid fare (rabbit with mustard, steak frites) and especially the low prices keep regulars coming back for more. It's always packed and the atmosphere is great. There are *menus* at 56FF (lunch only) and

PLACES TO EAT

118FF; plats du jour are 45FF. Expect to pay about 130FF à la carte. It's open daily except Saturday lunch and all day Sunday.

Asian

Le Fleuve de Chine (Map 1; ☎ 01 45 82 06 88; metro Porte de Choisy), 15 Ave de Choisy, or enter through the Tour Bergame housing estate at 130 Blvd Masséna, 13e. Take it from the experts, this place has the most authentic Cantonese food in Paris and, as is typical, both the surrounds and the service are as forgettable as Hong Kong post-1997. Main courses range from 40 to 95FF, but settle in around 40 to 50FF for chicken, prawn and superb clay pot dishes. Expect to pay about 110FF per person for a blowout. It's open for lunch and dinner seven days a week.

Orchidée Villa (Map 1; ☎ 01 45 82 18 81; metro Porte de Choisy), 44-46 Ave de Choisy, 13e. This Chinese-Vietnamese place has an all-you-can-eat buffet (15 starters and four mains) for 59/75FF at lunch/dinner on weekdays, 78/89FF on Saturday and 75 FF all day Sunday.

MONTPARNASSE AREA

Since the 1920s, the area around Blvd du Montparnasse (6e and 14e) has been one of the city's premier avenues for enjoying that most Parisian of pastimes: sitting in a café and checking out the passers-by. Many younger Parisians, however, now consider the area passé and dull.

There are several *crêperies* at 20 Rue d'Odessa (Map 4) and several more around the corner on Rue du Montparnasse. An alternative to the all-night Au Pied de Cochon – if the idea of a gelatinous pig's trotter at 5 am turns your stomach – is the *Mustang Café* (Map 4; ☎ 01 43 35 36 12; metro Montparnasse-Bienvenüe), at 84 Blvd du Montparnasse, 14e, with passable Tex-Mex (combination platters and chili con carne from 45FF; fajitas 98FF) available to 5 am.

French

Blvd du Montparnasse, around the Vavin metro stop (Map 4), is home to a number of legendary establishments, made famous between the wars by writers (F Scott Fitzgerald, Ernest Hemingway etc) and avant-garde artists (Dalí, Cocteau). Before the Russian Revolution, the area's cafés attracted exiled revolutionaries such as Lenin and Trotsky. The intellectual café scene shifted to Saint Germain des Prés after WWII.

L'Assiette (Map 1; ☎ 01 43 22 64 86; metro Gaîté), 181 Rue du Château, 14e. This engaging bistro, with its short but very fresh menu, is a bit off the beaten track south-west of the Cimitière du Montparnasse, but it has an unusual claim to fame: a woman chef. It's not cheap though; the dinner *menu* is 200FF (with wine) and you'll scarcely find a bottle of wine for less than 300FF. It's open Wednesday to Sunday for lunch and dinner until 10.30 pm (closed August).

La Cagouille (Map 1; ☎ 01 43 22 09 01; metro Gaîté), 10-12 Place Constantin Brancusi, facing 23 Rue de l'Ouest, 14e. Chef Gérard Allemandou, one of the flavours of the 1990s, gets rave reviews for his fish and shellfish dishes at this café-restaurant. The *formule* costs 150FF, a *menu* with wine is 250FF and bookings are essential.

Le Caméléon (Map 6; ☎ 01 43 20 63 43; metro Vavin), 6 Rue de Chevreuse, 6e. If you want to eat at a 'nouveau' bistro or brasserie – the distinction isn't that clear even to the French any more –which serves fresh, innovative food in a traditional setting, you couldn't do better than this place. Their lobster ravioli (82FF), among other dishes, is delicious. Starters range from 35 to 70FF, main courses from 82 to 135 and there's a lunchtime *menu* for 120FF. It also has an excellent wine selection.

Chez Dummonet (Map 4; ☎ 01 42 22 81 19 or 01 45 48 52 40; metro Falguière), 117 Rue du Cherche Midi, 6e. The rôtisserie *menu* costs 150FF, including wine and coffee; there are *formules* for 128 to 210FF. It is closed Monday and Tuesday and in August.

La Coupole (Map 4; ☎ 01 43 20 14 20; metro Vavin), 102 Blvd de Montparnasse, 14e. La Coupole's famous mural-covered columns (decorated by artists including Brancusi and Chagall), dark wood panelling and indirect lighting have hardly changed since the days of Sartre, Soutine, Man Ray and Josephine Baker. Mains at this 450-seat brasserie, which opened in 1927, cost about 100FF, so count on spending about 185FF per person for a meal. A lunchtime express *menu* is 89FF including 0.25L of wine; evening *menus* start at 123FFF. It is open daily from noon to 2 am. There's dancing on some nights and tea dances at the weekend (see Discos & Clubs in the Entertainment chapter for details).

French Chain Restaurants – There are branches of several chain restaurants on the Blvd du Montparnasse including *Pizza Pino* (Map 4; ☎ 01 45 48 94 77) at No 57; *Batifol* (Map 6; ☎ 01 43 20 63 02) at No 127; *Léon de Bruxelles* (Map 4; ☎ 01 42 71 75 56) at 82bis; and *Bistrot Romain* (Map 4; ☎ 01 45 48 38 01) at No 59. There are also a couple of *Hippos* (Maps 4 and 6) in the area.

Le Select (Map 4; ☎ 01 42 22 65 27; metro Vavin), 99 Blvd du Montparnasse, 6e. Another Montparnasse legend, the Select's décor has changed very little since 1923. The *menu* costs 90FF, and tartines (buttered bread with toppings) made with Poilâne bread start at 30FF. Drinks are served at the tiny, round sidewalk tables, each equipped with Parisian café-style rattan chairs. It is open daily from 7 am to 3 am.

Self-Catering

There's an *Inno* supermarket (Map 4), opposite the Tour Montparnasse, open Monday to Saturday from 9 am to 9 pm and a **food market** on Blvd Edgar Quinet open Wednesday and Saturday mornings until 1 pm. The *Laporte Fromagerie* (Map 4; ☎ 01 43 35 22 75; metro Vavin) at 8 Rue Delambre (14e) has a superb selection of cheeses.

15e ARRONDISSEMENT

There are quite a few places to eat to the south of Blvd de Grenelle.

Le Café du Commerce (Map 4; ☎ 01 45 75 03 27; metro Émile Zola), 51 Rue du Commerce. Inside this resolutely old-fashioned place you can enjoy traditional French dishes with *menus* at 85 or 115FF including a drink. All cheeses are 22FF, all desserts 24FF.

Feyrous (Map 4; ☎ 01 45 78 07 02; metro Dupleix), 8 Rue de Lourmel. A bright, busy and outgoing Lebanese traiteur-restaurant with *menus* at 60 and 85FF at lunch and 105FF at dinner. It's open daily from 7 am to 2 am.

L'Os à Moëlle (Map 1; ☎ 01 45 57 27 27; metro Lourmel), 3 Rue Vasco de Gama. In the far-flung south-western 15e, the 'Marrow Bone' is well worth the trip and chef Thierry Faucher (late of the Crillon) offers one of the best and most affordable (145FF at lunch, 190FF at dinner) *dégustation* menus in town. Its four courses include such niceties as creamed scallops in the shell with coriander, bass in cumin-flavoured butter and half a quail with endives and chestnuts, plus dessert. Wines are in the 95 to 160FF range and the list is very good. L'Os à Moëlle is open for lunch and dinner from Tuesday to Saturday.

Le Tipaza (Map 4; ☎ 01 45 79 22 25; metro Émile Zola), 150 Ave Émile Zola. This classy Moroccan restaurant has good couscous (65 to 82FF), tajines (76 to 80FF) and other Moroccan specialities with *menus* at 75FF at lunch and 130FF at dinner.

MONTMARTRE & PIGALLE

This area encompasses bits of the 9e, 17e and 18e. The restaurants along Rue des Trois Frères, 18e (Map 9) are a much better bet than their touristy counterparts at Place du Tertre. Many are open seven days a week but only for dinner.

French

Montmartre's French restaurants, like almost everything else on the Butte, are slightly offbeat.

Le Bateau Lavoir (Map 9; ☎ 01 42 54 23 12; metro Abbesses), 8 Rue Garreau, 18e. Named after the studio behind it on Place Émile Goudeau where Picasso and Co made art around the turn of the century, this wonderful old-style bistro has good value *menus* at 98 and 130FF. It's closed Saturday lunch and all day on Monday.

Charlot – Roi des Coquillages (Map 2; ☎ 01 53 20 48 00; metro Place de Clichy), 12 Place de Clichy, 9e. Some Parisians think this is the best place for no-nonsense seafood like perfect oysters, grilled sardines and sole meunière and we tend to agreed. *Menus* are 178FF and, after 11 pm, 123FF. It's open daily to 1 am.

French Chain Restaurants – *Léon de Bruxelles* (Map 9; ☎ 01 42 80 28 33; metro Pigalle) has a branch at 1 Place Pigalle (9e) and there's a *Batifol* at 3 Place Blanche, 18e (Map 9).

Macis et Muscade (Map 2; ☎ 01 42 26 62 26; metro La Fourche), 110 Rue Legendre, 17e. This is another example of an excellent restaurant du quartier with the fine menu changed by chef Thierry Arrouasse every season. The lunch *formule* is 65FF, the dinner *menu* is 120FF. À la carte entrées are 30 to 42FF, mains run from 50 to 80FF. Wines are in the 120 to 160FF range. It's open for lunch and dinner except midday Saturday and all day Sunday.

Le Refuge des Fondus (Map 9; ☎ 01 42 55 22 65; metro Abbesses or Anvers), 17 Rue des Trois Frères, 18e. This establishment has been a Montmartre favourite since 1966. For 87FF you get an aperitif, hors d'œuvre, red wine in a baby bottle (or beer or soft drink) and a good quantity of either fondue Savoyarde (cheese) or fondue Bourguignonne (meat; minimum order for two). It is open daily from 7 pm to 2 am (last seating at midnight or 12.30 am). It's a good idea to phone ahead (at 5 or 6 pm) for reservations, especially at the weekend.

Au Village de Michel (Map 1; ☎ 01 42 52 62 94; metro Marx Dormoy), 100 Rue Ordener, 18e. You wouldn't go out of your way to eat at this simple café-restaurant but should you be in the area the plat du jour at 50FF is one of the biggest bargains in Paris.

Other Cuisines

Il Duca (Map 9; ☎ 01 46 06 71 98; metro Abbesses), 26 Rue Yvonne Le Tac, 18e. A neat, tidy and intimate little Italian restaurant with good, straightforward food including a lunchtime *menu* for 69FF and main courses from 70 to 82FF. Home-made pasta dishes are 45 to 75FF.

Le Mono (Map 9; ☎ 01 46 06 99 20; metro Abbesses or Blanche), 40 Rue Véron, 18e. The friendly Togolese woman who runs this unpretentious restaurant has been serving great West African cuisine for more than 20 years. Specialities – made with special imported ingredients – include lélé (flat, steamed cakes made from white beans and shrimp and served with tomato sauce; 25FF), maffé (beef or chicken served with peanut sauce; 50FF), gbekui (a sort of goulash made with spinach, onions, beef, fish and shrimp; 55FF) and djenkommé (grilled chicken with special semolina noodles). Vegetarian dishes are prepared upon request. It is open from 7 to 11.30 pm (later on Friday and Saturday); closed on Wednesday.

Taj (Map 9; ☎ 01 42 59 88 80; metro Abbesses), 11 Rue des Trois Frères, 18e. This cosy little Indian restaurant has biryanis from 45 to 60FF, curries from 39 to 45FF and *menus* at 59 and 75FF.

Le Taroudant (Map 9; ☎ 01 42 64 95 81; metro Abbesses), 8 Rue Aristide Bruant, 18e. Couscous and tajines are served at this Moroccan restaurant for 65 to 100FF (for the fish tajine). It is closed on Wednesday.

Wou Ying (Map 9; ☎ 01 42 51 24 44; metro Abbesses), 24 Rue Durantin, 18e. Open daily from noon to 2.30 pm and 7 to 11.30 pm, this place is great for cheap Cantonese food (starters 19 to 43FF, main courses 36 to 80FF), including a *menu* for only 45FF available at lunch and at dinner until 9.30 pm.

Self-Catering

Towards Pigalle there are lots of groceries – many of them open until late at night – on the side streets (eg Rue Lepic) leading off Blvd de Clichy. Heading south from Blvd de Clichy, Rue des Martyrs, 9e (Map 3) is lined with **food shops** basically all the way to the Notre Dame de Lorette metro stop.

Les Caves de Nîmes (Map 9; metro Abbesses), 7bis Rue Tardieu, 18e. This wine and cheese shop, next door to Charcutier-Traiteur, is open daily except Wednesday from 8.30 am to 1.30 pm and 3.30 to 8.30 pm.

Charcutier-Traiteur (Map 9; metro Abbesses), 6 Rue des Trois Frères, 18e. This store sells ready-to-eat gourmet dishes daily from 9.30 am to 8.30 pm.

Franprix (Map 9; metro Lamarck Caulaincourt), 44 Rue Caulaincourt, 18e. This supermarket is open Monday to Saturday from 8.30 am to 7.25 pm (7.45 pm on Friday and Saturday). There's an *Ed l'Épicier* supermarket (Map 9; metro Anvers) a block south of the bottom of the funicular at 31 Rue d'Orsel (open Monday to Saturday from 9 am to 8 pm).

Fromagerie Tissot (Map 9; metro Abbesses), 32 Rue des Abbesses, 18e. This good fromagerie is open Tuesday to Saturday from 8 am to 1 pm and 4 to 7 pm. There is also an *alimentation générale* (grocery store; Map 9) on the same street at 37bis, open from 7.30 am to 9 or 9.30 pm (closed on Monday).

UNIVERSITY RESTAURANTS

Stodgy but filling food is available in copious quantities at Paris' 16 *restaurants universitaires* (student cafeterias), run by the Centre Régional des Œuvres Universitaires et Scolaires (CROUS; ☎ 01 40 51 36 00; Minitel 3615 CROUS). Tickets for three-course meals cost 14.10FF for students with ID, 23FF if you have an ISIC card (or Carte Jeune Internationale) and 27.90FF for nonstudent guests.

CROUS restaurants (usually referred to as *restos U)* have variable opening times which change according to school holiday schedules and weekend rotational agreements. Even during the academic year, only about half are open for dinner; the weekend selection is even more limited. Only one university restaurant stays open during July; a different one is on duty during August. Monthly schedules are generally posted at ticket windows, some of which are open only on weekdays at lunchtime. In general, lunch is served from 11.30 am to sometime between 1.45 and 3.30 pm, while dinner is served from 6 or 6.30 to 8 pm.

About half of the CROUS cafeterias are in the 5e and 6e arrondissements. They include:

Assas (Map 6; ☎ 01 46 33 61 25; metro Port Royal or Notre Dame des Champs), 92 Rue d'Assas (7th floor), 6e, in the Université de Paris' Faculté de Droit et des Sciences Économiques (Law and Economics Faculty). The ticket window is on the 6th floor.

Bullier (Map 6; ☎ 01 43 54 93 38; metro Port Royal), 39 Ave G Bernanos (2nd floor) in Centre Jean Sarrailh, 5e.

Châtelet (Map 6; ☎ 01 43 31 51 66; metro Censier Daubenton), 10 Rue Jean Calvin, just off Rue Mouffetard, 5e.

Mabillon (Map 6; ☎ 01 43 25 66 23; metro Mabillon), 3 Rue Mabillon (3rd floor), 6e.

PLACES TO EAT

Entertainment

LISTINGS

It's virtually impossible to sample the richness of Paris' entertainment scene without first perusing *Pariscope* (3FF) or *L'Officiel des Spectacles* (2FF), both of which come out on Wednesday and are available at any newsstand. *Pariscope* includes a five page insert in English courtesy of London's *Time Out* weekly events magazine.

For up-to-date information on clubs and the music scene, pick up a copy of *LYLO* (an acronym for *Les Yeux, Les Oreilles*; ie The Eyes, The Ears), a free magazine with excellent listings of rock concerts and other live music available at certain cafés and bars; information is also available on Minitel at 3615 LYLO. The monthly magazine *Nova* (10FF) is a more mainstream source, but its *Hot Guide* insert of listings is particularly useful. Check out any of the FNAC outlets (see Booking Agencies), especially the one in the Forum des Halles shopping mall, for free flyers and programs.

For less time-sensitive information on the hottest discos, bars and live music venues, the best source is *Le Fêtard en Poche* (Éditions Florent-Massot; 89FF), a 160-page guide to Paris after dark updated annually and available at bookshops and some newsstands.

You can hear recorded English-language information on concerts and other events, prepared by the Paris tourist office, by calling ☎ 01 49 52 53 56 (24 hours) though it's not always as up to date as it could be. Two other excellent sources for what's on are Radio FG on 98.2 MHz FM and Radio Nova on 101.5 MHz. For who and what is *caliente* in Latino music, check out Minitel 3615 LATINA.

BOOKING AGENCIES

You can buy tickets for many (but not all) cultural events at several ticket outlets, among them FNAC (rhymes with 'snack') outlets and Virgin Megastores. Both accept reservations and do ticketing by phone. Virgin Megastore will take Visa, MasterCard, American Express and Diners Club; FNAC will take Visa and MasterCard. Tickets cannot be returned or exchanged unless a performance is cancelled.

Reservations for a wide variety of theatre and opera productions can be made using the Minitel (3615 THEA).

FNAC (Map 7; ☎ 01 40 41 40 00 or ☎ 08 36 68 04 56 for information; metro Châtelet-Les Halles), 1-7 Rue Pierre Lescot (1er) in the FNAC Forum department store on the 3rd underground level of the Forum des Halles shopping mall. It is open Monday to Saturday from 10 am to 7.30 pm. The commission is 10 to 20FF a ticket. To purchase tickets by Minitel, key in 3615 FNAC and your credit card number – the tickets will be sent to you by mail.

FNAC has several other *billeteries* (ticket offices; *services des spectacles*) around the city including one at the FNAC Montparnasse department store (Map 4; ☎ 01 49 54 30 00; metro Saint Placide) at 136 Rue de Rennes (6e), about 600 metres north-east of Gare Montparnasse, open Monday to Saturday from 10 am to 7.30 pm; FNAC Musique Bastille (Map 5; ☎ 01 43 42 04 04; metro Bastille) at 4 Place de la Bastille (12e), open Monday to Saturday from 10 am to 8 pm (10 pm on Wednesday and Friday); and another FNAC Étoile department store (Map 2; ☎ 01 44 09 18 00; metro Ternes) at 26-30 Ave des Ternes (17e), open Monday to Saturday from 10 am to 7.30 pm.

Virgin Megastore (Map 2; ☎ 01 49 53 50 00; metro Franklin D Roosevelt), 52-60 Ave des Champs-Élysées, 8e. The billeterie (☎ 01 49 53 52 09 for both stores) in the basement, like the rest of this four-level emporium, is open daily from 10 am (noon on Sunday) to midnight. Virgin has a second store (Map 7; ☎ 01 49 53 52 90; metro Palais Royal) with a box office next to the inverted glass pyramid in the Carrousel du Louvre shopping mall at 99 Rue de Rivoli (1er). It is open daily from 11 am to 8 pm (to 10 pm Wednesday to Saturday).

Other booking agencies include:

Agence Perrossier (Map 2; ☎ 01 42 60 58 31; metro Madeleine), 6 Place de la Madeleine, 8e. Open Monday to Saturday 9.15 am to 7 pm.
Agence des Théâtres (Map 7; ☎ 01 42 97 46 70; metro Quatre Septembre), 7 Rue de Marivaux, 2e.
Cityrama (Map 7, ☎ 01 44 55 60 00; metro Louvre Rivoli), 147 Rue Saint Honoré, 1er.
SOS Théâtre (Map 2; ☎ 01 44 77 88 55; metro Madeleine), 6 Place de la Madeleine, 8e. Open Monday to Saturday from 10 am to 7 pm.

DISCOUNT TICKETS

On the day of a performance, the *Kiosque Théâtre* outlets (no phone) sell theatre tickets for 50% off the usual price (plus a commission of 16FF). The seats on offer are almost always the most desirable (in the orchestra or 1st balcony) and expensive. Tickets to concerts, operas and ballets may also be available.

Both outlets – one across from 15 Place de la Madeleine, 8e (Map 2; metro Madeleine) and the other halfway between Gare Montparnasse and the nearby Tour Montparnasse, 15e (Map 4; metro Montparnasse Bienvenüe) – are open Tuesday to Saturday from 12.30 to 8 pm and on Sunday from 12.30 to 4 pm. By contract, every Paris theatre – even if it has the most popular show in town – has to supply the outlet with at least four tickets, so bargain-hunting fans often arrive an hour or more before it opens. The earlier you come by, the better the chance of finding a ticket to the performance you want; your chances are also better during the week than on Saturday or Sunday.

CINEMA

Pariscope and *L'Officiel des Spectacles* list the cinematic offerings alphabetically by their French title followed by the English (or German, Italian, Spanish etc) one. Going to the movies in Paris does not come cheaply: expect to pay 45 to 50FF for a ticket. Students and people under 18 and over 60 usually get discounts of about 25% except on Friday, Saturday and Sunday nights. On Wednesday (and sometimes Monday), most cinemas give discounts to everyone.

If a movie is labelled 'VO' or 'v.o.' (for *version originale*) it means it will be subtitled rather than dubbed ('v.f.' or *version française*), so Hollywood movies will still be in English. French enthusiasm for cinema goes far beyond the borders of France; the French passion for Jerry Lewis is well known and Woody Allen movies have a huge following in Paris.

Cinéma des Cinéastes (Map 2; ☎ 08 36 68 97 17; metro Place de Clichy). This cinema at 7 Ave de Clichy (17e) is another good choice for art films.
Cinémathèque Française (☎ 01 45 53 21 86 or, for a recording, ☎ 01 47 04 24 24). This government-supported cultural institution almost always leaves its foreign offerings – often seldom-screened classics – in the original, nondubbed version. Screenings take place daily except Monday in the far-eastern tip of the Palais de Chaillot on Ave Albert de Mun, 16e (Map 4; metro Trocadéro or Iéna). Tickets cost 28FF (17FF reduced price).

DISCOS & CLUBS

A *discothèque* is just about any sort of place where music leads to dancing. The truly *branché* (trendy) crowd considers showing up before 1 am a serious breach of good taste.

The discothèques favoured by the Parisian 'in' crowd change frequently, and many are officially private. Single men may not be admitted, even if their clothes are subculturally appropriate, simply because they're single men. Women, on the other hand, get in for free on some nights. It's always easier to get into the club of your choice during the week – when things may be hopping even more than they are at the weekend. Remember that Parisians tend to go out in groups and don't mingle as much as Anglo-Saxons do.

Paris is a great city for music, especially techno, and there are some mighty fine DJs based here. Latino and Cuban salsa music is also huge. Theme nights at clubs are as common here as they are in, say, London so it's best to consult the sources mentioned in the Listings section of this chapter before making plans.

Les Bains (Map 8; ☎ 01 48 87 01 80; metro Étienne Marcel), 7 Rue du Bourg l'Abbé, 3e. Located in a renovated old Turkish bath, this club still manages to produce steam heat on particularly hot nights. Les Bains, once renowned for its surly, selective bouncers on the outside and trendy, star-struck revellers inside, has calmed down a bit under new management, but it's still very hard to get in at the weekend. Monday is theme night. Mostly techno with a healthy dash of 70s music attracts a mixed straight and gay crowd from 11.30 pm to 6.30 am (entry 100FF).

Le Balajo (Map 5; ☎ 01 47 00 07 87; metro Bastille), 9 Rue de Lappe, 11e. A mainstay of the Parisian dance-hall scene since 1936. Wednesday night is mambo night; the DJs spin the LPs and CDs (rock, 1970s disco, funk etc) Thursday to Saturday nights from 11.30 pm to 5.30 am; dancing begins in earnest at 2 or 3 am. Admission costs 100FF (80FF on Wednesday) and includes one drink. Women can wear pretty much whatever they want, but men should be a bit dressed up. On Sunday (and sometimes Saturday) afternoon from 3 to 7 pm, DJs play old-fashioned *musette* (accordion music) – waltz, tango, cha-cha – for aficionados of *rétro* tea dancing. Entry is 50FF (60FF with a drink).

La Casbah (Map 1; ☎ 01 43 79 69 04; metro Ledru Rollin), 18-20 Rue de la Forge Royale, 11e. You might want to brave the gorillas and the big egos of this club just to check out the décor: over-the-top pastel Moorish from floor to ceiling. The music is retro 80s, house and dance and the club is regaining popularity lost over the past few years. Entry costs 80FF on Thursday, 120FF on Friday and Saturday, including a drink.

La Chapelle des Lombards (Map 5; ☎ 01 43 57 24 24; metro Bastille), 19 Rue de Lappe, 11e. Antillean, African and Latin American beats make for a very lively dance scene. Something of a pick-up place, the club is open Tuesday to Saturday from 10.30 pm to 5 am (6 am on the weekend). Entry (including one drink) costs 100FF (120FF on Friday and Saturday night); it's free for women before midnight. Trainers (sneakers) are not permitted. There's usually a concert of some sort on Thursday at 8 pm (70FF).

Dancing de la Coupole (Map 4; ☎ 01 43 20 14 20; metro Vavin), 102 Blvd du Montparnasse, 14e.

Tuesday is salsa night at La Coupole (90FF) from 9.30 pm to 3 am, when a 15-member Latin American band plays and attracts a very mixed crowd. On Friday and Saturday from 9.30 pm to 4 am there's a retro disco (95FF) and tea dances (40FF) on Saturday from 3 to 7 pm and Sunday from 3 to 9 pm.

Ekivök (Map 8; ☎ 01 42 71 71 41; metro Rambuteau), 40 Rue des Blancs Manteaux, 4e. A new kid in town that dares to bill itself as *'la disco libertine du Marais'* (literally, the licentious disco of the Marais) must have something going for it. It's open daily from 11 pm to 6 am. There's a tea dance on Thursday from 3 to 8 pm.

Les Étoiles (Map 3; ☎ 01 47 70 60 56; metro Château d'Eau), 61 rue du Château d'Eau, 10e. A definite second choice to the Java (see below) for salsa but still worth a look. It's open Thursday to Saturday from 9 pm to 4 am. Entry is 100FF including drink.

Folies Pigalle (Map 9; ☎ 01 48 78 25 56; metro Pigalle), 11 Place Pigalle, 9e. A heaving, mixed place that is great for cruising from the balcony above the dance floor. It's open Thursday to Saturday from 11 pm till dawn. Entry costs 100FF.

Le Gibus (Map 3; ☎ 01 47 00 78 88; metro République), 18 Rue du Faubourg du Temple, 11e. A former cathedral of rock, this cave-like place now devotes itself to followers of techno (Wednesday and Thursday), trance (Friday) and house (Tuesday, Saturday and Sunday). There are concerts some nights so be sure to inquire. It's open Tuesday to Sunday from 11.30 pm till dawn. Entry is 20 to 70FF, depending on the night.

La Guinguette Pirate (Map 1; ☎ 01 44 24 89 89 or ☎ 01 53 82 02 04; metro Quai de la Gare), 157 Quai de la Gare, 13e. This club, situated on a three-masted Chinese junk on the Seine at the foot of the Bibliothèque National de France, is as eclectic as it gets: from reggae and ska to Breton rock. There's usually a concert at 10.30 pm (entry 30FF), and the crowd is young (25 to 30) and energetic. Weekend concerts feature French rock groups. It's open daily from about noon (7.30 pm on Monday) to 2 am.

La Java (Map 3; ☎ 01 42 02 20 52; metro Belleville), 105 Rue du Faubourg du Temple, 10e. The original dance hall where Piaf (see the boxed text) got her first break now reverberates to the sound of salsa at the 'Cuban Jam Sessions' Thursday and Friday (entry 80FF with drink) from 11 pm to 5 am.

Edith Piaf, the Urchin Sparrow

Like her contemporary Judy Garland in the USA, Edith Piaf (1915-63) was not just a singer but a tragic, stoical figure whom the nation took to its heart and never let go.

Born Edith Giovanna Gassion in the poor Belleville district of Paris, her father was a street acrobat and her mother a singer. Edith's early childhood was spent with her maternal grandmother, an alcoholic who neglected her, and later with her father's parents in Normandy who ran a local brothel. At age nine she toured with her father but left home at 15 to sing alone in the streets of Paris. Her first employer, Louis Leplée, called her *la môme piaf* (the urchin sparrow) and introduced her to the cabarets of Pigalle.

When Leplée was murdered in 1935, she faced the streets again. But along came Raymond Asso, an ex-Legionnaire who would become her Pygmalion, forcing her to break with her pimp and hustler friends, putting her in her signature black dress and inspiring her first big hit *(Mon Légionnaire*, 1937). When he succeeded in getting her a contract at what is now La Java, one of the most famous Parisian music halls of the time, her career skyrocketed.

This frail woman, who sang about street life, drugs, death and whores, seemed to embody all the miseries of the world yet sang in a husky, powerful voice with no self-pity. Her tumultuous love life earned her the reputation as *une dévoreuse d'hommes* (a man-eater), but she launched the careers of several, including Yves Montand and Charles Aznavour. Another of her many lovers was world middleweight boxing champion Marcel Cerdan; he was killed in a plane crash while joining her on her American tour in 1949. True to form, Piaf insisted that the show go on after learning of his death and fainting on stage in the middle of *L'Hymne à l'Amour*, a love song inspired by Cerdan.

After she was involved in a car accident in 1951, Piaf began drinking heavily and became addicted to morphine. Her health declined quickly but she continued to sing around the world (notably at New York's Carnegie Hall in 1956) and recorded some of her biggest hits, including *Je Ne Regrette Rien* and *Milord*. In 1962, frail and once again penniless, Piaf married a young hairdresser called Théo Sarapo, recorded the duet *À Quoi Ça Sert l'Amour?* (What Use Is Love?) with him and left Paris for southern France, where she died the following year. Around two million people attended her funeral in Paris, and the grave of the much missed Urchin Sparrow in Père Lachaise Cemetery, 20e (see the map on page 134) is still visited and decorated by thousands of her loyal fans each year.

La Locomotive (Map 9; ☎ 01 53 41 88 88; metro Blanche) in Pigalle at 90 Blvd de Clichy, 18e. An enormous, ever-popular disco that's long been one of the favourite dancing venues for teenage out-of-towners. Music at La Loco ranges from techno in the pulsating basement to groove and disco on the 1st floor loft; psychedelic, rock and the like dominate on the

huge ground floor. It is open nightly from 11 pm (midnight on Monday) to 6 am (7 am on weekends). Entrance costs 70/55FF with/ without a drink on weekdays, and women get in free before 12.30 am. On Friday and Saturday it costs 60FF with a drink before midnight and 100FF with one after that. Men pay 70FF and women get in free on Sunday. Dress rules are mellow: jogging suits and sandals are out but almost everything else is decidedly in. There's a popular gay tea dance here on Sunday from 5 to 11 pm. Entry costs 40/60FF before/after 6 pm.

L'Opus Café (Map 3; ☎ 01 40 34 70 00; metro Château Landon), 167 Quai de Valmy, 10e. Salsa, zouk (a blend of African and Latin American dance rhythms) and jazz are on offer in this former officers' mess by the Canal Saint Martin.

Le Pulp & Le Scorpion (Map 7; ☎ 01 40 26 01 93 or 01 40 26 01 30; metro Rue Montmartre), 25 Blvd Poissonnière, 2e. On the ground floor: Le Pulp, open Wednesday to Sunday from midnight to 6 or 7 am, is for lesbians only at the weekend (entry 50FF), mixed on the other nights. In the cellar: Le Scorpion, both gay and straight, is open nightly from midnight to 7 am. There's no cover charge except on Friday and Saturday nights (50FF). The music in both sections is mainly techno and themed disco. People wearing jogging suits or military-style clothes are not admitted.

Le Queen (Map 2; ☎ 01 53 89 08 90; metro George V), 102 Ave des Champs-Élysées, 8e. The king (as it were) of gay discos in Paris now reigns even more supreme with special theme parties open to all (eg 'Respect' on Wednesday) if they can get past the hostile bouncer. Queen is open seven days a week from midnight to 6 or 7 am. There's no cover charge except on Friday and Saturday nights (100FF, including a drink). Dress as outrageously as you can at the weekend.

Rex Club (Map 7; ☎ 01 42 36 83 98; metro Bonne Nouvelle), 5 Blvd Poissonnière, 2e. This huge, popular club is the undisputed king (for now) of techno and house. It has both a music DJ and a video one. It's open Tuesday to Saturday from 11 pm till dawn and entry is 60 to 70FF.

La Scala de Paris (Map 7; ☎ 01 42 61 64 00; metro Palais Royal), 188 Rue de Rivoli, 1er. A large, touristy disco whose three dance floors (all playing the same music) and five bars are lit by laser lights. The patrons are mostly Eurotrash in the 18-30 age group and come from all over Euroland and provincial France. It is open nightly from 10.30 pm to dawn. Entry costs 80FF (100FF on Saturday night), including one drink. Women get in for free from Sunday to Thursday except on the eve of public holidays. Jeans and running shoes are OK so long as they're clean and expensive.

Slow Club (Map 7; ☎ 01 42 33 84 30; metro Châtelet), 130 Rue de Rivoli, 1er. An unpretentious disco housed in a deep cellar once used to ripen Caribbean bananas. The live bands attract students as well as older couples. The music varies from night to night but includes jazz, boogie, bebop, swing and blues. It is open Tuesday to Saturday from 10 pm to 3 am (4 am on Friday and Saturday nights); often crowded after 1.30 am, especially on weekends. The cover charge is 60FF (75FF on Friday and Saturday with a drink); students get a small discount. Don't come in shorts, ripped jeans or running shoes.

Le Tango (Map 8; ☎ 01 42 72 17 78; metro Arts et Métiers), 13 Rue au Maire, 3e. An Afro-Caribbean club on the boil Thursday to Saturday night (60FF) and popular with the *frotti/frotta* (rubbing) set. Le Tango is *not* for the shy.

Club Zed (Map 5; ☎ 01 43 54 93 78; metro Maubert Mutualité), 2 Rue des Anglais, 5e, one block north of 70 Blvd Saint Germain. An arched stone basement where the DJs favour rock'n'roll, jazz and swing. It is open Wednesday to Saturday from 10.30 pm to 3 am (5 am on Friday and Saturday nights). Entrance costs 50FF (100FF on Friday and Saturday), including a drink. Don't come sloppily dressed (ie no T-shirts) and note that *garçons non accompagnés* (unaccompanied men) may not get in.

THEATRE

Almost all of Paris' theatre productions, including those written in other languages, are performed in French. There are a few English-speaking troupes around, though – look for ads on metro poster boards and in English-language periodicals (eg *France USA Contacts* – see Newspapers & Magazines in the Facts for the Visitor Chapter). Three theatres which occasionally stage productions in English are *Théâtre de Nesle* (Map 6; ☎ 01 46 34 61 04; metro Odéon or Mabillon), 8 Rue de Nesle, 6e; *Théâtre Les Déchargeurs* (Map 7; ☎ 01 42 36 00 02; metro Châtelet), 3 Rue des Déchargeurs, 1er; and *Bouffes du Nord* (Map 3; ☎ 01 46 07 34 50; metro La Chapelle), 37bis Blvd de la Chapelle, 10e. There's stand-up comedy in English from time to time at *Hôtel du Nord* (Map 3; ☎ 01 48 06 01 20;

metro Jacques Bonsergent) at 102 Quai de Jemmapes, 10e. For details on the *Théâtre du Tourtour*, which puts on plays as well as concerts, see Rock.

Comédie Française (Map 7; ☎ 01 40 15 00 15; metro Palais Royal), 2 Rue de Richelieu, next to the Palais Royal, 1er. The world's oldest national theatre, it was founded in 1680 under Louis XIV. Its repertoire is based on the works of such French theatrical luminaries as Corneille, Molière, Racine, Beaumarchais, Marivaux and Musset, though in recent years contemporary and even non-French works have been staged. As the beneficiary of some US$26 million in annual state subsidies, it is partly run by the 34 members of the permanent troupe, known as *sociétaires*, who enjoy job security and jealously guarded perks. The box office (☎ 01 44 52 15 15) is open daily from 11 am to 6 pm. Tickets for regular seats cost from 70 to 185FF and can be purchased up to 14 days ahead. Tickets for places near the ceiling (30FF) go on sale one hour before curtain time, which is when – subject to availability – those under 25 and students under 27 can purchase any of the better seats remaining for only 50FF. The discount tickets are available from the window around the corner from the box office and facing Rue de Montpensier.

Odéon Théâtre de l'Europe (Map 6; ☎ 01 44 41 36 36; Minitel 3615 ODEON; metro Odéon), 1 Place Paul Claudel, 6e. This huge, ornate theatre, built in the early 1780s, often puts on foreign plays in their original languages (subtitled in French) and hosts theatre troupes from abroad (30 to 170FF). The box office (☎ same) is open daily from 11 am to 7 pm (to 1 pm on Sunday). Tickets can be purchased over the phone with a credit card. People over 60 get a discount on the pricier tickets, while students and people under 26 who purchase a special discount card, the *Carte Complice Jeune,* can get good reserved seats at low prices. Half-price tickets are available to anyone 50 minutes before curtain time. During the first week of a play's run, some rush tickets are available one hour before curtain time for as little as 15 to 25FF.

La Patache (Map 3; ☎ 01 42 08 14 35; metro Jacques Bonsergent), 60 Rue de Lancry, 10e. Near the Canal Saint Martin, this is another good venue with a mixed bag of offerings. It's open daily from 6 pm to 2 am.

Point Virgule (Map 8; ☎ 01 42 78 67 03; metro Hôtel de Ville), 7 Rue Sainte Croix de la Bretonnerie, 4e. This is café-theatre at its best, with stand-up comics, performance artists, musical acts, you name it. There are three shows daily at 8, 9.15 and 10.15 pm. Entry costs 80/130/150FF for one/two/three shows (on show for students costs 65FF).

CABARET

Paris' risqué cancan revues – those dazzling, pseudo-bohemian productions featuring hundreds of performers, including female dancers both with and without elaborate costumes – are about as representative of late 1990s Paris as crocodile wrestling is of Australia or bronco busting is of the USA.

Crazy Horse Saloon (Map 2; ☎ 01 47 23 32 32; metro Alma Marceau), 12 Ave George V, 8e. The Crazy Horse boasts it has *l'art du nu*; it also had Woody Allen in its dressing (or undressing) rooms in his very first film (*What's New Pussycat?* 1965). There are two shows nightly Sunday to Friday at 8.30 and 11 pm, and three shows on Saturday at 7.30, 9.45 and 11.50 pm. Prices range from 220FF at the bar with one drink, up to 750 or 980FF for the show and dinner.

Folies Bergères (Map 7; ☎ 01 44 79 98 98; metro Cadet), 32 Rue Richer, 9e. This place is celebrated for its high-kicking, feather-clad dancers but lately it's been staging musicals such as *Fame* Tuesday to Sunday at 9 pm with matinees at 3 pm on Saturday and Sunday (100 to 350FF). When the dancers are on show entry costs 130 to 350FF; dinner and the show at 7.30 pm is 510 to 690FF.

Le Lido (Map 2; ☎ 01 40 76 56 10; metro George V), 116bis Ave des Champs-Élysées, 8e. The floor show gets top marks for the grandiose sets and lavish costumes. Operating since 1946, the nightly shows at 10 pm and midnight cost 540FF for the show with a half bottle of champagne, 365FF to watch from the bar with two drinks and 770, 880 or 990FF for the show and dinner.

Moulin Rouge (Map 9; ☎ 01 53 09 82 82; metro Blanche), 82 Blvd de Clichy, 18e. This legendary cabaret, whose dancers appeared in Toulouse-Lautrec's famous posters, sits under its trademark red windmill (a 1925 copy of the

ENTERTAINMENT

BRENDA TURNNIDGE
The Moulin Rouge, famous cabaret venue and
Paris icon.

original). The dinner show (at 7 or 8 pm, depending on the season) costs 750FF, including champagne. Tickets cost 350FF (including two drinks) if you stand at the bar; if you prefer to sit down the price jumps to 450 or 510FF including half a bottle of champagne. Apart from the dinner show, there are performances nightly at 9 or 10 pm and again at 11 pm or midnight, again depending on the season.

Paradis Latin (Map 5; ☎ 01 43 25 28 28; metro Cardinal Lemoine), 28 Rue du Cardinal Lemoine, 5e. This establishment is known for its extravagant, nonstop performances of songs, dances and nightclub numbers. All the staff, including the waiters, often participate. The show begins at 9.30 pm every night except Tuesday and costs 465FF, including half a bottle of champagne or two drinks. A ticket including dinner (680, 865 or 1250FF, depending on the *menu* you choose) begins at 8 pm.

OPERA & CLASSICAL MUSIC

The Opéra National de Paris now splits its performances between Opéra Garnier, its old home, and Opéra Bastille, which opened in 1989. Both opera houses also stage ballets and concerts put on by the Opéra National's affiliated orchestra, choir and ballet companies. The opera season lasts from mid-September to mid-July.

Paris plays host to dozens of orchestral, organ and chamber music concerts each week.

Cité de la Musique (Map 1; ☎ 01 44 84 45 45 or, for reservations, ☎ 01 44 84 44 84; Minitel 3615 CITEMUSIQUE; www.cite-musique.fr; metro Porte de Pantin), in the south-eastern tip of Parc de la Villette at 221 Ave Jean Jaurès, 19e. The oval, 1200-seat main auditorium, whose blocks of seats can be reconfigured to suit different types of performances, hosts every imaginable type of music and dance, from Western classical to North African and Japanese. Tickets, usually available from FNAC and Virgin, cost 75 to 200FF (60 to 170FF reduced rate) for evening concerts. Concerts in the little auditorium on Friday, Saturday and Sunday cost 80/60FF. The Sunday afternoon performances, which usually start at 3 pm, cost 80FF. The ticket office, open Tuesday to Saturday from noon to 6 pm and Sunday from 10 am, is opposite the main auditorium next to the Fontaine aux Lions (Lions Fountain).

Students at the *Conservatoire National Supérieur de Musique et de Danse* (National Higher Conservatory of Music and Danse; ☎ 01 40 40 45 45), which is also on the other side of the fountain from the Cité de la Musique, put on free orchestra concerts and recitals several times a week, in the afternoon and/or evening.

Opéra Bastille (Map 5; ☎ 01 44 73 13 99 or ☎ 08 36 69 78 68 for inquiries, ☎ 01 44 73 13 00 for reservations, ☎ 01 43 43 96 96 for a recording in French; Minitel 3615 OPERAPARIS; metro Bastille), 2-6 Place de la Bastille, 12e. Telephone lines are staffed from 11 am to 6 pm daily except Sunday and holidays. It's possible to make reservations by phone from abroad – just make sure you pay for the tickets at least one hour before curtain time. Credit cards are accepted only at the box office, which is open Monday to Saturday from 11 am to 6.30 pm.

MARK HONAN

MARK HONAN

Top: Palace of Versailles
Bottom: Interior, Palace of Versailles

Top: Hameau de la Reine (Queen's Hamlet), Versailles
Bottom: Versailles

Ticket sales begin 14 days before the date of the performance. According to Parisian opera buffs, however, the only way to ensure a certain reservation is by post some two months in advance: 120 Rue de Lyon, 75576 Paris Cedex 12. Opera tickets cost 145 to 635FF. To have a shot at the cheapest (ie worst) seats in the house (60FF), you have to stop by the ticket office the day tickets go on sale – exactly 14 days before the performance you'd like to see (on a Monday if the performance is on a Sunday). Ballets cost 70 to 280FF (45FF for the cheapest seats). Concerts are 85 to 240FF (45FF for the least expensive seats). If there are unsold tickets, people under 25 or over 65 and students can get excellent seats for about 100FF only 15 minutes before the curtain goes up. Ask for the *tarif spécial*.

Opéra Comique (Map 7; ☎ 01 42 44 45 46 for reservations; metro Richelieu Drouot), 5 Rue Favart, 2e. A century-old hall that plays host to classic and less well known works of opera. The season lasts from late October to early July. Tickets, available from FNAC or Virgin, cost 100 to 610FF; 50FF tickets with limited or no visibility are available up to 12 hours before the performance at the box office (opposite 14 Rue Favart), open Monday to Saturday from 11 am to 7 pm. Subject to availability, students, the young and the old can get big discounts 15 minutes before curtain time.

Opéra Garnier (Map 7; same ☎ and Minitel as Opéra Bastille; metro Opéra), Place de l'Opéra, 9e. Ticket prices and conditions (including last-minute discounts) are about the same as at Opéra Bastille. For certain non-opera performances, the cheapest regular tickets, which get you a seat with an obstructed view, cost as little as 20 or 30FF.

Salle Pleyel (Map 2; ☎ 01 45 61 53 00; metro Ternes), 252 Rue du Faubourg Saint Honoré, 8e. A highly regarded, 1920s-era hall that hosts many of Paris' finest classical music concerts and recitals. The box office is open Monday to Saturday from 11 am to 6 pm. Tickets are usually from 70 to 200FF.

Théâtre des Champs-Élysées (Map 2; ☎ 01 49 52 50 50; metro Alma Marceau), 15 Ave Montaigne, 8e. A prestigious Right Bank orchestral and recital hall with popular Sunday concerts (100FF) held year round at 11 am. The box office is open Monday to Saturday from 11 am to 7 pm.

Théâtre Musical de Paris (Map 6; ☎ 01 42 33 00 00 for information, ☎ 01 40 28 28 40 for reservations; Minitel 3615 CHATELET; metro Châtelet), 2 Rue Édouard Colonne, on the western side of Place du Châtelet, 1er. Also called the Théâtre Municipal du Châtelet or just the Théâtre du Châtelet, this hall hosts operas (200 to 750FF for the better seats, 50 to 80FF for seats with limited visibility), ballets (90 to 200FF), concerts (including some by the excellent Orchestre de Paris) and theatre performances. Classical music is performed on Sunday at 11.30 am (80FF; free for under 12s) and on Monday, Wednesday and Friday at 12.45 pm (50FF). The ticket office is open daily from 11 am to 7 pm (8 pm on performance nights); tickets go on sale 14 days before the performance date. Subject to availability, students and people under 25 or over 65 can get seats for all performances, except the operas, for 50FF starting 15 minutes before curtain time. There are no performances in July or August.

Théâtre de la Ville (Map 6; ☎ 01 42 74 22 77; Minitel 3615 THEAVILLE; metro Châtelet), 2 Place du Châtelet (on the eastern side), 4e. This municipal hall plays host to theatre, dance and all kinds of music, with tickets from 95 to 190FF. Depending on availability, people under 25 and students can buy up to two tickets at a 30 to 50% discount on the day of the performance. Credit cards are accepted at the ticket office, which is open Monday to Saturday from 9 am to 8 pm (6 pm on Monday) and on Sunday an hour before curtain time. There are no performances in July and August.

Church Venues

Some of the performances held in Paris' historic churches are free, such as those at Notre Dame Cathedral (Map 8) each Sunday at 5.30 pm (usually 80/60FF on certain other days of the week at 8.30 pm). From April to October, classical concerts are also held in the Sainte Chapelle (Map 6; ☎ 01 53 73 78 51) on the Île de la Cité (4e); the cheapest seats are about 110FF (80FF for students under 25). Other noted concert venues with similar admission fees are Église Saint Eustache, 1er (Map 7), Église Royale at the Val-de-Grâce, 5e (Map 6), Église Saint Sulpice, 6e (Map 6),

ENTERTAINMENT

Église Saint Germain des Prés, 6e (Map 6), Église de la Madeleine, 8e (Map 2) and Église Saint Pierre de Montmartre, 18e (Map 9).

Museum Venues

Museums featuring concert series include the Musée du Louvre (Map 7; ☎ 01 40 20 53 17), which holds a series of midday and evening chamber music concerts from September to June, and the Musée d'Orsay (Map 4; ☎ 01 40 49 48 14).

ROCK

Rock concerts are listed in *Pariscope* and *L'Officiel des Spectacles*, but you'll get a better idea of what's on by checking booking counters at Virgin or FNAC or by picking up a copy of *LYLO* or *Nova* (see the Listings section at the start of this chapter).

There's rock at numerous bars, cafés and clubs around Paris, plus a host of venues regularly put on acts by big international performers. It's often easier to see anglophone acts in Paris than back in their home countries. Typically, tickets cost 120 to 220FF. The most popular stadium venues for international acts include Le Zénith (Map 1; ☎ 01 42 08 60 00) at the Cité de la Musique in the 19e and the Palais Omnisports de Paris-Bercy (Map 1; ☎ 01 44 68 44 68) in the 12e. Other venues – though not exclusively for rock – include the following:

L'Ailleurs (Map 8; ☎ 01 44 59 82 82; metro Bastille), 13 Rue Jean Beausire, 4e. This tiny concert café showcasing local talent (mostly *chansons françaises*) is open seven nights a week. Concerts begin at 9.30 pm (though you should arrive an hour before) and finish at about 11 pm. Entry costs 30, 50 or 80FF depending on where you sit. It's open daily from 6.30 pm to 1.30 am.

Le Bataclan (Map 5; ☎ 01 49 23 96 33; metro Saint Ambroise), 50 Blvd Voltaire, 11e. A small concert venue with some big acts, Le Bataclan masquerades some weekend nights as a techno club. It's open from 11.30 pm to 5 am.

La Cigale (Map 9; ☎ 01 49 25 89 99; metro Pigalle), 102 Blvd Rochechouart, 18e. An enormous old music hall that hosts international rock acts as well as jazz occasionally. There's seating in the balcony and dancing up front. Admission runs from 80 to 120FF.

Café de la Danse (Map 5; ☎ 01 47 00 57 59; metro Bastille), 5 Passage Louis-Philippe, 11e. An auditorium with 300 to 500 seats located only a few metres from 23 Rue de Lappe. Almost every evening at 8 or 8.30 pm, it plays host to rock concerts, dance performances, musical theatre and poetry readings. Tickets (50 to 150FF) are available from FNAC.

Élysée Montmartre (Map 9; ☎ 01 44 92 45 45; metro Anvers), 72 Blvd Rochechouart, 18e. This huge old music hall is one of the better venues for one-off rock and indy concerts. La Java (see Discos & Clubs) brings its salsa here every third Saturday of the month (80FF), and the 'Scream' theme party (entry 100FF, drinks 50FF) held on another Saturday each month attracts big name DJs and a mixed crowd – from supermodels to drag queens. Women shouldn't have any problems getting in any time; single guys might have to wait till late.

Espace Voltaire (Map 1; ☎ 01 40 24 02 48; metro Voltaire), 4 Rue Camille Desmoulin, 11e. This large hall is hired out for special events and has some of the best musical entertainment in the city.

Le Divan du Monde (Map 9; ☎ 01 44 92 77 66; metro Pigalle), 75 Rue des Martyrs, 18e. One of the best concert venues in town with good visibility and sound; Latino figures at least once a week. It's also a popular club, open most nights till dawn.

L'Européen (Map 2; ☎ 01 49 87 50 50; metro Place de Clichy), 3-5 Rue Biot, 17e. A large music hall north-west of Place de Clichy that frequently hosts Latino concerts (tickets 100FF).

Théâtre du Tourtour (Map 8; ☎ 01 48 87 82 48; metro Châtelet), 20 Rue Quincampoix, 4e. This is an intimate, 123-seat theatre in a 15th-century cellar. There's something on every night from Tuesday to Saturday: plays by young theatre companies at 7 pm; classical or modern plays by more experienced actors at 8.30 pm; music – anything from rock to French chansons – at 10.15 pm. Ticket prices range from 70 to 100FF. Students and people under 25 or over 65 get a 20FF discount. Reservations can be made by phone, usually on the day of the performance, and you can pick up your tickets 20 minutes before show time. Tickets are also available at FNAC and the discount Kiosque Théâtre outlets.

JAZZ

After WWII, Paris was Europe's most important jazz centre and again the music is very much *à la mode* these days; the city's better *boîtes* (clubs) continue to attract top international stars. The Banlieues Bleues (☎ 01 42 43 56 66), a jazz festival held in Saint Denis and other Paris suburbs from late February to early April, attracts big-name talent.

All Jazz Club (Map 6; ☎ 01 42 61 53 53; metro Saint Germain des Prés), 7-11 Rue Saint Benoît, 6e. Formerly called Latitudes, this club features a more varied assortment of musicians in stylish club surroundings. The bar is open daily from 6 pm to 2 am; there are sessions every night except Sunday at 10 pm (10.30 on Friday and Saturday). The price of the first drink (120FF) usually gains entry; some special concerts cost 130 to 150FF.

Le Baiser Salé (Map 7; ☎ 01 42 33 37 71; metro Châtelet), 58 Rue des Lombards, 1er. One of three very hip jazz clubs on the same street (see the following two venues) at which a single membership card (150FF a year) gets you significant discounts. The *salle de jazz* on the 1st floor has concerts of Afro jazz, jazz fusion etc nightly from 10 pm to 3 am. The cover charge is 40 to 80FF; it's free on Sunday (when young musicians play) and during jam sessions on Monday night. The bar on the ground floor is open daily from 7 pm to 6 am.

Le Caveau de la Huchette (Map 6; ☎ 01 43 26 65 05; metro Saint Michel), 5 Rue de la Huchette, 5e. A medieval *caveau* (cellar) – used as a courtroom and torture chamber during the Revolution – where virtually all the jazz greats have played since 1946. It's touristy – no doubt about that – but the atmosphere can often be more electric than at the more 'serious' jazz clubs. It is open nightly from 9.30 pm to 2 am (4 am on Saturday, Sunday and the night before public holidays); sessions begin at 10.30 pm. The cover charge is 60FF (55FF for students) during the week, 70FF (no discounts) on Friday, Saturday and the night

before holidays. Fruit juice/beer start at 22/26FF. Details on coming attractions are posted on the door; the bands change every week or so.

Au Duc des Lombards (Map 7; ☎ 01 42 33 22 88; metro Châtelet), 42 Rue des Lombards, 1er. An ultra-cool venue decorated with posters of past jazz greats that attracts a far more relaxed (and less reverent) crowd than the other two venues on the street. The ground floor bar area vibrates nightly from 8 pm to 4 or 5 am. The cover charge is 50 to 100FF, depending on what's on; drinks are 28 (juice, beer) to 55FF (cocktails).

New Morning (Map 3; ☎ 01 45 23 51 41 for recorded information, ☎ 01 42 31 31 31 for reservations; metro Château d'Eau), 7-9 Rue des Petites Écuries, 10e. An informal auditorium that hosts concerts of jazz as well as rock, funk, salsa, Afro-Cuban and Brazilian music etc three to seven nights a week at 9 pm. The second set ends at about 1 am. Tickets (110 to 140FF), available from FNAC and Virgin, can usually be purchased at the door. There are concerts from time to time on Sunday at 3 pm (30FF).

Le Sunset (Map 7; ☎ 01 40 26 46 60; metro Châtelet), 60 Rue des Lombards, 1er. Musicians and actors (cinema and theatre) are among the jazz fans who hang out at this trendy club, whose cellar hosts live concerts of funk, Latino, bebop and the like nightly from 10.30 pm to 4 am; most of the big names play Wednesday to Saturday. Entry costs 80FF, including a drink; subsequent liquid refreshment is 28FF a go. At the ground floor bar and restaurant, you can eat until 3 am (closed Sunday); *menus* are 80 and 120FF.

La Villa (Map 6; ☎ 01 43 26 60 00; metro Saint Germain des Prés), 29 Rue Jacob, 6e. This very cool, high-tech place attracts big-name performers from the USA, the rest of Europe and Japan, with local talent thrown in for good measure between sets. You'll love the odd furniture – stools shaped like teardrops, 'crouching' chairs etc. It's open Monday to Saturday from 10.30 pm to 2 am and entry costs 150FF, including the first drink.

FRENCH CHANSONS

For details on accordion music at Le Balajo's weekend tea dances, see Discos & Clubs.

Chez Louisette (Map 1; ☎ 01 40 12 10 14; metro Porte de Clignancourt), in the Marché aux Puces de Saint Ouen. This is one of the highlights of a visit to Paris' largest flea market (see the Shopping chapter). Market-goers crowd around little tables to eat lunch and hear an old-time *chanteuse* belt out Edith Piaf numbers accompanied by accordion music. It is open from noon to 6 or 7 pm on Saturday, Sunday and Monday. Main dishes are 65 to 135FF. Chez Louisette is inside the maze of Marché Vernaison not far from 130 Ave Michelet, the boulevard on the other side of the highway from the Porte de Clignancourt metro stop (18e).

Le Croquenote (Map 7; ☎ 01 42 33 60 70; metro Rue Montmartre), 22 Passage des Panoramas, 2e. An intimate French restaurant with dinner (170FF) at 8 pm and chansons – in the styles of Brel, Brassens, Léo Ferré and Félix Leclerc – at around 10 pm. It is closed on Sunday and in August. Call ahead to book a table.

Le Lapin Agile (Map 9; ☎ 01 46 06 85 87; metro Lamarck Caulaincourt), 22 Rue des Saules, 18e. A rustic cabaret venue favoured by turn-of-the-century artists and intellectuals. The name derives from *Le Lapin à Gill*, a mural of a rabbit jumping out of a cooking pot by caricaturist André Gill, which can still be seen on the western exterior wall. In 1911 the writer Roland Dorgelès, known for his hatred of modern art, tied a paintbrush to the tail of a donkey and – with the unwitting help of Guillaume Apollinaire, a Lapin Agile regular and a noted exponent of Cubism – managed to get the resulting mess into the Salon des Indépendants art show under the title *Sunset over the Adriatic*. These days, chansons are performed and poetry read nightly, except Monday, from 9 pm to 2 am. Entry costs 130FF (90FF for students except on Saturday and holidays), including a drink.

Le Piano Zinc (Map 8; ☎ 01 42 74 32 42; metro Rambuteau), 49 Rue des Blancs Manteaux, 4e. An informal, mainly gay establishment with three levels, including a basement room where, after 10 pm, a pianist accompanies patrons overwhelmed by the desire to sing Piaf and Brel favourites. It is open from 6 pm to 2 am; the basements are closed on Monday. There's no cover charge except on Friday, Saturday and the eve of public holidays, when you have to buy a drink (19 to 42FF). Happy hour is from 6 to 8 pm.

Au Vieux Paris (Map 8; ☎ 01 48 87 55 56; metro Hôtel de Ville), 72 Rue de la Verrerie, 4e. A real period piece Parisian bar (closed Sunday and Monday) that hosts sing-alongs of French chansons, accompanied by an accordionist and Madame Françoise, the feisty proprietor (sheet music provided). The music begins at about 11.45 pm on Thursday, Friday and Saturday nights and carries on till 4 am. The patrons are mostly young Parisians. Come by at around 11 pm to get a seat.

PUBS, BARS & CAFÉS
Les Halles Area
The area around Forum des Halles is filled with 'in' places for a drink.

Café Beaubourg (Map 8; ☎ 01 48 87 63 96; metro Châtelet-Les Halles), 100 Rue Saint Martin, just opposite the Centre Pompidou, 1er. This minimalist café draws in an arty crowd, and there's always free entertainment on the large square in front. Sunday brunch (110FF) on the terrace is excellent. It's open daily from 8 am to 1 am (2 am on Friday and Saturday).

Café Oz (Map 7; ☎ 01 40 39 00 18; metro Châtelet), 18 Rue Saint Denis, 1er. An Aussie pub bubbling with the same Down Under (well, let's just say) enthusiasm as the original across the river on Rue Saint Jacques in the 5e. See the Latin Quarter section for details.

Marais
The 4e has quite a few lively places for daytime and after-hours drinks.

Amnésia Café (Map 8; ☎ 01 42 72 16 94; metro Hôtel de Ville), 42 Rue Vieille du Temple, 4e. A cosy, warmly lit and very popular place, most of whose clients – but not all – are gay. Beers start at 15FF (19FF after 10 pm), cocktails at 45FF. Breakfast is 70FF, *menus* at brunch (daily noon to 4 pm) are 90 and 130FF, and the plat du jour is 60FF. It is open daily from 11 am to 2 am.

Café des Phares (Map 5; ☎ 01 42 72 04 70; metro Bastille), 7 Place de la Bastille, 4e. A pioneering 'philosopher café' where you can argue the meaning of life from 11 am on Sundays. Attempts to resurrect the Paris of Jean-Paul Sartre, but on a commercial basis, are very popular in the 1990s.

La Chaise au Plafond (Map 8; ☎ 01 42 76 03 22; metro Hôtel de Ville), 10 Rue du Trésor, 4e. Owned by the same people as Le Petit Fer à Cheval (and with a similar cybertoilet), this place is warm and wooden with tables outside on a pedestrian-only backstreet. Open daily from 9.30 am to 2 am.

Les Étages (Map 8; ☎ 01 42 78 72 00; metro Hôtel de Ville), 35 Rue Vielle du Temple, 4e. Head upstairs to the two upper floors for grunge, with graffiti on the walls and big leather armchairs. The drinks aren't cheap (55 to 60FF for spirits), but you do get to phone through your order on an ancient 1950s phone. Happy hour is from 5 to 9 pm.

Louis-Philippe Café (Map 8; ☎ 01 42 72 29 42; metro Pont Marie), 66 Quai de l'Hôtel de Ville, 4e, facing the Seine. A mirror-lined café, founded in 1840, with a large terrace. It is open daily from 9 am to 2 am; coffee is 6/10FF at the bar/seated. The brasserie on the 1st floor, reached via a spiral staircase, is open from noon to 3 pm and 7.30 to 11.30 pm. The 82FF weekday *menu* is not available in the evening during the warm months. The *plat du jour* is 68FF.

Mixerl Bar (Map 8; ☎ 01 48 87 55 44; metro Hôtel de Ville), 23 Rue Sainte Croix de la Bretonnerie, 4e. The name says it all – straight, gay, eclectic music. It's open daily from 4 pm to 2 am.

Le Petit Fer à Cheval (Map 8; ☎ 01 42 72 47 47; metro Hôtel de Ville or Saint Paul), 30 Rue Vieille du Temple, 4e. A slightly offbeat bar/restaurant named after its horseshoe-shaped counter; often filled to overflowing with friendly, mostly straight young regulars. The plat du jour changes each day. The all stainless-steel bathroom is straight out of a Flash Gordon film. It is open daily from 9 am (11 am at the weekend) to 2 am. Food *(plat du jour* 60FF, sandwiches around 20FF) is available nonstop from noon to 1.15 am.

Le Pick Clops (Map 8; ☎ 01 40 29 02 18; metro Hôtel de Ville), 16 Rue Vieille du Temple, at the corner of Rue de Roi du Sicile, 4e. In a very gay neighbourhood, this straight, rock bar with cheap drinks is a great place to watch the world go by. The brief happy hour is from 8 to 9 pm.

Piment Café (Map 8; ☎ 01 42 74 33 75; metro Saint Paul), 15 Rue de Sévigné, 4e. This small and cosmopolitan bar changes face frequently, with tranquil moments punctuated by live music, art on show and good, reasonably

priced food (30 to 70FF for main courses; 45FF for the plat du jour). It's open daily from noon (6 pm on Sunday) to 1 am.

Stolly's (Map 8; ☎ 01 42 76 06 76; metro Hôtel de Ville), 16 Rue de la Cloche Percée, 4e. Just off Rue du Rivoli, this anglophone bar is always overcrowded, particularly during the 5 to 8 pm happy hour. It's open daily, there are chairs on the pavement and a demi/pint of Guinness is 20/35FF. A 1.6L pitcher of cheap *blonde* (house lager) is 50FF.

La Tartine (Map 8; ☎ 01 42 72 76 85; metro Saint Paul), 24 Rue de Rivoli, 4e. A wine bar where little has changed since the days of gas lighting (the fixtures are still in place). It offers 15 selected reds, whites and rosés for 9.50 to 15.50FF a glass. There's not much to eat except sandwiches (14 to 45FF) and, of course, lots of *tartines*. It is open from 8.30 am (noon on Wednesday) to 10 pm (closed Tuesday).

Île de la Cité

The island (1er) is not exactly hopping after dark but there is a good wine bar here.

Taverne Henri IV (Map 6; ☎ 01 43 54 27 90; metro Pont Neuf), 13 Place du Pont Neuf, 1er. A decent restaurant as well as a serious wine bar, this place attracts lots of people in the legal profession from the nearby Palais de Justice. It's open weekdays from noon to 9 pm, on Saturday to 4 pm.

Latin Quarter

The Latin Quarter (5e) has Paris' highest concentration of bars catering to anglophones.

Café Oz (Map 6; ☎ 01 43 54 30 48; metro Luxembourg), 184 Rue Saint Jacques, 5e. A casual, friendly Australian pub with Fosters on tap for 22FF (35FF for a schooner or 0.4L) and VB, Coopers, Cascade and Redback as other amber options, plus Australian wines from 22FF a glass. A pie lunch with salad is 45FF. It is open daily from 4 pm to 2 am (happy hour from opening to 9.30 pm), and the Australian staff are clued in about jobs, apartments etc.

Le Cloître (Map 6; ☎ 01 43 25 19 92; metro Saint Michel), 19 Rue Saint Jacques, 5e. An unpretentious, relaxed place where the mellow background music goes down well with the students who congregate here. There's beer and Guinness on tap, and you can play chess in the back except after 10 pm on weekends and holidays, when it gets too crowded. It is open daily from 3 pm to 2 am.

Polly Maggoo (Map 6; ☎ 01 46 33 33 64; metro Saint Michel), 11 Rue Saint Jacques, 5e. An informal, friendly bar founded in 1967 and still spinning discs from the 1960s. The regulars include English speakers resident in Paris. Chess and backgammon can be played from noon to 8 pm and beer starts at 13FF (18FF after 10 pm). It is open daily from 1 pm to 3 or 4 am.

Le Rallye (Map 8; ☎ 01 43 54 29 65; metro Maubert Mutualité), 11 Quai de la Tournelle, 5e. A 1950s-style Provençal café whose speciality is, as you'd expect, *pastis*. Most of the daytime clients come from the quartier, some in search of the 50FF lunch *menu*, others to pick up their *boules* for a game of riverbank *pétanque*. The evening crowd is young, lively and from all over the city. It is open daily from 7 am (9.30 am on Sunday) to 2 am.

Le Violon Dingue (Map 6; no phone; metro Maubert Mutualité), 46 Rue de la Montagne Sainte Geneviève, 5e. A loud, lively and none-too-spotless American-style bar that attracts lots of English speakers in their early 20s. A pint of beer costs 20FF during the 6 to 10 pm happy hour – when most drinks are half-price – and from 32FF the rest of the time. American sporting events like the Superbowl (football) and the NBA (basketball) play-offs are shown on the large-screen TV. It is open daily from 6 pm to 1.30 am (4 am on Friday and Saturday).

6e Arrondissement

The 6e has some of Paris' most famous cafés – and quite a few decent newcomers.

Café de Flore (Map 6; ☎ 01 45 48 55 26; metro Saint Germain des Prés), 172 Blvd Saint Germain. An Art Deco-style café less touristy than the Deux Magots where the red banquettes, mosaic floors, mirrors and marble walls haven't changed since the days when Jean Paul Sartre, Simone de Beauvoir, Albert Camus and Picasso sipped the house Pouilly Fumé. The outdoor terrace (glassed-in in winter) is a sought-after place to sip beer (41FF for 0.4L), wine (32FF) or coffee (23FF). It is open daily from 7 am to 1.30 am.

Café de la Mairie (Map 6; ☎ 01 43 26 67 82; metro Saint Sulpice), 8 Place Saint Sulpice. A bustling and slightly tacky café on two floors frequented by students, writers and, since the late 1980s, film producers attracted by its tattered Left Bank ambience and tired of the Flore. A beer costs 11FF at the counter, 20FF if you sit down. It is open Monday to Saturday from 7 am to 11 pm or midnight (2 am in the warm months).

Chez Georges (Map 6; ☎ 01 43 26 79 15; metro Mabillon), 11 Rue des Canettes. A friendly bar popular with people of all ages, whose smoke-darkened walls are decorated with photos of musicians who played here in the 1960s and 1970s. Beer in bottles starts at 16FF (20FF after 10 pm, 30FF in the cellar), and coffee is 6 to 9FF. It is open Tuesday to Saturday from noon to 2 am (closed in August). The dank cellar, suffused with live mellow music at the weekend, opens at 10 pm.

Coolin (Map 6; ☎ 01 44 07 00 92; metro Mabillon), 15 Rue Clément. The only Irish bar we intend to include in this chapter, the Coolin stands out for its location (it's in a renovated old covered market) and its odd fusion of Dublin pub and Parisian café. It's open daily from 10 am (noon on Sunday) to 2 am.

Cubana Café (Map 4; ☎ 01 40 46 80 81; metro Vavin), 45 Rue Vavin. The perfect place for a couple of 'starter' drinks before carrying on to the nearby Coupole for a night of salsa and mambo. For those who indulge in cigars, there's a *fumoir* (smoking room) equipped with a bunch of comfy sofas and live Cuban music on Wednesday evenings and on Sunday at 2 pm.

Les Deux Magots (Map 6; ☎ 01 45 48 55 25; metro Saint Germain des Prés), 170 Blvd Saint Germain. There's been a café here since 1881 but the present one – whose name derives from the two wooden *magots* (grotesque figurines) of Chinese dignitaries at the entrance – dates from 1914. It is perhaps best known as the haunt of Jean-Paul Sartre, André Breton and Hemingway. On the huge terrace (enclosed in winter), you can sip coffee (22FF), beer on tap (28FF) and their famous home-made hot chocolate (30FF) in steaming porcelain pitchers, served by waiters clad in long white aprons. A continental breakfast costs 80FF; light meals (34 to 48FF) are also available. It is open daily from 7.30 am to 1.30 am.

Le 10 (Map 6; ☎ 01 43 26 66 83; metro Odéon), 10 Rue de l'Odéon. A pub whose orange lighting adds a warm glow to the smoke-darkened posters on the walls. Popular with local and foreign university students and au pairs, many in their late teens or early 20s. The taped music ranges from jazz and the Doors to Yves Montand. The house speciality is sangria (38FF for 0.5L). Beer in bottles is 22 to 32FF. It is open daily from 6 pm to 2 am. Odéon is also a good area to hang out in if you miss your curfew or last metro as there are a few cafés and always lot of people around.

La Paillotte (Map 6; ☎ 01 43 26 45 69; metro), 45 Rue Monsieur le Prince. This dimly lit bar, open daily from 9 pm till late, plays excellent canned jazz.

La Palette (Map 6; ☎ 01 43 26 68 15; metro Mabillon), 43 Rue de Seine. This turn-of-the-century café, stomping ground of both Cézanne and Braque, attracts dealers and shoppers from the local art galleries. Open Monday to Saturday to 2 am.

Champs-Élysées Area

Once considered hopelessly tacky, the Ave des Champs-Élysées (8e) and surrounds has got a new lease of life since its costly renovation.

Cricketer Pub (Map 2; ☎ 01 40 07 01 45; metro Saint Augustin), 41 Rue des Mathurins, 8e. This is a genuine English pub – supposedly transported to Paris from Ipswich – and the last refuge for homesick Brits, with darts, quiz nights and Adams on tap (25FF). It's open daily from 11 am to 2 am.

Buddha Bar (Map 2; ☎ 01 53 05 90 00; metro Concorde), 8 Rue Boissy d'Anglas, 8e. At centre stage in the cavernous cellar of this restaurant-bar frequented by suits, supermodels and hangers-on is an enormous bronze Buddha. Everyone should go at least once for a look, but stick with the drinks (cocktails from 60FF); a Pacific Rim-style meal will cost you upwards of 300FF. The bar is open daily from 6 pm to 2 am.

Montecristo Café (Map 2; ☎ 01 45 62 30 86; metro Franklin D Roosevelt), 68 Ave des Champs-Élysées, 8e. This bar-restaurant, which bills itself as 'Havana in Paris', brings Latino mainstream and the tourists love it. The music is

decent, there's a great bar and the place never closes – it's open 24 hours seven days a week. The first drink costs 100FF on Friday and Saturday. Happy hour is from 3 to 8 pm and Sunday brunch (90 to 110FF) is from 11 am to 5 pm.

Grands Boulevards Area

The Grands Boulevards (2e and 9e) are one of the Right Bank's major areas for a night on the town.

Harry's New York Bar (Map 7; ☎ 01 42 61 71 14; metro Opéra), 5 Rue Daunou, 2e. Back in the prewar years, when there were several dozen American-style bars in Paris, Harry's was one of the most popular – habitués included Ernest Hemingway and Scott Fitzgerald. The Cuban mahogany interior dates from the mid-19th century and was brought over lock, stock and barrel from Manhattan's Third Ave in 1911. Beer costs 28FF (35FF after 10 pm). Drinks at the basement piano bar – there's live music (usually soft jazz) nightly from 10 pm to 2 or 3 am – cost 40 to 70FF. It is open every day of the year except 24 and 25 December from 10.30 am to 4 am. The copyrighted advertisement for Harry's in the *International Herald Tribune* still reads: 'Tell the Taxi Driver Sank Roo Doe Noo'.

Bastille Area

The area just north and east of Place de la Bastille (11e) has become enormously popular for dining, drinking and dancing until all hours. Rue de Lappe, a dreary narrow lane in the daytime, comes alive at night. See the Places to Eat chapter for details of some of the many popular bar-restaurants along Rue de Lappe, like the popular Cuban *Havanita*, *La Pirada Bar Tapas*, *Café 66* and *Del Rio Café*. The area to the south-east of the square (12e) has a number of excellent after-dark venues.

Boca Chica (Map 5; ☎ 01 43 57 93 13; metro Ledru Rollin), 58 Rue de Charonne, 11e. An enormous, almost industrial place close to Suds (see Bastille Area in the Places to Eat chapter) with three large bars on two floors. Friendly, lively and young crowd. Happy hour is from 4 to 8 pm daily when a 0.5L beer is 20FF and all cocktails half price. It's open daily till 2 am.

Le Café du Passage (Map 5; ☎ 01 49 29 97 64; metro Ledru Rollin), 12 Rue de Charonne, 11e. A modern but laid-back wine bar where you can relax in upholstered armchairs while sampling 70 varieties of wine, 16 of them available by the glass (from 23 to 37FF). Light food such as pâtés, risotto and salads (48 to 65FF) is also available. It is open Monday to Saturday from 6 pm (noon on Saturday) to 2 am.

China Club (Map 5; ☎ 01 43 43 82 02; metro Ledru Rollin), 50 Rue de Charenton, 12e. If you've got the rich uncle (he's the 'American uncle' in French, surprise, surprise) or aunt in tow, drag them to this stylish establishment just behind the Hôpital Quinze Vingts and the Opéra Bastille. It's got a huge bar with high ceilings on the ground floor, a fumoir (in case your uncle's into Havanas) open from 7 pm to 2 am (3 am on Friday and Saturday) on the 1st floor and a jazz club in the cellar open till 3 am – all done up to look like Shanghai circa 1930. The restaurant here (7 pm to 12.30 am) is just so-so and expensive (starters from 50FF, main courses from 90FF) though there's a *menu* at 155FF (100FF on Sunday) and dim sum assortment for 47FF. Happy hour is from 7 to 9 pm daily when all drinks are 35FF.

Iguana Café (Map 5; ☎ 01 40 21 39 99; metro Bastille), 15 Rue de la Roquette, 11e. A chic, two-level café-pub that attracts exceptionally trendy people in their 20s and early 30s. Cocktails are 42 to 55FF (46 to 59FF after 10 pm); beer on tap is 20 to 28FF (or 24 to 32FF). It is open daily from 9 am to 5 am.

Le Viaduc Café (Map 5; ☎ 01 44 74 70 70; metro Gare de Lyon), 43 Ave Daumesnil, 12e. The terrace of this very trendy café in one of the glassed-in arches of the Viaduc des Arts (see Bastille Area in the Things to See & Do chapter) is an excellent spot to while away the hours, and the jazz brunch on Sunday is very popular (see Breakfast in the Places to Eat chapter). It's open seven days a week until 4 am.

Oberkampf & Ménilmontant Areas

East of Place de la République, Rue Oberkampf (11e) and its extension, Rue de Ménilmontant (20e) are the up-and-coming *branché* areas of Paris with a number of interesting cafés and bars, like the popular *Le Charbon* (see the Places to Eat chapter).

Café Cannibale (Map 3; ☎ 01 49 29 95 59; metro Couronnes), 93 Rue Jean Pierre Timbaud, 11e. So laid-back it's almost asleep, this cosy café and bar is a place where you can either linger over a coffee (10FF) or grab a quick beer at the bar (12FF) or *à table* (20FF). The lunch *formule* is 60FF and brunch *menus*, served from noon to 4 pm, are 75 and 85FF. It's open daily from 8 am to 2 am.

Le Cithéa (Map 3; ☎ 01 40 21 70 95; metro Parmentier), 114 Rue Oberkampf, 11e. This place has bands playing acid and jungle jazz, Latin, drum and bass, and funk. Wine and beer costs 25FF, cocktails from 60FF. It is open daily from 8 pm till dawn and it's where most people from the Charbon end up in the wee hours.

Le Mécano Bar (Map 3; ☎ 01 40 21 35 28; metro Parmentier), 99 Rue Oberkampf, 11e. Housed in a former tool shed, this ultra-cool place attracts those who wouldn't be caught dead in the Cannibale. It's open daily from 8 pm to 2 am.

Le Troisième Bureau (Map 3; ☎ 01 43 55 87 65; metro Oberkampf), 74 Rue de la Folie Méricourt, 11e. A pubby *bistrot* with an interesting clientele where you can read, listen to music and even send or receive a fax. Decent dishes are available for 50 to 82FF. It's open daily from 11.30 am (6.30 on Sunday) to 2 am.

Montparnasse

The most popular places to while away the hours over a drink or coffee in this area (14e and 6e) are the large café-restaurants like *La Coupole* and *Le Select* on the Blvd du Montparnasse. See the Places to Eat chapter for details.

La Closerie des Lilas (Map 6; ☎ 01 40 51 34 50; metro Port Royal), 171 Blvd du Montparnasse, 6e. Anyone who's ever read Hemingway knows he did a lot of writing, drinking and eating of oysters here, and little brass tags on the tables tell you exactly where he (and other luminaries such as Picasso, Apollinaire etc) whiled away the hours making art or just gossiping. It's open daily from 11.30 am to 2 am.

Montmartre & Pigalle

In between the sleaze there are some interesting bars at the bottom of the hill in Montmartre (9e and 18e).

Chao Ba Café (Map 2; ☎ 01 46 06 72 90), 22 Blvd de Clichy, 18e. This café-restaurant, transformed from an old-style brasserie into something straight out of Saigon, is open from Sunday to Wednesday to 2 am and the rest of the week to 5 am.

Le Dépanneur (Map 9; ☎ 01 40 16 40 20; metro Blanche), 27 Rue Fontaine, 9e. American diner meets the 1980s round the clock with plenty of tequila and fancy cocktails (60FF). Beer is 28 to 35FF (though cheaper from 7 to 10 pm) and happy hour is from 4 to 8 pm. The lunch *menu* is 65FF, the dinner one 89FF. Come to this place and you may never leave. It's open 24 hours a day, seven days a week.

Le Moloko (Map 9; ☎ 01 48 74 50 26; metro Blanche), 26 Rue Fontaine, 9e. An incredibly 'in' *bar de nuit* whose décor is an eclectic mix of the classic (red velvet) and the provocative. There's jukebox dancing (soul, hip-hop) on the ground floor. Entry is free most nights, but not on Saturdays, when there are live shows (concerts, striptease etc). It is open daily from 10 pm to 5.30 or 6 am, but things don't start to pick up until after midnight.

Le Salsa Loco (Map 3; ☎ 01 40 82 91 56; metro Pigalle), 70 Rue Condorcet, 9e. Yet another place with a Cuban theme and salsa music, this is the place to come in Pigalle when everything else is shutting down. *Mojitos*, rum-based Cuban cocktails, are reasonable at 30FF. It's open daily from 7 pm to 3 am (5 am on Saturday).

Le Sancerre (Map 9; ☎ 01 42 58 08 20; metro Abbesses), 35 Rue des Abbesses, 18e. A popular, lively bistro/bar that's often crowded in the evening. The cheapest beers cost between 10FF (at the bar during the day) and 20FF (after 10 pm). It is open daily from 7 am to 1.30 or 2 am. Food, including two *plats du jour* (60FF), is served from noon to 11 pm.

Le Wepler Café (Map 2; ☎ 01 45 22 53 24; metro Place de Clichy), 14 Place de Clichy, 18e. Though this large café-restaurant is celebrated for its oysters (120FF) and other seafood, we go to Charlot-Roi des Coquillages (see Montmartre & Pigalle in the Places to Eat chapter) for those sorts of things and come here to sit in the large covered terrace, enjoying the hubbub and scenery of Place de Clichy. It's open daily from 8 am to 1 am.

20e Arrondissement

La Flèche d'Or Café (Map 1; ☎ 01 43 72 04 23; metro Porte de Bagnolet), 102bis Rue de Bagnolet, 20e. This bar – in a disused train station south-east of Père Lachaise Cemetery – attracts a trendy and arty young crowd; this may as well be Berlin. It's open daily except Tuesday from 10 am to 2 am (6 am at the weekend) and the big café here does a decent brunch on Sunday.

GAY PARIS

The Marais (4e) – especially the areas along around the intersection of Rue des Archives and Rue Sainte Croix de la Bretonnerie and westward to Rue Vieille du Temple – has been Paris' main centre of gay social life since the early 1980s.

L'Arène (Map 8; no telephone; metro Hôtel de Ville), 80 Quai de l'Hôtel de Ville, 4e. For those seriously OFB (out for business), this place can oblige. It's got dark rooms and cubicles on three levels and heats up (boils over, rather) from around midnight. Take the usual precautions. It's open daily from 2 pm to 6 am (7 am on the weekend).

Bar de l'Hôtel Central (Map 8; ☎ 01 48 87 99 33; metro Hôtel de Ville), 33 Rue Vieille du Temple, 4e. Founded in 1980, this is one of the oldest gay bars in the city, but it's pretty comatose these days. A demi costs 15FF (18FF after 10 pm). It is open daily from 4 pm (2 pm on Saturday and Sunday) to 1 am (2 am on Friday and Saturday nights).

Café Cox (Map 8; ☎ 01 42 72 08 00; metro Hôtel de Ville), 15 Rue des Archives, 4e. OK, it's got an in-your-face name but this small bar attracts an interesting, rather friendly crowd. It's open from 1 pm to 2 am.

Coffee Shop (Map 8; ☎ 01 42 74 46 29; metro Hôtel de Ville), 3 Rue Sainte Croix de la Bretonnerie, 4e. A small, almost exclusively gay café that's open daily from noon to 2 am. Bottled beer, officially served only with the two-course meals (60FF; available all day long), costs 17FF. Coffee is 16FF.

Duplex Bar (Map 8; ☎ 01 42 72 80 86; metro Rambuteau), 25 Rue Michel Le Comte, 3e. Also one of the oldest gay bars in Paris (in every sense), this dark, avant-garde place doubles as something of a gallery with art shows every month. It is open daily from 8 pm to 2 am.

Open Café (Map 8; ☎ 01 42 72 26 18; metro Hôtel de Ville), 17 Rue des Archives, 4e. This is where most people head after work or where they start the evening. It's so packed at those times that the clientele usually spills out onto the pavement. It's open from 10 am to 2 am. Happy hour is from 6 to 8 pm.

QG Bar (Map 8; ☎ 01 48 87 74 18; metro Rambuteau), 12 Rue Simon Le Franc, 4e. Not as popular as L'Arène but the same type of place so come prepared. It's open seven days a week from 5 pm to 6 am (8 am on the weekend).

Quetzal Bar (Map 8; ☎ 01 48 87 99 07; metro Hôtel de Ville), 10 Rue de la Verrerie, at the corner of Rue des Mauvais Garçons (literally, 'Street of the Bad Boys), 4e. A neon-lit, ultra-modern bar popular with gay men in the 30-something age group. A demi on tap is 18FF. It is open daily from 5 pm to 3 am (4 am on Friday and Saturday). Happy hour is from 5 to 8 pm and 11 pm to midnight.

Le Skeud (Map 8; ☎ 01 40 29 44 40; metro Hôtel de Ville), 35 Rue Sainte Croix de la Bretonnerie, 4e. This place has a more clubby feel than the Open Café and Cox around the corner and attracts a lot of neighbourhood regulars. It's open daily from 3 pm to 2 am.

While the Marais is the main centre of gay life in Paris, there are some decent bars west of Blvd de Sébastopol in the 1er and 2e as well.

Banana Café (Map 7; ☎ 01 42 33 35 31; metro Châtelet-Les Halles), 13 Rue de la Ferronnerie, 1er. This ever popular cruise bar on two levels has a nice enclosed terrace with stand-up tables and attracts a young crowd. Happy hour (drinks half-price) is between 4.30 and 7.30 pm. It's open daily from 4.15 pm to 6 am.

La Champmeslé (Map 7; ☎ 01 42 96 85 20; metro Pyramides), 4 Rue Chabanais, 2e. A relaxed, dimly lit place that plays mellow music for its patrons, about 75% of whom are lesbians (the rest are mostly gay men). The back room is reserved for women only. Works by a different woman artist are displayed each month. Beer or fruit juice is about 30FF. It is open Monday to Saturday from 5 pm to 2 am, and traditional French chansons are performed live every Thursday at 10 pm.

Le Mercury Bar (Map 7; ☎ 01 40 41 00 01; metro Châtelet-Les Halles), 5 Rue de la Ferronnerie,

1er. The Mercury is not as popular as its neighbour, but it's convenient should you get tired of the Banana. The ground floor is open from 4 pm till dawn, the basement from 9 pm.

Le Vagabond (Map 7; ☎ 01 42 96 27 23; metro Pyramides), 14 Rue Thérèse, 1er. A bar/restaurant long popular with older gay men, some of whom have been patrons since the place was founded in 1956. It is open from 6 pm to 2 am (closed Monday) and drinks are 26 to 32FF. French cuisine is served from 8.30 pm to 12.15 am; the *menus* are 110 and 140FF. To gain entry, push the white button to the left of the door.

SPECTATOR SPORTS

For details on upcoming sporting events, consult the sports daily *L'Équipe* (4.90FF) or the *Figaroscope* published by *Le Figaro* each Wednesday.

Football & Rugby

The Paris-Saint Germain (PSG) football club, one of the best teams in the French first division, often plays at the 50,000-seat Parc des Princes, 16e (Map 1; metro Porte de Saint Cloud). Tickets to see PSG in action (usually on Saturday night) are available through FNAC and the Virgin Megastore on the Ave des Champs-Élysées (see Booking Agencies at the start of this chapter) as well as at the Parc des Princes box office (☎ 01 49 87 29 29 or ☎ 01 42 88 02 76 for a recording; metro Porte de Saint Cloud) at 24 Rue du Commandant Guilbaud (16e), open weekdays from 9 am to 8 pm and Saturday from 10 am to 5 pm. The Coupe de France finals take place at the Stade de France (SDF; see the boxed text) in early May, the Tournoi de Paris in late July.

The Parc des Princes sometimes hosts rugby matches as well, a sport particularly popular in south-west France, and local rugby champions Le Racing Club de France (☎ 01 45 67 55 86) also play at the SDF. The highlights of the rugby season are the championship finals in early June and the Tournoi des Cinq Nations (Five Nations Tournament), involving France, England, Scotland, Wales, Ireland and, from 2000, Italy in March/April.

Stade de France

With a sigh of relief heard round Paris and the nation, the purpose-built 80,000-seat Stade de France (SDF) in the northern suburb of Saint Denis opened with ample time to spare for the World Cup football finals (won by France) of June/July 1998. Built at a cost of 2.7FF billion in just two years, this futuristic and very beautiful structure had been from the start the target of much criticism in the French press.

The controversy began early on. In 1991, when France was proposed as host for the 1998 World Cup, the site picked for the new stadium was Melun-Sénart, 35km east of Paris. But two years later, after a certain amount of funding had been earmarked for Melun-Sénart, then-Prime Minister Édouard Balladur abruptly changed the location to Saint Denis, which did in fact have the benefit of being closer to Paris and on a metro line.

The polemics continued as the stadium was being built. Would it be ready on time? What should it be called? (A national debate on that point finally arrived at a consensus: the less-than-inspiring Stadium of France). For many years even the grass on the pitch wasn't growing fast enough.

On the eve of the World Cup, the next question on everyone's lips was: what the heck would this fantastic stadium do for a living afterward? The Paris-Saint Germain (PSG) football club, which usually attracts some 37,000 spectators at the Parc des Princes in the 16e, bowed out as new tenant, citing the high costs of using the SDF. Other more modest clubs, among them Le Racing Club de France (rugby and athletics) and Red Star (second division football) were also being considered. Meanwhile the SDF will continue to welcome international matches and national finals in football and rugby and 'big event' concerts by foreign and home-grown sensations like the Rolling Stones and Johnny Halliday.

In July 1998 France won the World Cup soccer championships for the first time. The French team defeated the reigning champions Brazil, 3 – 0. Vive la France!

Tennis

Les Internationaux de France de Tennis (French Open), the second of the four Grand Slam tournaments, is held in late May/early June on red clay at Stade Roland Garros (Map 1; ☎ 01 47 43 48 00; metro Porte d'Auteuil) at 2 Ave Gordon Bennett (16e). The capacity of the stadium's main section, Le Central, is about 16,500. Tickets are expensive and hard to come by; bookings are usually made by March at the latest.

The top indoor tournament is the Open de Tennis de la Ville de Paris (Paris Tennis Open), which takes place in late October/early November at the Palais Omnisports de Paris-Bercy (Map 1; ☎ 01 43 46 12 21; metro Bercy) at 8-12 Blvd de Bercy (12e).

Cycling

The final stage (of a total of 21) of the world's most prestigious cycling event, the Tour de France, has, since the 1970s, ended with a dash up the Ave des Champs-Élysées on the third or fourth Sunday in July sometime between noon and 6 pm.

The second biggest 'Parisian' event on the cycling calendar no longer begins in Paris. It's the gruelling, one-day Paris-Roubaix race held on the first Sunday after Easter. The race actually begins in Compiègne, 82km north-east of Paris, and continues for 280km over some 20 different sections of cobblestones (*pavé*) before reaching the *vélodrome* at Roubaix, north-east of Lille.

The biggest indoor cycling event is the Grand Prix des Nations, held in October and pitting the best cyclist from the world's eight best teams against one another on a 250m vélodrome at the Palais Omnisports de Paris-Bercy (Map 1).

ENTERTAINMENT

Horse Racing

One of the cheapest ways to spend a relaxing afternoon in the company of Parisians of all ages, backgrounds and walks of life is to go to the races. The most accessible of Paris' six racecourses is Hippodrome d'Auteuil (Map 1; ☎ 01 45 27 12 25 or ☎ 01 49 10 20 30; metro Porte d'Auteuil) in the south-eastern corner of the Bois de Boulogne (16e), which hosts steeplechases from February to early July and from early September to early December.

Races are held on Sunday as well as some other days of the week, with half a dozen or so heats scheduled between 2 and 5.30 pm. There's no charge to stand on the *pelouse* (lawn) in the middle of the track; a seat in the *tribune* (stands) costs 25FF (40FF on Sunday and holidays, 50FF during special events). Race schedules are published in almost all national newspapers. If you can read a bit of French, pick up a copy of *Paris Turf* (Minitel 3615 TURF for results), the horse-racing daily available at newsstands for 7FF.

To buy yourself a stake in the proceedings, you can place a bet – the minimum is only 10FF. Information on the horses and their owners, trainers and jockeys is available from the free programs; additional statistics are printed in *Paris Turf*. The odds are displayed on TV screens near the betting windows. You can bet that your horse will come in *gagnant* (1st place), *placé* (1st or 2nd place) or *placé jumelé* (1st, 2nd or 3rd place). If your horse wins, take your ticket back to any betting window to collect your windfall, which, if you're lucky, will be enough for a beer or two.

Show jumping is all the rage in Paris and the Jumping International de Paris, held in March at the Palais Omnisports de Paris-Bercy (Map 1), attracts thousands of fans.

Shopping

Paris has shopping options to suit all tastes and all budgets. Garments, for instance, can be selected at the ultra-chic couture houses along Ave Montaigne or plucked from flea-market tables. And certain streets still specialise in certain products. Rue du Pont Louis-Philippe, 4e (Map 8; metro Pont Marie), for example, has all manner of paper goods and stationery, while Rue de Paradis, 10e (Map 3; metro Château d'Eau), is famed for its crystal, glass and tableware shops. If you're in the market for a sewing machine, turn south from Rue de Paradis onto Rue Martel – it's chock-a-block with the things. Walk along Rue Victor Massé in the 9e (Map 3), and you'll see more musical instruments than you thought existed. The shops on Rue Drouot in the 9e (Map 7) sell almost nothing but old postage stamps.

BOOKSHOPS

Paris is justly famous for the writers who have graced its cafés, backstreets and boulevards. But a city's literary culture is only as good as its bookshops, and Paris has many excellent English language ones.

Abbey Bookshop (Map 6; ☎ 01 46 33 16 24; metro Cluny-La Sorbonne), 29 Rue de la Parcheminerie, 5e. A mellow place, not far from Place Saint Michel, known for having free tea and coffee, a supply of Canadian newspapers and a good selection of new and used works of fiction – plus readings of prose and poetry once a week, usually on Wednesday night. It's not far from Place Saint Michel, and is open Monday to Saturday from 10 am to 7 pm; Sunday hours vary according to the owner's whim.

Australian Bookshop (Map 6; ☎ 01 43 29 08 65; metro Saint Michel), 33 Quai des Grands Augustins, 6e. Open Tuesday to Sunday from 11 am to 7 pm. This bookshop, which opened in 1996, specialises in Australian literature in both English and French, has a wealth of Australian state tourist brochures and maps, schedules regular readings and stocks Lonely Planet guidebooks.

Brentano's (Map 7; ☎ 01 42 61 52 50; metro Opéra), 37 Ave de l'Opéra, 2e. Midway between the Louvre and Opéra Garnier, this shop specialises in books from the USA and is open Monday to Saturday from 10 am to 7.30 pm.

La Maison de l'Expatriée (Map 4; ☎ 01 53 59 33 00; metro Assemblée Nationale), 7 Rue de Bourgogne, 7e. This bookshop/newsagent due south of the Assemblée Nationale has one of the largest selections of English-language newspapers and magazines in Paris. It's open weekdays from 7 am to 8 pm and on Saturday and Sunday from 9 am to 1 pm and 2 to 7 pm.

Les Mots à la Bouche (Map 8; ☎ 01 42 78 88 30; metro Hôtel de Ville), 6 Rue Sainte Croix de la Bretonnerie, 4e. Paris' premier gay bookshop specialises in books written by homosexuals or with gay or lesbian themes, and periodicals, including some in English. Most of the back wall is dedicated to English-language books, including lots of novels. It is open Monday to Thursday from 11 am to 11 pm, till midnight on Friday and Saturday, and on Sunday from 2 to 8 pm.

Shakespeare & Company (Map 6; ☎ 01 43 26 96 50; metro Saint Michel), 37 Rue de la Bûcherie, 5e. Paris' most famous English-language bookshop has a varied and unpredictable collection of new and used books in English, including novels from 10FF. They also have a large selection of books in Russian, German, Spanish and Italian. It is open daily from noon till midnight. Poetry readings are held on most Mondays at 8 pm, and there are two libraries on the 1st floor. The shop is named after Sylvia Beach's bookshop – famous for publishing James Joyce's *Ulysses* in 1922 – at 12 Rue de l'Odéon, which was closed by the Nazis in 1941.

Village Voice (Map 6; ☎ 01 46 33 36 47; metro Mabillon), 6 Rue Princesse (6e), two blocks south of Saint Germain des Prés. A friendly, helpful shop with an excellent selection of contemporary North American fiction and European literature in translation. It often sponsors readings, usually on Thursday (and perhaps Tuesday) at around 7 pm. It is open on Monday from 2 to 8 pm and Tuesday to Saturday from 10 am to 8 pm.

WH Smith (Map 2; ☎ 01 44 77 88 99; metro Concorde), 248 Rue de Rivoli, 1er. Situated one block east of Place de la Concorde, WH Smith is open from Monday to Saturday from 9.30 am to 7 pm and on Sunday from 1 to 7 pm. Brace yourself for the imported prices.

DEPARTMENT STORES

Paris' 'big three' department stores are Printemps, Galeries Lafayette and La Samaritaine.

BHV (Bazar de l'Hôtel de Ville), (Map 8; ☎ 01 42 74 90 00; metro Hôtel de Ville), 52-64 Rue de Rivoli, 4e. BHV is a straightforward department store – apart from its enormous but hopelessly chaotic hardware/DIY department in the basement, with every type of hammer, power tool, nail, plug or hinge you could ask for (which is what you'll have to do since you'll never find it on your own). It's open Monday to Saturday from 9.30 am to 7 pm (to 10 pm on Wednesday).

Le Bon Marché (Map 4; ☎ 01 44 39 80 00; metro Sèvres Babylone), 24 Rue de Sèvres, 7e. Paris' first department store, housed in two adjacent buildings, is less fancy (and expensive) than its upmarket rivals across the river. It's open Monday to Saturday from 9.30 am to 7 pm; the famed grocery department is now a separate store called La Grande Épicerie de Paris at No 26 of the same street. It is open from 8.30 am to 9 pm.

Galeries Lafayette (Map 7; ☎ 01 42 82 36 40; metro Auber or Chaussée d'Antin), 40 Blvd Haussmann, 9e. This huge store, housed in two adjacent buildings linked by a pedestrian bridge, features over 75,000 brand-name items, and has a wide selection of fashion accessories. It is open Monday to Saturday from 9.30 am to 6.45 pm (9 pm on Thursday). There's a fine view from the rooftop restaurant.

Marks & Spencer (Map 2; ☎ 01 47 42 42 91; metro Auber or Chaussée d'Antin), 35 Blvd Haussmann, 9e. If you can't survive Paris without your Marks & Sparks knickers, cashmere jumper or faux crab meat on whiter-than-white bread, you're in luck. It's open Monday to Saturday from 9 am (9.30 am on Tuesday) to 8 pm (9 pm on Thursday).

Printemps (Map 2; ☎ 01 42 82 57 87 or 01 42 82 50 00; metro Havre Caumartin), 64 Blvd Haussmann, 9e. Printemps has one of the world's largest perfume and cosmetics departments, and is open Monday to Saturday from 9.35 am to 7 pm (to 10 pm on Thursday). You can take in the outstanding rooftop view from building No 2 for free (see the Things to See & Do chapter).

La Samaritaine (Map 7; ☎ 01 40 41 20 20; metro Pont Neuf), in four buildings between Pont Neuf and 142 Rue de Rivoli, 1er. A colour-coded brochure in English is available. Arrowhead-shaped building No 1 is devoted solely to toys, stuffed animals and games; building No 4 has a big supermarket in the basement. The main store is in building No 2. It is open Monday to Saturday from 9.30 am to 7 pm (10 pm on Thursday). You can take in the outstanding rooftop view from building No 2 for free (see the Things to See & Do chapter).

Tati (Map 4; ☎ 01 45 48 68 31; metro Saint Placide), 140 Rue de Rennes, 6e. Paris' great working-class department store.

CLOTHES & FASHION ACCESSORIES

New collections are released twice a year – for spring/summer and autumn/winter. There are city-wide end-of-season sales from the end of June until sometime in August and from late December to January/February.

Triangle d'Or

Some of the fanciest clothes in Paris are sold by the *haute couture* houses of the Triangle d'Or (1er and 8e), an ultra-exclusive neighbourhood whose corners are at Place de la Concorde, the Arc de Triomphe and Place de l'Alma. The clients, including (as you'd expect) elegantly dressed women accompanied by immaculately coiffed poodles, are at least as interesting as the garments.

Along the even-numbered side of Ave Montaigne, 1er (Map 2; metro Franklin D Roosevelt or Alma Marceau), you'll find Prada at No 10, Inès de la Fressange at No 14, Celine at No 38 and Chanel at No 42. On the odd side, you'll pass Valentino at No 17, Nina Ricci at No 39 and Thierry Mugler at No 49. Givenchy (metro Alma Marceau) is nearby at 3 Ave George V, 8e; Hermès is at No 42 of the same street.

Rue du Faubourg Saint Honoré & Rue Saint Honoré

Another grouping of couture houses and exclusive clothing and accessories stores is just north of Place de la Concorde along Rue du Faubourg Saint Honoré, 8e (Map 2; metro Madeleine or Concorde), and its eastern continuation, Rue Saint Honoré (metro Tuileries). Guy Laroche is at 28 Rue du Faubourg Saint Honoré, Christian Lacroix at No 73.

Place des Victoires

Trendy designer boutiques at Place des Victoires, 1er and 2e (Map 7; metro Bourse or Sentier), include Kenzo at No 3, Cacharel at No 5, Stephane Kélian at No 6 and Thierry Mugler at No 8. Rue Étienne Marcel, which runs to the east from the Place des Victoires, is the home of Comme des Garçons at No 40 (for men) and No 42 (for women), Yohji Yamamoto at Nos 45 and 47, Chevignon Trading Post at No 49 and Junko Shimada at No 54.

The postmodern designs of Jean-Paul Gaultier are on sale a few blocks west of Place des Victoires at 6 Rue Vivienne, 2e (metro Bourse). Towards Forum des Halles on Rue du Jour (1er), near Église Saint Eustache, the modern, casual styles of Agnès B (Map 7; metro Les Halles) are available in the shops at No 3 (for men) and No 6 (for women).

Marais

In recent years, Rue des Rosiers, 4e (Map 8; metro Saint Paul) has attracted a growing number of fashionable clothing shops. Tehen is at No 5bis, L'Éclaireur at No 3, while Lolita Lempicka is not far away at No 2. Under the exclusive arcades of Place des Vosges, Issey Miyake is tucked away at No 3-5. There are other interesting shops along Rue des Francs Bourgeois, leading out of the Place des Vosges.

For more everyday clothing, there are lots of shops along Rue de Rivoli, which gets less expensive as you move east from the 1er into the 4e.

6e Arrondissement

The largest grouping of chic clothing boutiques in the fashionable 6e – many of them run by younger and more daring designers – is north-west of Place Saint Sulpice (Map 6; metro Saint Sulpice or Saint Germain des Prés). Ultra-chic clothing, footwear and leather goods shops along Rue du Cherche Midi (Map 4) include Il Bisonte at No 17. Along Blvd Saint Germain, Sonia Rykiel has shops at No 175 (for women) and No 194 (for men). Rue de Rennes has Celine at No 58, Kenzo (Map 6) at No 60 and Benetton shops, including one for kids, at Nos 61 and 63. At Place Saint Sulpice, you can pop into Yves Saint Laurent Rive Gauche at No 12 and their Boutique Femme at No 6.

A bit to the south-west, just south of Le Bon Marché, Rue Saint Placide (Map 4; metro Sèvres Babylone) has lots of attractive shops selling clothes and shoes, mainly (but not exclusively) for women.

Reasonably priced clothing and shoe shops are legion along the southern half of Rue de Rennes (metro Rennes or Saint Placide).

Rue d'Alésia

The part of Rue d'Alésia, 14e (Map 1; metro Alésia), between No 54 (just east of Place Victor et Hélène Baschand) and No 149 is lined with places which sell relatively inexpensive brand-name clothes and accessories, including *dégriffés* (discounted designer seconds with their labels removed). Most of the shops are cramped and chaotic, with poorly displayed merchandise and disinterested staff – this is especially true west of Nos 110 and 125. More shops can be found on Ave du Général Leclerc, both north and south of Place Victor et Hélène Baschand.

JEWELLERY

Around Place Vendôme, 1er (Map 2; metro Tuileries), Cartier has shops at Nos 7 and 23, Philippe Patek is at No 10 and Van Cleef & Arpels is at No 22. There are more expensive jewellery shops along nearby Rue de Castiglione (1er) and Rue de la Paix (2e).

Less expensive jewellery is sold at various places around the city. Funky items, many of them imported, can be found in the Marais, including along Rue des Francs Bourgeois, 3e and 4e (Map 5). Costume jewellery is available at the flea markets.

Galerie d'Amon (Map 6; ☎ 01 43 26 96 60; metro Saint Sulpice), 28 Place Saint Sulpice, 6e. Specialises in modern glass and jewellery. It's open Monday to Saturday from 11 am to 6.45 pm.

Galerie Alain Carion (Map 8; ☎ 01 43 26 01 16; metro Pont Marie), 92 Rue Saint Louis en l'Île, 4e. This shop has a stunningly beautiful collection of museum-quality minerals, crystals, fossils and meteorites from 40 different countries, some of them in the form of earrings, brooches and pendants. Prices range from 5 to 80,000FF (for a 60kg meteorite). It is open Tuesday to Saturday from 10.30 am to 1 pm and 2 to 7.30 pm.

Méllerio Dits Meller (Map 2; ☎ 01 42 61 57 53; metro Opéra), 9 Rue de la Paix, 2e. Has jewellery ranging from the sublime (rings copied from medieval styles) to the ridiculous (traditional swords carried by the Immortals of the Académie Française).

Sic Amor (Map 8; ☎ 01 42 76 02 37; metro Pont Marie), 20 Rue du Pont Louis-Philippe, 4e. Sells contemporary jewellery done by local designers.

MUSIC

A vast selection of recorded music is available at the Virgin Megastores and FNAC outlets (see Booking Agencies in the Entertainment chapter). CDs are generally more expensive in France than in North America – count on paying 100 to 150FF. Virgin lets you listen to many of the CDs before buying them.

Second-hand CDs (50 to 70FF) can be purchased from two shops on Rue Linné (metro Jussieu) in the 5e: Jussieu Classique (Map 5; ☎ 01 47 07 60 45) at No 16 and Jussieu Music (Map 5; ☎ 01 43 31 14 18) at No 19. Both are open Monday to Saturday from 11 am to 7.30 pm and on Sunday from 2 to 7 pm.

CAMPING & SPORTS EQUIPMENT

Au Vieux Campeur, 5e (Map 6; ☎ 01 43 29 12 32; metro Maubert Mutualité), has 17 shops in the Latin Quarter just east of Rue Saint Jacques between Blvd Saint Germain and Rue des Écoles. Each specialises in equipment for a specific kind of outdoor activity: hiking, mountaineering, cycling, skiing, snowboarding, scuba diving etc. Camping equipment is sold at several shops, including those at 18 Rue du Sommerard, at 2 and 3 Rue de Latran and at 6 Rue Thénard. Opening hours vary wildly but most are open Monday to Saturday from 10.30 am to 7.30 pm (though sometimes from 2 to 7pm only on Monday, and 10.30 am to 10 pm on Wednesday).

ANTIQUES

For details on shopping for antiques at Le Louvre des Antiquaires (Map 7), see the Louvre Area section in the Things to See & Do chapter.

In the 6e, there are a number of shops selling antique maps and antiquarian books around Rue Bonaparte (Map 6; metro Saint Germain des Prés) and Rue Jacob.

For information on Paris' legendary flea markets, see the Flea Markets section later in this chapter.

FOOD & WINE

Caviar Kaspia (Map 2; ☎ 01 42 65 33 52; metro Madeleine), 17 Place de la Madeleine, 8e. This place sells caviar from the Iranian and Russian sections of the Caspian Sea for 450 to 1200FF per 100g, depending on the quality. It is open from 9 am to 1 am (closed on Sunday and some holidays). The *salle de dégustation* (tasting room; ☎ 01 42 65 33 32) is open from noon to 1 am.

Fauchon (Map 2; ☎ 01 47 62 60 11; metro Madeleine), 26-30 Place de la Madeleine, 8e. Six departments sell the most incredibly mouth-watering (and expensive) delicacies, such as foie gras for 1000 to 2000FF per kilogram. The fruits – the most perfect you've ever seen – include exotic items from South-East Asia (mangosteens, rambutans etc). Fauchon is open daily except on Sunday and holidays, and also has several eat-in options.

To place an order from abroad, contact Fauchon's *service export* (☎ 01 47 62 60 11; fax 01 47 42 83 75).

Hédiard (Map 2; metro Madeleine), 21 Place de la Madeleine, 8e. This famous luxury food shop consists of two adjacent sections selling prepared dishes, tea, coffee, jams, wine, pastries, fruit and vegetables etc. It is open from 9.30 am to 9 pm (closed on Sunday and certain holidays).

Jadis et Gourmande (Map 5; ☎ 01 43 26 17 75; metro Port Royal), 88 Blvd Port Royal, 5e. One of four branches of shops selling chocolate, chocolate and more chocolate in every conceivable shape and size.

La Maison du Miel (Map 2; ☎ 01 47 42 26 70; metro Madeleine), 24 Rue Vignon, a block north of Fauchon, 9e. This store stocks over 40 kinds of honey (17.50 to 42FF for 500g) made from the pollen of different types of flowers. It is open Monday to Saturday from 9 am to 7 pm.

Maison de la Truffe (Map 2; ☎ 01 45 65 53 22 or 01 42 66 10 01; metro Madeleine), 19-21 Place de la Madeleine, 8e. If you've always wanted to taste fine truffles – black French ones from late October to March, white Italian ones from mid-October to December (over 2000FF per 100g) – this may be your chance. This place also has a small sit-down area (open from noon to closing time) where you can sample dishes made with the prized fungus (300FF for the *menu*) or fresh foie gras (125 to 240FF); a cheaper three-course seasonal *menu* is 100FF. It is open Monday to Saturday from 9 am to 9 pm.

Mariage Frères (Map 8; ☎ 01 42 72 28 11; metro Hôtel de Ville), 30-32 Rue du Bourg Tibourg, 4e. Paris' premier tea shop, with 450 to 500 varieties from 32 countries; the most expensive is a variety of Japanese *thé vert* (green tea) which costs about 50FF for 100g. It is open daily from 10.30 am to 7.30 pm. The 19th-century *salon de thé* (tearoom), where in summer you can cool off with five kinds of tea-flavoured ice cream, is open from noon to 7 pm. A tea lunch here is 140FF. Mariage Frères (founded in 1854) has another shop at 13 Rue des Grands Augustins, 6e (Map 6; ☎ 01 40 51 82 50; metro Odéon). It keeps the same hours.

À l'Olivier (Map 8; ☎ 01 48 04 86 59; metro Saint Paul), 23 Rue de Rivoli, 4e. *The* place in Paris for oil – from olive to walnut – with a good selection of vinegars and olives too.

Produits des Monastères (Map 8; ☎ 01 48 04 39 05; metro Hôtel de Ville or Pont Marie), 10 Rue des Barres, 4e. Sells jams, biscuits, cakes, muesli (granola), honey, herbal teas etc made at Benedictine and Trappist monasteries. It is open Tuesday to Saturday from 10 am to 6.30 pm, with breaks for prayers from 12.15 to 2 pm; Sunday hours are 12.30 to 1 pm only.

GIFTS & SOUVENIRS
Paris has a huge number of speciality shops offering unique gift items.

Album (Map 6; ☎ 01 43 25 85 19; metro Maubert Mutualité), 8 Rue Dante, 5e. This shop specialises in *bandes dessinées* (comic books), which have an enormous following in France. Album has everything from *Tintin* to erotic comics and French editions of the latest Japanese *manga*.

Alexandre de Paris (Map 2; ☎ 01 42 61 41 34; metro Tuileries), 235 Rue Saint Honoré, 1er. More than 200 different hair accessories: clips, ties, slides, nets, combs.

Bains Plus (Map 8; ☎ 01 48 87 83 07; metro Hôtel de Ville), 51 Rue des Francs Bourgeois, 3e. This shop stocks everything the bathroom of the late 1990s could possibly want or need.

E Dehillerin (Map 7; ☎ 01 42 36 53 13; metro Les Halles), 18-20 Rue Coquillère, 1er. This shop (founded in 1820) carries the most incredible selection of professional-quality cookware – you're sure to find something even the most well equipped kitchen is lacking. It is open Monday to Saturday from 8 am to 6 pm (closed on Monday from 12.30 to 2 pm).

EOL' Modelisme (Map 6; ☎ 01 43 54 01 43; metro Maubert Mutualité), 55 Blvd St Germain, 5e, and two other locations at Nos 62 and 70 of the same street. This shop sells expensive toys for big boys and girls, including every sort of model imaginable – from radio-controlled aircraft to huge wooden yachts. The main shop, right by the metro entrance, has an amazing collection of tiny cars and is open weekdays from 8 am to 8 pm.

Galerie Inard (Map 6; ☎ 01 45 44 66 88; metro Saint Germain des Prés), 179 Blvd Saint Germain, 6e. This gallery sells stunning Aubusson tapestries from the postwar period and imaginative, contemporary glass (open Tuesday to Saturday from 10 am to 12.30 pm and 2 to 7 pm). You won't get much change from 350,000FF for a medium-sized tapestry by a well known artist.

Génération Condom (Map 5; ☎ 01 43 54 43 42; metro Cardinal Lemoine), 6 Rue Thouin, 5e. Every sort of condom (little ones, big ones, sophisticated ones, comic ones etc) and condom-related items you could ask for. Open Monday to Saturday from 11 am to 7 pm.

Il pour l'Homme (Map 7; ☎ 01 42 60 43 56; metro Tuileries), 209 Rue Saint Honoré, 1er. Housed in an old paint shop with Victorian era display counters and chests of drawers, 'It for the Man' has, well, everything a man could want or not need – from tie clips and cigar cutters to DIY tools and designer tweezers.

Madeleine Gély (Map 4; ☎ 01 42 22 63 35; metro Saint Germain des Prés), 218 Blvd Saint Germain, 7e. If you're in the market for a bespoke cane or umbrella, this shop (founded in 1834) will supply.

Mélodies Graphiques (Map 8; ☎ 01 42 74 57 68; metro Pont Marie), 10 Rue du Pont Louis-Philippe, 4e. This shop carries all sorts of items made from exquisite Florentine *papier à cuve* (paper hand-decorated with marbled designs). It is open from 11 am (2 pm on Sunday and Monday) to 7 pm. There are several other fine stationery shops along the same street.

Odimex Paris (Map 6; ☎ 01 46 33 98 96; metro Odéon), 17 Rue de l'Odéon, 6e. This shop sells teapots: little ones, big ones, sophisticated ones, comic ones and very expensive ones.

Paris Accordéon (Map 1; ☎ 01 43 22 13 48; metro Denfert Rochereau), 80 Rue Daguerre, 14e. If you're looking for a gift of revenge, head for this shop south of the Cimitière du Montparnasse: it sells accordions and accordions only in every size and shape possible. It's worth coming here just for a look.

Robin des Bois (Map 8; ☎ 01 48 04 09 36; metro Saint Paul), 15 Rue Fernand Duval, 4e. A shop strictly for environmentalists, this place sells everything and anything made from recycled things – from jewellery to stationery.

A Simon (Map 7; ☎ 01 42 33 71 65; metro Étienne Marcel), 36 Rue Étienne Marcel, 2e. Another supplier of kitchenware with more saucepans and mixing bowls than you thought imaginable.

La Vaisellerie (Map 2; ☎ 01 42 60 64 50; metro Tuileries), 332 Rue Saint Honoré, 1er. This shop between the Louvre and Place Vendôme specialises in innovative tableware – from decorative butter knives to silver-plated napkin rings.

FLEA MARKETS

Paris' *marchés aux puces* (flea markets), easily accessible by metro, can be great fun if you're in the mood to browse for unexpected treasures among the *brocante* (second-hand goods) and bric-a-brac on display. Some new goods are also available, and a bit of bargaining is expected.

Marché d'Aligre (Map 5; metro Ledru Rollin). Smaller and more central than the other three, this market in the 12e at Place d'Aligre – 700m south-east of Place de la Bastille – is one of the best places in Paris to rummage through cardboard boxes filled with old clothes and one-of-a-kind accessories worn decades ago by fashionable (and not-so-fashionable) Parisians. It is open Tuesday to Sunday until about 1 pm.

Marché aux Puces de Montreuil (Map 1; metro Porte de Montreuil). Established in the 19th century, this market is in the south-eastern corner of the 20e on Ave de la Porte de Montreuil, between the Porte de Montreuil metro stop and the ring road. It is known for having good quality second-hand clothes and designer seconds. The 500 stalls also sell engravings, jewellery, linen, crockery, old furniture and appliances. It is open on Saturday, Sunday and Monday from 7 am to about 7 pm.

Marché aux Puces de Saint Ouen (Map 1; metro Porte de Clignancourt). This vast flea market, founded in the late 19th century and said to be Europe's largest, is at the northern edge of the 18e arrondissement. The stalls – of which there are over 2000 – are grouped into nine *marchés* (market areas), each with its own specialities (antiques, cheap clothing etc). It is open to the public on Saturday, Sunday and Monday from 7.30 am to 7 pm (later during summer). If you arrive by metro, walk north along Ave de la Porte de Clignancourt and cross under the Blvd Périphérique to the inner suburb of Saint Ouen. The market is centred around Rue des Rosiers and nearby Ave Michelet, Rue Voltaire, Rue Paul Bert and Rue Jean-Henri Fabre. While shopping, watch out for pickpockets.

Marché aux Puces de la Porte de Vanves (Map 1; metro Porte de Vanves). This market in the far south-western corner of the 14e arrondissement is known for its fine selection of junk. Ave Georges Lafenestre looks like a giant car-boot sale, with lots of 'curios' which aren't quite old (or classy) enough to qualify as antiques. Ave Marc Sangnier is lined with stalls selling new clothes, shoes, handbags and household items. It is open Saturday and Sunday from 7 am to 6 ▶ pm (7.30 pm in summer).

Excursions

The region surrounding Paris is known as the Île de France (Island of France; 12,000 sq km) because of its position between four rivers: the Aube, the Marne, the Oise and the Seine. It was from this relatively small area that, beginning in around 1100, the kingdom of France began to expand.

Today, the region's excellent rail and road links with the French capital and its exceptional sights – the cathedrals of Saint Denis, Chartres, Beauvais and Senlis, the châteaux of Versailles, Fontainebleau and Chantilly and, of course, Disneyland Paris – make it especially popular with day-trippers. The many woodland areas around the city, which include the forests of Fontainebleau and Chantilly, offer unlimited outdoor activities.

Information
The Espace du Tourisme Île de France (☎ 01 42 44 10 50), which is in the lower level of the Carrousel du Louvre shopping mall next to I M Pei's inverted glass pyramid, is open daily, except Tuesday, from 10 am to 7 pm. Before you head out pick up a copy of Michelin's 1:200,000-scale *Île de France* map (No 237) or its 1:100,000-scale *Environs de Paris* map (No 106).

PARC ASTÉRIX
⬚ *postcode 60128*
A home-grown alternative to Disneyland Paris, the Parc Astérix (☎ 03 44 62 31 31; fax 03 44 62 34 56; Minitel 3615 PARC ASTERIX) is 36km north of Paris, just beyond Roissy Charles de Gaulle airport. Like Disneyland it's divided into a variety of areas – Astérix Village, the Roman City, Ancient Greece and so on – and there are lots of rides, including a particularly hair-raising roller coaster. The park is open daily from early April to mid-October from 10 am to 6 pm. Entry to the park and all the rides is 160FF for adults, 110FF for children under 12.

Getting There & Away
Take RER line train B3 as if you're going to the airport. From the Charles de Gaulle 1 train station, Courriers Île-de-France buses depart for the park every half-hour from 9.30 am to 1.30 pm. They return from the park every half-hour from 4.30 pm until 30 minutes after the park closes.

SAINT DENIS
• *pop 97,000* ⬚ *postcode 93200*
For 1200 years, Saint Denis was the burial place of the kings of France; today it is an industrial suburb just north of Paris' 18th arrondissement. The ornate royal tombs, adorned with some truly remarkable statuary, and the basilica that contains them – the world's first major Gothic structure – are an easy half-day excursion by metro. Saint Denis' more recent claim to fame is the Stade de France (see Spectator Sports in the Entertainment chapter) just south of the Canal de Saint Denis, the futuristic stadium where nine matches of the World Cup were held in June/July 1998.

Information
The tourist office (☎ 01 55 87 08 70; fax 01 48 20 24 11) at 1 Rue de la République is open Monday to Saturday from 9.30 am to 12.30 pm and 1.30 to 6 pm; from April to September, afternoon hours on those days are 2 to 6.30 pm. On Sunday, it's open from 12.30 to 4.30 pm (to 6.30 from mid-June to mid-September).

Basilique Saint Denis
The basilica of Saint Denis (☎ 01 48 09 83 54), part of which is currently undergoing renovation, served as the burial place for all but a handful of France's kings from Dagobert I (ruled 629-39) to Louis XVIII (ruled 1814-24). Their tombs and mausoleums constitute one of Europe's most important collections of funerary sculpture.

EXCURSIONS

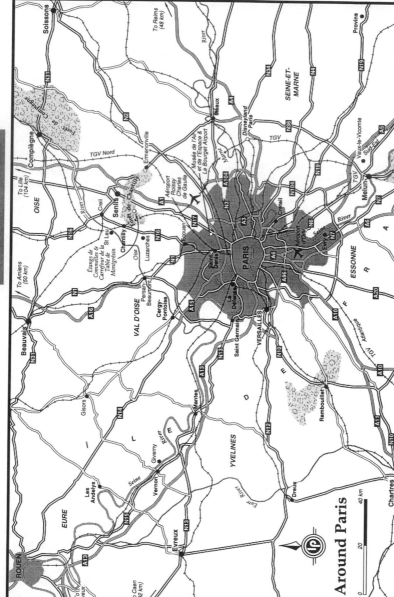

Around Paris

The present basilica, begun in around 1135 by the irrepressible Abbot Suger, changed the face of western architecture. It was the first major structure to be built in the Gothic style, and it served as a model for many other 12th-century French cathedrals, including the one at Chartres. Features illustrating the transition from Romanesque to Gothic can be seen in the choir and ambulatory, which are adorned with a number of 12th-century stained-glass windows. The narthex (the portico running along the western end of the basilica) also dates from this period. The nave and transept were built a century later.

During the Revolution, the basilica was devastated – the royal tombs were emptied of their human remains, which were then dumped in pits outside the church – but the mausoleums, put into storage in Paris, survived. They were brought back in 1816, and the royal bones were reburied in the crypt a year later. Restoration of the structure was begun under Napoleon, but most of the work was carried out by Viollet-le-Duc from 1858 until his death in 1879.

You can visit the nave for free, but to get to the interesting bits in the transept and chancel there's a charge of 32FF (21FF for those aged 12 to 25, students and seniors; free for those under 12). The basilica is open daily, except on five major holidays, from 10 am (noon on Sunday) to 5 pm (7 pm from April to September). The ticket counters close 30 minutes earlier.

Tombs

The tombs – all of which are now empty – are decorated with life-size figures of the deceased. Those built before the Renaissance are adorned with gisants (recumbent figures). Louis IX (Saint Louis; 1214-70) decided that all his royal predecessors should have elaborate tombs of their own, so though he had little idea what they looked like, he commissioned reclining figures for each of them. Those made after 1285 were carved from death masks and are thus fairly, well, life-like. The oldest tombs (dating from around 1230) are those of Clovis I (died 511) and his son Childebert I (died 558), brought to Saint Denis during the early 19th century. The finest Renaissance tombs include those of Louis XII (1462-1515) and Anne of Brittany (1476-1514); François I (1494-1547) and Claude de France (1499-1524), whose mausoleum is in the form of a Roman triumphal arch; and Henri II (1519-59) and Catherine de Médicis (1519-89).

Musée d'Art et d'Histoire

Saint Denis' excellent Museum of Art and History (☎ 01 42 43 05 10) at 22bis Rue Gabriel Péri occupies a restored Carmelite convent founded in 1625 and later presided over by Louise de France, the youngest daughter of Louis XV. Displays include reconstructions of the Carmelites' cells, an 18th-century apothecary and, in the archaeology section, fascinating items found during excavations around Saint Denis. There's also a section on modern art and, on the 2nd floor, politically charged posters, cartoons, lithographs and paintings from the 1871 **Paris Commune**. The museum is open daily, except Tuesday and holidays; opening hours are 10 am to 5.30 pm (2 to 6.30 pm on Sunday). Entry costs 20FF (10FF for students, teachers and seniors; free for those under 16).

Getting There & Away

Take metro line No 13 to the Saint Denis-Basilique terminus for the basilica and tourist office or Saint Denis-Porte de Paris for the Museum of Art and History, and the Stade de France. Make sure you don't get on one of the trains going to Asnières-Gennevilliers; the line splits at La Fourche station.

DISNEYLAND PARIS
✉ *postcode 77777*

It took US$4.4 billion and five years of work to turn the beet fields 32km east of Paris into Disneyland Paris, which opened as Euro-Disney in 1992 amid much fanfare and controversy. Although Disney stockholders were less than thrilled with the bottom line for the first few years, Disneyland Paris is now in the black, and the many visitors – mostly families with young children – seem to be having a great time exploring the gleaming facilities and carefully tended gardens. The park is now the most popular tourist destination in Europe, having received 12.6 million visitors in 1997.

Information

The park is bilingual. There are information booths scattered around the park, including one in City Hall. By phone, information is available (and hotel reservations can be made) in France on ☎ 01 60 30 60 30 (fax 01 60 30 30 99), in the UK on ☎ 0990 030 303, and in the USA on ☎ 407-WDISNEY. By Minitel, dial 3615 DISNEYLAND. The park's Web site is at www.disneyland paris.com.

Disneyland Paris Theme Park

The theme park, isolated from the outside world by a clever layout and grassy embankments, is divided into five *pays* (lands). **Main Street, USA**, just inside the main entrance, is a spotless avenue reminiscent of Norman Rockwell's idealised small-town America, circa 1900. The adjacent **Frontierland** is a re-creation of the 'rugged, untamed American West'.

Adventureland, intended to evoke the Arabian Nights and the wilds of Africa among other exotic lands, is home to that old favourite, Pirates of the Caribbean, as well as the Indiana Jones roller coaster. **Fantasyland** brings fairy-tale characters such as Sleeping Beauty, Snow White and Pinocchio to life. And in **Discoveryland**, the high-tech rides (including the Space Mountain and Big Thunder Mountain) and futuristic movies pay homage to Leonardo da Vinci, H G Wells, George Lucas and – for a bit of local colour – Jules Verne.

Opening Hours & Entry Fees

Disneyland Paris is open 365 days a year. From early September to late June, the hours are 10 am to 6 pm (8 pm on Saturday, some Sundays and perhaps during school holiday periods). In summer it's open daily from 9 am to 11 pm.

The one-day entry fee, which includes unlimited access to all rides and activities (except the shooting gallery and the video games arcade) costs 200FF (155FF for children aged three to 11) from late March to October. The rest of the year, except during the Christmas holidays, prices drop to 160/130FF. Multiple-day passes are also available.

Places to Stay

Camping *Davy Crockett Ranch* (☎ 01 60 45 69 00), a lovely forested area whose entrance is 7km south-west of the theme park, is open year round. It costs 400FF to park a caravan or pitch a tent at the 97 camping sites. There are also some 500 bungalows for four to six people costing 400 to 815FF a night, depending on the season. Each has two double beds (plus two bunk beds in the six-person models) and a kitchenette.

Hotels Each of the park's six enormous hotels has its own all-American theme, reflected in the architecture, landscaping, decor, restaurants and entertainment. All the rooms have two double beds (or, in the case of the Hôtel Cheyenne, one double bed and two bunk beds) and can sleep four people; certain rooms can be linked up to form suites. Rooms specially equipped for disabled guests are available.

Rates depend on the dates of stay. Prices are highest during July and August and around Christmas; on Friday and Saturday nights and during holiday periods from April to October; and on Saturday nights from mid-February to March. The least expensive rates are available on most weeknights (ie Sunday to Thursday or, sometimes, Friday) from January to mid-February, from mid-May to June, for most of September, and from November to mid-December.

The cheapest hotel is the 1000-room, New Mexico-style *Hôtel Santa Fe* (☎ 01 60

45 78 00), which charges 435 to 780FF for a room. The 14 buildings of the 1000-room *Hôtel Cheyenne* (☎ 01 60 45 62 00) – each with its own hokey name – are arranged to resemble a Wild West frontier town, Hollywood-style. Rooms cost 535 to 925FF.

Places to Eat
There are about 10 American-style restaurants in Disney Village, including *Planet Hollywood* (☎ 01 60 43 78 27), open daily from 11 or 11.30 am to about midnight. Lots of eateries, takeaway food booths etc are found all over the theme park. Most offer reasonable value.

Getting There & Away
Marne-la-Vallée-Chessy (Disneyland's RER station) is served by RER line A4, which runs every 15 minutes or so. Tickets, available at metro stations, cost 39FF (35FF from the Nation metro stop; 35 to 40 minutes). Trains that go all the way to Marne-la-Vallée-Chessy have four-letter codes beginning with the letter 'Q'. The last train back to Paris leaves Disneyland a bit after midnight. A taxi to/from the centre of Paris costs about 350FF (450FF from 7 pm to 8 am and on Sunday and holidays).

VERSAILLES
• *pop 95,000* ⊠ *postcode 78000*
Paris' prosperous, leafy and very bourgeois suburb of Versailles is the site of the grandest and most famous château in France. It served as the kingdom's political capital and the seat of the royal court for almost the entire period between 1682 and 1789 – the year Revolutionary mobs massacred the palace guard and dragged Louis XVI and Marie-Antoinette to Paris.

Because so many people consider Versailles a must-see destination, the château attracts more than three million visitors a year. The best way to avoid the queues is to arrive first thing in the morning; if you're interested in just the Grands Appartements, you can also come around 3.30 or 4 pm. Versailles is 23km south-west of Paris.

Information
The tourist office (☎ 01 39 50 36 22; fax 01 39 50 68 07) is at 7 Rue des Réservoirs (a bit beyond the northern end of the château). From mid-September to April, it is open Monday to Saturday from 9 am to 12.30 pm and 1.30 to 6 pm; the rest of the year, daily hours are 9 am to 7 pm. English-language brochures on the town are available.

The tourist office has an annexe (☎ 01 39 53 31 63) in the Îlot de Manèges shopping complex at 10 Ave du Général de Gaulle almost diagonally opposite the Versailles-Rive Gauche train station. It is open Tuesday to Saturday from 10 am to 6 pm.

Château de Versailles
This enormous château (☎ 01 30 84 74 00 or, for a recording, ☎ 01 30 84 76 76; Minitel 3615 VERSAILLES) was built in the mid-1600s during the reign of Louis XIV – the Roi Soleil (Sun King) – to project both at home and abroad the absolute power of the French monarchy, then at the height of its glory. Its scale and décor also reflect Louis XIV's taste for profligate luxury and his near boundless appetite for self-glorification. Some 30,000 workers and soldiers toiled on the structure, whose construction bills wrought havoc on the kingdom's finances.

The château complex consists of four main parts: the palace building, a 580m-long structure with innumerable wings, grand halls and sumptuous bedchambers (only parts are open to the public); the vast gardens west of the palace; and two outbuildings, the Grand Trianon and, a few hundred metres to the north-east, the Petit Trianon. The château has undergone relatively few alterations since its construction, though almost all the interior furnishings disappeared during the Revolution and many of the rooms were rebuilt by Louis-Philippe (ruled 1830-48).

Architecture About two decades into his 72-year reign (1643-1715), Louis XIV decided to enlarge the hunting lodge his father had built at Versailles and turn it into

EXCURSIONS

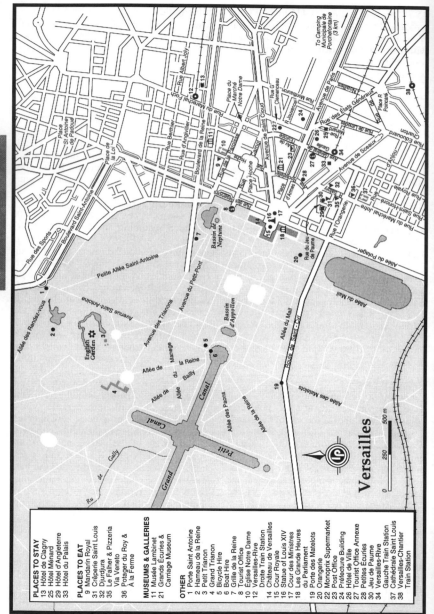

PLACES TO STAY
13 Hôtel de Clagny
25 Hôtel Ménard
29 Hôtel d'Angleterre
33 Hôtel du Palais

PLACES TO EAT
9   Mandarin Royal
31 Crêperie Saint Louis
32 Djurdjura
35 Le Falher & Pizzeria
     Via Veneto
36 Potager du Roy &
     À la Ferme

MUSEUMS & GALLERIES
11 Musée Lambinet
21 Grands Écuries &
     Carriage Museum

OTHER
1   Porte Saint Antoine
2   Hameau de la Reine
3   Petit Trianon
4   Grand Trianon
5   Bicycle Hire
6   Boat Hire
7   Grille de la Reine
8   Tourist Office
10 Versailles-Rive
     Droite Train Station
12 Église Notre Dame
14 Château de Versailles
15 Cour Royale
16 Statue de Louis XIV
17 Cour des Ministres
18 Les Grande Heures
     du Parliament
19 Porte des Matelots
20 Orangerie
23 Monoprix Supermarket
24 Post Office
26 Préfecture Building
27 Hôtel de Ville
28 Tourist Office Annexe
30 Petites Écuries
32 Jeu de Paume
34 Versailles-Rive
     Gauche Train Station
37 Cathédrale Saint Louis
38 Versailles-Chantier
     Train Station

Versailles

0   250   500 m

a palace big enough for the entire court, which numbered some 6000 people. To accomplish this task he hired four supremely talented people: the architect Louis Le Vau; his successor Jules Hardouin-Mansart, who took over in the mid-1670s; the painter and interior designer Charles Le Brun; and the landscape artist André Le Nôtre, whose workers flattened hills, drained marshes and relocated forests as they laid out the seemingly endless gardens, ponds and fountains.

Le Brun and his hundreds of artisans decorated every moulding, cornice, ceiling and door of the interior with the most luxurious and ostentatious of appointments: frescoes, marble, gilt woodcarvings and the like. Many of the themes and symbols used by Le Brun are drawn from Greek and Roman mythology. The **Grand Appartement du Roi** (King's Suite), for example, includes rooms dedicated to Hercules, Venus, Diana, Mars and Mercury. The ornateness reaches its peak in the **Galerie des Glaces** (Hall of Mirrors), a 75m-long ballroom with 17 huge mirrors on one side and, on the other, an equal number of windows looking out on the gardens and the setting sun. The mirrors were designed to reflect the ceiling frescoes (which relate the history of Louis XIV's early life) and allowed the splendidly arrayed guests to watch themselves – and each other – while dancing.

Gardens & Fountains The section of the vast gardens nearest the palace, laid out between 1661 and 1700 in the formal French style, is famed for its geometrically aligned terraces, flower beds, tree-lined paths, ponds and fountains. The many statues of marble, bronze and lead were made by the finest sculptors of the period. The **English-style garden** just north of the Petit Trianon is more pastoral and has meandering paths.

The **Grand Canal**, 1.6km long and 62m wide, is oriented to reflect the setting sun. It is intersected by the 1km **Petit Canal**, creating a cross-shaped body of water with a perimeter of over 5.5km. Louis XIV used to hold boating parties here. From May to mid-October, you too can paddle around the

Grand Canal. Four-person rowing boats (☎ 01 39 54 22 00) cost 70FF an hour. The dock is at the canal's eastern end. The **Orangerie**, built under the Parterre du Midi (flower bed) on the south-west side of the palace, is used for the wintertime storage of exotic plants.

The gardens' largest fountains are the 17th-century **Bassin de Neptune** (Neptune Fountain), 300m north of the main palace building, whose straight side abuts a small, round pond graced by a winged dragon, and, at the eastern end of the Grand Canal, the **Bassin d'Apollon**, in whose centre Apollo's chariot, pulled by rearing horses, emerges from the water.

Sunday from early May to early October, the fountains are turned on at 11.15 am for the 20-minute **Grande Perspective** and from 3.30 pm to 5.30 pm for the longer and more elaborate **Grandes Eaux**. On the days when the fountain shows take place, there is a 25FF fee to get into the gardens.

The Trianons In the middle of the park, about 1.6km north-west of the main building, are Versailles' two smaller palaces, each surrounded by neatly tended flower beds. The pink-colonnaded **Grand Trianon** was built in 1687 for Louis XIV and his family, who used it as a place of escape from the pressures and rigid etiquette of court life. Napoleon I had it redone in the Empire style. The much smaller **Petit Trianon**, built in the 1760s, was redecorated in 1867 by the Empress Eugénie, who added Louis XVI-style furnishings similar to the uninspiring pieces that now fill its 1st floor rooms.

A bit farther north is the **Hameau de la Reine** (Queen's Hamlet), a mock rural village of thatch-roofed cottages constructed from 1775 to 1784 for the amusement of Marie-Antoinette. You can wander around its gardens for no charge.

Opening Hours & Entry Fees The **Grands Appartements** (State Apartments), the main section of the palace that can be visited without a guided tour, include the Galerie des Glaces and the Appartement de la Reine (Queen's Suite). Except on Monday and five public holidays, they are open from 9 am to 5.30 pm (6.30 pm from May to September); the ticket windows close 30 minutes earlier. Entry costs 45FF (35FF for people aged 18 to 25 and, after 3.30 pm daily and on Sunday, for everyone; free for under 18s). Tickets are on sale at Entrée A (also known as Porte A), which, as you approach the palace, is off to the right from the equestrian statue of Louis XIV. The queues are worst on Tuesday, when many Paris museums are closed, and on Sunday.

A new exhibit called **Les Grandes Heures du Parlement** (Famous Events of Parliament; ☎ 01 39 67 07 73), which focuses on the history of France's Assemblée Nationale (National Assembly) is in the château's south wing. It keeps the same hours as the château though the ticket office closes one hour earlier. Entry costs 20FF (15FF for those aged 18 to 25; free for under 18s).

From October to April, the Grand Trianon (25FF; 15FF reduced price; free for under 18s) is open Tuesday to Sunday, 10 am to 12.30 pm and 2 to 5.30 pm (no midday closure on weekends). The rest of the year, hours are 10 am to 6.30 pm. The last entry is 30 minutes before closing time. The Petit Trianon, open the same days and hours, costs 15FF (10FF reduced price; free for under 18s). A combined ticket for both will set you back 30FF (20FF reduced price).

The gardens are open seven days a week (unless it's snowing) from 7 am to nightfall (between 5.30 and 9.30 pm, depending on the season). Entry is free *except* on Sunday from early May to early October, when the fountains are in operation and entry is 25FF.

If you have a Carte Musées et Monuments, you don't have to wait in the queue – go straight to Entrée A2.

Guided Tours One of the best ways to get a sense of the Grands Appartements is to rent the state-of-the-art recorded tour available for 30FF at Entrée A, right behind the ticket booths. The excellent commentary lasts 80 minutes.

The **Appartement de Louis XIV** and the **Appartements du Dauphin et de la Dauphine** can be toured with a 55-minute audioguide, available at Entrée C, for 25FF (17FF for children aged seven to 17). You can begin your visit between 9 am and 3.30 pm (4.15 pm from May to September). This is also a good way to avoid the queues at Entrée A.

Several different guided tours are available in English from 9 am to 3.30 pm (4 pm from May to September). They last one, 1½ and two hours and cost 25FF *per hour* (17FF per hour for people aged seven to 17). Tickets are sold at Entrée D; tours begin across the courtyard at Entrée F.

All the tours require that you also purchase a ticket to the Grands Appartements. If you buy it at Entrée C or Entrée D when paying for your tour, you can later avoid the Grands Appartements queue at Entrée A by going straight to Entrée A2.

The Town of Versailles

Like the château, the attractive town of Versailles, crisscrossed by wide boulevards, is a creation of Louis XIV. However, most of today's buildings date from the 18th and 19th centuries.

Grandes & Petites Écuries Ave de Paris, Ave de Saint Cloud and Ave de Sceaux, the three wide thoroughfares that fan out eastward from Place d'Armes, are separated by two large, late 17th-century stables: the Grandes Écuries (presently occupied by the army) and the Petites Écuries, which contains an architectural unit and restoration workshops. The **Carriage Museum** in the Grandes Écuries can be visited daily May to September from 12.30 to 6.30 pm. In April and October the hours on Saturday and Sunday only are 9 am to 12.30 pm and 2 to 5.30 pm. Entry costs 12FF (free for under 18s).

Jeu de Paume The Jeu de Paume, built around 1686, is 350m south-east of the château on Rue du Jeu de Paume. It is open to the public from May to September, when

---

The Tennis Court Oath

In May 1789, in an effort to deal with the huge national debt and to moderate dissent by reforming the tax system, Louis XVI convened at Versailles the États-Généraux (States General), a body made up of over a thousand deputies representing the three estates: the Nobility and the Clergy (most of whom were exempt from paying taxes) and the Third Estate, representing the middle classes. When the Third Estate, whose members constituted a majority of the delegates, was denied entry to the usual meeting place of the États-Généraux, it met separately in the Salle de Jeu de Paume (Royal Tennis Court), where its members constituted themselves as the National Assembly on 17 June. Three days later they took the famous Tennis Court Oath, swearing not to dissolve the assembly until Louis XVI had accepted a new constitution. This act of defiance sparked protests of support and, a short while later, open rebellion. Less than a month after the Tennis Court Oath, a Parisian mob would storm the Bastille prison.

---

it can be visited Wednesday and Saturday, 2 to 5 pm. Contact the château's Bureau d'Action Culturelle (☎ 01 30 84 76 18) for details.

Cathédrale Saint Louis This neoclassical (and slightly baroque) cathedral, a harmonious if austere work by Hardouin-Mansart at 4 Place Saint Louis, was built between 1743 (when Louis XV himself laid the first stone) and 1754. It is known for its 3131-pipe Cliquot organ and is decorated with a number of interesting paintings and stained-glass panels. Opening hours are 9 am to noon and 2 to 6 or 7 pm.

Musée Lambinet Housed in a lovely 18th-century residence, the Musée Lambinet (☎ 01 39 50 30 32) at 54 Blvd de la Reine displays 18th-century furnishings (ceram-

ics, sculpture, paintings, furniture) and objects connected with the history of Versailles (including the Revolutionary period). The museum is open Tuesday and Friday from 2 to 5 pm, Wednesday and Thursday from 1 to 6 pm and on Saturday and Sunday from 2 to 6 pm. Entry costs 25FF (15FF reduced tariffs).

Église Notre Dame Built by Hardouin-Mansart in 1684, this church at 35 Rue de la Paroisse served as the parish church of the king and his courtiers. It has a fine sculpted pulpit. It is generally open from 8.30 am till noon and 2 to 7.30 pm.

Places to Stay

Camping Municipale de Porchefontaine (☎ 01 39 51 23 61), about 3km south-east of the centre at 31 Rue Berthelot, is 500m from the Versailles-Porchefontaine train station (on RER line C5) and in the Parc Forestier des Nouettes. It charges 50FF per site and 30FF per adult.

The friendly, 17-room *Hôtel Ménard* (☎ 01 39 50 47 99) at 8 Rue Ménard has simple, spotless singles with washbasin from 100 to 130FF, doubles for 150 to 170FF. Singles/doubles with shower are 170/190FF.

Across the street from the Versailles-Rive Gauche station is the *Hôtel du Palais* (☎ 01 39 50 39 29; fax 01 39 50 80 41) at 6 Place Lyautay (2nd floor). This well kept hotel has doubles with washbasin for 170FF, with shower for 220 to 250FF.

Around the corner from the Jeu de Paume, the two-star, 18-room *Hôtel d'An-gleterre* (☎ 01 39 51 43 50; fax 01 39 51 45 63) at 2bis Rue de Fontenay has attractive singles/doubles from 150/250FF (300FF with bath).

The *Hôtel de Clagny* (☎ 01 39 50 18 09; fax 01 39 50 85 17) is at 6 Impasse de Clagny, a block from 91 Blvd de la Reine and behind the Versailles-Rive Droite station. Singles with washbasin and toilet at this 21-room, two-star place are 200FF. Doubles with shower and toilet are 280FF (300FF with bath and toilet).

EXCURSIONS

Places to Eat

Restaurants The quiet, elegant *Restaurant Le Falher* (☎ 01 39 50 57 43) at 22 Rue Satory has French gastronomic *menus* for 115FF (at lunch) and 128, 160 (with wine) and 180FF (closed on Saturday at midday and Sunday).

Traditional French *menus* at the refined *Potager du Roy* (☎ 01 39 50 35 34) at 1 Rue du Maréchal Joffre go for 130FF (Tuesday to Saturday at lunch only) and 175FF (closed Sunday night and Monday). Two doors away at No 3 is *À la Ferme* (☎ 01 39 53 10 81), an establishment specialising in fish and grilled meats. Two-course *formules* and *menus* cost 87 to 117FF (closed all day Monday and Tuesday at lunchtime.

The *Crêperie Saint Louis* (☎ 01 39 53 40 12) is at 33 Rue du Vieux Versailles, around the corner from 22bis Rue Satory. The Breton specialities at this cosy place include sweet and savoury crêpes (18 to 45FF), and there are *menus* for 55, 65 and 85FF. It is open daily.

The couscous at the friendly *Djurdjura* (☎ 01 39 50 47 49) at 5 Rue Satory is prepared in the manner of the Kabyles of eastern Algeria and costs from 49FF; the excellent mixed one is 69FF while couscous royal is 85FF. It's open daily till midnight.

There are a dozen other restaurants in the immediate vicinity, including *Pizzeria Via Veneto* (☎ 01 39 51 03 89) at 20 Rue Satory which has pizzas (39 to 50FF) and pasta dishes (43 to 57FF) and is open daily.

The *Mandarin Royal* (☎ 01 39 50 48 03), a Chinese restaurant with some Thai and Vietnamese dishes at 5 Rue de Sainte Geneviève just west of the Église Notre Dame, has a lunch *menu* for 49FF and dinner *menus* for 68, 88 and 118FF. It's open for lunch and dinner daily, except Sunday night and midday Monday.

Self-Catering There's an outdoor food market at Place du Marché Notre Dame open Tuesday, Friday and Sunday from 8 am to 1 pm; the food stalls in the covered market are open every morning. There also are a lot of nearby food shops, open daily except Sunday afternoon and Monday.

The *Monoprix* supermarket at 9 Rue Georges Clemenceau, north of the Ave de Paris, is open Monday to Saturday from 8.30 am to 9 pm.

Getting There & Around

Each of Versailles' three train stations is served by RER and/or SNCF trains coming from a different set of Paris stations.

RER line C5 takes you from Paris' Left Bank RER stations to Versailles-Rive Gauche station (14FF), which is only 700m from the château. From Paris, catch any train whose four-letter code begins with the letter 'V'. There are 60 trains a day (35 on Sunday); the last train back to Paris leaves just after midnight. Tickets are not sold at regular metro ticket windows.

RER line C7 links Paris' Left Bank with Versailles-Chantiers station (14FF), a 1.3km walk from the château. From the city, take any train whose code begins with 'S'. Versailles-Chantiers is also served by 36 SNCF trains a day (20 on Sunday) from Gare Montparnasse (14FF; 14 minutes); all trains on this line continue on to Chartres.

From Paris' Gare Saint Lazare and La Défense, the SNCF has about 70 trains a day (19FF including a metro journey) to Versailles-Rive Droite, which is 1200m from the château. The last train to Paris leaves a bit past midnight.

From late February to December, Astel (☎ 01 39 66 97 66) hires out bicycles both at Petite Venise (the eastern end of the Grand Canal) and next to Grille de la Reine (entrance to the château grounds). Hours are 10 am to at least 5 pm (later as the days get longer). Fees are a steep 20/30FF per half-hour/hour at Petite Venise and 15/25FF at Grille de la Reine.

FONTAINEBLEAU

• *pop 18,000* ✉ *postcode 77300*

The town of Fontainebleau, 65km southeast of Paris, is renowned for its elegant Renaissance château – one of France's largest royal residences – whose splendid

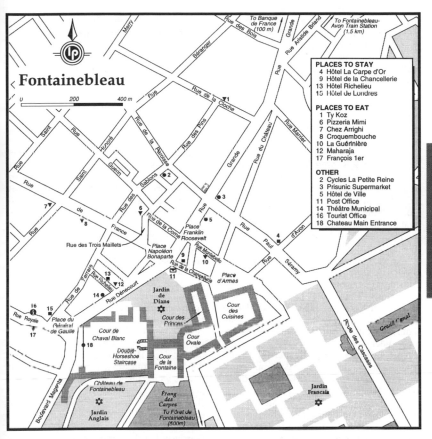

Fontainebleau

PLACES TO STAY
4 Hôtel La Carpe d'Or
9 Hôtel de la Chancellerie
13 Hôtel Richelieu
15 Hôtel de Londres

PLACES TO EAT
1 Ty Koz
6 Pizzeria Mimi
7 Chez Arrighi
8 Croquembouche
10 La Guérinière
12 Maharaja
17 François 1er

OTHER
2 Cycles La Petite Reine
3 Prisunic Supermarket
5 Hôtel de Ville
11 Post Office
14 Théâtre Municipal
16 Tourist Office
18 Chateau Main Entrance

EXCURSIONS

furnishings make it particularly worth a visit. It's much less crowded and pressured than Versailles. The town itself has a number of fine restaurants and night spots and is surrounded by the beautiful Forêt de Fontainebleau, a favourite hunting ground of a long line of French kings.

Information

The tourist office (☎ 01 60 74 99 99; fax 01 60 74 80 22; Minitel 3615 FONTAINEBLEAU), 4 Rue Royale, is open May to September from Monday to Saturday from 9.30 am to

6.30 and from 10 am to 6 pm on Sunday. During the rest of the year, it is open weekdays from 9.30 am to 5.30 pm, on Saturday from 10 am to 6 pm and on Sunday from 10 am to 12.30 pm and 3 to 5.30 pm. The very helpful staff here can provide information on *chambres d'hôte* and *gîtes ruraux*. They also rent self-paced audioguide tours of the city, in English, lasting 1½ hours (30FF).

Château de Fontainebleau

The enormous, 1900-room Château de Fontainebleau (☎ 01 60 71 50 70), whose list of former tenants reads like a Who's Who of French royal history, is one of the most beautifully ornamented and furnished châteaux in France. Every centimetre of the wall and ceiling space is richly adorned with wood panelling, gilded carvings, frescoes, tapestries and paintings. The parquet floors are of the finest woods, the fireplaces ornamented with exceptional carvings, and many of the pieces of furniture are Renaissance originals.

Courtyards & Rooms As successive monarchs added their own wings to the château, five irregularly shaped courtyards were created. The oldest and most interesting is the **Cour Ovale** (Oval Courtyard), no longer oval due to Henri IV's construction work. It incorporates the sole remnant of the medieval castle, the keep.

The largest is the **Cour du Cheval Blanc** (Courtyard of the White Horse), also known as the Cour des Adieux (Farewell Courtyard). The second name dates from 1814 when Napoleon, about to be exiled to Elba, bid farewell to his guards from the famous **double-horseshoe staircase**, built under Louis XIII in 1634.

The **Grands Appartements** (State Apartments) include a number of outstanding rooms. The spectacular **Chapelle de la Trinité** (Trinity Chapel), whose ornamentation dates from the first half of the 17th century, is where Louis XV married Marie Leczinska in 1725 and where the future Napoleon III was christened in 1810. **Galerie François 1er**, a gem of Renaissance architecture, was decorated from 1533 to 1540 by Il Rosso, a Florentine follower of Michelangelo. In the wood panelling, François I's monogram, a letter 'F', appears repeatedly along with his emblem, a dragon-like salamander.

The **Salle de Bal**, a ballroom 30m long that was also used for receptions and banquets dating from the mid-16th century, is renowned for its mythological frescoes, marquetry floor and Italian-inspired coffered ceiling. The large windows afford views of the Cour Ovale and the gardens.

The gilded bed in the 17th and 18th-century **Chambre de l'Impératrice** was never used by Marie-Antoinette, for whom it was built in 1787. The gilding in the **Salle du Trône**, the royal bedroom before the Napoleonic period, is in shades of gold, green and yellow.

The **Petits Appartements** were the private apartments of the emperor and empress. They do not have fixed opening hours but are always open on Monday from 9 am to 5 pm (call ☎ 01 60 71 50 70 for other times). Entry is 16FF (12FF reduced tariff).

Museums The **Musée Napoléon 1er** within the château has a collection of personal effects (uniforms, hats, coats, ornamented swords) and knick-knacks that belonged to Napoleon and his relatives. Not surprisingly, a lot of the items are gilded, enamelled or bejewelled.

The four rooms of the **Musée Chinois** (Chinese Museum), which charges a separate admission, are filled with beautiful ceramics and other objects brought to France from East Asia during the 19th century. Some of the items, from the personal collection of Empress Eugénie (wife of Napoleon III), were gifts of a delegation that came from Siam (Thailand) in 1861. Others were stolen by a Franco-British expeditionary force sent to China in 1860. Both museums keep the same hours as the château.

Gardens On the north side of the château, the **Jardin de Diane**, a formal garden created by Catherine de Médicis, is home to a flock of noisy *paons* (peacocks). The marble fountain in the middle of the garden, decorated with a statue of Diana, goddess of the hunt, and four urinating dogs, dates from 1603.

Le Nôtre's formal, 17th-century Jardin Français (French Garden), also known as the Grand Parterre, is to the east of the Cour de la Fontaine (Fountain Courtyard) and the Étang des Carpes (Carp Pond). The **Grand Canal** further east was excavated in 1609 and predates the canals at Versailles by over half a century. The informal Jardin Anglais

(English Garden), laid out in 1812, is west of the Carp Pond. The Forêt de Fontainebleau, crisscrossed by paths, begins 500m south of the château.

Opening Hours & Entry Fees The interior of the château (enter from the Cour du Cheval Blanc) is open daily (except Tuesday) from 9.30 am to 12.30 pm and 2 to 5 pm (no midday closure from June to September and until 6 pm in July and August). The last visitors are admitted an hour before closing time. Tickets for the Grands Appartements and the Musée Napoléonien, valid for the day, cost 35FF (23FF for people aged 18 to 25 and, on Sunday, for everyone; free for under 18s). The Musée Chinois is an extra 16FF (12FF reduced price). Conducted tours in English of the Grands Appartements depart several times a day from the staircase near the ticket windows.

The gardens (free entry) are open daily from early morning until sundown. In winter, parts of the garden may be closed if personnel are in short supply.

Forêt de Fontainebleau

This 250-sq-km forest, which surrounds the town of Fontainebleau, is one of the loveliest wooded tracts in the Paris region, boasting oaks, beeches, birches and planted pines. The many trails – including parts of the **GR1** and **GR11** – are great for jogging, hiking, cycling and horse riding. The area is covered by IGN's 1:25,000-scale map No 2417OT, entitled *Forêt de Fontainebleau* (57FF). Michelin's *Île de France* (63FF) green guide has several detailed hiking itineraries. The tourist office sells a small topoguide, *Guide des Sentiers de Promenades dans le Massif Forestier de Fontainebleau* (50FF), whose maps and text (in French) cover almost 20 walks in the forest.

Places to Stay

The two-star, 25-room Hôtel de la Chancellerie (☎ 01 64 22 21 70; fax 01 64 22 64 43) at 1 Rue de la Chancellerie has old-fashioned singles/doubles/triples with shower and toilet for 180/250/320FF from November to March and 240/300/380FF the rest of the year. You might also try the 14-room Hôtel La Carpe d'Or (☎ 01 64 22 28 64) at 21bis Rue Paul Séramy (enter from 7 Rue d'Avon), where singles/doubles/triples with washbasin, bidet and toilet cost 162/194/306FF and 177/224/358FF with shower and toilet.

The 18-room *Hôtel Richelieu* (☎ 01 64 22 26 46; fax 01 64 23 40 17), just north of the château at 4 Rue Richelieu, has singles with shower from 240 to 270FF, depending on the season, and doubles from 290 to 310FF. If you want to splurge you should choose the 12-room *Hôtel de Londres* (☎ 01 64 22 20 21; fax 01 60 72 39 12) opposite the château's main entrance on Place du Général de Gaulle. Doubles with everything go for 350 to 450FF in winter and 550 to 650FF in summer.

Places to Eat

Restaurants Two excellent choices on Rue de France are *Chez Arrighi* (☎ 01 64 22 29 43) at No 53, whose *menus* cost 95, 125 and 175FF (closed Monday) and *Croquembouche* (☎ 01 64 22 01 57) at No 43, where the *menus* go for 88FF (at lunch), 125FF (till 10 pm) and 195FF. The latter is closed all day Wednesday and at lunch on Thursday. The *François 1er* (☎ 01 64 22 24 68) opposite the tourist office at 3 Rue Royale has excellent specialities from Normandy and Brittany (especially seafood) and *menus* at 98, 125 and 150FF. Expect to pay about 230FF per person if ordering à la carte.

La Guérinière (☎ 01 60 72 04 05) at 10-12 Rue Montebello is an excellent choice for quality French cuisine at affordable prices. The lunch *formule* is 75FF, four-course dinner *menus* are 108 and 160FF and there's a simple buffet of salads and cold meats available any time for 55FF. It is open for lunch and dinner, except all day Tuesday and Wednesday evening.

The *Maharaja* (☎ 01 64 22 14 64), an Indian restaurant at 15 Rue Dénecourt, has curries (46 to 69FF) and tandoori dishes (29 to 46FF) as well as starters like pakoras and samosas for 20 to 24FF. There are lunch *menus* for 59 and 89FF and one at dinner for 99FF. It closes on Sunday.

For Breton crêpes and galettes, head for *Ty Koz* (☎ 01 64 22 00 55) down the little alleyway from 18 Rue de la Cloche. It is open daily to 10 pm.

Pizzeria Mimi (☎ 01 64 22 70 77) at 17 Rue des Trois Maillets has pizzas (43 to 56FF), pastas (42 to 58FF) and more elaborate Italian main courses available daily at lunch and dinner.

Self-Catering The *Prisunic* at 58 Rue Grande is open Monday to Saturday from 8.45 am to 7.45 pm; the food section is on the 1st floor.

Getting There & Around
Between 22 and 25 daily commuter trains link Paris' Gare de Lyon with Fontainebleau-Avon (47FF; 40 to 60 minutes); in off-peak periods, there's about one train an hour. The last train back to Paris leaves Fontainebleau a bit after 9.45 pm (just after 10.30 pm on Sunday and holidays).

Cycles La Petite Reine (☎ 01 60 74 57 57) at 32 Rue des Sablons rents mountain bikes year round for 60/80FF per half/full day (80/100FF on weekends). A 2000FF deposit is required. The shop is open Monday to Saturday from 9 am to 7.30 pm and to 6 pm on Sunday. During the warm months, bikes can be hired at the train station for 80/120 for a half/whole day. Ring ☎ 01 64 22 36 14 for information.

CHANTILLY
• *pop 11,3000*   ✉ *postcode 60500*

The elegant town of Chantilly, 48km north of Paris, is best known for its heavily restored but imposing château, surrounded by gardens, lakes and a vast forest. The château is slightly over 2km east of the train station. The most direct route is to walk through the Forêt de Chantilly along Route de l'Aigle, but you'll get a better sense of the town by taking Ave du Maréchal Joffre and Rue de Paris to Rue du Connétable, Chantilly's thoroughfare.

Information
The tourist office (☎ 03 44 57 08 58; fax 03 44 57 74 64) at 60 Ave du Maréchal Joffre is open daily April to September from 9 am to 7 pm. During the rest of the year the Monday to Saturday hours are 9.15 am to 12.45 pm and 2.15 to 6.15 pm.

Château de Chantilly
Chantilly's château (☎ 03 44 62 62 62), left in a shambles after the Revolution, is of interest mainly because of its gardens and a number of superb paintings. It consists of two attached buildings entered, through the same vestibule. The **Petit Château** was built around 1560 for Anne de Montmorency (1492-1567), who served six French kings as *connétable* (high constable), diplomat and warrior and died in battle against the Protestants. The attached Renaissance-style **Grand Château**, completely demolished during the Revolution, was rebuilt by the Duc d'Aumale in the late 1870s. It served as a French military headquarters during WWI.

The Grand Château, to the right as you enter the vestibule, contains the **Musée Condé**. Its unremarkable, 19th-century rooms are adorned with furnishings, paintings and sculptures haphazardly arranged according to the whims of the Duc d'Aumale, son of King Louis-Philippe, who donated the château to the Institut de France at the end of the 19th century on condition that the exhibits not be reorganised. The most remarkable works are hidden away in a small room called the **Sanctuaire**, including paintings by Raphael (1483-1520), Filippino Lippi (1457-1504) and Jean Fouquet (1425-80).

The Petit Château contains the **Appartements des Princes** (Princes' Apartments), which, from the entrance, are straight ahead. Their highlight is the **Cabinet des Livres** (library), a repository of 700 manuscripts and over 12,000 other volumes including a

Gutenberg Bible and a facsimile of the **Très Riches Heures du Duc de Berry**, an illuminated manuscript dating from the 15th century which illustrates the calendar year for the peasantry and the nobility. The **chapel**, to the left as you walk into the vestibule, is made up of mid-16th century woodwork and windows assembled by the Duc d'Aumale in 1882.

The château is open daily, except Tuesday, from 10 am to 6 pm; from November to February, hours arc 10.30 am to 12.45 pm and 2 to 5 pm (the same entry ticket is good both before and after the midday break). Ticket sales end 45 minutes before closing time. Entry to the château and its park (open daily) costs 39FF (34FF for those aged 12 to 17; 12FF for under 12s). Entry to the park alone costs 17FF (10FF reduced tariff).

Gardens The château's lovely but long-neglected gardens were once among the most spectacular in France. The formal **Jardin Français**, whose flower beds, lakes and Grand Canal were laid out by Le Nôtre in the mid-17th century, is directly north of the main building. To the west is the informal **Jardin Anglais**, begun in 1817. East of the Jardin Français is the rustic **Jardin Anglo-Chinois** (Anglo-Chinese Garden), created in the 1770s. Its foliage and silted-up waterways surround the **Hameau** (hamlet), a mock rural village whose mill and half-timbered buildings, built in 1774, inspired the Hameau de la Reine at Versailles.

Musée Vivant du Cheval
The château's Grandes Écuries (stables), built from 1719 to 1740 to house 240 horses and over 400 hunting hounds, are next to Chantilly's famous Champ de Course (racecourse), inaugurated in 1834. They house the Living Horse Museum ☎ 03 44 57 40 40 or, for a recording, ☎ 03 44 57 13 13), whose equines live in luxurious wooden stalls built by Louis-Henri de Bourbon, the seventh Prince de Condé. Displays, in 31 rooms, include everything from riding equipment to horse toys and paintings of famous nags. The museum is open April to October from 10.30 am to 5.30 pm (6 pm on weekends); it's closed on Tuesday except in May and June (open on Tuesday afternoons in July and August). From November to March, the weekday hours are 2 to 5 pm; at the weekend it's open from 10.30 am to 5.30 pm. Entry costs 50FF (40FF for those aged three to 17).

The 30-minute **Présentation Équestre Pédagogique** (Introduction to Dressage Riding), included in the entry price, generally takes place at 11.30 am, 3.30 pm and 5.15 pm (3.30 pm only from November to March). More elaborate, hour-long demonstrations of dressage riding (80FF, 70FF for children) are held on the first Saturday of the month at 8.30 pm and the first Sunday of the month at 3.15 pm (with an additional one at 4.45 from April to October).

Forêt de Chantilly
The Chantilly Forest, once a royal hunting estate, covers 63 sq km. Its tree cover, patchy in places because of poor soil and overgrazing by deer, includes beeches, oaks, chestnuts, limes and pines.

The forest is crisscrossed by a variety of walking and riding trails. In some areas, straight paths laid out centuries ago meet at multi-angled *carrefours* (crossroads). Long-distance trails which pass through the Forêt de Chantilly include the **GR11**, which links the château with the town of Senlis (see the following section); the **GR1**, which goes from Luzarches (famed for its 16th-century cathedral) to Ermenonville; and the **GR12**, which goes north-eastward from four lakes known as the **Étangs de Commelles** to the Forêt d'Hallate.

The area is covered by IGN's 1:25,000-scale map No 2412OT (57FF), which is entitled *Forêts de Chantilly, d'Halatte and d'Ermenonville*. The *Carte de Découverte des Milieux Naturels et du Patrimoine Bâti* (40FF), a 1:100,000-scale map available at the tourist office, indicates places of historic importance and tourist interest (eg churches, châteaux, museums and ruins). *Randonnées autour de Chantilly et Senlis* (24FF), an unbound topoguide available at the tourist office, has details in French on 10 hikes in the vicinity of Chantilly and Senlis.

Places to Stay

The seven-room *Auberge Le Lion d'Or* (☎ 03 44 57 03 19; fax 03 44 57 92 31) at 44 Rue du Connétable has large and cheery singles with washbasins for 110FF and shower-equipped rooms for two/three people for 180/230FF, or four/five people for 280/330FF. Reception (in the restaurant) is closed on Wednesday. The hotel shuts down from 20 December to 20 January.

Hôtel La Calèche (☎ 03 44 57 02 55) at No 3 on the busy Ave du Maréchal Joffre has rooms for up to three people uniformly priced at 240FF. *Hôtel de la Gare* (☎ 03 44 62 56 90; fax 03 44 62 56 99) just opposite the train station on Place de la Gare is a surprisingly pleasant place with shower-equipped doubles for 290FF.

Places to Eat

The restaurant and crêperie at the Auberge Le Lion d'Or, with *menus* at 114 and 142FF, is highly recommended. Other restaurants on the Rue du Connétable include the bistro-like *L'Adresse* (☎ 03 44 57 27 74) at No 49 and *Maison Mandarin* (☎ 03 44 57 00 29), a Chinese restaurant at No 62. L'Adresse has starters from 35 to 48FF, mains for 65 to 90FF, a formule at 95FF and a *menu* for 145FF. It's open for lunch and dinner, except Sunday evening and all day Monday, from noon to 2 pm and 7 to 10 pm. The Maison Mandarin has starters in the 25 to 35FF range and main courses are 40 to 68FF. It is open for lunch and dinner Tuesday to Sunday.

Midway between the train station and the château, the *Atac* supermarket at Place Omer Vallon is open Monday to Saturday from 8.30 am to 7.30 pm.

Getting There & Around

Paris' Gare du Nord is linked to Chantilly-Gouvieux train station (☎ 03 44 21 50 50; 41FF; 30 to 45 minutes) by a mixture of RER and SNCF commuter trains, a total of almost 40 a day (26 on Sunday and holidays). In the morning, there are departures from Gare du Nord at least twice an hour; in the evening, there are generally trains back to Paris every hour or so until just before midnight.

The two dozen weekday trains – signposted for a variety of destinations including Creil, Amiens, Compiègne and Saint Quentin – start at Gare du Nord, where Chantilly-bound trains use both the Grandes Lignes and Banlieue platforms. The bus station is next to the train station.

SENLIS

• *pop 15,200* ✉ *postcode 60300*

Senlis, just 10km north-east of Chantilly through the forest, is an attractive medieval town of winding, cobblestoned streets, Gallo-Roman ramparts and towers. It was a royal seat from the time of Clovis to Henri IV and contains several fine museums and an important 12th-century cathedral. Buses (15FF; 20 minutes) link Senlis with Chantilly about every half-hour.

The Gothic **Cathédrale de Notre Dame**, which is entered through the south portal on Place Notre Dame, was consecrated in 1191. The cathedral is unusually bright but the stained glass, though original, is unexceptional. The magnificent carved stone **Grand Portal** on the west side facing the Place du Parvis Notre Dame has statues and a relief relating to the life of Mary. It was the inspiration for the one at the cathedral in Chartres.

The tourist office (☎ 03 44 53 06 40; fax 03 44 53 29 80) is on the Place du Parvis Notre Dame just opposite (and west) of the cathedral. It is open Wednesday to Monday from 10 am till noon and 2.15 to 6.15 pm.

CHARTRES

• *pop 40,000* ✉ *postcode 28000*

The magnificent 13th-century cathedral of Chartres, crowned by two soaring spires – one Gothic, the other Romanesque – rises from rich farmland 90km south-west of

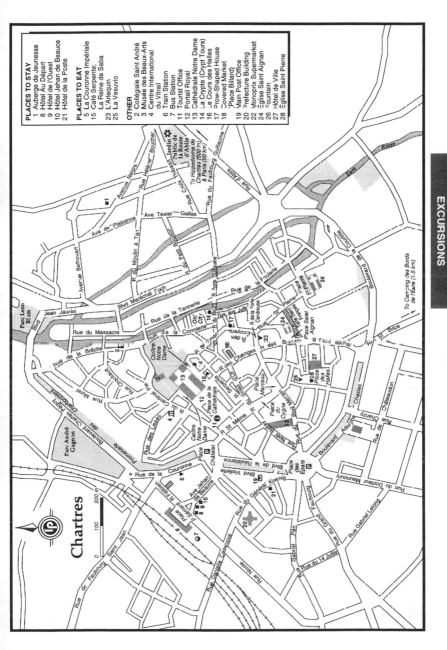

Chartres

PLACES TO STAY
1 Auberge de Jeunesse
8 Hôtel Au Départ
9 Hôtel de l'Ouest
10 Hôtel Jehan de Beauce
21 Hôtel de la Poste

PLACES TO EAT
5 La Couronne Impériale
15 Café Serpente;
   La Reine de Saba
23 L'Arlequin
25 La Vesuvio

OTHER
2 Collégiale Saint André
3 Musée des Beaux-Arts
4 Centre International
   du Vitrail
6 Train Station
7 Bus Station
11 Tourist Office
12 Portail Royal
13 Cathédrale Notre Dame
14 La Crypte (Crypt Tours)
16 Le Cours des Halles
17 Prow-Shaped House
18 Covered Market
   (Place Billard)
19 Main Post Office
20 Prefecture Building
22 Monoprix Supermarket
24 Église Saint Aignan
26 Fountain
27 Hôtel de Ville
28 Église Saint Pierre

Paris and dominates the medieval town around its base.

The cathedral's varied collection of relics – particularly the Sainte Chemise, a piece of cloth said to have been worn by the Virgin Mary when she gave birth to Jesus – attracted many pilgrims during the Middle Ages. Indeed, the town of Chartres has been attracting pilgrims for over 2000 years. Gallic Druids may have had a sanctuary here, and the Romans apparently built themselves a temple dedicated to the Dea Mater (mother goddess), later interpreted by Christian missionaries as prefiguring the Virgin Mary.

Information

The tourist office (☎ 02 37 21 50 00; fax 02 37 21 51 91) is across Place de la Cathédrale from the cathedral's main entrance. From April to September it's open Monday to Saturday from 9 am to 7 pm and on Sunday from 9.30 am to 5.30 pm. During the rest of the year, the Monday to Saturday hours are 10 am to 6 pm and the Sunday ones from 10 am to 1 pm and 2.30 to 4.30 pm. Hotel reservations in the department of Eure-et-Loir cost 10FF (plus a 50FF deposit). The tourist office rents self-guided, one-hour Walkman tours of the old

---

Saved by Red Tape

The cathedral at Chartres survived the ravages of the Revolution for the same reason that everyday life in France can seem so complicated – the vaunted French bureaucratic approach to almost everything. As antireligious fervour was nearing fever pitch in 1791, the Revolutionaries decided that the cathedral deserved something more radical than mere desecration – demolition. The question was how to accomplish that. To find an answer, they appointed a committee, whose admirably thorough members deliberated for four or five years, by which time the Revolution's fury had been spent and the plan was shelved.

---

city for 35FF for one person, 40FF for two people sharing (plus a 100FF deposit).

Cathédrale Notre Dame

Chartres' 130m-long cathedral (☎ 02 37 21 75 02), one of the crowning architectural achievements of western civilisation, was built in the Gothic style during the first quarter of the 13th century to replace a Romanesque cathedral that had been devastated – along with much of the town – by fire on the night of 10 June 1194. Because of effective fund raising among the aristocracy and donations of labour by the common folk, construction took only 25 years, resulting in a high degree of architectural and iconographical unity. It is France's best preserved medieval cathedral, having been spared both post-medieval modifications and the ravages of war and revolution.

The cathedral is open daily from 7.30 am (8.30 am on Sunday) to 7.15 pm except during Mass, weddings and funerals. English-language tours conducted by Chartres expert Malcolm Miller (☎ 02 37 28 15 58; fax 02 37 28 33 03) last one hour to 1½ hours and are held twice daily at noon and 2.45 pm, except Sunday and holidays, from Easter to sometime in November. The cost is 30FF (20FF for students).

Portals & Towers All three of the cathedral's entrances have magnificently ornamented triple portals, but the west entrance, known as the Portail Royal (Royal Portal), is the only one that predates the fire. Carved from 1145 to 1155, its superb statues, whose features are elongated in the Romanesque style, represent the glory of Christ. The structure's other main Romanesque feature is the 105m Clocher Vieux (Old Bell Tower), also known as the Tour Sud (South Tower), which was begun in the 1140s. It is the tallest Romanesque steeple still standing.

A visit to the 115m-high **Clocher Neuf** (New Bell Tower) or the **Clocher Gothique** – also known as the Tour Nord (North Tower) – is well worth the ticket price and the long, spiral climb. Access is via the north transept arm. A 70m-high platform on the lacy, Flamboyant Gothic spire, built from 1507 to 1513 by Jehan de Beauce after an earlier wooden spire burned down, affords superb views of the three-tiered flying buttresses and the 19th-century copper roof, turned green by verdigris. Except on Sunday morning, certain major holidays and in icy weather, the Clocher Neuf is open from 9.30 or 10 to 11.30 am, and 2 pm to 4 pm from November to February, 5 pm in September, October, March and April, and 6 pm from May to August. The fee is 20FF (free for under 12s).

Stained-Glass Windows The cathedral's extraordinary stained-glass windows, almost all of which are 13th-century originals, form one of the most important ensembles of medieval stained glass in Europe. The three most important windows dating from before the 13th century are in the wall above the west entrance, below the rose window. Survivors of the fire of 1194 (they were made around 1150), the windows are renowned for the depth and intensity of their blue tones, known as Chartres blue.

Trésor Chapelle Saint Piat, up the stairs at the far end of the choir, houses the cathedral's treasury, including the Sainte Chemise, which is also known as the Voile de Notre Dame (Veil of Our Lady). From April to October, it is open from 10 am to noon and 2 to 6 pm (closed on Sunday and holiday mornings and on Monday). The rest of the year, hours are 10 am to noon and 2.30 to 4.30 pm (5 pm on Sunday and holidays). Entry is free.

Crypte The cathedral's 110m-long crypt, a tombless Romanesque structure built from 1020 to 1024 around a 9th-century crypt, is the largest in France. Guided tours in French (with a written English translation) lasting 30 minutes start at La Crypte (☎ 02 37 21 56 33), the cathedral-run souvenir shop at 18 Cloître Notre Dame. There are four or five tours a day (two a day from No-

vember to March); year round, there are departures at 11 am and 4.15 pm. Tickets cost 11FF (8FF for students and seniors).

Musée des Beaux-Arts
Chartres' Fine Arts Museum (☎ 02 37 36 41 39) at 29 Cloître Notre Dame (through the gate next to the cathedral's north portal) is housed in the former **Palais Épiscopal** (Bishop's Palace), most of which was built in the 17th and 18th centuries. Its collections include mid-16th century enamels of the 12 Apostles made by Léonard Limosin for François I, paintings from the 16th to 19th century and wooden sculptures from the Middle Ages. It is open from 10 am to noon and 2 to 5 pm (6 pm from October to May; closed Tuesday and on Sunday morning all year). Entry costs 10FF (5FF for students and people over 60).

Centre International du Vitrail
The International Centre of Stained Glass (☎ 02 37 21 65 72), in a half-timbered former granary at 5 Rue du Cardinal Pie (down the hill from the cathedral's north portal), has three exhibitions a year of contemporary stained glass. It can be visited daily from 9.30 am to 12.30 pm and 1.30 to 6 pm (closed for about two weeks between exhibitions). The entry fee is 20FF (12FF for children, students and seniors).

Old City
Chartres' carefully preserved old city is north-east and east of the cathedral along the narrow western channel of the Eure River, which is spanned by a number of footbridges. From Rue du Cardinal Pie, the stairs known as **Tertre Saint Nicolas** and **Rue Chantault** – the latter is lined with old houses – lead down to the empty shell of the mid-12th century **Collégiale Saint André**, a Romanesque collegiate church closed in 1791 and severely damaged in the early 19th century and 1944.

Rue de la Tannerie and its continuation along the river's east bank, **Rue de la Foulerie**, are lined with flower gardens, millraces and the restored remnants of riverside trades: wash houses, tanneries and the like. **Rue aux Juifs** (Street of the Jews) has been extensively renovated, but half a block down the hill there's a riverside promenade and up the hill **Rue des Écuyers** has many houses from around the 16th century, including a prow-shaped, half-timbered structure with its upper section supported by beams at No 26. **Rue du Bourg** also has some old half-timbered houses.

From Place Saint Pierre, you get a good view of the flying buttresses holding up the 12th and 13th-century **Église Saint Pierre**. Once part of a Benedictine monastery founded in the 7th century, it was outside the city walls and therefore vulnerable to attack; the fortress-like, pre-Romanesque **bell tower** attached to it was used as a refuge by monks and dates from around 1000. The fine, brightly coloured **clerestory windows** in the nave, choir and apse are from the mid-13th and early 14th centuries. It is open daily from 9 am to 5 pm (7 pm in summer).

Église Saint Aignan at Place Saint Aignan, built in the early 16th century, is interesting for its wooden barrel-vault roof (1625) and its painted interior of faded blue and gold floral motifs (circa 1870). The stained glass and the Renaissance **Chapelle de Saint Michel** dates from the 16th century. It's open daily from 8 am to 5 pm (7 pm in summer).

Places to Stay

Camping About 2.5km south-east of the train station *Camping des Bords de l'Eure* (☎ 02 37 28 79 43) at 9 Rue de Launay is open from late April to early September. To get there from the train station or Place des Épars take bus No 8 to the Vignes stop.

Hostel The 70-bed Auberge de Jeunesse (☎ 02 37 34 27 64; fax 02 37 35 75 85) at 23 Ave Neigre is about 1.5km east of the train station via Blvd Charles Péguy and Blvd Jean Jaurès. A bed in this pleasant and calm hostel costs about 65FF, including breakfast. Reception is open daily from 2 to

10 pm. Curfew is 10.30 pm in winter and 11.30 pm in summer. To get there from the train station, take bus No 3 to the Rouliers stop.

Hotels The two-star, 29-room *Hôtel de l'Ouest* (☎ 02 37 21 43 27) at 3 Place Pierre Sémard has somewhat dingy, carpeted doubles/triples ranging from 120/170FF (with washbasin and bidet) to 210/260FF (with shower and toilet). The hall shower costs 10FF.

Almost next door is the *Hôtel Jehan de Beauce* (☎ 02 37 21 01 41; fax 02 37 21 59 10) at 19 Ave Jehan de Beauce (1st floor). This two-star, 46-room hotel has clean, decent singles/doubles from 140/160FF (195/225FF with shower and toilet). Triples are also available for 300FF.

You might also try the eight-room *Hôtel Au Départ* (☎ 02 37 36 80 43) at 1 Rue Nicole where doubles/triples with washbasin and bidet are 110/170FF. Reception (at the bar) is closed on Sunday. The *Hôtel de la Poste* (☎ 02 37 21 04 27; fax 02 37 36 42 17), with 57 rooms at 3 Rue du Général Koenig near Place des Épars, has singles with shower for 230FF with shower and toilet (330FF with bath and toilet). Triples and rooms for five cost 370/440FF.

Places to Eat

Restaurants *L'Arlequin* (☎ 02 37 34 88 57) at 8 Rue de la Porte Cendreuse features freshly caught fish dishes for 65 to 85FF, with starters for 42 to 70FF and a lunchtime *plat du jour* at 56FF. It's open for lunch and dinner till 11 pm, except midday Saturday and all day Sunday.

The *Café Serpente* (☎ 02 37 21 68 81), a brasserie and *salon de thé* at 2 Cloître Notre Dame, serves meals daily from 9 am to 1 am. The plat du jour is 98FF, salads are 35 to 42FF. *La Reine de Saba* (☎ 02 37 21 89 16), 8 Cloître Notre Dame, has four lunch *menus* for 59 to 99FF. This casual French restaurant is open from 8.30 am to 8 pm (9.30 or 10 pm on weekends and from July to mid-September).

At *La Vesuvio* (☎ 02 37 21 56 35), 30

Place des Halles, pizzas (35 to 60FF), salads (42 to 48FF) and light meals are served daily from noon to 3 pm and 7 to 11 pm. *La Couronne Impériale* (☎ 02 37 21 87 59) at 7-9 Rue de la Couronne has Chinese and Vietnamese starters for 25 to 42FF, main courses for 38 to 45FF and dim sum for 25FF. *Menus* are available at 58 and 79FF. It's closed on Monday.

Self-Catering There are a number of *food shops* around the *covered market* on Rue des Changes (open Saturday until about 1 pm). The *Monoprix* supermarket at 21 Rue Noël Ballay is open Monday to Saturday from 9 am to 7.30 pm. In the old city, *Le Cours des Halles*, a grocery at 19 Rue du Bourg, is open daily from 8 am to 7.30 pm (closed on Sunday after 1 pm).

Getting There & Around
There are 36 round trips a day (20 on Sunday) to/from Paris' Gare Montparnasse (71FF one way; 55 to 70 minutes) and Versailles' Chantiers station (59FF; 50 minutes). The last train back to Paris leaves Chartres a bit after 9 pm (7.40 pm on Saturday, sometime after 10 pm on Sunday and holidays).

BEAUVAIS
• *pop 55,000* ✉ *postcode 60000*
The soaring Cathédrale Saint Pierre, whose 48m-high choir has the highest Gothic vaults ever built, and the town's fine museums make Beauvais a great day trip from Paris – or a fine stopover on your way between northern France and the French capital. Beauvais, prefecture of the Oise département, is 81km north of Paris.

Information
The tourist office (☎ 03 44 45 08 18; fax 03 44 45 63 95) at 1 Rue Beauregard, on the other side of the Galerie Nationale de la Tapisserie from the cathedral, is open May to October on Monday from 10 am to 1 pm and 2 to 6 pm, Tuesday to Saturday from 9.30 am to 7 pm and Sunday from 10 am to 5 pm. During the rest of the year the hours

Monday to Saturday are 9.30 am to 6.30 pm and the Sunday ones 10 am to 1.30 pm.

Cathédrale Saint Pierre
Beauvais' unfinished Gothic cathedral (☎ 03 44 48 11 60) is to church architecture what the Venus de Milo is to sculpture – to some, a fantastically beautiful work with certain key extremities missing, in this case the nave; to others it looks like an up-ended dinosaur, frightening in its sheer mass. When the town's Carolingian cathedral was partly destroyed by fire in 1225, a series of ambitious local bishops and noblemen decided that its replacement should surpass anything ever built. Unfortunately, their soaring and richly adorned creation surpassed not only its rivals but the limits of technology, and in 1272 and again in 1284 the 48m-high vaults collapsed.

The cathedral is open daily from 9 am to 12.15 pm and 2 to 5.30 pm (6.15 pm from May to October). The **astronomical clock** (built 1868) sounds at 10.40 am (Monday to Saturday) and daily at 2.40, 3.40 and 4.40 pm (22FF for adults; 15FF for students; 5FF for children aged four to 14).

Église Saint Étienne
This church on Rue Angrand Leprince, begun in the 12th century but dating mostly from the 16th century, is much smaller than the cathedral. It has a Romanesque nave and a Gothic choir, which some historians believe was the birthplace of that style. The church, which keeps the same hours as the cathedral, contains some superb 16th-century stained glass (notably the one named *L'Arbre de Jessé,* or Jesse's Tree).

Museums
The outstanding Musée Départemental de l'Oise (☎ 03 44 48 48 88) at 1 Rue du Musée is just west of the cathedral in the former Bishops' Palace. It has sections dedicated to archaeology, medieval wood carvings, French and Italian paintings (including a number of gruesome 16th century works depicting decapitations), ceramics and Art Nouveau. It is open from 10 am to noon and

2 to 6 pm (closed Tuesday). Entry costs 16FF (8FF for under 25s and seniors; free for under 18s and, on Wednesday, for everyone).

The **Galerie Nationale de la Tapisserie** (☎ 03 44 05 14 28) on Rue Saint Pierre has permanent and temporary tapestry exhibitions. From April to September, it's open from 9.30 to 11.30 am and 2 to 6 pm (closed Monday); the rest of the year, hours are 10 to 11.30 am and 2.30 to 4.30 pm. Entry costs 22FF (15FF for seniors and those aged 18 to 25; free for under 18s).

Places to Stay

The *Hôtel Normandie* (☎ 03 44 45 07 61) at 19 Rue Beauregard, a half-block south of the tourist office, has utilitarian doubles from 120FF (140FF with toilet). Reception is closed on Monday.

The cheaper *Hôtel du Commerce* (☎ 03 44 48 17 84) at 11-13 Rue Chambiges has basic singles/doubles with washbasin for 100/110FF and ones with shower for 134/144FF. More central is the *JP Pub Hôtel* (☎ 03 44 45 07 51; fax 03 44 45 71 25) at 15 Place Jeanne Hachette, with singles/doubles with shower from 120/180FF. The *Hôtel de la Poste* (☎ 03 44 45 14 97; fax 03 44 45 02 31) at 19 Rue Gambetta has singles/doubles with washbasin and toilet for 145/195FF and rooms with shower for 155/205FF.

Places to Eat

Les Petits Trucs (☎ 03 44 48 31 31) at 6 Rue Philippe de Dreux is a crêperie with galettes and crêpes for 15 to 48FF and *menus* at 58FF (weekday lunch only) and 70FF. It is open daily, except Sunday, to 10 pm. *La Tourtière* (☎ 03 44 45 86 32) at 3 Rue Ricard has savoury and sweet tartes (17 to 20FF) and tourtes (20 to 28FF) as well as salads from 35FF available Monday to Saturday from 11.30 am to 2 pm (to 9 pm on Friday).

The *Nouvelles Galeries*, one block east of the tourist office at 2 Rue Carnot, has a basement supermarket open Monday to Saturday from 9 am to 7 pm (closed on Monday between noon and 2 pm). The *market* on Place des Halles is open on Wednesday and Saturday mornings.

Getting There & Away

The train station on Ave de la République has an information office (☎ 03 44 21 50 50) open from 8.15 to 11.45 am and 12.15 to 7.30 pm (closed Sunday). Beauvais is on the secondary line linking Creil (on the Paris-Amiens line) with the Channel beach resort of Le Tréport. Travel to/from Paris' Gare du Nord (64FF; 1½ hours for direct services; 16 a day, nine on Sunday and holidays) often requires a change at Persan Beaumont.

Index

TEXT

BOXED TEXT

LONELY PLANET PHRASEBOOKS

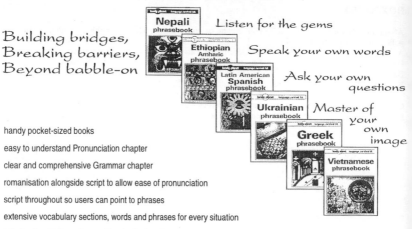

Building bridges,
Breaking barriers,
Beyond babble-on

Listen for the gems

Speak your own words

Ask your own
questions

Master of
your
own
image

- handy pocket-sized books
- easy to understand Pronunciation chapter
- clear and comprehensive Grammar chapter
- romanisation alongside script to allow ease of pronunciation
- script throughout so users can point to phrases
- extensive vocabulary sections, words and phrases for every situation
- full of cultural information and tips for the traveller

'...vital for a real DIY spirit and attitude in language learning' – Backpacker

'the phrasebooks have good cultural backgrounders and offer solid advice for challenging situations in remote locations' – San Francisco Examiner

'...they are unbeatable for their coverage of the world's more obscure languages' – The Geographical Magazine

---

Arabic (Egyptian)
Arabic (Moroccan)
Australia
 Australian English, Aboriginal and Torres Strait languages
Baltic States
 Estonian, Latvian, Lithuanian
Bengali
Brazilian
Burmese
Cantonese
Central Asia
Central Europe
 Czech, French, German, Hungarian, Italian and Slovak
Eastern Europe
 Bulgarian, Czech, Hungarian, Polish, Romanian and Slovak
Ethiopian (Amharic)
Fijian
French
German
Greek

Hindi/Urdu
Indonesian
Italian
Japanese
Korean
Lao
Latin American Spanish
Malay
Mandarin
Mediterranean Europe
 Albanian, Croatian, Greek, Italian, Macedonian, Maltese, Serbian and Slovene
Mongolian
Nepali
Papua New Guinea
Pilipino (Tagalog)
Quechua
Russian
Scandinavian Europe
 Danish, Finnish, Icelandic, Norwegian and Swedish

South-East Asia
 Burmese, Indonesian, Khmer, Lao, Malay, Tagalog (Pilipino), Thai and Vietnamese
Spanish (Castilian)
 Basque, Catalan and Galician
Sri Lanka
Swahili
Thai
Thai Hill Tribes
Tibetan
Turkish
Ukrainian
USA
 US English, Vernacular, Native American languages and Hawaiian
Vietnamese
Western Europe
 Basque, Catalan, Dutch, French, German, Irish, Italian, Portuguese, Scottish Gaelic, Spanish (Castilian) and Welsh

---

LONELY PLANET JOURNEYS

JOURNEYS is a unique collection of travel writing – published by the company that understands travel better than anyone else. It is a series for anyone who has ever experienced – or dreamed of – the magical moment when they encountered a strange culture or saw a place for the first time. They are tales to read while you're planning a trip, while you're on the road or while you're in an armchair, in front of a fire.

JOURNEYS books catch the spirit of a place, illuminate a culture, recount a crazy adventure, or introduce a fascinating way of life. They always entertain, and always enrich the experience of travel.

THE GATES OF DAMASCUS
Lieve Joris
Translated by Sam Garrett

This best-selling book is a beautifully drawn portrait of day-to-day life in modern Syria. Through her intimate contact with local people, Lieve Joris draws us into the fascinating world that lies behind the gates of Damascus. Hala's husband is a political prisoner, jailed for his opposition to the Assad regime; through the author's friendship with Hala we see how Syrian politics impacts on the lives of ordinary people.

Lieve Joris, who was born in Belgium, is one of Europe's leading travel writers. In addition to an award-winning book on Hungary, she has published widely acclaimed accounts of her journeys to the Middle East and Africa. *The Gates of Damascus* is her fifth book.

'Expands the boundaries of travel writing' – Times Literary Supplement

---

KINGDOM OF THE FILM STARS
Journey into Jordan
Annie Caulfield

Kingdom of the Film Stars is a travel book and a love story. With honesty and humour, Annie Caulfield writes of travelling in Jordan and falling in love with a Bedouin. Her book offers fascinating insights into the country – from the traditional tent life of nomadic tribes to the first woman MP's battle with fundamentalist colleagues. *Kingdom of the Film Stars* unpicks some of the tight-woven Western myths about the Arab world, presenting cultural and political issues within the intimate framework of a compelling love story.

Annie Caulfield, who was born in Ireland and currently lives in London, is an award-winning playwright and journalist. She has travelled widely in the Middle East.

'Annie Caulfield is a remarkable traveller. Her story is fresh, courageous, moving, witty and sexy!' – Dawn French

LONELY PLANET TRAVEL ATLASES

Lonely Planet has long been famous for the number and quality of its guidebook maps. Now we've gone one step further and produced a handy companion series: Lonely Planet travel atlases – maps of a country produced in book form.

Unlike other maps, which look good but lead travellers astray, our travel atlases have been researched on the road by Lonely Planet's experienced team of writers. All details are carefully checked to ensure the atlas corresponds with the equivalent Lonely Planet guidebook.

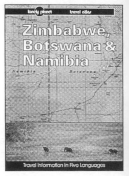

The handy atlas format means no holes, wrinkles, torn sections or constant folding and unfolding. These atlases can survive long periods on the road, unlike cumbersome fold-out maps. The comprehensive index ensures easy reference.

- full-colour throughout
- maps researched and checked by Lonely Planet authors
- place names correspond with Lonely Planet guidebooks
  – no confusing spelling differences
- legend and travelling information in English, French, German,
  Japanese and Spanish
- size: 230 x 160 mm

Available now:
Chile & Easter Island • Egypt • India & Bangladesh • Israel & the Palestinian Territories •Jordan, Syria & Lebanon • Kenya • Laos • Portugal • South Africa, Lesotho & Swaziland • Thailand • Turkey • Vietnam • Zimbabwe, Botswana & Namibia

---

LONELY PLANET TV SERIES & VIDEOS

Lonely Planet travel guides have been brought to life on television screens around the world. Like our guides, the programmes are based on the joy of independent travel, and look honestly at some of the most exciting, picturesque and frustrating places in the world. Each show is presented by one of three travellers from Australia, England or the USA and combines an innovative mixture of video, Super-8 film, atmospheric soundscapes and original music.

Videos of each episode – containing additional footage not shown on television – are available from good book and video shops, but the availability of individual videos varies with regional screening schedules.

Video destinations include: Alaska • American Rockies • Australia – The South-East • Baja California & the Copper Canyon • Brazil • Central Asia • Chile & Easter Island • Corsica, Sicily & Sardinia – The Mediterranean Islands • East Africa (Tanzania & Zanzibar) • Ecuador & the Galapagos Islands • Greenland & Iceland • Indonesia • Israel & the Sinai Desert • Jamaica • Japan • La Ruta Maya • Morocco • New York • North India • Pacific Islands (Fiji, Solomon Islands & Vanuatu) • South India • South West China • Turkey • Vietnam • West Africa • Zimbabwe, Botswana & Namibia

The Lonely Planet TV series is produced by:
Pilot Productions
The Old Studio
18 Middle Row
London W10 5AT UK

For video availability and ordering information contact your nearest Lonely Planet office.

Music from the TV series is available on CD & cassette.

PLANET TALK

Lonely Planet's FREE quarterly newsletter

We love hearing from you and think you'd like to hear from us.

*When...*is the right time to see reindeer in Finland?
*Where...*can you hear the best palm-wine music in Ghana?
*How...*do you get from Asunción to Areguá by steam train?
*What...*is the best way to see India?

For the answer to these and many other questions read PLANET TALK.

Every issue is packed with up-to-date travel news and advice including:

* a letter from Lonely Planet co-founders Tony and Maureen Wheeler
* go behind the scenes on the road with a Lonely Planet author
* feature article on an important and topical travel issue
* a selection of recent letters from travellers
* details on forthcoming Lonely Planet promotions
* complete list of Lonely Planet products

To join our mailing list contact any Lonely Planet office.

Also available: Lonely Planet T-shirts. 100% heavyweight cotton.

LONELY PLANET ONLINE

Get the latest travel information before you leave or while you're on the road

Whether you've just begun planning your next trip, or you're chasing down specific info on currency regulations or visa requirements, check out Lonely Planet Online for up-to-the-minute travel information.

As well as travel profiles of your favourite destinations (including maps and photos), you'll find current reports from our researchers and other travellers, updates on health and visas, travel advisories, and discussion of the ecological and political issues you need to be aware of as you travel.

There's also an online travellers' forum where you can share your experience of life on the road, meet travel companions and ask other travellers for their recommendations and advice. We also have plenty of links to other online sites useful to independent travellers.

And of course we have a complete and up-to-date list of all Lonely Planet travel products including guides, phrasebooks, atlases, Journeys and videos and a simple online ordering facility if you can't find the book you want elsewhere.

www.lonelyplanet.com
or
AOL keyword: lp

LONELY PLANET PRODUCTS

Lonely Planet is known worldwide for publishing practical, reliable and no-nonsense travel information in our guides and on our web site. The Lonely Planet list covers just about every accessible part of the world. Currently there are nine series: *travel guides, shoestring guides, walking guides, city guides, phrasebooks, audio packs, travel atlases, Journeys – a unique collection of travel writing and Pisces Books - diving and snorkeling guides.*

EUROPE

Amsterdam • Austria • Baltic States phrasebook • Berlin • Britain • Canary Islands• Central Europe on a shoestring • Central Europe phrasebook • Czech & Slovak Republics • Denmark • Dublin • Eastern Europe on a shoestring • Eastern Europe phrasebook • Estonia, Latvia & Lithuania • Finland • France • French phrasebook • Germany • German phrasebook • Greece • Greek phrasebook • Hungary • Iceland, Greenland & the Faroe Islands • Ireland • Italian phrasebook • Italy • Lisbon • London • Mediterranean Europe on a shoestring • Mediterranean Europe phrasebook • Paris • Poland • Portugal • Portugal travel atlas • Prague • Romania & Moldova • Russia, Ukraine & Belarus • Russian phrasebook • Scandinavian & Baltic Europe on a shoestring • Scandinavian Europe phrasebook • Slovenia • Spain • Spanish phrasebook • St Petersburg • Switzerland •Trekking in Spain • Ukrainian phrasebook • Vienna • Walking in Britain • Walking in Italy • Walking in Switzerland • Western Europe on a shoestring • Western Europe phrasebook

Travel Literature: The Olive Grove: Travels in Greece

NORTH AMERICA

Alaska • Backpacking in Alaska • Baja California • California & Nevada • Canada • Chicago • Deep South• Florida • Hawaii • Honolulu • Los Angeles • Mexico • Mexico City • Miami • New England • New Orleans • New York City • New York, New Jersey & Pennsylvania • Pacific Northwest USA • Rocky Mountain States • San Francisco • Southwest USA • USA phrasebook • Washington, DC & the Capital Region

Travel Literature: Drive thru America

CENTRAL AMERICA & THE CARIBBEAN

•Bahamas and Turks & Caicos •Bermuda •Central America on a shoestring • Costa Rica • Cuba •Eastern Caribbean •Guatemala, Belize & Yucatán: La Ruta Maya • Jamaica

SOUTH AMERICA

Argentina, Uruguay & Paraguay • Bolivia • Brazil • Brazilian phrasebook • Buenos Aires • Chile & Easter Island • Chile & Easter Island travel atlas • Colombia Ecuador & the Galápagos Islands • Latin American Spanish phrasebook • Peru • Quechua phrasebook • Rio de Janeiro • South America on a shoestring • Trekking in the Patagonian Andes • Venezuela

Travel Literature: Full Circle: A South American Journey

ISLANDS OF THE INDIAN OCEAN

Madagascar & Comoros • Maldives• Mauritius, Réunion & Seychelles

AFRICA

Africa - the South • Africa on a shoestring • Arabic (Moroccan) phrasebook • Cairo • Cape Town • Central Africa • East Africa • Egypt • Egypt travel atlas• Ethiopian (Amharic) phrasebook • Kenya • Kenya travel atlas • Malawi, Mozambique & Zambia • Morocco • North Africa • South Africa, Lesotho & Swaziland • South Africa, Lesotho & Swaziland travel atlas • Swahili phrasebook • Tunisia • Trekking in East Africa • West Africa • Zimbabwe, Botswana & Namibia • Zimbabwe, Botswana & Namibia travel atlas

Travel Literature: The Rainbird: A Central African Journey • Songs to an African Sunset: A Zimbabwean Story

MAIL ORDER

Lonely Planet products are distributed worldwide. They are also available by mail order from Lonely Planet, so if you have difficulty finding a title please write to us. North American and South American residents should write to 150 Linden St, Oakland CA 94607, USA; European and African residents should write to 10a Spring Place, London NW5 3BH; and residents of other countries to PO Box 617, Hawthorn, Victoria 3122, Australia.

NORTH-EAST ASIA

Beijing • Cantonese phrasebook • China • Hong Kong • Hong Kong, Macau & Guangzhou • Japan • Japanese phrasebook • Japanese audio pack • Korea • Korean phrasebook • Mandarin phrasebook • Mongolia • Mongolian phrasebook • North-East Asia on a shoestring • Seoul • Taiwan • Tibet • Tibet phrasebook • Tokyo

Travel Literature: Lost Japan

MIDDLE EAST & CENTRAL ASIA

Arab Gulf States • Arabic (Egyptian) phrasebook • Central Asia • Central Asia phrasebook • Iran • Israel & the Palestinian Territories • Israel & the Palestinian Territories travel atlas • Istanbul • Jerusalem • Jordan & Syria • Jordan, Syria & Lebanon travel atlas • Lebanon • Middle East • Turkey • Turkish phrasebook • Turkey travel atlas • Yemen

Travel Literature: The Gates of Damascus • Kingdom of the Film Stars: Journey into Jordan

ALSO AVAILABLE:

Brief Encounters • Travel with Children • Traveller's Tales

INDIAN SUBCONTINENT

Bangladesh • Bengali phrasebook • Delhi • Goa • Hindi/Urdu phrasebook • India • India & Bangladesh travel atlas • Indian Himalaya • Karakoram Highway • Nepal • Nepali phrasebook • Pakistan • Rajasthan • Sri Lanka • Sri Lanka phrasebook • Trekking in the Indian Himalaya • Trekking in the Karakoram & Hindukush • Trekking in the Nepal Himalaya

Travel Literature: In Rajasthan • Shopping for Buddhas

SOUTH-EAST ASIA

Bali & Lombok • Bangkok • Burmese phrasebook • Cambodia • Ho Chi Minh City • Indonesia • Indonesian phrasebook • Indonesian audio pack • Jakarta • Java • Laos • Lao phrasebook • Laos travel atlas • Malay phrasebook • Malaysia, Singapore & Brunei • Myanmar (Burma) • Philippines • Pilipino phrasebook • Singapore • South-East Asia on a shoestring • South-East Asia phrasebook • Thailand • Thailand's Islands & Beaches • Thailand travel atlas • Thai phrasebook • Thai audio pack • Thai Hill Tribes phrasebook • Vietnam • Vietnamese phrasebook • Vietnam travel atlas

AUSTRALIA & THE PACIFIC

Australia • Australian phrasebook • Bushwalking in Australia • Bushwalking in Papua New Guinea • Fiji • Fijian phrasebook • Islands of Australia's Great Barrier Reef • Melbourne • Micronesia • New Caledonia • New South Wales • New Zealand • Northern Territory • Outback Australia • Papua New Guinea • Papua New Guinea phrasebook • Queensland • Rarotonga & the Cook Islands • Samoa • Solomon Islands • South Australia • Sydney • Tahiti & French Polynesia • Tasmania • Tonga • Tramping in New Zealand • Vanuatu • Victoria • Western Australia

Travel Literature: Islands in the Clouds • Sean & David's Long Drive

ANTARCTICA

Antarctica

THE LONELY PLANET STORY

Lonely Planet published its first book in 1973 in response to the numerous 'How did you do it?' questions Maureen and Tony Wheeler were asked after driving, busing, hitching, sailing and railing their way from England to Australia.

Written at a kitchen table and hand collated, trimmed and stapled, *Across Asia on the Cheap* became an instant local bestseller, inspiring thoughts of another book.

Eighteen months in South-East Asia resulted in their second guide, *South-East Asia on a shoestring*, which they put together in a backstreet Chinese hotel in Singapore in 1975. The 'yellow bible', as it quickly became known to backpackers around the world, soon became *the* guide to the region. It has sold well over half a million copies and is now in its 9th edition, still retaining its familiar yellow cover.

Today there are over 350 titles, including travel guides, walking guides, language kits & phrasebooks, travel atlases and travel literature. The company is the largest independent travel publisher in the world. Although Lonely Planet initially specialised in guides to Asia, today there are few corners of the globe that have not been covered.

The emphasis continues to be on travel for independent travellers. Tony and Maureen still travel for several months of each year and play an active part in the writing, updating and quality control of Lonely Planet's guides.

They have been joined by over 80 authors and 200 staff at our offices in Melbourne (Australia), Oakland (USA), London (UK) and Paris (France). Travellers themselves also make a valuable contribution to the guides through the feedback we receive in thousands of letters each year and on our web site.

The people at Lonely Planet strongly believe that travellers can make a positive contribution to the countries they visit, both through their appreciation of the countries' culture, wildlife and natural features, and through the money they spend. In addition, the company makes a direct contribution to the countries and regions it covers. Since 1986 a percentage of the income from each book has been donated to ventures such as famine relief in Africa; aid projects in India; agricultural projects in Central America; Greenpeace's efforts to halt French nuclear testing in the Pacific; and Amnesty International.

'I hope we send people out with the right attitude about travel. You realise when you travel that there are so many different perspectives about the world, so we hope these books will make people more interested in what they see. Guidebooks can't really guide people. All you can do is point them in the right direction.'

– Tony Wheeler

---

lonely planet

LONELY PLANET PUBLICATIONS

Australia
PO Box 617, Hawthorn 3122, Victoria
tel: (03) 9819 1877 fax: (03) 9819 6459
e-mail: talk2us@lonelyplanet.com.au

USA
150 Linden St
Oakland, CA 94607
tel: (510) 893 8555 TOLL FREE: 800 275-8555
fax: (510) 893 8572
e-mail: info@lonelyplanet.com

UK
10a Spring Place,
London NW5 3BH
tel: (0171) 428 4800 fax: (0171) 428 4828
e-mail: go@lonelyplanet.co.uk

France:
71 bis rue du Cardinal Lemoine, 75005 Paris
tel: 01 44 32 06 20 fax: 01 46 34 72 55
e-mail: bip@lonelyplanet.fr

World Wide Web: http://www.lonelyplanet.com
or AOL. keyword: lp

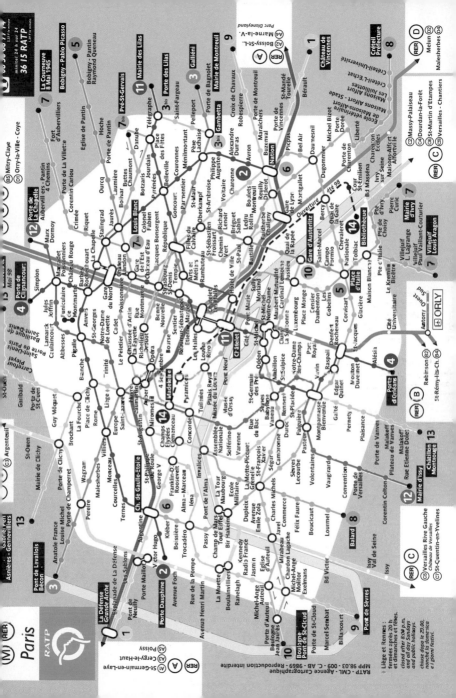

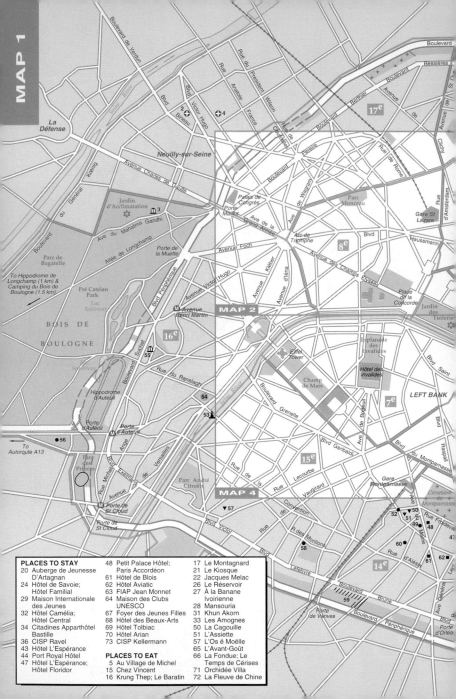

MAP 1

La Défense

Neuilly-sur-Seine

Jardin d'Acclimatation

Parc de Bagatelle

To Hippodrome de Longchamp (1 km) & Camping du Bois de Boulogne (1.5 km)

Pré Catelan Park

Lac Inférieur

BOIS DE BOULOGNE

Lac Supérieur

Hippodrome d'Auteuil

Porte d'Auteuil

Porte d'Auteuil

To Autoroute A13

Parc des Princes

Porte de St Cloud

Porte de St Cloud

Seine River

Avenue Charles de Gaulle

Avenue du Mahatma Gandhi

Allée de Longchamp

Bois de Boulogne

Boulevard du Général Koenig

Boulevard

Boulevard Victor Hugo

Bld Bineau

Rue Anatole France

Rue du (President) Wilson

Palais des Congrès

Porte Maillot

Ave de la Grande Armée

Avenue Foch

Avenue Victor Hugo

Avenue Henri Martin

16e

Rue du Ranelagh

Blvd Périphérique

Bld Suchet

Boulevard Exelmans

Rue Michel Ange

Avenue de Versailles

Parc André Citroën

Boulevard Victor

Rue Lecourbe

Rue de la Convention

Boulevard Lefebvre

Porte de Vanves

Boulevard Brune

Périphérique

Boulevard de Verdun

Rue d'Amsterdam

Gare St Lazare

Parc Monceau

Arc de Triomphe

Avenue des Champs Elysées

8e

Haussmann

Place de la Concorde

Jardin des Tuileries

Eiffel Tower

Champ de Mars

Esplanade des Invalides

Hôtel des Invalides

7e

LEFT BANK

Boulevard Grenelle

Boulevard Garibaldi

15e

Ave de Breteuil

Blvd du Montparnasse

Gare Montparnasse

Cimetière du Montparnasse

14e

Porte d'Orléans

MAP 2

MAP 4

Clichy

17e

Boulevard Berthier

Boulevard Bessières

PLACES TO STAY
20 Auberge de Jeunesse D'Artagnan
24 Hôtel de Savoie; Hôtel Familial
29 Maison Internationale des Jeunes
32 Hôtel Camélia; Hôtel Central
34 Citadines Apparthôtel Bastille
36 CISP Ravel
43 Hôtel L'Espérance
44 Port Royal Hôtel
47 Hôtel L'Espérance; Hôtel Floridor

48 Petit Palace Hôtel; Paris Accordéon
61 Hôtel de Blois
62 Hôtel Aviatic
63 FIAP Jean Monnet
64 Maison des Clubs UNESCO
67 Foyer des Jeunes Filles
68 Hôtel des Beaux-Arts
69 Hôtel Tolbiac
70 Hôtel Arian
73 CISP Kellermann

PLACES TO EAT
5 Au Village de Michel
15 Chez Vincent
16 Krung Thep; Le Baratin

17 Le Montagnard
21 Le Kiosque
22 Jacques Melac
26 Le Réservoir
27 À la Banane Ivoirienne
28 Mansouria
31 Khun Akorn
33 Les Amognes
50 La Cagouille
51 L'Assiette
57 L'Os è Moëlle
65 L'Avant-Goût
66 La Fondue; Le Temps de Cérises
71 Orchidée Villa
72 La Fleuve de Chine

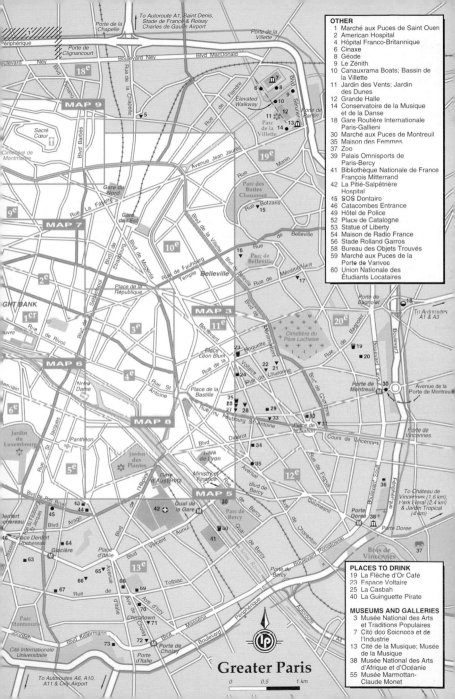

Greater Paris

OTHER
1 Marché aux Puces de Saint Ouen
2 American Hospital
4 Hôpital Franco-Britannique
6 Cinaxe
8 Géode
9 Le Zénith
10 Canauxrama Boats; Bassin de la Villette
11 Jardin des Vents; Jardin des Dunes
12 Grande Halle
14 Conservatoire de la Musique et de la Danse
18 Gare Routière Internationale Paris-Gallieni
30 Marché aux Puces de Montreuil
35 Maison des Femmes
37 Zoo
39 Palais Omnisports de Paris-Bercy
41 Bibliothèque Nationale de France François Mitterrand
42 La Pitié-Salpêtrière Hospital
45 SOS Dentairo
46 Catacombes Entrance
49 Hôtel de Police
52 Place de Catalogne
53 Statue of Liberty
54 Maison de Radio France
56 Stade Rolland Garros
58 Bureau des Objets Trouvés
59 Marché aux Puces de la Porte de Vanves
60 Union Nationale des Étudiants Locataires

PLACES TO DRINK
19 La Flèche d'Or Café
23 Espace Voltaire
25 La Casbah
40 La Guinguette Pirate

MUSEUMS AND GALLERIES
3 Musée National des Arts et Traditions Populaires
7 Cité des Sciences et de l'Industrie
13 Cité de la Musique; Musée de la Musique
38 Musée National des Arts d'Afrique et d'Océanie
55 Musée Marmottan-Claude Monet

0   0.5   1 km

PLACES TO STAY
17 Atlantic Hôtel
18 Hôtels Du Calvados
   & Britannia
62 Hôtel Ritz
65 Hôtel de Crillon
72 Hôtel Brighton
73 Hôtel Meurice

PLACES TO EAT
1 Macis et Muscade
5 Charlot-Roi des Coquillages
22 L'Étoile Verte
25 Maison Prunier
33 Chicago Pizza Pie Factory
35 Planet Hollywood; Batifol
39 La Maison d'Alsace
43 Pizza Pino
52 Hédiard
55 Fauchon
69 L'Ardoise

PLACES TO DRINK
3 L'Européen
4 Le Wepler Café
7 Chao Ba Café
32 Le Queen

36 Montecristo Café
47 Cricketer Pub
61 Buddha Bar

MUSEUMS AND GALLERIES
15 Musée Cernuschi
16 Musée Nissim de Camondo
20 Musée Jacquemart-André
74 Jeu de Paume
75 Musée de l'Orangerie
77 Musée des Beaux-Arts;
   Musée du Petit Palais
78 Nationales Galeries
   du Grand Palais
83 Panthéon Bouddhique
   (Musée Guimet Annexe)
85 Musée Guimet
86 Musée de la Mode et du
   Costume; Palais Galliera
89 Musée d'Art Moderne
   de la Ville de Paris

OTHER
2 Cinéma des Cinéastes
6 Pharmacie Européenne
8 ADA Car Rental
9 Banque de France
10 FNAC Étoile Department
   Store

11 Palais de Congrès
   de Paris
12 ADA Car Rental
13 American Express
14 Salle Pleyel
19 FNAC Department Store
21 Saint Joseph's Church
23 Air France Buses
24 Irish Embassy
26 New Zealand Embassy
27 Rue Copernic Liberal
   Synagogue
28 Main Tourist Office
29 Air Inter
31 Le Lido
34 Pharmacie des Champs
   (24 Hours)
37 Air France
38 Post Office
40 Prisunic Supermarket
44 Bureau de Change
45 Théâtre Marigny
46 Palais de l'Elysée
48 Printemps Department
   Store
49 Marks & Spencer
   Department Store
50 American Express

51 La Maison du Miel
53 Maison de la Truffe;
   Caviar Kaspia
54 Kiosque Théâtre
56 Méllerio Dits Meller
57 Historic Public Toilet
58 Église de la Madeleine
59 SOS Théâtre; Agence
   Perossier (Ticket Offices)
60 UK Consulate
64 Van Cleef & Arpels
64 Colonne Vendôme
67 US Consulate
68 WH Smith Bookshop
70 Alexandre de Paris
71 La Vaisellerie
76 Obelisk
79 Palais de la Découverle
80 Church of Scotland
81 Canadian Embassy
82 German Consulate
84 Goethe Institute
87 Crazy Horse Saloon
88 Théâtre des
   Champs-Élysées
90 Liberty Flame;
   Diana Memorial
91 Bateaux Mouches

Central Paris
North-West

0   200   400 m

MAP 3
MAP 9
MAP 7
MAP 4

17e
18e
9e
8e
1er

Cimetière
de Montmartre

Boulevard   Pereire

Square
des
Batignolles

Rue   Legendre

Rue   de   Rome

Rue   Jouffroy   d'Abbans

Boulevard   Malesherbes

Rue   Legendre

Place de Clichy
Place
de Clichy

Avenue de Clichy

Place du
Général Catroux

Avenue de Villiers

Villiers

Boulevard de Courcelles

Monceau

Monceau

Rue   de   Constantinople

Rue   de   Rome

Rue   de   Pétersbourg

Rue   d'Amsterdam

Rue   Cardinal
Mercier

Rue   de   Clichy

Liège

Parc de
Monceau

Avenue
Velasquez

Rue   de

Boulevard   Malesherbes

Rue   de   Vienne

Rue   de   Madrid

Place de
l'Europe

Europe

Rue   de   Madrid

Rue   de

Londres

Rue   de   Lisbonne

Rue   Murillo

Rue   de

Rue   de   Monceau

Avenue   N.   Messine

Avenue   de   Lisbonne

Rue   de

Boulevard   Haussmann

Place
St Augustin

St Augustin

Rue   de   la   Pépinière

Gare
Saint Lazare

St Lazare

Saint   Lazare

Rue

Rue   de   Caumartin

St Lazare

Boulevard   Haussmann

Rue   Tronchet

Rue   de   l'Arcade

Rue   de   Caumartin

Havre
Caumartin

Auber

Auber

Rue   la   Boétie

Rue   de

Miromesnil

Rue   de

Boulevard   Malesherbes

Rue   de   l'Arcade

Rue   Vignon

Rue   Auber

Rue   Scribe

Avenue   de   Friedland

Rue   La   Boétie

St Philippe
du Roule

St
Honoré

Rue   du
Colisée

Avenue   Franklin   Roosevelt

Avenue   Matignon

Rue   de   Faubourg   Saint   Honoré

Rue   d'Anjou

Rue   Royale

Rue   Tronchet

Boulevard   des
Capucines

Rue   de   la   Paix

Franklin D
Roosevelt

Rue   de   Marignan

Rond-Point des
Champs-Elysées

Franklin D
Roosevelt

Avenue   Gabriel

Avenue   de   Marigny

Rue   de   Faubourg   Saint   Honoré

Rue   d'Anjou

Rue   Boissy

La   Madeleine

Madeleine

Blvd   de   la   Madeleine

Rue   St   Honoré

Place
Vendôme

Rue   de   la   Paix

Montaigne

Champs Elysées
Clemenceau

Avenue   des   Champs   Elysées

Rue   Royale

Rue   St   Florentin

Rue   Cambon

St   Honoré

Rue   de   Rivoli

Grand
Palais

Petit
Palais

Cours   la   Reine

Place   de   la
Concorde

Concorde

Jardin
des
Tuileries

Tuileries

Pont
Alexandre   III

Seine   River

Albert   1er

MAP 3

Montmartre

Basilique du Sacré Cœur

18ᵉ

Boulevard Barbès

Lariboisière

Rue de Douai

Boulevard de Clichy

Boulevard de Rochechouart

Pigalle

Rue de Dunkerque

Lycée J Decours

Avenue Trudaine

Rue Ambroise Paré

MAP 9

Rue Fontaine

Rue Victor Massé

Rue Condorcet

2

Rue Clauzel

13

12

11

10

15

9ᵉ

Rue Notre Dame de Lorette

16

Rue Rochambeau

18

17

Place Franz Liszt

19

20

Rue de Chabrol

Poissonnière

MAP 7

Cadet

Rue Bleue

21

Rue de Paradis

Rue d'Hauteville

Rue des Petites Écuries

41

40

39

42

Rue du Faubourg Poissonnière

Rue d'Enghien

Passage Brady

43

44

45

Porte Saint Denis

Porte Saint Martin

Boulevard Poissonnière

Boulevard de Bonne Nouvelle

Bourse des Valeurs

2ᵉ

Rue Réaumur

Rue des Petits Champs

Place des Victoires

Jardin du Palais Royal

1ᵉʳ

Rue Étienne Marcel

Rue du Louvre

PLACES TO STAY	MUSEUMS AND GALLERIES
2 Grand Hôtel Magenta	16 Musée Gustave Moreau
7 Hôtel La Vieille France	21 Baccarat Crystal Museum
8 Nord Hôtel	
12 Hôtel Bonne Nouvelle	**OTHER**
13 Woodstock Hostel	1 Bouffes du Nord
15 Résidence Hôtel des	3 Bus Terminal
Trois Poussins	4 RATP Bus No 350 to Charles
22 Hôtel de Milan	de Gaulle Airport
23 Hôtel Français	6 Post Office
24 Hôtel d'Alsace	17 Allostop Pravoya
28 Sibour Hôtel	18 Église Saint Vincent de Paul
29 Grand Hôtel de Paris	20 Marché Saint Quentin
34 Hôtel Liberty	25 RATP Bus No 350 to Charles
38 Hôtel Pacific	de Gaulle Airport
39 Hôtel Château d'Eau	26 Post Office
55 Auberge de Jeunesse	30 Église Saint Laurent
Jules Ferry	31 Hôtel du Nord
	32 Franprix Supermarket
PLACES TO EAT	35 La Patache
9 Brasserie Terminus Nord	40 Franprix Supermarket
10 Batifol	42 Fromagerie
11 Hippopotamus	44 Food Shops
19 Le Chalet Maya	45 Porte Saint Denis
27 Le Pavillon Puebla	46 Porte Saint Martin
33 Restaurant Paris-Dakar	48 Franprix Supermarket
36 Au Gigot Fin	56 Franprix Supermarket
43 Pooja & South Asian	59 ADA Car Rental
Restaurants	60 Langue Onze (Language
50 Naouri	School)
51 Felafel Ely Gel	65 Bains-Douches Oberkampf
52 Chez Lalou	
54 Aux Délices du Cameroun	
58 Café Florentin	
62 Le Charbon	
63 Favela Chic	
66 Le Villaret	

PLACES TO DRINK
5 L'Opus Café
14 Le Salsa Loco
37 Les Étoiles
41 New Morning
47 Le Gibus
49 La Java
57 Café Cannibale
57 Le Troisième Bureau
61 Le Mécano Bar
64 Le Cithéa

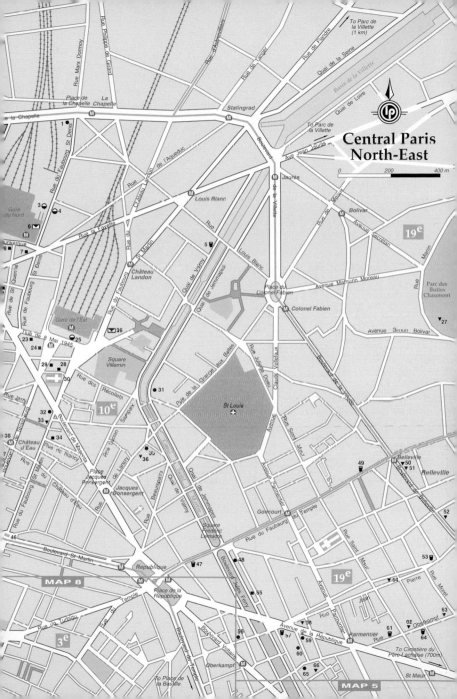

Central Paris
North-East

To Parc de la Villette (1 km)

0   200   400 m

19ᵉ

10ᵉ

3ᵉ

19ᵉ

Gare du Nord

Gare de l'Est

Parc des Buttes Chaumont

Bassin de la Villette

St Louis

Place de la Chapelle

La Chapelle

Stalingrad

Jaurès

Louis Blanc

Bolivar

Avenue Secrétan

Place du Colonel Fabien

Colonel Fabien

Avenue Mathurin Moreau

Avenue Simon Bolivar

Château Landon

Square Villemin

Rue des Récollets

Château d'Eau

Place Jacques Bonsergent

Jacques Bonsergent

Square Frédéric Lemaître

Belleville

Belleville

Goncourt

République

Place de la République

MAP 8

Oberkampf

Parmentier

St Maur

MAP 5

To Parc de la Villette

To Parc de la Villette

To Cimetière du Père-Lachaise (700m)

To Place de la Bastille

Streets and places (as labelled)

Rue Marx Dormoy
Rue Philippe de Girard
Rue d'Aubervilliers
Rue de Jessaint
Rue de Flandre
Quai de la Seine
Quai de Loire
Ave Jean Jaurès
e la Chapelle
Rue du Faubourg St Denis
Boulevard de la Villette
Rue de Meaux
Rue de l'Aqueduc
Rue Château Landon
Rue La Fayette
Rue de Dunkerque
Rue de St Quentin
Rue St Denis
Rue du Faubourg St Martin
Rue St Martin
Quai de Jemmapes
Quai de Valmy
Rue Louis Blanc
Rue de Meaux
Avenue Mathurin Moreau
Rue Manin
Rue de 8 Mai 1945
Rue de la Grange aux Belles
Rue Juliette Dodu
Rue Claude Vellefaux
Boulevard de la Villette
Rue de Strasbourg
Boulevard de Magenta
Rue de Nancy
Rue de Lancry
Rue Yves Toudic
Rue Beaurepaire
Rue du Faubourg du Temple
Rue Saint Maur
Avenue Parmentier
Boulevard St Martin
Boulevard Jules Ferry
Avenue de la République
Rue Oberkampf
Rue du Turbigo
Rue du Temple
Boulevard Voltaire
Boulevard du Temple
Rue St Maur
Rue Morel
Rue Pierre
Rue Jean
Rue Parmentier

MAP 4

16ᵉ

Central Paris South-West

0   200   400 m

M Trocadéro

Place du Trocadéro et du 11 Novembre

Palais de Chaillot

Jardins du Trocadéro

M Passy

Pont de Bir Hakeim

Seine River

Quai de Grenelle

M Bir Hakeim

Champ de Mars-Tour Eiffel

Eiffel Tower

Rue Jean Rey

Avenue de Suffren

Pont d'Iéna

Place de Varsovie

Place d'Iéna

Quai Branly

Avenue de New York

Avenue des Nations Unies

Pont de l'Alma

M Pont de l'Alma

Place de la Résistance

Quai Branly

Rue de l'Université

Rue du Général-Camou

Avenue Rapp

Avenue Bosquet

Rue Sa

Avenue de la Bourdonnais

Bouleva

Champ de Mars

Avenue Charles Risler

Place Joffre

École Militaire

Avenue de la Motte-Picquet

Boulevard de Grenelle

Rue de la Fédération

Rue Desaix

Rue du Docteur Finlay

Rue du Théâtre

Rue Linois

Rue Émeriau

Rue Saint Charles

Rue Viala

Rue Rouelle

Rue Lourmel

Rue Duplex

M Dupleix

Boulevard de Grenelle

La Motte Picquet Grenelle

M

Place Cambronne

Cambronne

15ᵉ

Rue Violet

Rue Fondary

Rue Frémicourt

Avenue Émile Zola

M

Rue du Commerce

Rue du Théâtre

Rue de la Croix Nivert

Rue Lecourbe

Rue Miollis

Rue Cambronne

M Commerce

Rue Mademoiselle

Place Étienne Pernet

Rue de Vaugirard

Rue Blomet

Vaugirard

Rue des Laos

PLACES TO STAY
27 Flatotel International
28 Hôtel Saphir Grenelle
40 Three Ducks Hostel
41 Aloha Hostel
43 Hôtel Miramar
49 Celtic Hôtel
56 Hôtel des Académies

PLACES TO EAT
26 Feyrous
29 Le Tipaza
30 Café du Commerce
32 Chez Dummonet
36 Bistrot Romain
37 Pizza Pino
38 Hippopotamus
50 Crêperies
51 Léon de Bruxelles
54 Mustang Café
54 Le Select
57 Le Dôme
58 La Coupole

PLACES TO DRINK
55 Cubana Café

MUSEUMS AND GALLERIES
2 Entrance to Musée des Égouts de Paris
9 Musée d'Orsay
16 Musée Rodin
39 Musée Bourdelle
42 Musée de la Poste

OTHER
1 Cinémathèque Française
3 American Church
4 Aérogare des Invalides
5 Air France Buses
6 Ministère des Affaires Étrangères
7 Assemblée Nationale
8 Batobus Stop
10 La Maison de l'Expatriée
11 British Council
12 American Library in Paris
13 Bateaux Parisiens
14 Australian Embassy
15 Église du Dôme
17 Hôtel Matignon
18 Madeleine Gély
19 Galerie Inard
20 Centaur Statue
21 Boulangerie Poilâne
22 Banque de France
23 Le Bon Marché
24 La Grande Épicerie
25 Institut Parisien de Langue et de Civilisation Françaises
31 Carte de Séjour Office for Students
33 FNAC Montparnasse Department Store
34 Alliance Française
35 Tati Department Store
44 Kiosque Théâtre
45 Tour Montparnasse
46 Inno Supermarket
47 Food Market
48 Hi Tech Café
53 Église Notre Dame des Champs
59 Laporte Fromagerie
60 Air France Buses

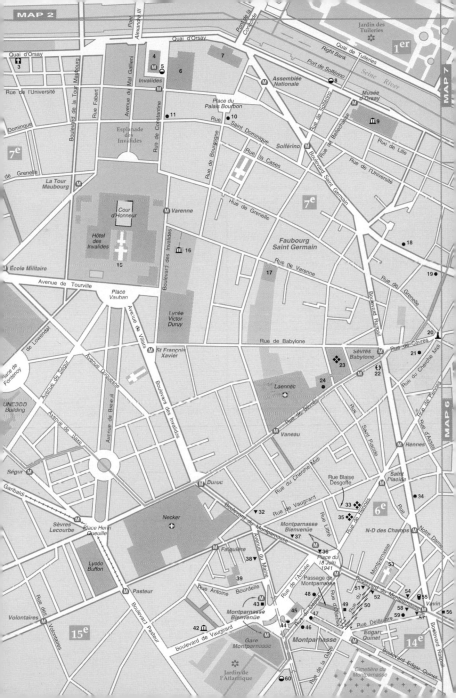

MAP 5

Rue de Rivoli

Louvre

Quai du Louvre

Seine

River

1er

Forum
des
Halles

Centre
Pompidou

Rue

Rue de Rivoli

Rue des Halles

Boulevard de Sébastopol

Rue

Rue Beaubourg

Rue du Renard

MAP 7

Quai de la Mégisserie

Conciergerie

Hôtel
de Ville

Palais
de Justice

Préfecture
de Police

Île de la Cité

Notre Dame

Quai St Michel

Quai de Montebello

Quai de la Tournelle

Boulevard Saint Germain

Boulevard Saint Germain

Rue de Bernardins

MAP 6

Rue

Rue Lemoine

Rue des Fossé

PLACES TO STAY
8 Résidence Bastille;
   Hôtel de France
9 Hôtel Lyon Mulhouse
15 Hôtel Bastille Opéra;
   Hôtel Bastille
23 Vix Hôtel
27 Hôtel Baudin
29 Hôtel Pax; Le Café du Passage
31 Hôtel des Alliés
33 Hôtel et Résidence Trousseau
34 Auberge Internationale des
   Jeunes; Hôtel Saint Amand
44 Hôtel Au Royal Cardinal
46 Familia Hôtel
53 Hôtel des Grands Écoles
54 Résidence Monge
65 Hôtel Saint Christophe
70 Y & H Hostel

PLACES TO EAT
2 La Piragua
3 Le Camelot
4 Le Tabarin
5 Café Le Serail
6 Café de l'Industrie
7 Les Galopins
10 Restaurant Relais du
   Massif Central
11 Restaurant Babylon
13 Havanita Café;
   La Pirada Bar Tapas;
   Café de la Danse
16 Chez Heang
17 Hippopotamus; Léon de
   Bruxelles
22 Crêpes Show
25 Suds
28 Chez Paul
35 Café Cannelle
36 Le Square Trousseau
38 L'Encrier
43 Moissonnier
47 La Voie Lactée
48 Restaurant Koutchi
49 Le Petit Légume
51 Savannah Café
56 L'Arbre à Cannelle
64 Jardin des Pâtes
68 Crêpes Stand
82 Founti Agadir

PLACES TO DRINK
1 Le Bataclan
12 Iguana Café
14 Le Balajo; La Chapelle
   des Lombards
18 Café des Phares
26 Boca Chica
37 China Club
40 Le Viaduc Café
45 Paradis Latin

MUSEUMS AND GALLERIES
42 Musée de Sculpture en Plein Air
72 Grande Galerie de l'Évolution
73 Galerie de Minéralogie
   et Paléobotanie
74 Galerie d'Entomologie
75 Galerie d'Anatomie Comparée
   et de Paléontologie

OTHER
19 Banque de France Branch
20 Colonne de Juillet
21 FNAC Musique Bastille
24 Centre Gai et Lesbien
30 Canauxrama Dock
32 Monoprix Supermarket
39 Marché d'Aligre
41 Capitainerie & Europ' Yachting
50 Shopi Supermarket
52 Génération Condom
55 Arènes de Lutèce
57 Jussieu Classique
58 Jussieu Music
59 Ménagerie Entrance
60 Ménagerie
61 Jardin Alpin; Gardens of the
   École de Botanique
62 Children's Playground
63 Serres Tropicales
66 Bains-Douches Municipaux
67 Ed l'Épicier Supermarket
69 Franprix Supermarket
71 Mosquée de Paris
76 Cour Départ
77 Post Office
78 Cour d'Arrivée
79 La Pitié-Salpêtrière Hospital
80 Paris Vélo
81 Food Market
83 Jadis et Gourmande

6e

Rue des Écoles

Jardin
Carré

43
45
46
47
48
44
Cardinal
Lemoine
49 Jussieu

Rue Saint Jacques

Rue Soufflot

Panthéon

Jardin
du
Luxembourg

Boulevard Saint Michel

**Central Paris
South-East**

0   200   400 m

Latin
Quarter

Rue Clovis

Rue Thouin

50
51
52 53
5e
55
56
54
58

Place de la
Contrescarpe

66
67

Rue Rollin

Place
Monge

Lapcépède   64
65

Rue Monge

Rue Mouffetard

Rue Tournefort

68   Place
Monge

69
70

Rue Jean
Calvin

Rue Claude Bernard

Rue Monge

Rue Georges

Rue Daubenton

de l'Arbalète

81

Centre
Daubenton

Rue Censie

Rue du Fer à Moulin

82

83

Hôtel
de Ville

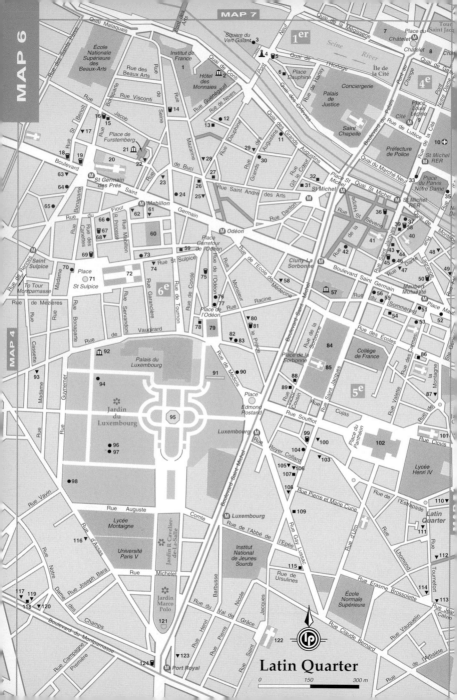

Latin Quarter

PLACES TO STAY

6 Hôtel Henri IV
13 Hôtel de Nesle
15 Hôtel des Deux
 Continents; Hôtel
 des Marronniers
26 Hôtel Petit Trianon
27 Hôtel Saint André
 des Arts
31 Hôtel Saint Michel
32 Delhy's Hôtel; Osteria
 del Passe-Partout
39 Hôtel Esmeralda
43 Hôtel du Centre
54 Hôtel Marignan
59 Hôtel du Globe
78 Hôtel Michelet Odéon
86 Hôtel Saint Jacques
88 Hôtel Cluny Sorbonne
89 Grand Hôtel
 Saint Michel
107 Hôtel de Médicis
109 Hôtel Gay Lussac
115 Grand Hôtel du Progrès
118 Citadines Apparthôtel
 Raspail Montparnasse

PLACES TO EAT

17 Le Petit Zinc;
 All Jazz Café
22 Guenmaï
23 L'Arbuci
25 Chez Jean-Mi
28 Chez Albert
29 Rôtisserie d'En Face
44 Le Navigator; Chez Maï
47 Au Coin des Gourmets
48 Les Bouchons
 de François Clerc
49 Al Dar
58 Pâtisserie Viennoise
61 Le Golfe de Naples
62 Mabillon University
 Restaurant
63 Brasserie Lipp
68 Le Mâcon d'Henri
74 Lina's
80 Restaurant Polidor
82 Restaurant Indonesia
87 L'Étoile de Berger;
 Le Violon Dingue
93 Les Mouettes
100 Perraudin
103 Tashi Delek
105 Machu Picchu
106 Douce France

108 Tao
110 La Truffière
111 Castor et Pollux
112 Le Vigneron
113 Châtelet University
 Restaurant
114 Chez Léna et Mimille
116 Assas University
 Restaurant
117 Hippopotamus
119 Le Caméléon
120 Batifol
123 Bullier University
 Restaurant;
 OTU Voyages

PLACES TO DRINK

5 Taverne Henri IV
14 La Palette
16 La Villa Jazz Club
18 Café de Flore
19 Les Deux Magots
36 Le Caveau
 de la Huchette
38 Tea Caddy
45 Le Cloître & Polly
 Maggoo Pubs
50 Club Zed
60 Coolin; Marché
 Saint Germain
67 Chez Georges
69 Café de la Mairie
75 Le 10
81 La Paillotte
99 Café Oz
124 La Closerie des Lilas

MUSEUMS AND
GALLERIES

2 Musée de la Monnaie
21 Musée Eugène
 Delacroix
57 Musée National
 du Moyen Age
92 Musée du Luxembourg

OTHER

1 Institut de France;
 Bibliothèque Mazarine
3 Vedettes du Pont Neuf
4 Statue of Henri IV
7 Théâtre Musical
 de Paris
8 Théâtre de la Ville
9 Flower Market
10 Hôtel Dieu Hospital

11 Australian Bookshop
12 Théâtre de Nesle
20 Église Saint Germain
 des Prés
24 Champion Supermarket
30 Mariage Frères
33 Crypte Archéologique
34 Tower Entrance
35 Point Zéro
37 Shakespeare &
 Company Bookshop
40 Église Saint Julien
 le Pauvre
41 Église Saint Séverin
42 Abbey Bookshop
46 Album
51 EOL' Modelisme
52 Food Market; Food
 Shops; Fromagerie
53 Au Vieux Campeur
 Shop
55 Au Vieux Campeur
 Shop
56 Eurolines Office
64 Monoprix Supermarket
65 Kenzo
66 Village Voice Bookshop
70 La Maison de la Chine
71 Fontaine des
 Quatre Évêques
72 Église Saint Sulpice
73 Galerie d'Amon
76 Odimex Paris
77 Council Travel
79 Odéon Théâtre
 de l'Europe
83 USIT
84 Sorbonne
 (Université de Paris)
85 Chapelle de
 la Sorbonne
90 Café Orbital
91 Fontaine des Médicis
94 Chess & Card Games
95 Grand Bassin
96 Théâtre du Luxembourg
97 Playground
98 Beehives
101 Église Saint Étienne
 du Mont
102 Panthéon
104 Food Shops;
 Fromagerie
121 Fontaine de
 l'Observatoire
122 Église Val-de-Grace

MAP 7

MAP 3

MAP 2

MAP 6

Les Halles
& Louvre Areas

0   150   300

Trinité

Rue Lamartine

Rue de Châteaudun

Notre Dame
de Lorette

Cadet

Rue La Fayette

Bleue

Rue La Fayette

10e

9e

Le Peletier

Galeries
Lafayette

Chaussée d'Antin

Boulevard Haussmann

Richelieu
Drouot

Boulevard Montmartre

Boulevard des Italiens

Boulevard Poissonnière

Place
de
l'Opéra

Opéra

Quatre
Septembre

Bourse

Bourse
des
Valeurs

2e

Pyramides

Jardin
du
Palais
Royal

Banque
de
France

1er

Palais
Royal

Place
André
Malraux

Place
des
Pyramides

Place
Royal

Palais
Royal

Rue Saint Honoré

Rue de Rivoli

Jardin
du
Carrousel

Musée
du
Louvre

Cour
Carrée

Louvre-Rivoli

Quai des Tuileries

Châtelet
Les Halles

Les
Halles

Square des
Innocents

Châtelet

Place
Sainte
Opportune

Châtelet

Quai
Voltaire

Seine   River

Pont-Neuf

Quai

La Samaritaine department store on Rue de Rivoli

PLACES TO STAY

51 Hôtel Central Marais;
 Bar de l'Hôtel Central;
 Les Étages; Les Mots
 à la Bouche Bookshop
69 Hôtel Axial Beaubourg
75 Hôtel Rivoli
76 Hôtel de Nice
77 Hôtel Le Palais des Fès
79 Hôtel Le Compostelle
84 Grand Hôtel Malher
87 Hôtel Moderne;
 Hôtel Pratic
89 Hôtel Sully
90 Hôtel de la Place
 des Vosges
95 Hôtel de la Herse d'Or
102 MIJE Fourcy
108 MIJE Maubuisson
116 MIJE Fauconnier
118 Hôtel Castex
123 Hôtel Saint Louis
124 Hôtel des Deux Îles
131 Centre International BVJ
 Paris-Quartier Latin

PLACES TO EAT

2 Au Bascou
5 404
6 Chinese Restaurants
9 Le Valet du Carreau
10 Au Trou Normand
11 Le Clown Bar
13 Madame Sans Gêne
14 Chez Omar
18 Mélodine Cafeteria
25 Le Repaire
 de Cartouche
28 Robert et Louise
32 Le Studio
38 Restaurant China;
 Au Vieux Paris
40 Le Gai Moulin
41 Aquarius; Le Petit Picard
46 Le Petit Gavroche
52 La Truffe; Coffee Shop
55 Chez Rami et Hanna
57 Chez Marianne
59 Caves Saint Gilles
61 Marais Plus
62 Café des Psaumes
63 Jo Goldenberg
67 Minh Chau; Quetzal Bar
71 Au P'tit Rémouleur
81 Piccolo Teatro
93 Brasserie Bofinger;
 Bistrot du Dôme
96 L'Impasse
97 Vins des Pyrénées
104 Amadeo
106 La Perla
117 L'Enoteca
119 Woolloomooloo
120 Les Fous de l'Île
121 Brasserie de
 l'Île Saint Louis
132 Restaurant A
133 La Tour d'Argent;
 Le Rallye

PLACES TO DRINK

4 Les Bains
7 Le Tango
8 Web Bar
15 Duplex Bar
22 QG Bar
30 Ekivök
31 Le Piano Zinc
33 Café Beaubourg
42 Le Skeud
43 Café Cox
44 Open Café
45 Mixeri Bar
53 Le Petit Fer à Cheval
54 Amnésia Café
66 La Chaise au Plafond
78 Le Pick Clops
80 Stolly's
82 La Tartine
85 Piment Café
92 L'Ailleurs
111 L'Arène
112 Louis-Philippe Café

MUSEUMS AND GALLERIES

19 Galerie Zabriskie
21 Centre Pompidou
24 Archives Nationales;
 Musée de l'Historie
 de France
26 Musée Picasso
27 Musée de la Serrure
58 Musée Cognacq-Jay
60 Musée Carnavalet
88 Hôtel de Sully
91 Maison de Victor Hugo
103 Maison Européenne
 de la Photographie
114 Mémorial du Martyr
 Juif Inconnu

OTHER

1 Oldest House in Paris
3 Église St Nicholas
 des Champs
12 Cirque d'Hiver
16 Le Défenseur du Temps
 (Clock)
17 Bibliothèque Publique
 d'Information (BPI)
20 AJF
23 Allô Logement
 Temporaire
29 Bains Plus
34 Fountains
35 Théâtre du Tourtour
36 Pharmacie des Halles
37 Église Saint Merri
39 Bains-Douches
 Municipaux
47 Post Office
48 Mariage Frères
49 Point Virgule
50 Les Mots à la Bouche
56 Sacha Finkelsztajn
64 Robin des Bois
65 Florence Finkelsztajn
68 BHV Department Store
70 Ed l'Épicier Supermarket
72 Noctambus Stops
73 Post Office
74 Hôtel de Ville
83 Guimard Synagogue
86 Ma Bourgogne
94 Flo Prestige
98 Monoprix Supermarket;
 G Millet Fromager
99 Gourmaud
100 Supermarché G20
101 Franprix Supermarket
105 À l'Olivier
107 Église Saint Gervais-
 Saint Protais
109 Sic Amor
110 Produits des
 Monastères
113 Melodies Graphiques
115 Hôtel de Sens
122 Galerie Alain Carion
125 Le Moule à Gâteau
126 Berthillon Ice Cream
127 Église Saint Louis
 en l'Île
128 Bains-Douches
 Municipaux
129 Mémorial des Martyrs
 de la Déportation
130 Bateaux Parisiens Dock
134 Institut du Monde Arabe
135 Children's Playground

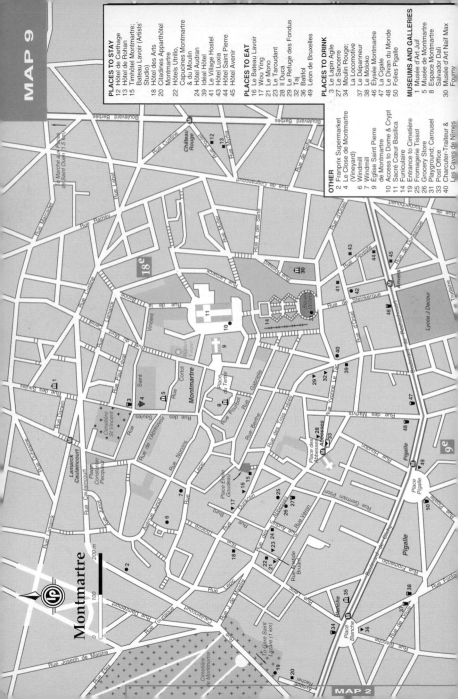

MAP 9

Montmartre

PLACES TO STAY
12 Hôtel de Carthage
13 Hôtel de Rohan
15 Timhôtel Montmartre; Bateau Lavoir (Artists' Studio)
18 Hôtel des Arts
20 Citadines Apparthôtel Montmartre
22 Hôtels Utrillo, Capucines Montmartre & du Moulin
24 Hôtel Audran
39 Ideal Hôtel
41 Le Village Hostel
43 Hôtel Luxia
44 Hôtel Saint Pierre
45 Hôtel Avenir

PLACES TO EAT
16 Le Bateau Lavoir
17 Wou Ying
21 Le Mono
23 Le Taroudant
28 Il Duca
29 Le Refuge des Fondus
32 Taj
36 Batifol
49 Léon de Bruxelles

PLACES TO DRINK
3 Le Lapin Agile
27 Le Sancerre
34 Moulin Rouge; La Locomotive
37 Le Dépanneur
38 Le Moloko
46 Elysee Montmartre
47 La Cigale
48 Le Divan du Monde
50 Folies Pigalle

MUSEUMS AND GALLERIES
1 Musée d'Art Juif
5 Musée de Montmartre
8 Espace Montmartre Salvador Dali
30 Musée d'Art Naïf Max Fourny

OTHER
2 Franpix Supermarket
4 Le Clos de Montmartre (Vineyard)
6 Windmill
7 Windmill
9 Église Saint Pierre de Montmartre
10 Access to Dome & Crypt
11 Sacré Cœur Basilica
14 Funiculaire
19 Entrance to Cimetière
25 Fromagerie Tissot
26 Grocery Store
31 Playground; Carousel
33 Post Office
40 Charcuter-Traiteur & Les Caves de Nîmes

TONY WHEELER

SIMON BRACKEN

Top: View of the Arc de Triomphe from the Eiffel Tower
Bottom: Gare du Nord, one of Paris' six major train stations

Map Legend

BOUNDARIES

.... International Boundary
.... Provincial Boundary

ROUTES

[A25] .... Freeway, with Route Number
.... Major Road
.... Minor Road
.... Minor Road - Unsealed
.... City Road
.... City Street
.... City Lane
.... Train Route, with Station
.... Metro Route, with Station
.... Cable Car or Chairlift
.... Ferry Route
.... Walking Track

AREA FEATURES

.... Building
.... Cemetery
.... Forest
.... Hotel
.... Market
.... Park, Gardens
.... Pedestrian Mall
.... Urban Area

HYDROGRAPHIC FEATURES

.... Canal
.... Coastline
.... Creek, River
.... Lake
.... Rapids, Waterfalls

SYMBOLS

✪ **CAPITAL** ...... National Capital
● **CITY** .... City
● **Town** .... Town
● Village .... Village
....
■ .... Place to Stay
▼ .... Place to Eat
🍺 .... Pub or Bar

✈ .... Airport
...... Ancient or City Wall
⁂ ... Archaeological Site
Θ .... Bank
🁢 ..... Buddhist Temple
🀫 .... Castle or Fort
✚ 🛈 .... Church
... Cliff or Escarpment
ⵙ .... Embassy
✛ .... Hospital
⁑ .... Lookout
⚲ .... Monument
◖ .... Mosque
🏛 .... Museum

← ...... One Way Street
🅿 .... Parking
○ ....Point of Interest
★ .... Police Station
✉ .... Post Office
❖ ..... Shopping Centre
🏰 .... Stately Home
▭ .... Swimming Pool
⬚ .... Synagogue
☎ .... Telephone
◼ .... Tomb
ℹ ... Tourist Information
⬭ .... Transport
🐘 .... Zoo

Note: not all symbols displayed above appear in this book